THE CASE FOR REDUCTION

Cultural Inquiry

EDITED BY CHRISTOPH F. E. HOLZHEY
AND MANUELE GRAGNOLATI

The series 'Cultural Inquiry' is dedicated to exploring how diverse cultures can be brought into fruitful rather than pernicious confrontation. Taking culture in a deliberately broad sense that also includes different discourses and disciplines, it aims to open up spaces of inquiry, experimentation, and intervention. Its emphasis lies in critical reflection and in identifying and highlighting contemporary issues and concerns, even in publications with a historical orientation. Following a decidedly cross-disciplinary approach, it seeks to enact and provoke transfers among the humanities, the natural and social sciences, and the arts. The series includes a plurality of methodologies and approaches, binding them through the tension of mutual confrontation and negotiation rather than through homogenization or exclusion.

Christoph F. E. Holzhey is the Founding Director of the ICI Berlin Institute for Cultural Inquiry. Manuele Gragnolati is Professor of Italian Literature at the Sorbonne Université in Paris and Associate Director of the ICI Berlin.

THE CASE FOR REDUCTION

EDITED BY
CHRISTOPH F. E. HOLZHEY
JAKOB SCHILLINGER

ISBN (Hardcover): 978-3-96558-039-8
ISBN (Paperback): 978-3-96558-040-4
ISBN (PDF): 978-3-96558-041-1
ISBN (EPUB): 978-3-96558-042-8

Cultural Inquiry, 25
ISSN (Print): 2627-728X
ISSN (Online): 2627-731X

Bibliographical Information of the German National Library
The German National Library lists this publication in the Deutsche Nationalbibliografie
(German National Bibliography); detailed bibliographic information is available online at
http://dnb.d-nb.de.

In Europe, volumes are printed by Lightning Source UK Ltd., Milton Keynes, UK. See the
final page for further details.

Digital editions can be viewed and downloaded freely at: https://doi.org/10.37050/ci-25.

ICI Berlin Press is an imprint of
ICI gemeinnütziges Institut für Cultural Inquiry Berlin GmbH
Christinenstr. 18/19, Haus 8
D-10119 Berlin
publishing@ici-berlin.org
www.ici-berlin.org

Contents

Introduction
CHRISTOPH F. E. HOLZHEY AND JAKOB SCHILLINGER 1

The Case and the Signifier: Generalization in Freud's *Rat Man*
IRACEMA DULLEY 13

Haptic Reductions: A Sceptic's Guide for Responding to the
Touch of Crisis
RACHEL AUMILLER 39

Disalienation and Structuralism: Fanon with Lévi-Strauss
CHRISTOPHER CHAMBERLIN 61

Black Box Allegories of Gulf Futurism: The Irreducible Other
of Computational Capital
ÖZGÜN EYLÜL İŞCEN 91

Lines that Reduce: Biography, Palms, Borders
SAM DOLBEAR 117

Post-anti-identitarianism: The Forms of Contemporary
Gender and Sexuality
BEN NICHOLS 135

Nothing Beyond the Name: Towards an Eclipse of Listening in
the Psychotherapeutic Enterprise
SARATH JAKKA 155

Reduction in Computer Music: Bodies, Temporalities, and
Generative Computation
FEDERICA BUONGIORNO 175

Reduction in Time: Kinaesthetic and Traumatic Experiences
of the Present in Literary Texts
ALBERICA BAZZONI 191

Seeking *Home*: Vignettes of Homes and Homing
AMINA ELHALAWANI 213

Law Is Other Wor(l)ds
XENIA CHIARAMONTE 227

EXCURSUS

On the List
SAM DOLBEAR, BEN NICHOLS, AND CLAUDIA PEPPEL 253

White Supremacist Capitalist Patriarchy
BEN NICHOLS 263

Proust List Impulse
SAM DOLBEAR 267

A List of Fears: Eva Kot'átková's *Asylum*
CLAUDIA PEPPEL 271

How to Bake X Cake: Notes on the Recipe
IRACEMA DULLEY 277

Walking Away, Walking in Circles, Writing Lists
RACHEL AUMILLER 281

References 287
Notes on the Contributors 311
Index 315

Introduction

CHRISTOPH F. E. HOLZHEY AND JAKOB SCHILLINGER

Critical discourse has little patience with reduction. One of the most devastating charges levelled against theories, analyses, and descriptions is that of being reductive. Conceptual frameworks are dismissed for being impoverished, ontologies rejected for being too poor, descriptions for being too sparse or flat. And conversely, to call something 'irreducible' seems to confer an immediate and indisputable dignity to it. Yet the history of knowledge and in particular the history of science cannot be told without acknowledging the importance of reductionist paradigms, from Stoic physics or mechanistic materialism to cybernetics and structuralism. Any attempt to reject these paradigms has to contend with their ambiguous effects, such as their ability to generate radical innovations even when they are ultimately considered to have failed. Reductionisms indeed make the theoretical landscape more complex even as they seek to account for more with less and to achieve deeper understanding through unified theories.

What lies at the root of such different attitudes towards 'reduction' and what can be made of their tensions? A polar opposition of reductionist and anti-reductionist positions is often aligned with the alleged split of the 'two cultures' — the natural sciences and the humanities, with the social sciences somewhere in between and internally split. Yet, 'reduction' itself has always had at least two distinct meanings: following the Latinate root 're-ducere', it means bringing something back to something else, whereas in the more common, vernacular sense it means a decrease in quantity. The latter furthermore has the almost irresistible connotation of devaluation.[1] To what extent do anti-reduction reflexes rely on the conflation of these different meanings, and to what extent can re-duction help establish relations between terms and dissolve boundaries between fields without implying a hierarchy in quantity, scale, or value? How might reduction, in its contraction of multiple dimensions and its extension across virtually all fields of inquiry, generate unexpected or errant resonances, interferences, and entanglements without losing its sense of direction, orientation, and analytical purchase?

The significance of reduction is perhaps most evident in relation to complexity. Quite plausibly, nothing could be described, understood, or done without reducing complexity. While this insight deflates accusations of reductiveness and establishes a common ground across all fields, it also shifts attention to the ways in which reductions are performed: Reduction can be done sparingly — taking complexity as a limited resource to be saved and economized — or liberally, treating complexity as a bounded, even conserved quantity that can be differently distributed. In the latter case, the relevant question is not how much one reduces, but which complexities one seeks to enhance at the price of which reductions, or which focus one sets and narrows in order to allow for greater complexity within it. While a trade-off between reduced complexity in some respects and increased complexity in others suggests a zero-sum game of reduction and complexity — or a competition over finite attention — reduction can also be reconciled with a logic of growth. For instance, division of labour increases overall production by reducing the individual's work to a limited range of often very mechanical activities. But it can also promise the emergence of new and greater complexities for everyone involved. Such is the premise of intersectional, trans- or multidisciplinary endeavours that combine different knowledge systems, each defined by its specific

---

1   This may be due to 'up' functioning as an orientational metaphor for 'more', 'good', and 'happy', or 'increase', 'growth', and 'progress'. See George Lakoff and Mark Johnson, *Metaphors We Live By* (Chicago: University of Chicago Press, 2003), chapters 4 ('Orientational Metaphors') and 5 ('Metaphor and Cultural Coherence').

epistemic reduction, with the expectation that complexities not merely add up but multiply.

Yet the belief in unlimited growth, fuelled in the second half of the twentieth century by a new, post-Newtonian science of complexity, emergence, and self-organization, may well be the product of a selective perception: the constructive interferences that are welcomed get balanced by destructive ones, and periods of catastrophic collapse are an integral part of self-organizing systems maximizing complexity.[2] In a different register, lateral to visions of accumulated reductions and emergent complexities, there remains in all fields of inquiry the guiding ideal — epistemological as much as aesthetic — of being clear and distinct, even simple. The sciences may be more deliberately reductive in their theorizing and experimenting, but attempting to grasp the core of a phenomenon, issue, or question by stripping away all that is incidental and distracting also characterizes writing and modelling practices within the humanities, the arts, and design. No doubt resonances exist with ideas of efficiency and parsimony, even ascesis or austerity, yet techniques of concentration and condensation, in-

---

2   For an early, powerful, and highly influential argument for a new science of complexity, emergence, and self-organization, see Ilya Prigogine and Isabelle Stengers, *Order Out of Chaos: Man's New Dialogue with Nature* (London: Heinemann, 1984). The authors here propose a science that would overcome the 'static view of nature' (p. 11) of Newtonian mechanics and its deterministic laws, in which past and future are in principle fully determined for all times. Central to their argument is the second law of thermodynamics, commonly understood as an irreversible tendency towards decay, dissipation, and death — and, more technically, towards the degradation and dissipation of energy and temperature gradients. Against this usual reading, Prigogine and Stengers turn the second law into a principle for self-organized growth of order, complexity, and ultimately life. While Prigogine and Stengers re-animated Henri Bergson's conception of duration and creative vitalism, much of current new materialism repeats the same arguments of a post-Newtonian science that would, yet again, recognize the fundamental activity, vitality, and creativity of matter. See, e.g., *New Materialisms: Ontology, Agency, and Politics*, ed. by Diana Coole and Samantha Frost (Durham, NC: Duke University Press, 2010). However, the theories of self-organization from the 1970s and 80s were more ambivalent insofar as they included notions such as 'self-organized criticality' or the tendency of systems moving to the 'edge of chaos', where the rate of evolution is arguably at a maximum, but only because growth is balanced by catastrophic avalanches occurring on all scales, and both growth and collapse equally contribute to the emergence of new structures. See, e.g., Stuart A. Kauffman, *The Origins of Order: Self-Organization and Selection in Evolution* (Oxford: Oxford University Press, 1993) and Per Bak, *How Nature Works: The Science of Self-Organized Criticality* (New York: Springer, 1996).

tensification and subtraction also exceed economic considerations and constitute arts of knowing and forms of life.

The ancient technologies of the self, whose practitioners sought to rid themselves of the devastating effects of the passions, were compared by Plotinus to sculpture, regarded at the time as the paradigmatic art of reduction: while a painter proceeded through addition, a sculptor was thought to free an image from a block of marble through subtraction alone.[3] Pierre Hadot has argued that Western philosophy was initially a 'spiritual exercise' aimed at transforming the self and its vision of the world. On his account, Western philosophy was 'emptied of its spiritual exercises' under the influence of medieval scholasticism, which had philosophy's role 'reduced to the rank of a "handmaid of theology"'; it 'was henceforth to furnish theology with conceptual — and hence purely theoretical — material'. At the same time, practices of the self were 'relegated to Christian mysticism and ethics'.[4] Medieval female mystics, in particular, intensified such practices and retained a strong bodily dimension in ways that would resonate through the centuries — from Catherine of Siena to Simone Weil — but techniques of the self are also present in René Descartes's *Meditations* and in Edmund Husserl's 'eidetic' and 'transcendental reductions'. And reductive paradigms have periodically revitalized the arts, from neo-classicism to modernist design, from abstraction to diverse minimalisms or self-imposed arbitrary restrictions and aleatoric principles.

The present volume is the first publication to come out of the core project 'Reduction' that the ICI Berlin launched in autumn 2020. Defined along the lines just sketched, the aim was to explore the critical potentials of notions and practices of reduction within and across different fields and approaches — from the sciences, technology, and the arts, to feminist, queer, and decolonial approaches — and to inquire, in particular, into the ways different economies of reduction travel and the possibilities of escaping the seemingly unquestionable premium placed on production.

---

3   Plotinus, *Enneads* 1.6.9.
4   Pierre Hadot, *Philosophy as a Way of Life: Spiritual Exercises from Socrates to Foucault*, ed. by Arnold I. Davidson, trans. by Michael Chase (Malden, MA: Blackwell, 1995), p. 107.

Formulated at the end of the 'ERRANS, environ/s' project, which culminated in the volume *Weathering: Ecologies of Exposure*,[5] the project's inquiry was meant to resonate also with demands for reduction that acquired unprecedented public visibility in the context of climate change, partially due to movements such as Fridays for Future and Extinction Rebellion.[6] By the time the project started, COVID-19 led to other, unexpected resonances. The collective project began shortly before the second partial shutdown in autumn 2020 and was accompanied by repeated experiences of reduction in several domains: little mobility, few possibilities of exchange (cultural, economic, or otherwise), and limited social contacts — both quantitatively and qualitatively, as those that did occur were for the most part reduced to the two-dimensional screen. Yet such reductions by no means implied a uniformity or greater simplicity of experience, which was instead often characterized by new difficulties, complexities, temporalities, and intensities.

In weekly meetings over a period of almost two years, the contributors to this volume thus discussed reduction not only as a concept and method but also in its experiential dimensions. They inquired into possibilities of understanding and experiencing reduction as generative as well as diminishing. Phenomenological reduction was soon evoked as a model joining method with experience and the generative with the limiting aspects of reduction. Insofar as it can be understood as a method of bracketing preconceptions and judgments about reality

---

5   See 'ERRANS environ/s: ICI Focus 2018–20', ICI Berlin <https://www.ici-berlin.org/projects/errans-environs-2018-20/> [accessed 22 July 2022] and *Weathering: Ecologies of Exposure*, ed. by Christoph F. E. Holzhey and Arnd Wedemeyer, Cultural Inquiry, 17 (Berlin: ICI Berlin Press, 2020) <https://doi.org/10.37050/ci-17>.

6   Of course, critiques of growth have a long tradition and have already been well publicized since at least the 1970s and its so-called 'oil crisis'. While the 1972 Club of Rome Report *The Limits of Growth* advocated zero-growth, the notion of 'degrowth' — from the French *décroissance* — appeared around the same time. First employed by André Gorz in 1972, the term was used for the French translation of selected articles by Nicholas Georgescu-Roegen under the title *Demain la décroissance: Entropie — Écologie — Économie* (1979). The degrowth movement took off in the early 2000s, arguably from a 'convergence between the criticism of development in southern countries, and critiques of consumer society in northern ones'. See Timothée Duverger, 'Degrowth: The History of an Idea', *Encyclopédie d'histoire Numérique de l'Europe* <https://ehne.fr/en/encyclopedia/themes/material-civilization/transnational-consumption-and-circulations/degrowth-history-idea> [accessed 12 June 2022].

and causality, time and space, physical and social determination, phenomenological reduction promises a fuller experience of the present in its duration, a richer description of this experience, and a better account of how it is embodied and arises in perception through memory and expectation.

While some contributions explicitly engage with phenomenology, the multidisciplinary group moved on to considering reduction as a practice in a more general sense and inquired into the possibility of distinguishing different styles, genres, or aesthetics of reduction. Minimalist and abstract art here provided a case with which to reflect on the possibilities and risks of thinking reduction as expansion. Subtracting specificities opens (re)presentations up to the general and even universal, but it also risks perpetuating the privilege of unmarked subjects at the expense of gendered, sexualized, and racialized others. While especially mid-twentieth century artistic movements can and have been problematized along these lines,[7] important developments in Black and queer abstraction suggest that it may be time to revisit the well-rehearsed critiques of abstraction as a claim to universality and explore its potentials.[8]

Considering diverse genres of reduction — among them the vignette, the list, and the dictionary, which all figure in this volume — the group was ultimately most attracted to that of 'the case'. It first discussed the case in the context of law and psychoanalysis, to which discussions ended up returning as much as to phenomenology and to questions of style, genre, and aesthetics. But a 'thinking in cases' — which John Forrester proposed as a 'style of reasoning' alongside others, such as 'postulation and deduction', 'experimental exploration',

---

7   See e.g. Anna C. Chave, 'Minimalism and Biography', *The Art Bulletin*, 82.1 (2000), pp. 149–63 <https://doi.org/10.2307/3051368>.

8   See e.g. David J. Getsy, *Reduction as Expansion: The Queer Capacities of Abstract Art*, lecture, ICI Berlin, 1 February 2021, video recording, mp4, 55:44 <https://doi.org/10.25620/e210201>; Darby English, *1971: A Year in the Life of Color* (Chicago: University of Chicago Press, 2016) <https://doi.org/10.7208/chicago/9780226274737.001.0001>; Huey Copeland, 'One-Dimensional Abstraction', *Art Journal*, 78.2 (2019), pp. 116–18 <https://doi.org/10.1080/00043249.2019.1626161>; Adrienne Edwards, 'Blackness in Abstraction', *Art in America*, 103.1 (2015), pp. 62–69; Sampada Aranke, 'Material Matters: Black Radical Aesthetics and the Limits of Visibility', *e-flux Journal*, 79 (2017) <https://www.e-flux.com/journal/79/94433/material-matters-black-radical-aesthetics-and-the-limits-of-visibility/>.

or 'hypothetical construction of models by analogy'[9] — also seemed to characterize well the subsequent trajectory of the conversations, from reduction as metaphor and event to reduction as experience structured, and possibility curtailed, by habitus and class, sexuality and racialization, colonization and migration, technology and capital, etc.

The case is indeed a paradigmatic form of reduction, one that ties together two opposite poles: an incommensurable singularity that cannot be reduced further and a general theory or structure to which it could be reduced. The case is of particular interest when it mediates between the two and brackets both, reducing the complexity of empirical reality in view of more general schemata or rules that allow for comparison with similar cases, but at same time remaining in excess of, and irreducible to, the general it nonetheless conjures up, affirms, or even founds.

As a form, the case thus emblematically articulates the tension between singularity and generalization that the contributions to this volume explore in different ways and with different emphases, often associating singularity with experience and generalization with structure, concept, or category. Some contributions push the logic of the case to its limit and are perhaps better understood as presenting no longer cases of something more general, but rather pure cases — i.e. the contingent facticity of what is the case — that seek to resist subsumption and instead enter constellations with other singular cases.

The volume's title should be read in this light. Of course, at first glance it probably reads rather as 'making the case for reduction', that is, as polemically arguing for reduction and defending it as one might in a court case. Such a provocative resonance is not entirely unintended, but it should be clear that there is no single such case: there are many meanings and forms of reduction and, for each of them, one could no doubt make many different cases. Nor should the title be understood as a snappy shorthand for 'Cases for Reduction', as if each contribution

---

9   John Forrester, 'If p, Then What? Thinking in Cases', *History of the Human Sciences*, 9.3 (1996), pp. 1–25 (p. 2) <https://doi.org/10.1177/095269519600900301>. For 'styles of reasoning', Forrester refers to Ian Hacking's *The Taming of Chance* (Cambridge: Cambridge University Press, 1990), which in turn refers to Ian Hacking, 'Styles of Reasoning', in *Postanalytic Philosophy*, ed. by John Rajchman and Cornel West (New York: Columbia University Press, 1985), pp. 145–64.

was arguing one such case. In this volume, the case for reduction serves rather as a heuristic device: To push back against — or at least temporarily suspend — anti-reductionist reflexes is to allow critical attention to dwell on different notions and practices of reduction and also to explore their generative potentials.

As the cover design is meant to evoke, the case is also to be heard as a 'box' or 'receptacle, designed to contain an item or items for safe keeping, transportation, or display'.[10] Instead of shunning reduction as such, that is, in general, the case showcases it to explore its potentials and dangers. It particularizes reductions so as to inquire about their ethics and politics: Which reductions are to be avoided and which are to be endorsed? Can the benefits of reductions be transported and can the violences of reductions be contained? The case — now again in the sense of a form evoking the thorny practice of negotiating singularity and generality, bottom-up and top-down determination, and ultimately also agency and justice — may be more essential than ever to identify not only the 'reductions to be avoided', but also those to be fostered.[11]

The volume opens with an analysis of how the case study as method proposes generalizations based on singularity and how it may mediate between the individual and the social. Focusing on Sigmund Freud's Rat Man case, Iracema Dulley explores the chain of signification that emerges in Freud's articulation of the rat-related signifiers through which his patient's neurosis is expressed. She shows that the general claim this case makes is one that asserts the singularity of each

---

10   See the entry 'case, n.2', in *OED Online* (Oxford: Oxford University Press, 2020) <https://www.oed.com/view/Entry/28394> [accessed 23 July 2022].

11   In the introduction to Georges Canguilhem's *The Normal and the Pathological*, Michel Foucault characterizes Canguilhem's understanding of vitalism as a 'critical indicator of reductions to be avoided' and specifies that these reductions are 'those which tend to ignore the fact that the life sciences cannot do without a certain position of value indicating preservation, regulation, adaptation, reproduction, etc.). "A demand rather than a method, a morality more than a theory"'. In other words, the reductions to be avoided here are those dismissing the situated, always contingent norms and reductions imposed by the living. See Michel Foucault, 'Introduction', in Georges Canguilhem, *The Normal and the Pathological*, trans. by Carolyn R. Fawcett (New York: Zone Books, 1991), pp. 7–24 (p. 18). Cf. also Astrid Deuber-Mankowsky and Christoph F. E. Holzhey, 'Vitalismus als kritischer Indikator: Der Beitrag der Kulturwissenschaften an der Bildung des Wissens vom Leben', in *Der Einsatz des Lebens*, ed. by Deuber-Mankowsky and Holzhey (Berlin: b_books, 2009), pp. 9–30.

particular case, namely that any individual neurosis finds its expression in a unique chain of signifiers. Dulley's reflection is furthermore guided by a concern to question the divide between the individual and the social by showing how signifiers are one of the ways in which the symbolic inscribes itself onto the subject.

A similar intertwinement of the individual and the social, in this case effected by an oscillation between different reductions, is at work in Rachel Aumiller's contribution. 'Haptic Reductions' puts forth a feminist ethic grounded in phenomenological scepticism. Identifying two contrasting methodological reductions utilized in philosophical scepticism — 'withdrawal/doubt' and 'immersion/attention' — it explores how reduction relates to experiences of personal and global uncertainty during a pandemic. Reduction, Aumiller argues, involves the entire embodied being, challenging how one is fundamentally in touch with the world.

The case study's inherent tension between general and particular and the technique of bracketing either pole open up the field that this volume measures out in different ways. In Aumiller and Dulley, the social, symbolic, and abstract appear relatively fixed and inaccessible to transformation by the subject, who instead moves laterally within, seeking to override fixations or dogmatisms through therapeutic or bodily techniques. Other contributions focus rather on how the general enacts reduction and how it may be historicized and possibly transformed.

Christopher Chamberlin's chapter does so by identifying how structural anthropology, long maligned for its conceptual reductions and politics, has exerted a hidden influence on Frantz Fanon's theory of the 'sociogenesis' of mental illness. His text outlines how Fanon's belief in the therapeutic capacity of 'socialization' critically absorbs Claude Lévi-Strauss's examination of the link between 'madness' and the symbolic structure of society. These innovations, Chamberlin argues, pushed Fanon to institute 'semi-hospitalization' as a radically dialectical method of treatment in his final role as a clinician at the Neuropsychiatric Day Centre in Tunis. Functioning as a *heterotopia*, the Fanonian hospital partially brackets the colonized world to allow for the patients' disalienation, but it also creates the space for them to act politically back onto the social field.

In 'Black Box Allegories of Gulf Futurism', Özgün Eylül İşcen historically situates contemporary Gulf Futurism within the cybernetic undercurrent of today's smartness mandate. Her text revisits Fredric Jameson's cognitive mapping as a model for grasping the structures and processes of computational capital along with their inherent frictions. It highlights that cognitive mapping poses the aesthetic problem of mediation between different fields and scales — such as the global and local, or the social and psychic — and explores this issue in the work of Kuwaiti artist Monira Al Qadiri. Mobilizing the concept of allegory, İşcen engages with the fundamental paradox, also addressed by Chamberlin, that identifying, mapping, or otherwise representing structures or systems in order to counter their reductive effect is itself a form of reduction.

The ambivalence of mapping is also central in Sam Dolbear's 'Lines that Reduce'. The text moves from biography to a diagram of 'primal acquaintances' drawn by Walter Benjamin, which it transposes to other linear or lineal forms, such as a family tree, a diagram of chemical affinity, an astral chart, and the lines of a palm. Dolbear highlights the entangled constellations and rich lives these reductions can evoke and contrasts them to the reductive use of fingerprints performed by border guards. Moving from case to case, the essay suggests that the singularity of individual lives may be redeemed not by an evasion of reduction but by juxtaposing different kinds of temporal, historical, epistemic, and aesthetic reductions in a non-hierarchical, open-ended list.

While these contributions, which unveil the analytical potential of reduction, tend to emphasize the — often violent — losses it imparts on lived experience, Ben Nichols's 'Post-Anti-Identitarianism' focuses on its enabling and generative dimension. Nichols, too, engages with open-ended lists. While feminist, queer, and trans studies are all influenced significantly by anti-identitarian thought, contemporary gender and sexual identities only seem to be proliferating: nonbinary, graysexual, demigender, and more. Nichols's contribution focuses on a series of reference guides that schematize this recent expansion, often miming reductive formats, such as the dictionary or the A–Z list. These texts and the questions they raise, Nichols argues, help to rethink the place of 'identity' across gender and sexuality studies.

If Nichols's text could be said to bracket the totality of 'identitarian thinking' in order to focus on specific cases and concrete functions, such a bracketing of the general is the explicit method of other contributions. The point here is not just epistemological — to bring into focus experiential particularities that would otherwise be elided through subsumption under the general — but also performative, linked to the claim that such bracketing or suspension might counteract the reductive effects of generalization. In 'Reduction in Time' Alberica Bazzoni explores the experience of what she terms 'the living present' as a form of temporal reduction that brackets past and future, but is also different from a still, eternal moment. Examining its articulations in literary texts, Bazzoni contrasts the living present with the temporal reduction at work in trauma. Her contribution identifies the affective, ethical, and political dimensions of the living present as a site of subjectivation, as a form of reduction that counters the reduction effected by normative discourses.

A similar bracketing involving temporal experience allows Federica Buongiorno to reconceptualize agency as well as the role that the relation between human bodies and technology plays in constituting reality during an age of pervasive computing. The decreasing role played by embodiment is a problem in computer music in particular, since the latter relies heavily on different layers of (digital) technology and mediation in both its production and its performance. In her contribution, Buongiorno argues that such a mediation should not be conceived of as an obstacle but rather as a constitutive element of a permanent, complex negotiation between the artist, the machinery, and the audience. Focusing on the artist Caterina Barbieri, she outlines the aim of shaping a musical temporality that could resist the synchronizations of collective entrainment by mainstream music.

Sarath Jakka's 'Nothing Beyond the Name' directly juxtaposes the reduction performed by generalization with the reduction performed by bracketing generalization. The text considers the agonistic relation between a *listening* to patients and a diagnostic *naming* to be constitutive for various psychotherapeutic paradigms. Yet, as different schools compete and struggle for institutional legitimacy, Jakka argues, they all tend to subordinate the names and concepts they use to a property regime, thereby obscuring or compromising forms of listening that occur on the threshold of naming and meaning.

Yet other contributions take an operational, processual view of the general, conceiving it not as a fixed structure but as constantly actualized and reconstituted through techniques in the widest sense. Noting that the notion of home does not just point to a location but also involves a complex process of 'homing', Amina ElHalawani insists that it can only be studied by conjuring it through individual cases. ElHawani's text thus engages in a close reading of key moments in the film *Salt of this Sea* by Annemarie Jacir and the collection of essays *The Idea of Home* by John Hughes. These 'vignettes of homes and homing' allow her to identify what constitutes or recreates home for displaced individuals.

Drawing on the thought of legal historian Yan Thomas, Xenia Chiaramonte's contribution examines law as a casuistic practice, focusing on the interplay between cases and legal institutions. The art of law, she argues, is characterized by the reduction of the 'things' of the social world through the construction of categories, and by the use of these same categories to conduct legal operations. Based on the observation that the quintessential legal performance is that of instituting, Chiaramonte raises the question of how to exercise a legal imagination for Gaia. Her chapter thus calls for a new way of instituting nature: not as a foundation, as is the case in natural law, but rather as a fiction, following the tradition of Roman law.

Seeking to mediate between the reductive poles of singularity and generalization, the case at once participates in these reductions and exceeds them. It thereby calls for its own proliferation, for a movement from case to case within an open-ended list. The device of the list indeed not only features prominently in several contributions but also sparked additional projects, whose outcomes are included at the end of this volume. The 'Excursus' on lists, collected and introduced by Sam Dolbear, Ben Nichols, and Claudia Peppel, and containing contributions by these authors as well as Rachel Aumiller and Iracema Dulley, thus stands as a reminder of the remainder in excess of any reduction.

The Case and the Signifier
Generalization in Freud's *Rat Man*
IRACEMA DULLEY

This piece explores Sigmund Freud's 'Notes upon a Case of Obsessional Neurosis (1909)', a.k.a. the Rat Man case.[1] In this classical case
study, Freud describes the articulation of the symptoms of his patient
Ernst Lanzer, a twenty-nine-year-old upper-middle-class lawyer from
Vienna who is given the epithet of Paul. Through the reception of
Freud's description in psychoanalysis, the Rat Man became a paradigmatic case of obsessional neurosis. Yet, Jacques Lacan draws our
attention to the fact that 'the main interest of this case lies in its particularity'.[2] As the Rat Man case reduces obsessional neurosis to a
particular instantiation of it — that of Paul's subjectivity —, it simultaneously leaves open the scope of its generalization to the extent

*   I thank Cheryl Schmitz, José Jakousi Castañeda Vázquez, Xenia Chiaramonte, Christopher Chamberlin, Jakob Schillinger, Daniel Barber, and Christoph Holzhey for their
comments on previous versions of this text.

1   Sigmund Freud, 'Notes upon a Case of Obsessional Neurosis (1909)', in Freud, *The
Standard Edition of the Complete Psychological Works of Sigmund Freud*, ed. and trans.
by James Strachey and others, 24 vols (London: Hogarth Press, 1953–74), X (1955),
pp. 153–318. Sigmund Freud, 'Bemerkungen über einen Fall von Zwangsneurose', in
Freud, *Gesammelte Werke*, 17 vols (Frankfurt a.M.: Fischer, 1940–52), VII: *Werke aus
den Jahren 1906–1909* (1941), pp. 380–463.

2   Jacques Lacan, 'Le mythe individuel du névrosé', *Ornicar?*, 17–18 (1979), pp. 289–307
(p. 295). All English translations are mine unless otherwise specified.

that it points to singularity as constitutive of subjectivity. In this essay, I propose that the particularity that makes this case study suitable to become paradigmatic is the clarity obtained from the reductiveness with which Freud articulates the chain of signification related to Paul's symptoms in his case description. This seems to have happened through linguistic contagion.

Two central concerns guide my reflection: (i) to question the divide between the individual and the social by showing how signifiers are one of the ways in which the symbolic, that is, language as the Other, inscribes itself onto the subject; and (ii) to discuss how the case study as method proposes generalizations based on a singularity. In order to do so, I investigate both the description of obsessional neurosis proposed by Freud in his 1909 publication and the manuscript containing the notes that he produced during Paul's treatment.[3] The manuscript, one of the few that survived Freud's habit of destroying his notes after his texts were published, is of interest because his notes contain signifiers that are either absent from or not fully explored in his account of the case in 1909. Thus, although it is not possible to return to the scene of analysis itself, through the combination of Freud's notes with his case description one can reconstitute how Freud articulates the chain of signifiers that, according to him, articulated Paul's symptoms in speech even though Paul's capacity to hear the signifiers he uttered only emerged in the course of his analysis. This essay shows how, many decades before Lacan proposed that the meaning of the signifier is not fixed ('le signifiant ne signifie absolument rien'),[4] Freud used transference to draw on the metaphorical malleability of language in neurosis and thereby to displace the fixation that happens in the reduction of signification by the symptom.

---

3   Sigmund Freud, *L'homme aux rats: journal d'une analyse* (Paris: Presses Universitaires de France, 1974). The complete manuscript was published in the German original and its French translation by Elza Ribeiro Hawelka with the collaboration of Pierre Hawelka and the authorization of Anna Freud. In this publication, the German original is published side-by-side with the French translation in a text that has a French title (*L'homme aux rats: journal d'une analyse*). Quotes are from the German original and translations are mine.

4   Jacques Lacan, 'Ouverture à la section clinique', *Ornicar?*, 9 (1977), pp. 7–14 (p. 7).

THE CASE: UNVEILING GENERALIZATION

The case points to the possibility of generalization while retaining the idea that, since what it portrays is a singularity, it also resists generalization. As Lauren Berlant affirms, 'as genre, the case hovers about the singular, the general, and the normative.'[5] The Rat Man case does not claim to contain all the features of obsessional neurosis; nor does it claim to state unequivocally what it is. Yet, to the extent that it names and describes a configuration of symptoms, it establishes a unit of analysis (obsessional neurosis as instantiated in Paul) in relation to which one can discuss both its conclusions and the way in which this unit of analysis is circumscribed. The case makes it possible to include in the narrative the aspects that one thinks constitute its most relevant features without necessarily excluding the existence of other relevant but unexplored ones. It is 'actuarial', i.e. it 'bear[s] the weight of an explanation worthy of attending to and taking a lesson from'.[6] Thus, it implies that something like it has existed in the past and will probably exist in the future. It can serve as a parameter for elucidation to the extent that it is exemplary: as 'an instance of something', the case 'is a genre that organizes singularities into exemplary, intelligible patterns, enmeshing realist claims [...] with analytic aims'.[7]

According to Jean-Claude Passeron and Jacques Revel, the case points in the direction of the laws of the general and the universal without dissolving into them.[8] In presenting the way in which a particular signifier — *Ratte* — makes obsessional neurosis apprehensible in Paul's speech, Freud's case makes the general claim that a singular chain of signifiers articulates the obsessional neurosis of particular subjects. In this process, Rat Man acquires the opacity and malleability of a signifier. As a deictic, it 'blindly directs the attention towards its referent without ever being able to completely define it': Rat Man, as a proper name, allows the different understandings of those who are

---

5   Lauren Berlant, 'On the Case', *Critical Inquiry*, 33.4 (2007), pp. 663–72 (p. 664).

6   Ibid., p. 666.

7   Ibid., p. 670.

8   Jean-Claude Passeron and Jacques Revel, *Penser par cas* (Paris: Enquête, 2005), p. 12 <https://doi.org/10.4000/books.editionsehess.19921>.

familiar with this Freudian case to be indexed to it.[9] Yet, if a case is 'the exploration and deepening of the properties of a *singularity* accessible to the observation' with the purpose of 'extracting from it an argumentation of more general import, the conclusions of which could be reused to ground other intelligibilities or justify other decisions', comparison becomes an implicit procedure.[10] In its self-referentiality, the case generalizes through its singularity.[11] The articulation of signifiers that gives expression to the Rat Man's subjectivity is singular. Yet, it is generalizable that the configuration of a particular chain of signifiers occurs in the constitution of singular subjects — and this is something one verifies by comparing cases qua singularities that are both exceptional and exemplary.

The fact that Freud considers this case a successful one is an exception.[12] His Dora case, for instance, is presented as an example of failed management of transference that led to the patient interrupting her treatment.[13] In the Rat Man case, Freud claims not to fully grasp the mechanisms that lead to the formation of obsessional neurosis in this and other cases despite having been able to cure it. This notwithstanding, through his simultaneous consideration of other cases

---

9   Ibid., p. 12.

10   Ibid., p. 9, their emphasis.

11   Susan Wells, 'Freud's Rat Man and the Case Study: Genre in Three Keys', *New Literary History*, 34.2 (2003), pp. 353–66 (p. 357).

12   In *Freud and the Rat Man* (New Haven, CT: Yale University Press, 1986), Patrick Mahony disagrees on the effectiveness of the treatment in his analysis of transference in the Rat Man case (p. 129), whereas in *Rat Man: Freud's 1909 Case* (New York: New York University Press, 1986), Stuart Schneiderman considers the treatment to have been effective despite the fact that the analysis was interrupted. Both point to Freud's refusal to deal with the role of the mother in the structuring of Paul's symptoms. I would suspend judgment on the question of effectiveness, not only because what cure is remains uncertain to the extent that defining it would depend on an impossible definition of normality, but also because Ernst Lanzer died in WWI a couple of years after the end of his treatment. Yet, I would argue that the capacity he acquired to hear his own signifiers in the course of analysis did displace his symptom — the fact that he got married to Gisela and regained his capacity to work is one of the indexes thereof. For different assessments of Freud's treatment of Paul, see Jerome Beigler, 'A Commentary on Freud's Treatment of the Rat Man', *Annual of Psychoanalysis*, 3 (1975), pp. 271–85 and Samuel Lipton, 'The Advantages of Freud's Technique as Shown in his Analysis of the Rat Man', *International Journal of Psychoanalysis*, 58 (1977), pp. 255–73.

13   Sigmund Freud, 'Fragment of an Analysis of a Case of Hysteria (1905 [1901])', in Freud, *The Standard Edition*, VII (1953), pp. 1–122.

of obsessional neurosis, he attempts to generalize on 'the genesis and finer psychological mechanism of obsessional processes' by means of implicit comparison.[14] As his conclusions are presented as 'some disconnected statements of an aphoristic character' — a characteristic Freud ascribes to obsessional discourse in general —, he recognizes the limited scope of his generalizations.[15] This remark makes one wonder how much the disconnected character of aphorisms bears a resemblance to the aleatoric laws that govern obsessional neurosis. That is, if one considers with Lacan that the analyst is a symptom,[16] to what extent does Freud's account mime the operation of obsessional neurosis? As will become clear in what follows, Freud's account of the case is pervaded by rat-related signifiers that seem to have entered it through obsessional contagion.

According to Freud, Paul sought treatment after having read a few pages of *The Psychopathology of Everyday Life*. Paul said he was impressed by Freud's 'explanation of some curious verbal associations' (Aufklärung sonderbarer Wortverknüpfungen) in that work.[17] Thus, it seems that the patient's transference with Freud, based on which he attributed to the psychoanalyst the capacity to deal with the causes that lead to paralysis in his life, was related to Freud's capacity to explain the strange association of words through which the patient's symptoms — 'fears' (Befürchtungen), 'compulsive impulses' (Zwangsimpulse), and 'prohibitions' (Verbote) — were articulated.[18] According to Freud, the unconscious is expressed in language differently in each kind of neurosis: while the language of hysteria leads to conversion into bodily symptoms, in obsessional neurosis the meaning of the patient's spoken language is to be discovered behind the veil of generalization and indeterminateness.

This is what Freud says regarding the way in which generalization operates in obsessional neurosis — the example refers to Paul's simultaneous fear of and wish for his father's death:

---

14   Freud, 'Notes upon a Case', p. 155.
15   Ibid.
16   Jacques Lacan, *Le séminaire de Jacques Lacan*, ed. by Jacques-Alain Miller (Paris: Seuil, 1973–), XXIII: *Le Sinthome (1975–1976)* (2005).
17   Freud, 'Notes upon a Case', p. 159; 'Bemerkungen', p. 385.
18   Ibid., p. 158; p. 384.

Side by side with the obsessive wish, and intimately associated
with it, was an obsessive fear: every time he had a wish of
this kind he could not help fearing that something dreadful
would happen. This something dreadful was already clothed
in a characteristic indeterminateness [Unbestimmtheit] which
was thenceforward to be an invariable feature of every manifestation of the neurosis. But in a child it is not hard to discover
what it is that is veiled behind an indeterminateness of this
kind. If the patient can once be induced to give a particular
instance in place of the vague generalities [verschwommenen
Allgemeinheiten] which characterize an obsessional neurosis,
it may be confidently assumed that the instance is the original
and actual thing which has tried to hide itself behind the generalization [Verallgemeinerung]. Our present patient's obsessive
fear, therefore, when restored to its original meaning, would
run as follows: 'If I have this wish to see a woman naked, my
father will be bound to die.'[19]

Thus, according to Freud, the idiom of generalization serves as a veil to
the patient's actual wish: Paul says 'something dreadful' could happen
when he actually means that his father could die. For Freud, the difference between this procedure and what one finds in hysteria is not only
of the order of sexuality, but also of the order of language:

The language of an obsessional neurosis — the means by which
it expresses its secret thoughts — is, as it were, only a dialect
of the language of hysteria; but it is a dialect in which we
ought to be able to find our way about more easily, since it is
more nearly related to the forms of expression adopted by our
conscious thought than is the language of hysteria. Above all,
it does not involve the leap from a mental process to a somatic
innervation — hysterical conversion — which can never be
fully comprehensible to us.[20]

Freud seems to be saying that differently from hysteria, in which conversion inscribes the symptom onto the body (as Lacan would put it,

---

19   Ibid., p. 163; pp. 388–89.
20   Ibid., pp. 156–57. Freud relates that patients suffering from obsessional neurosis have
      an early interest in and beginning of sexual activity, which is absent in the constitution
      of hysteria. This corresponds to the coupling of hysteria with a shock related to
      the experience of passive presexual stimulation experienced as disgusting and the
      coupling of obsessional neurosis with active presexual activity experienced as pleasant
      (Mahony, *Freud and the Rat Man*). Yet, this opposition is undone if one considers this
      quoted passage, in which obsessionality is understood to be 'a dialect of hysteria', i.e.,
      hysteria of a certain kind.

the signifier as metaphor), obsessional neurosis manifests itself mostly at the level of spoken language (the signifier as metonymy). When Freud says that obsessional neurosis is a dialect whose meaning is easier to grasp because it is 'more nearly related to the forms of expression adopted by our conscious thought', one wonders whether the majestic plural refers to Freud himself. In Freud's conception of language, language bears a homological, that is, representational, relation to the world — his reality principle resides in this supposition.[21] Thus, he conceives of language in the constative mode, that is, in the mode in which statements are judged to be true or false descriptions of a world external to language.[22] Yet, Freud recognizes that the relationship between language and its supposed referents is not straightforward. For while the language of hysteria leads to conversion into bodily symptoms, in obsessional neurosis the meaning of the patient's spoken language is to be discovered behind the veil of generalization.

In a footnote, Freud attempts to generalize the way in which 'names and words' are employed by obsessive and hysterical subjects. His contrastive generalization depends on a comparison of degree:

> Names and words [Namen und Worten] are not nearly so frequently or so recklessly employed in obsessional neuroses as in hysteria for the purpose of establishing a connection [Verknüpfung] between unconscious thoughts (whether they are impulses or phantasies) and symptoms.[23]

Hysteria is said to employ *more* 'names and words' to connect symptoms to the unconscious, whereas obsessional neurosis would employ *fewer*. Yet, Freud's observation is made in relation to a situation in which names and words play a crucial role. Paul starts to be concerned about his weight after meeting a man he considered a competitor for Gisela's love, whose nickname was Dick, which in German means 'fat' as an adjective. After this attempted generalization, in which Freud claims that the example he gave is a somewhat rare one, he contradicts himself as he offers one more empirical instance in which a signifier

---

21   Susan Gal, 'Politics of Translation', *Annual Review of Anthropology*, 44 (2015), pp. 225–40.

22   John Austin, *How to Do Things with Words* (Oxford: Oxford University Press, 1962); Mary Pratt, 'Ideology and Speech Act Theory', *Poetics Today*, 7.1 (1986), pp. 59–72.

23   Freud, 'Notes upon a Case', p. 189; 'Bemerkungen', p. 411.

(in this case a related one) operates in the same way in another case of obsessional neurosis:

> I happen, however, to recollect another instance in which the very same name, Richard, was similarly used by a patient whom I analysed a long time since. After a quarrel with his brother he began brooding over the best means of getting rid of his fortune, and declaring that he did not want to have anything more to do with money, and so on. His brother was called Richard, and 'richard' is the French for 'a rich man'.[24]

One could say that just as behind Paul's generalizations there is an attempt to disguise his simultaneous fear of and desire for the death of people towards whom his feelings are ambivalent, behind Freud's generalizations on obsessional neurosis one finds the Rat Man case.[25] Yet, Freud's move is an ingenuous one: in presenting obsessional neurosis in the form of a case study that lays the ground for generalization, he both unveils the singularities on which his generalizations draw (the case that he describes and the other cases he mentions in footnotes) and points to the veil of generalization through which obsessional neurosis is constituted as a generalizable phenomenon. The example thus emerges as the singularity that generalization seeks to veil. According to Freud, this very procedure — that of producing a generalization based on singularities that are not always made explicit

---

24   Ibid.

25   Freud centres these wishes on the figure of the father, but his notes also reveal Paul's mother and Gisela's grandmother as the objects of similar wishes (Freud, *L'homme aux rats*, p. 156). For an assessment of the role of female figures in Paul's neurosis, see Ruth Abraham and K. H. Blacker, 'The Rat Man Revisited: Comments on Maternal Influences', *International Journal of Psychoanalytic Psychotherapy*, 9 (1982–1983), pp. 705–27. Freud's notes indeed reveal that Paul's mother was a domineering figure who controlled his money (Freud, *L'homme aux rats*, p. 182). I agree with Schneiderman's interpretation that Paul's oscillation between the richer cousin and the cousin he loved is related not only to the fact that Paul interiorized his mother's interpretation that his father chose her over the poorer woman he loved but also to Paul's oscillation between his sisters, who appear in Freud's notes as early objects of his desire (Schneiderman, *Rat Man*; Freud, *L'homme aux rats*, pp. 140–42, 164, and 246). The governess who is mentioned as Paul's first seducer and is remembered by her 'masculine-sounding' last name, Rudolf, also appears to have been a domineering woman — which also calls into question Freud's affirmation that obsessional neurosis is related to the early enjoyment of an active sexual role. Béla Grunberger ('Some Reflections on the Rat Man', *International Journal of Psycho-Analysis*, 47 (1966), pp. 160–68 (p. 162)) points to Paul's 'hesitat[ion] [...] over his desire to identify with the anal-sadistic mother' and Beigler ('A Commentary', p. 273) to his 'intense identification' with his mother.

— also characterizes obsessional neurosis. Freud's procedure bears a strange familiarity with that of his patient but differs from it in that the disclosure of his method renders the similarity between their procedures ironic.

Just like the rat-related signifiers employed in chain by Paul articulate his symptoms, Freud's naming and description of the Rat Man case constitute it as a paradigmatic case of obsessional neurosis. 'Rat Man' (Rattenmann) is the epithet given by Freud to both the case and the individual at its core.[26] This act of naming brings to the fore the torture method by which Paul was disturbed and the centrality of the rat-related signifiers in the articulation of his symptoms. Naming the case after the rat that obsessively occupied Paul's thoughts approximates him to the animal he feared. Implicitly, the compulsion that characterizes obsession is thus compared to the rat whose means of escaping from its own conundrum implies trying, but failing, to escape. This is why Lacan affirms that the case receives its name from a fantasy.[27]

The Rat Man is singularized through the making proper of that which was originally a common name or, better said, two common names: 'rat' (Ratte) and 'man' (Mann). In this juxtaposition, the autonomy of man as human is questioned by the contagion of animality that emerges when this man is said to be of the rat kind: *Rattenmann* can be translated as (i) 'Rat Man', that is, a man who is a rat; (ii) 'the man of rats', that is, the man who has something to do with rats ('l'homme aux rats', as the case is known in French); (iii) through approximated homophony, it can also mean 'the indebted man', for *Ratenmann*, 'installment man', points to debt of a postponed kind, postponement being one of the effects of debt in Paul's life.[28] Whereas for Freud Paul's neurosis revolves around his paralysis by doubt and indecision, Lacan relates it to debt:[29] Paul's unpayable debt to his

---

26   The epithet already appears in a letter sent to C. G. Jung in 1909.

27   Lacan, 'Le mythe'.

28   *Rattenmännchen*, the diminutive of *Rattenmann*, is used in reference to male rats (I thank Jakob Schillinger for this insight). This signifier does not appear in Freud's account but resonates the association between rats and children discussed below.

29   Lacan, 'Le mythe'. On the role of debt in obsessional neurosis, see Moustapha Safouan, 'The Signification of Debt in Obsessional Neurosis', pp. 77–82, and Charles Melman, 'The Rat Man', in *Obsessional Neurosis: Lacanian Perspectives*, ed. by Astrid Gessert (London: Routledge, 2018), pp. 83–92 as well as Martha N. Evans, 'Introduction to

father; the debt of his father towards the friend who saved his father from ruin after his father gambled away the military's money (which is rearticulated in Paul's imaginary as his debt to one of his colleagues); his father's indebtedness to his mother, a rich woman, to whom his father owed his upward social mobility; Paul's guilt over the suicide of a woman whose love he dismissed. The automatism of repetition in Paul's compulsions and thoughts, overdetermined by the paralysing manifestation of debt in the form of guilt, fear, and compulsion, bears a strange resemblance to the instinctual nature of rats. This resemblance is captured in the name Freud attributed to this case.

SINGULARITY AND THE SIGNIFIER

As already stated, my reading of the work of the signifier in the Rat Man case is based on the chain of signification found in the case and in Freud's notes. As far as the relationship between the utterances proffered in the analytic setting and the publication of the case in writing is concerned, the psychoanalytic case stands in between what Lacan calls *énonciation* and *énoncé*, for the signifiers that appear in the case were once uttered but have been reduced to writing. Whereas the *énoncé*, i.e. that which is uttered, can be fixated in writing, the *énonciation*, i.e. the performative act of uttering as it happens in analysis, is not transposable to the written form. Yet, the chain of signification that emerged in the analysis of Paul can be retraced through Freud's writing, in which the Lacanian concept of the signifier is absent but the role of *Wortlaut* (roughly translatable as 'wording') in the articulation of neurosis is underlined.

What are the effects of the chain of signifiers mobilized in the Rat Man case? The work of the signifier in analysis depends on its being voiced in the psychoanalytic situation. In the latter, through transference, the subject emerges as it articulates the chain of signification that constitutes it. Thus, in relation to the dynamic situation of analysis, the articulation of a chain of signification in the case study might appear as

---

Jacques Lacan's Lecture: The Neurotic's Individual Myth', *The Psychoanalytic Quarterly*, 48.3 (1979), pp. 386–404. Evans highlights how the institution of the name of the father entails the connection between the subject and the symbolic through an unpayable debt.

a reduction of the transferential work through which Paul emerged as a subject to an empty and opaque chain of signification. Yet, as the analytical process is fixated in writing, this chain of signification appears to be made up of signifiers that, in their opacity, are simultaneously subjective and social, singular and generalizable.

As already mentioned, it is impossible to have direct access to the work of the signifier as it happened in Paul's analysis through Freud's text. Writing indexes the situation in which signifiers were uttered (*énonciation*) but halts the potential for flotation that resides in the act of speaking, for writing reduces signifiers to meaning as it fixates them (thus transforming them into *énoncé*). Yet, this question can be displaced if one thinks of the chain of signifiers that emerges in the Rat Man case as a production resulting from the encounter of the unconscious of Paul and the unconscious of Freud mediated through the German language, the medium through which contagion was possible. In this case, the opposition between the written and the oral, the individual and the social, is blurred, for spacing and displacement in time characterize the work of the signifier in both its oral and written instantiations.[30] In what follows, transference appears as the medium for transposing the work of the signifier through which Paul emerged as a subject in the analytic setting into a chain of signification made up of opaque signifiers that are simultaneously subjective and social, singular and generalizable, and can therefore be displaced as they float.

In Freud's case, the rat-related chain of signification articulates Paul's symptoms: doubt, indecision, paralysis. It operates in a reductive mode to the extent that the way in which signifiers are articulated overdetermines the possibilities of action and experience of this particular subject. And yet, the emergence of this specific articulation of signifiers in the course of Paul's analysis is the condition of possibility for their displacement — and their displacement, to the extent that it relies on analysis, i.e. on the encounter with Freud's unconscious, is social. After Lacan, one can advance the claim that this is the reason why Freud could consider Paul to be 'cured', that is, relieved of these specific symptoms. The chain of signifiers articulated by Paul reveals

---

30   Jacques Derrida, 'Plato's Pharmacy', in Derrida, *Dissemination*, trans. by Barbara Johnson (Chicago: University of Chicago Press, 1981), pp. 61–171.

what Lacan calls the 'individual myth of the neurotic' to which his symptoms are connected. Through transference with Freud, in whom the signifiers voiced by Paul resonate *nachträglich* (afterwards or a posteriori), i.e. can be attached to different signifieds as they are allowed to float through Freud's *Deutung* ('interpretation' or, more literally, 'indication'), the fixity of their relation to his symptom is undone. Let us explore the particularity of the chain of signifiers the case mobilizes and its relationship to 'the individual myth of the neurotic'.

In the beginning of his narrative, Freud poses the following question:

> What can have been the meaning of the child's idea that if he had this lascivious wish [of seeing a woman naked] his father would be bound to die? Was it sheer nonsense? Or are there means of understanding the words and of perceiving them as a necessary consequence of earlier events and premises?[31]

In the original in German, Freud speaks not of 'words' but of a 'sentence': 'Ist das barer Unsinn, oder gibt es Wege, diesen Satz zu verstehen, ihn als notwendiges Ergebnis früherer Vorgänge und Voraussetzungen zu erfassen?'.[32] This combination of words is indeed not only a sentence in the grammatical sense, as implied by the German *Satz*, but also one in the legal sense if one thinks of a legal sentence in English. Thus, the rules that guide the Rat Man's 'individual myth' articulate the relationship between language and the law frequently pointed at in Lacanian psychoanalysis. The language in which this injunction is articulated produces effects: Paul's desire to see a naked female body leads to his fear (and wish) that his father, who stood in the way of the concretization of his desire, might die. Paralysis in his life is related to this sentence, in both senses of the word. One more sentence is to be added to it — the one pronounced by Paul's father in the childhood scene recounted by his mother, in which upon being beaten by his father for having bitten his nurse, Paul calls his father the names of various objects. His father's reaction is to stop beating him and pronounce the following sentence directed at Paul's mother:

---

31   Freud, 'Notes upon a Case', p. 164.
32   Freud, 'Bemerkungen', p. 389.

'The child will grow up to be either a great man or a great criminal!'.[33] Where Freud and his commentators have usually seen in this scene Paul's imperfect mastery of language, for Stuart Schneiderman this sentence both puts Paul in the position of an object that is talked about and points to the centrality of the mother, for whom the father might have been a decorative object in the house like the ones Paul named.[34]

'A captain with a Czech name' is presented by Freud as the person who unleashed the worsening of Paul's symptoms by telling him about a 'horrible punishment used in the East': 'the criminal [der Verurteilte] was tied up ... [...] a pot was turned upside down on his buttocks ... some *rats* were put into it ... and they ... [...] *bored their way in* ...'.[35] Paul, who accused himself of being a 'criminal' to both the friend who advised him to be treated and to Freud, was unable to complete the sentence he uttered only with much difficulty, having the analyst fill in the gap by naming the victim's anus. Paul feared that this punishment might be inflicted on the woman he loved and on his father, although the latter was deceased. To avoid that this fantasy might happen, he adopted two 'defensive measures' (*Abwehrmassregel*): a 'but' (in German, *aber*, later modified to *abér*, a signifier whose sound approximates *Abwehr*, 'defense') accompanied by a gesture of repudiation, and the phrase 'whatever are you thinking of?' (Was fällt dir denn ein?).[36] Here, the distinction between word and gesture collapses as both are reduced to the status of a ritual of avoidance in which signifiers that were part of his analysis seem to take part (analysis is thus literally transformed into a defense mechanism). As in magic, the performative juxtaposition of words and their effects is to be contrasted with 'the peculiar indeterminateness of all his remarks' (die eigentümliche Un-

---

33   Freud, 'Notes upon a Case', p. 205.

34   Schneiderman, *Rat Man*.

35   Freud, 'Notes upon a Case', p. 166; 'Bemerkungen', pp. 391–92.

36   Ibid., p. 167; p. 392. Mahony associates the stress placed on the last syllable of the word with Paul's anal fixation. He brilliantly reads the contamination of defense by drive in time as he foregrounds the ambiguity contained in the conjunction *aber*, both disjunction (but) and conjunction (again). The same seems to be the case in the 'apotropaic formula' *Glej(i)samen*, which Paul employed to prevent evil from happening to Gisela as he masturbated thinking of her. In this formula, Gisela's name is coupled to *Samen*, sperm, hinting at the possibility of producing children (Mahony, *Freud and the Rat Man*, pp. 58–59). Yet, the addition of *ohne Ratten* (Freud, *L'homme aux rats*, p. 176) to the formula undoes this imaginary action.

bestimmtheit aller seiner Reden).[37] Such indeterminateness, which
Freud also associates with Paul's tendency to vaguely generalize, was
overdetermined by the singular articulation of a chain of signifiers.

This strange juxtaposition of language, gesture, and the magical effects of their conjunction is followed, in Freud's case, by Paul's account
of his debt. His account brings to the fore one aspect Freud presents as
central to obsessional neurosis: the 'mésalliance [...] between an affect
and its ideational content' (eine Mesalliance zwischen Vorstellungsinhalt und Affekt).[38] During his military exercises, Paul received a pair
of glasses that had been paid for by someone else. He was therefore to
reimburse this person. He rationally knew that he merely had to send
the payment to the woman who worked at the post office. Yet, in his
mind, he came up with a myriad of complicated forms of repaying this
debt in order to follow the self-imposed command that he should pay a
specific colleague, in a phantasmatic instantiation of his father's unpaid
debt to his friend. Thus, a situation that could have easily been solved
gave rise to Paul's state of anguish. Freud recognizes the role of chance
and wording in the unleashing of Paul's neurosis both in his notes and
in the case description:

> Now it happened by chance — for chance may play a part in the
> formation of a symptom, just as the wording may help in the
> making of a joke — that one of his father's little adventures had
> an important element in common with the captain's request.
> His father, in his capacity as non-commissioned officer, had
> control over a small sum of money and had on one occasion lost
> it at cards. (Thus he had been a 'Spielratte' [literally 'game rat';
> gambler].) He would have found himself in a serious position
> if one of his comrades had not advanced him the amount.[39]

Paul's father now appears in the position of the rat, and the kind of
rat he is said to be — a 'game rat' (a gambler) — is one determined
by debt. It so happened that the captain who had told Paul the story of
the rat torture also mistakenly told him that he was to reimburse one of
his comrades (a 'Kamerad') who had paid for his glasses — 'Kamerad'

---

37   Freud, 'Notes upon a Case', p. 167; 'Bemerkungen', p. 392.
38   Ibid., p. 175; p. 399.
39   Freud, 'Notes upon a Case', p. 210; 'Bemerkungen', p. 430. For Freud's discussion of
      chance and wording, see Freud, L'homme aux rats, p. 216.

being another word in which the rat insinuates itself through homophony, establishing the bond between the gambler and the friend
who saved his reputation as a bond between rats.[40] Paul's extreme
affective reaction was unleashed by this chance happening: a person
who Paul thought to be violent articulated two signifiers of the chain
that was connected to the configuration of his symptoms. As the captain reminds Paul of the debt he unwillingly acquired when someone
paid for his glasses, Paul is put in a similar position to his father — a
position he associates with rats. He does not know whether his father
ever managed to pay the debt that haunts him. Moreover, to his father's
debt towards his friend is added his father's debt towards Paul's mother.
This debt, which is replicated in the suggestion by Paul's mother that
he marry a well-off cousin instead of the poor woman he loved, is
connected to Paul's obsessional complex through the word *heiraten*, in
German, 'to marry'. Through marriage, he would reproduce his father's
action and thus become indebted like his father, a *Spielratte*, a man
whose actions of gambling and marrying up are connected, in Paul's
spoken unconscious, to the parasitical being of the rat: both tormentor
and victim.

Freud is very clear about the fact that in this case, association is
also related to the sound of words, not only to their content. Although
the writing of the case might have the effect of congealing words, when
Freud speaks of *Wortlaut* he is pointing to both the articulation of
ideas and the dynamic character of sound in speech: He speaks of the
'Wortbrücke Raten-Ratten', that is, of a 'verbal bridge' between these
two words.[41] For Freud, cure would follow the discovery of the unconscious content (Vorstellung) that lies at the origin of this heightened
affective load, whereas for Lacan this affect is related to the signifier.[42]
Since signifiers float, the relationship between affect and signifier can
undergo a short-circuit in the course of analysis through which fixation
in the coupling of signifier and affect is undone. That is, there is no ori-

---

40   The word *Kamerad* is to be found in Freud, 'Bemerkungen', p. 430.
41   Freud, 'Notes upon a Case', p. 213; 'Bemerkungen', p. 433.
42   Lacan is frequently credited with a re-reading of Freud in which the unconscious is
      thought of as being structured as a language. Although Freud did not engage with the
      linguistic turn, I agree with Lacan's affirmation in 'Ouverture à la section clinique' that
      the centrality of language is already to be found in Freud.

ginal content to be excavated; there are relations whose displacement can occur as they are repeated in speech. There is no concept of the signifier in Freud, but the 'symbolic' does make an adjectival appearance: 'rats had acquired a series of symbolic meanings, to which, during the period which followed, fresh ones were continually being added' (die Ratten hatten [...] eine Reihe von symbolischen Bedeutungen erworben, zu welchen in der Folgezeit immer neue hinzutraten).[43] It is thus the 'verbal bridge' that connects installments (*Raten*) and debt to rats (*Ratten*) and torture that unleashes Paul's 'anal erotism', which Freud connects to imaginary anal penetration. Although not present in the case description, one more signifier is mentioned by Freud in the meeting of the Vienna Psychoanalytic Society on 8 April 1908, the first occasion on which he presented the case while still working on it: *raten*, as Freud states that Paul 'admits that he does not distinguish between *Ratten* (rats) and *raten* (to guess)'.[44]

TRANSFERENCE AS *RATEN*

Freud associates the rat with the penis based on the fact that 'rats are carriers of dangerous infectious diseases' and being in the army was associated with the possibility of acquiring syphilis.[45] It is unclear from his case account whether this association was established by the patient or by himself, but the notes reveal that it was Freud who interpreted that a rat was a penis, following which Paul developed a sequence of Oedipal associations.[46] In the case notes, Freud clearly states: 'rats mean fear of syphilis' (Ratten bedeutet Syphilis-Angst).[47] For Patrick Mahony, the association between rat and penis points to

---

43   The references for this and the next quote are: Freud, 'Notes upon a Case', p. 213; 'Bemerkungen', p. 432.

44   Mahony, *Freud and the Rat Man*, p. 80. Otto Rank, who wrote a brief report of Freud's presentation on the occasion, does not make any reference to the role played by language in obsessional neurosis. Instead, he highlights the role played by the coexistence of feelings of love and hate towards the same person and its manifestation in the forms of obsession, doubt, and a paralysis of will. It might be the case that the role of language in the manifestation of Paul's symptoms had not yet been articulated by Freud. See Otto Rank, 'Bericht über die I. private Psychoanalytische Vereinigung in Salzburg am 27. April 1908', *Zentralblatt für Psychoanalyse*, 1.3 (1910), pp. 125–26.

45   Freud, 'Notes upon a Case', p. 214.

46   Beigler, 'A Commentary', p. 278.

47   Freud, *L'homme aux rats*, p. 166.

Paul's ambivalence, castration anxiety, and fear of success.[48] This also appears in Freud's notes, in which Paul's dream of having a tooth extracted is interpreted by Freud as castration and Paul's loss of his glasses — which, according to Schneiderman, enabled him to exercise his voyeurism — as establishing an association between loss of erection and cowardice.[49] In line with his downplaying of female figures in the case analysis, Freud leaves out of the case description the association between rat as penis and Paul's mother's braid, which he used to hold as a child and which he designated as a 'Rattenschweif' (a rat's tail).[50] It was probably the phallic character of Paul's mother — who was similar to Freud's own mother in that respect, this being a possible reason for her elision from the case description — that contributed to Paul's development of the theory that sexual intercourse happens through the anus.[51] This is probably why he came to the conclusion, also absent from the case description and written down only in the notes, that 'to be married consists of showing each other one's buttocks' (verheiratet sein besteht darin, dass man sich gegenseitig den Po zeige) — a conclusion to which Paul came as he saw his mother's buttocks while lying in bed with her.[52]

It is the sound of *rat*, in German, that promotes the association between rats (*Ratten*), debt (implicit in *Raten*, 'installments'), and marriage (*heiraten*). There is one German word that is not mentioned by Freud as a relevant signifier but would easily fit into this chain of associations and could be related to Paul's transference: *Rat*, that is, 'advice',[53] which can also mean a way out of a difficult situation — in this case, Paul's identification with both the criminal and the rat.[54] Freud, as a *Berater* or *Ratgeber*, i.e. advisor, stood in a hierarchical relation to Paul, who usually looked up to him as the person who could put an end

---

48 Mahony, *Freud and the Rat Man*, p. 53.

49 Freud, *L'homme aux rats*, p. 248. Schneiderman, *Rat Man*.

50 Freud, *L'homme aux rats*, pp. 172 and 134.

51 Ibid., p. 230.

52 Ibid., p. 234.

53 However, 'to give advice' (Rat geben) appears in Freud's notes (Freud, *L'homme aux rats*, p. 236).

54 This also seems to be the case in Frederick Wertz's depiction of Paul as a 'jailed criminal' in 'Freud's Case of the Rat Man Revisited: An Existential-Phenomenological and Socio-Historical Analysis', *Journal of Phenomenological Psychology*, 34.1 (2003), pp. 47–78.

to his neurosis. This relationship, both friendly — Freud sounds very similar to *Freund*, 'friend' in German — and hierarchical, is hinted at by Freud as he discusses how transference places him in the position of Paul's father. This is made clear through a further association between rats and children: Paul pitied rats out of his own identification with them since childhood, when he was violently punished by his father for biting someone. Yet, as will become clear below, Freud also occupied a hierarchically subordinate position in transference despite not having acknowledged this in the case description.[55]

In Paul's speech, rats also stand for children. Freud says that as Paul was talking about the Rat-Wife in Ibsen's *Little Eyolf*, who in Freud's notes is identified with Paul's mother, it 'became impossible to escape the inference that in many of the shapes assumed by his obsessional deliria rats had another meaning still — namely, that of *children*'.[56] This is, according to Freud, the original reason why Paul identified with the rat: a sharpened-teeth animal that can bite but is persecuted by humans with cruelty. He pitied rats out of his own identification with them since childhood, and the reason for his indecision as to whether he should marry (*heiraten*) the woman he loved was connected to the rat complex in one more way: he loved children and she had undergone an operation that made her incapable of bearing any. Yet, at the same time, Freud's notes also reveal that since Paul did not identify with his father's choice of marrying up, he also did not want to 'betray' (verraten) the woman he loved.[57] Simultaneously, as an ambivalent son, he reproached himself for not having 'advised' (zuraten) his father to take care of his health as much as he thought he should.[58]

There are further transferential associations connected to the rat-related chain of signification that Freud does not explore. In Freud's interpretation, the rat is also connected to money, a relation that appears in transference as Paul comes up with a 'rat currency' to calculate the price of his analysis sessions: 'Soviel Gulden soviel Ratten', that is, 'So many florins, so many rats'.[59] This association acquires sex-

---

55   The fact that one of Freud's children was also called Ernst might have played a role in Freud's understanding of his place in transference as that of the father.

56   Freud, 'Notes upon a Case', p. 215.

57   Freud, *L'homme aux rats*, p. 194.

58   Ibid., p. 198.

59   Freud, 'Notes upon a Case', p. 213. 'Bemerkungen', p. 433.

ual meaning as Paul associates Freud's name with 'Freudenhaus' (a brothel):[60] the sessions were conducted in the analyst's home; one of his daughters appears in Paul's dream and deliria as having feces (i.e. money) in the place of her eyes and is assimilated to the rat complex in the position of the richer woman Paul's mother wanted him to marry; one of Paul's dreams instantiates his childhood fantasy that children are produced through the contact between the anuses of the parents: it pictures a coitus between Freud's wife and Freud's mother in which their anuses are united by a herring, the same fish Paul was served and refused to eat when he was offered a meal at Freud's house.[61]

As Ruth Abraham and K. H. Blacker suggest, despite Freud's tendency to see himself as occupying the position of Paul's father in transference, the association between *Gulden* and *Ratten* actually put him in the position of a prostitute, 'certainly a reflection of [Paul's] attitude toward his own women-dominated house, with his mother viewed as the Madame who charges her fee'.[62] It was indeed the case that the person who put pressure on Paul for him to marry the richer cousin and was in charge of the money he inherited upon his father's death was his mother, with whom he seems to have identified Freud. To the extent that Paul's delirium about the price of the session — 'Soviel Gulden soviel Ratten' — also appears as Paul considers how much money he needs to disburse to have sex with his lover, it points to the fact that he sees the price of the analysis session as equivalent to the price of a session of sexual intercourse.[63]

Freud occupies the position of a prostitute in a different way as he tries to guess — in German, *raten* or *erraten* — in order to fill in the gaps in Paul's narrative. As Paul mentions the narrative that unleashed the crisis that led him to seek Freud, he puts the analyst in the position of the torturer who will punish the 'criminal' (Paul), something that is marked by him calling Freud 'Captain' (Hauptmann).[64] Mahony proposes to see this scene of analysis as one of 'acting in':

60   Freud, *L'homme aux rats*, p. 158.
61   For an appreciation of the impact of Freud's feeding Paul on his analysis, see Beigler, 'A Commentary'.
62   Abraham and Blacker, 'Rat Man Revisited', p. 718.
63   Freud, *L'homme aux rats*, pp. 190–92.
64   Freud, 'Notes upon a Case', p. 169; 'Bemerkungen', p. 394.

the very mimetic manner of the Rat Man's expression turned it from being a discourse that simply narrates to one that enacts, performs; its very style and delivery *in* and *through* themselves constituted an enactive meaning. To be more specific: after initially voicing his resistance, the Rat Man went on, for one long uninterrupted paragraph in Freud's text, to introduce the narrative setting of the rat torture. With that accomplished, his gaping delivery elicited Freud's narrative participation in a complementary movement of thrust and counterthrust.[65]

In Mahony's reading, Freud's guessing of the missing signifiers in this scene is the equivalent of the anal penetration that Paul both feared and desired: a 'verbal happening' in which 'the Rat man multiplied holes in his sentences which Freud filled with correct guessing — *erraten*'.[66] Freud recognized the sexual component of this session but did not explore anality in his case description as much as he explored other aspects of obsessionality. As far as transference is concerned, his silence on the matter fits well with his striving towards the sublimation of homosexuality. The same kind of defensiveness seems to contagiously affect Mahony's language as he speaks of 'anal rape in lexical installments' where one might also have asked whether this was not a mutually enjoyable (in the Lacanian sense) situation.[67] This notwithstanding, I agree with Mahony that as Paul paid in rats, he both submitted to Freud and treated him as a prostitute.[68] Here the signifier *Unrat*, absent from both the case and the notes, but still implied as the imperfect opposite of *Rat*, points to the analyst's position as rest, waste, and excess — which Freud acknowledges in the notes as he affirms 'but I cannot guess' (ich kann aber nicht erraten [*sic*]).[69] From this position, which supposes the acceptance of castration, it becomes visible that the only alternative to anguish is to relinquish the fantasies that lead to imaginary castration: Paul's conundrum as Rat Man lies in his incapacity to choose, that is, to relinquish (*entraten*).

As a guessing prostitute, Freud was, according to Mahony, looking for 'the locality at which the repressed breaks through' in obsessional

---

65   Mahony, *Freud and the Rat Man*, p. 103, his emphasis.
66   Ibid., pp. 104 and 105.
67   Ibid., p. 106.
68   Ibid., p. 107.
69   Freud, *L'homme aux rats*, p. 158.

neurosis, which is 'word presentation and not the concept attached to it'.[70] Thus, for Mahony, obsessional ideas are said to unite 'the most disparate things under a single word with multiple meanings': Through words that are ambiguous, 'obsessional ideas are clothed in a characteristic verbal vagueness in order to permit such multiple development'.[71] That is, the vagueness of obsessional discourse is related to the way in which different ideas can be organized around the materiality and opacity of the signifier: *Wortlaut*.

CONCLUDING REMARKS: *WORTLAUT*, THE SUBJECT, AND THE SOCIAL

Freud calls the reader's attention to the role of wording in the chance articulation of Paul's neurosis: 'It was almost as though Fate, when the captain told him his story, had been putting him through an association test: she had called out a "complex stimulus-word" [...], and he had reacted to it with his obsessional idea' (Das Schicksal hatte ihm in der Erzählung des Hauptmannes sozusagen ein Komplexreizwort zugerufen, und er versäumte nicht, mit seiner Zwangsidee darauf zu reagieren).[72] Paul does not hear the rat-related chain of signifiers before analysis although he is the one who articulates it. This is because, paradoxically, 'the patients themselves do not know the wording [Wortlaut] of their own obsessional ideas' (die Kranken den Wortlaut ihrer eigenen Zwangsvorstellungen nicht kennen).[73] They do not know the wording of their ideas, but place value in how they sound: 'words have value for him' (Worte haben Wert für ihn).[74] In his notes, Freud associates Paul's interrogation of death with the sound of the word *sterben* as he reproduces the scene in which the patient asks this question: 'What does death mean? As if the sound of the word should tell him' (Was heißt denn 'sterben'? Als ob der Laut des Wortes es ihm sagen müßte).[75] The centrality of death and the desire to control it is also related to rats in Paul's speech as he 'wishes people rats' (jeman-

---

70   Mahony, *Freud and the Rat Man*, p. 287.
71   Ibid., pp. 287 and 288.
72   Freud, 'Notes upon a Case', p. 216; 'Bemerkungen', p. 435.
73   Ibid., p. 223; p. 441.
74   Freud, *L'homme aux rats*, p. 216.
75   Ibid., p. 202.

dem Ratten wünschen), that is, wants them to die, whenever they force him to make a decision.[76]

The fixed and partially unrecognized articulation of signifiers that is connected to the fully functioning neurosis is destabilized during the work of analysis, when 'the patient, who has hitherto turned his eyes away in terror from his own pathological productions, begins to attend to them and obtains a clearer and more detailed view of them'.[77] This idea is in itself not new to those familiar with the psychoanalytical technique. What is of special interest to our discussion is how one of the precepts of obsessional thought attributed by Freud to his patients guides his own analysis of the case. It is the extraordinary character of the articulation of signifiers that express Paul's symptoms that allows Freud to articulate his generalizations on obsessional neurosis. Like his obsessive patient, Freud generalizes based on one example. Yet, to the extent that this is brought to the fore, the case remains open to being displaced by other cases labeled as cases of obsessional neurosis. The singularity of the Rat Man case relates to the fact that in it the role played by signifiers in the dialect spoken by the subject as he articulates his neurosis is especially clear. Through the depiction of this singularity, Freud is able to state that this occurs in obsessional neurosis in general as he implicitly compares this case with other cases and chooses it for its exemplary character.

According to John Forrester, the case, the 'style of reasoning dominant in psychoanalysis', opposes the Aristotelian idea that 'there can only be a science of the universal and the necessary'.[78] Since practical wisdom, which is based on individuals, and therefore on particulars, is not considered knowledge in the Aristotelian tradition, no knowledge of individuals is possible. Yet, the syllogistic reasoning proposed by Aristotle depends on 'an inductively derived generalization to further particulars'.[79] This proposition by Forrester comes from John Stuart Mill's idea that the general is only necessary because people's memory is insufficient and general propositions are derived from inferences that

---

76   Ibid., p. 222.
77   Ibid., p. 223.
78   John Forrester, *Thinking in Cases* (Cambridge: Polity, 2017), p. 4.
79   Ibid., p. 5.

involve only particulars. In Forrester's reading of Mill, 'reasoning is always from particulars to particulars, because the general form of a proposition, or the general class to which particulars belong, are simply names, or *marks* as he calls them, which we employ because of our fallible memories.'[80]

Thus, the names employed in generalizing processes bear a relation of non-juxtaposition with the things they name, i.e. no relation of correspondence between labels and what they designate follows from the fact that they try to make up for the limitations of memory. The case study as method recognizes this fact to the extent that the scope of the generalization it claims remains open. As implied by Forrester, reasoning goes from particulars to generals (which are themselves particulars) and then back to particulars. This is to say that the insights it produces will be based on the possibility that they might be applicable in the next instance of a given named phenomenon, but whether this will be the case or not can only be decided in view of a particular situation. Since the 'permeability [of the case] invites corrective or amplifying uptake', the extent to which it might be generalizable in the future remains uncertain.[81] It will be provisionally determined upon encountering another case.

As far as the relationship between the individual and the social or the particular and the general is concerned, one cannot tell beforehand in what ways it will be manifested in each case. However, one can expect it to be found in processes of subject constitution, for if the signifier 'represents a subject [...] for another signifier' and the signifier pertains to the realm of the symbolic, there is no such thing as an individual subject.[82] Because subject constitution is both singular and social, it is not possible to fully distinguish the articulation of the rat-related chain of signification by Paul during analysis from its rendering in Freud's narrative. In Freud's notes, it is not always possible to differentiate Paul's speech from Freud's writing, and 'rat' as a core signifier seems to have emerged gradually during analysis: 'the rat story becomes more and more of a node' (die Rattengeschichte wird immer

---

80   Ibid., p. 6.

81   Wells, 'Freud's Rat Man', p. 363.

82   Jacques Lacan, *The Four Fundamental Concepts of Psychoanalysis*, ed. by Jacques-Alain Miller, trans. by Alan Sheridan (London: Routledge, 1998), p. 198.

mehr ein Knotenpunkt), Freud observed in his notes on 8 December 1907.[83] This is due (i) to the impossibility of accessing the 'original' scene, in which analysis took place and words were uttered, through a written text that tries to make sense of it a posteriori in order to propose a somewhat unified narrative of how obsessional neurosis operates and (ii) to the fact that signifiers pertain to the realm of the symbolic, and as such are social.

On 3 June 1909, Freud wrote a letter to C. G. Jung in which he stated: 'I suddenly feel like writing about the Salzburg rat man.' On 30 June of the same year, he told his then friend: 'I am too deep into my rats', while at the same time admitting that the case study he was writing was far from being an exact reproduction of what he actually found in the clinic.[84] Paul's rats became Freud's rats through the medium of language. Freud acknowledged this and joked about it with Jung, the friend from whom he expected recognition as he asked his opinion on the case in a letter from the same year. Jung not only reassured him that his manuscript was good but also shared with Freud his own considerations on rats. In the course of this exchange, Paul's rats became Freud's rats and then Jung's rats — as Octave Mannoni reminds us, Freud's *Deutung* of the connections between rats, syphilis, children, and penis in Paul's analysis owes much to Jung's archetype of the rat.[85]

Paul's signifiers articulate his symptoms in a very particular way, but in so doing reveal the general mechanism of obsessional neurosis. It is thus through the singular instantiation of obsessionality in Paul's symptom that one can grasp its general, and therefore social, character. If the signifier does not mean anything, it is because its crystallization is as arbitrary as it is necessary.[86] Not meaning anything in particular, the

---

83   Freud, *L'homme aux rats*, p. 178.

84   These two quotes are to be found in Mahony, *Freud and the Rat Man*, p. 84. What follows is my translation of Freud's remark to Jung concerning the distance between the case study and clinical experience: 'What bungling are our reproductions, how wretchedly do we tear the great works of art of psychic nature' (Was für Pfuschereien sind unsere Reproduktionen, wie jämmerlich zerpflücken wir die großen Kunstwerke der psychischen Natur!), in Sigmund Freud and Carl Jung, *Briefwechsel* (Frankfurt a.M.: Fischer, 1984), p. 117.

85   Octave Mannoni, 'L'homme aux rats', *Les temps modernes*, 20.228 (1965), pp. 2028–47.

86   Lacan, 'Ouverture'.

signifier is both material and opaque, and these characteristics make it possible for meaning to be both condensed in the chain of signification that articulates Paul's symptoms and displaced in analysis as Paul gradually hears the import of the sound of the words he articulates as he speaks about his symptoms.

Something similar seems to happen with the German word *Wortlaut*, the term employed by Freud to refer to Paul's phrasings. One might say that the erasure of sound and emphasis on wording in the common use of the German word *Wortlaut* points to a repression of the materiality of this signifier that is similar to the one occurring in obsessional neurosis, in which one utters an idea but does not listen to what its sound implies. Paul did not perceive the import of the rat-related signifiers he articulated because (and although) they were at the surface of his discourse. Similarly, *Wortlaut* contains in its materiality the importance of sound to wording that its use tends to erase. *Nachträglich*, one can hear in Freud's *Wortlaut* echoes of the materiality of Lacan's signifier. For like the signifier, theorization, and thus generalization, is also social.

Haptic Reductions
A Sceptic's Guide for Responding to the Touch of Crisis
RACHEL AUMILLER

GLOSSARY

Dogmatism

> The reduction of existence to a system of beliefs or a world-view. A necessarily conscious or unconscious reduction that provides orientation. Reduction for the sake of stability and confidence. The appearance of a fixed position. The condition for a subjective stance.

Haptic Dogmatism

> Conscious and unconscious beliefs that belong to my body. The way my body is accustomed to come into touch with itself, with others, and with the world. The way I grasp myself (as self) through my grasp of the world. Belief in the form of personal and cultural habits and practices involving touching and not touching.

Scepticism

> Modes of reduction that disrupt dogmatic reductions. Reduction that results in instability, disorientation, momentary or prolonged self-doubt. The (negative) reduction of (positive) reduction without its own content. The condition for subjective or epochal shifts.

Haptic Scepticism

> Experiences of touch that call touch itself into question. The
> disruption and disorientation of our beliefs and practices in-
> volving touch and belonging to touch. The possibility for
> transformed touch-relations.

Equipollence

> To be caught between two who each demand one's full fidelity.
> Two in the form of equally viable dogmatic reductions, two
> contradictory convictions, two equally intoxicating jealous
> lovers, two overwhelming but conflicting sensations or urges.
> The splitting of the subject who is stuck in the middle. The
> splitting which is subject.

Epochē A methodological suspension of belief/disbelief performed at
> the beginning of phenomenological reduction (Husserl). The
> affective experience of being suspended at the end of phe-
> nomenological reduction (Pyrrhonism). A dead end where
> beginning begins (Hegel). The repeated collapse of epistemo-
> logical enquiry, which drives enquiry. The opening of the
> possibility for ethical responsiveness in the space of uncer-
> tainty and undecidability.

Withdrawal [R–]

> Methodological reduction in the form of stripping away
> assumptions, beliefs, and experiences that can be initially
> doubted. Holding open distance between subject and
> object, reducer and reduced. The sensation of isolation and
> deprivation.

Immersion [R+]

> Methodological reduction in the form of the accumulation of
> phenomenological standpoints. The reduction of all beliefs,
> affects, and sensation to impressions. Attention to the surface.
> Closing distance between subject and object, the one employ-
> ing reduction and the one reduced. The sensation of sensual
> excess and being-with-others.

INTRODUCTION

Epistemology questions what we can know. It aims at producing dog-matic reductions in the form of stable positions that securely orient us in the world. From one perspective, scepticism trolls epistemology by performing different modes of reduction that dismantle dogmatic reductions and belief. From another perspective, sceptical disruption is the internal engine that drives enquiry, allowing for the transform-ation of knowledge and belief.

This chapter reduces the rich history of philosophical scepticism to two modes of reduction: *Reduction as Modes of Withdrawal* [R–] and *Reduction as Modes of Immersion* [R+]. I turn to early modern philosophy to illustrate the first mode of reduction. Here I highlight Descartes's appropriation of a classical sceptical method for the sake of dogmatic proof. Reduction as withdrawal systematically strips away layers of belief about the world until it reaches the one thing that can't be reduced any further. In my reading of Descartes for the purpose of this discussion, 'the irreducible' is in the position of the one who employs reduction without fully calling himself into question.

I locate the second mode in ancient scepticism with a focus on the birth of phenomenology in Pyrrhonism. Reduction as immersion provisionally welcomes all descriptive accounts of belief or experi-ence. In the context of phenomenological scepticism, reduction does not have to do with the distillation of excess to an essence. Instead all beliefs, judgements, ideas, sensations, emotions are reduced to the same playing field, treated equally as impressions (phenomena). This reduction accumulates impressions [R+] rather than stripping away what can be doubted [R–]. Rather than questioning what is real/truthful/right, reduction as immersion attends to the surface: the sensational and affective points of contact between one's body and the world. Phenomenological scepticism is a reduction to the surface or skin. Yet, the surface is limitless insofar as relationality is infinite.

Like the mode of withdrawal, the mode of immersion also ap-pears to reach a dead end, an *epochē* as it is first defined in ancient phenomenological scepticism. In this case, reduction in the form of attention to the surface often leads to an irreducible in the form of a contradiction between impressions or within a single impression.[1]

Despite the sceptic's attempt to remain epistemologically indifferent or neutral, the encounter with contradiction within our impressions challenges our ability to move through the world. An encounter with contradiction is an embodied experience sometimes leading to the experience of mental and psychological paralysis. Yet, life demands that we make a move (even in the form of not moving or not making a choice). But once again, I argue, the one employing or attending to reduction does not fully allow himself to be called into question by reduction. He fails to fully grasp himself within the contradiction of his own impressions.[2] *Immersion withdraws,* finding tranquil release from the tension and overwhelming fullness of reduction.

The two contrasting movements — withdrawal and immersion — lead to the same place: an epistemological crisis. But sceptical method, which is stunted by a premature stopping point (an 'irreducible' subject who may be disrupted further), shields the sceptic from experiencing this crisis as personal, which is to say, from experiencing it at all.

My own desire is to give method a little push, making reduction personal. When followed through to its own logical end, reduction gives rise to personal disorientation and radical self-doubt.[3] At the end of methodological reduction is the experience of reduction when reduction bites the hand that first employed it on another.[4]

---

1   The Pyrrhonists refrain from speculating whether contradiction itself exists in reality or in our accounts of the world. They do however describe how contradiction can be experienced at the level of affect and sensations. Impressions of all kinds fall into contradiction. Although there are different modes that lead to *epochē*, I highlight equipollence and contradiction because they are critical for how ancient scepticism is taken up in German idealism and twentieth-century phenomenology.

2   Hegel's sceptical phenomenology locates the subject in the very crack or contradiction within substance. Although ancient philosophy does not share a sense of modern subjectivity, Hegel argues that the shadow of the modern 'self' is born in this very moment of disruption in ancient scepticism. The experience of self-doubt precedes and conditions the self.

3   Socratic and Pyrrhonist dialectic shows us that a challenge to one's belief needn't come from the outside. Contradiction is encountered within the logic of one's own beliefs. Critique is internal, a form of self-relation. This sceptical insight is the foundation for nineteenth-century philosophy having different implications for German idealism, Marxism, psychoanalysis.

4   Methodological reduction may be employed for the sake of a proof or refutation. In this case, the end point or conclusion is predetermined from the beginning. Reduction

Methodological reduction has to do with epistemology and its limits. Experiential reduction implicates the reducer in his method, demanding accountability precisely when an individual is in a state of paralysis (*epochē*). Experiential reduction is the condition for a kind of ethical responsiveness and responsibility, which takes places from a space of ambiguity and undecidability. Ethics is set into motion from a place of being suspended.

I give reduction a little nudge, by highlighting the role of haptic sensation in the formation and disruption of belief. Knowledge and belief are impressions inscribed on our skin from infancy onwards, finding a home in our body and between bodies through our haptic relations and rituals: what I call 'haptic dogmatism'.

The history of epistemology and its negative double, scepticism, utilizes the sense of touch as a tool to question what we can know. These traditions also question touch itself as the object of enquiry. Is touch reliable? Can we trust our own sensation? By relocating both dogmatic and sceptical reductions in the body and between bodies-in-touch, I explore how different modes of reduction bring us into touch with ourselves, others, and the world. I turn to touch as a primary mode of being-with-others-in-the-world.

Touch is informative both in its knowledge and in the limits of its knowledge. However, the reduction of touch to its epistemic or negative epistemic character represses a deeper ontological significance of being-in-touch. Touch is sensational (a matter of phenomenology and aesthetics), cultural (a matter of society and politics), relational, and reciprocal (a matter of intimacy and ethics). How does method isolate these different registers of being-in-touch? When do these layers of touch come back into touch?

From a phenomenological perspective, an individual may try to describe how different sensational encounters impress themselves against her being. From a metaphysical or ontological view, we may question how existence is in touch with itself. Ancient philosophers and natural scientists approached this question through different

---

reveals nothing, but instead supports positive or negative dogma. The conclusion is determined from the start. 'To follow reduction to its own logical end' means to pursue method until it cannot be performed further. The path of reduction self-destructs when it encounters the appearance of a dead end or 'the irreducible'.

modes of 'micro-reductions'.[5] What is the most fundamental unit of existence? How do these units touch? Is existence held together through the mediation of gaps and cracks? Or is existence fully immersed in itself, in the way that the ocean touches itself through waves enveloping waves?

The question of how we come into touch as individuals is a question of how existence as a whole is in touch with itself. How does existence touch itself through our individual touching? How is my ontological relationship to existence expressed in my individual touch? How can singular experiences of touch transform my relationship to existence?

One of my motivations for engaging the history of phenomenological scepticism is to practice a feminist ethics that attends to the experience of radical uncertainty brought about by today's global crises. The path of reduction — both through withdrawal and immersion — leads me to a new beginning, a heightened sensitivity to the sensation of the unknown. This chapter concludes with the introduction of 'haptic scepticism', which I identify as an oscillating movement between withdrawal and immersion in the embodied experience of *epochē*, taken equally as an end and a beginning. Haptic scepticism is a moment of call-and-response. It is found in the sensation of being disoriented, of being suspended, of being acted upon. It is equally in our active response to disorientation, resulting in a transformed relationship to self and other in the experience of uncertainty.

TWO MODES OF SCEPTICAL REDUCTION:
WITHDRAWAL AND IMMERSION

In the following, I offer a snapshot of two varieties of scepticism that initially seem to have very different methods. I'm interested in how these philosophical methods resonate with our everyday experiences, especially during periods of intense uncertainty brought about by an event such as a pandemic.

One method offers insight into the experience of isolation, while the other offers insight into the experience of being immersed amongst

---

5   Hanna Andersen, 'The History of Reductionism versus Holistic Approaches to Scientific Research', *Endeavour*, 25.4 (2001), pp. 153–56.

many bodies. The latter touches upon the experience of an over-abundance of competing desires and sensory overload. The excess of Being. The former touches upon the overwhelming sensation of absence and deprivation. The excess of Nothingness.

Reduction as withdrawal can be represented in the model of the sceptic who takes a step back to gain critical distance from an object of enquiry or desire. Reduction as immersion can be represented by the sceptic who immediately takes an eager step forward without hesitation, walking directly into a new encounter.[6]

As I retell this history, I relocate these methods in the body and between bodies. To this end, I've been reimagining sceptical methods by pairing them with movements that represent different impulses and relations. I use these simple gestures as a way to meditate on different concepts with my body.

When people think of the sceptic, they may imagine someone with crossed arms and a furrowed brow, someone who approaches all subject matter with a hesitant reluctance even before a new proposal has been introduced. This popular image of the 'doubting Thomas' is echoed in the history of philosophy in early modern scepticism. It is the variety of scepticism that Descartes performs in the first books of his *Meditations* when he employs a method driven by a hyperbolic doubt.[7]

---

6   I've returned to this trope of two sceptics in several publications to tease out different registers of what I see as contrasting impulses within the history of phenomenological scepticism. See for example, 'Sensation and Hesitation: Haptic Scepticism as the Ethics of Touching', in *A Touch of Doubt: On Haptic Scepticism*, ed. by Rachel Aumiller (Berlin: De Gruyter, 2020), pp. 3–29 <https://doi.org/10.1515/9783110627176-002>. My division of the history of scepticism into two models is itself a practice of reduction. A model can function as a caricature, reducing a complex set of practices or beliefs to one defining feature, which is exaggerated to represent the whole. Reduction as exaggeration allows a model to play out the internal logic of the principles that it represents. As the model plays out its comic role, the cracks and contradictions of a complex system rise to the surface. From one perspective, internal contradiction might be evaluated as the shortcomings of methods or beliefs: a cause for critique or rejection of the entire system. From another perspective, the place where a system pulls at the seams reveals a new kind of value that the system itself had not anticipated or that it sensed but attempted to suppress: a cause for questioning, for reflection, revaluation, and transformation. From both perspectives, contradiction is the irreducible that can be interpreted as an end or new beginning.

7   René Descartes, *Meditations on First Philosophy*, trans. by John Cottingham (Cambridge: Cambridge University Press, 2017). Descartes is interesting for a study of

Suspicion	movement: stepping back; pushing away
Doubt	I hold open a negative space between my outstretched arms,
Hesitation	hollowed belly, and chest with a curved cat spine and inward tilted pelvic.
Subtraction	
Negation	
Distance	

Table 1. Modes of Withdrawal [R–].

Descartes employs a sceptical method to the end of upsetting that method, following its own logic and arriving instead at a conclusion that is contrary to its premise (a sceptical move if there ever was one). We may question however, as many have, whether Descartes reached his conclusion prematurely without thoroughly following the sceptical reduction to its own logical end. Descartes systematically strips away each layer of his beliefs about existence until he reaches certainty, 'the irreducible' that he perhaps did not have the courage to cast into question (his self).

Reduction in the form of withdrawal casts everything under suspicion until it encounters the one thing that proves itself worthy of trust. Methodological doubt or suspicion is the process of keeping the other at an arm's length. By pushing the other (in question) away and taking a step back, withdrawal maintains a critical distance between oneself and other, between the inquiring subject and object of enquiry.

During heightened periods of pandemic, we became familiar with living in a constant state of withdrawal, treating the other as a potential contagion, navigating our way through crowded streets while main-

---

reduction, because many of the countless critical references to his name across contemporary scholarship in the humanities employs a caricature. Descartes's philosophy is dogmatically reduced to the word 'dualism', without pausing to question the complexity or potential value of dualities. Descartes himself was not a sceptic, but ironically became equated with doubt, since his most celebrated work employs a well-known sceptical method, which traditionally leads the reducer to a space of uncertainty.

taining a calculated distance whenever possible. I cast the proximity of the other into doubt, until they receive a negative test result.

In order to be certain, in order to be safe, I isolate myself. From a space of isolation, I can at the very least have some confidence in my own precautions. Yet, self-certainty secured in isolation soon gives rise to the most extreme forms of self-doubt. With her arms stretched out in front of her in an effort to hold the other back, the sceptic finds herself gazing at the back of her own hand.

The ego that is secured through withdrawal proves to be an uncertain foundation to support the structure of one's entire systems of beliefs. As Descartes questions the existence of the parchment in his hands, his eyes drift to his own hands, which he also must doubt. I think therefore I am. Am I? The suspicion cast on the other falls back onto the self. Can I trust this other existence? Can I trust? Can I trust myself?

Prolonged distance and isolation amplify self-doubt to more extreme existential levels, resulting in the experience of radical scepticism, the experience of being-reduced. In isolation, it is difficult to know if what one experiences is similar to others' experience. The shadow of self-doubt calls into question what one is experiencing and thinking.

Reduction as withdrawal is the experience of falling out of touch with the world and thus with one's self. And yet, this negative space that separates us — that separates me from myself — also becomes a new medium through which we remain in touch without touching.

I am neither critiquing nor prescribing withdrawal. Rather I'm curious about how self-disruption opens up possibilities for new kinds of relations when crisis requires us to radically question our personal, communal, and global beliefs and practices. What happens when we lean into the sensation of self-doubt? For the moment, I leave aside the self-doubting subject in her isolation, but will return to question both the risks and ethical value of dwelling in the experience of reduction as withdrawal.

The second sceptical mode of reduction arguably has little to do with suspicion or doubt. I identify this second kind of reduction with varieties of ancient scepticism and phenomenology. I associate this sceptic with charismatic figures such as Socrates, Pyrrho, Apuleius,

Sensation	movement: overstepping; drawing near; leaning in
Addition	I fold over myself, intertwining limbs, breathing into twists
Accumulation	and binds, filling in the cracks with fat and flesh.
Yea-saying	
Affirmation	
Proximity	

Table 2. Modes of Immersion [R+].

and the young Augustine: philosophers who wandered outside of the city walls, participating in the local customs of the towns they passed through, enthusiastically entertaining the views of each new companion that they encountered along the way.[8] From this perspective, the sceptic is someone who is willing to occupy an interlocutor's narrative at least for the length of their shared journey.

On the surface, the fantasy of ancient scepticism is to live a life free of dogma. You might imagine that being without dogma would entail a categorical rejection of all beliefs. Paradoxically, this mode of reduction instead entertains a fantasy of a kind of polyamorous-bliss,

---

8   Although Socrates preferred to engage his interlocutors in Athens, Plato offers one account of Socrates seducing his walking companion beyond the city walls (Plato, *Phaedrus*, trans. by Alexander Nehamas and Paul Woodruff (Indianapolis, IN: Hackett, 1995)); some say that Pyrrho entertained every person who crossed his path for hours on hours (Diogenes Laertius, *Lives of Eminent Philosophers*, trans. by R. D. Hicks, 2 vols, Loeb Classical Series (London: Heinemann, 1925; repr. Cambridge, MA: Harvard University Press, 1972), II: *Books 6–10*). I read Apuleius, a student of Plutarch, as a sceptic, although he is too much of a sceptic to commit to any doctrine, even one that denies having a doctrine. Apuleius, much like his protagonist Lucius from *The Golden Ass*, was happy to adapt to the customs of the places that he passed through on his travels. Augustine recounts his participation in the foreign ideas and customs of the groups of which he was a temporary member (Augustine, *Confessions*, trans. by Garry Wills (New York: Penguin, 2006)). In his first autobiographical dialogue, *Soliloquies: Augustine's Inner Dialogue*, trans. by Kim Paffenroth (Hyde Park, NY: New City Press, 2000), Augustine confessions to his inability to fully adhere to the new dogma of his post-conversion beliefs.

in which one partakes in a bit of everything without fully giving oneself over to any One (dogma, god, truth, emotion, sensation, lover).[9]

If there is something prudish or frigid in modes of withdrawal, phenomenological scepticism requires promiscuity.[10] Like Apuleius, who filled his bag with forbidden foreign objects that he collected along his travels, the phenomenological-sceptic is a collector of impressions: shiny novelties gathered along her adventures, including her own impressions and the second-hand impressions of her interlocutors. She can hardly choose a favourite standpoint amongst the accumulation of so many impressions collected along the way.

Reduction may be viewed as the process of keeping the other at an arm's length [R−]. However, reduction can also be viewed as the practice of leaning into another, leaning into the sensational otherness of another, the practice of yea-saying without committing oneself to any one thing completely [R+].

When something unfamiliar brushes up against us — a way of being in touch with existence that is unlike our own — it is often difficult to distinguish attraction from anxiety or stimulation from irritation. The new sensation threatens to change us in ways we cannot predict or control.

In response to the unfamiliar, both dogmatic reduction (which explains the strange sensation in familiar terms) and sceptical withdrawal (which pushes the strange out of reach) can be utilized as modes of avoidance to shut down a potential disruption. Ironically, the phenom-

---

9   The authors of the original accounts of these sceptics employ excess or exaggeration as methodological reduction. Apuleius's and Augustine's hyperbolic autobiographical narratives present caricatures of the authors themselves, self-consciously blurring the line between fact and fiction. We only know of the lives of Socrates and Apuleius through second-hand or third-hand accounts, often self-consciously presented as unreliable gossip, hearsay of hearsay: a narrative device employed by Plato and Diogenes Laertius. The ancient sceptic is a model of the living embodiment of contradiction: represented by the competing contradictory accounts of Pyrrho's life, the performative contradiction between Plato's philosophy and Socrates's life, Apuleius's epistemological and erotic infidelity, and Augustine's inability to reconcile his pre-conversion and post-conversion selves.

10   In fact, each of the philosophers I mentioned above participated in his fair share of touching. Apuleius was even put on trial for over-touching. He was charged on eleven counts of forbidden touch, ranging from magical objects to a widowed matron. Apuleius, *Apologia; Florida; De deo Socratis*, trans. by Christopher P. Jones (Cambridge, MA: Harvard University Press, 2017).

enological sceptic, who is marked by a refusal to assent to anything, is most likely to respond to the touch of a stranger (at least for the sake of experimentation). Her refusal to commit to anything in particular allows her to be open to the equal consideration of everything that happens to come her way.

In theory, the sceptic practices openness and indifference. In practice, however, the sort of phenomenological or romantic polyamory that aims at attending equally to all involved parties is rarely sustainable. The fantasy of neutrality is frustrated by the emergence of asymmetrical relations and the demand to choose between competing commitments.

The ancient sceptics who adopted the life of Pyrrho as a model, aptly called the Pyrrhonists or Pyrrhonians, approached their dream of a (non)position with some irony. As they acknowledge, even committing oneself to remaining committed to nothing is itself a commitment.[11] They could only offer observations: experience seems to show us that it is exceedingly difficult to share oneself equally and unproblematically with all or none (without eventually needing to make a choice); yet it seems equally impossible to remain committed to one, especially for very long.

Phenomenological attention seeks to keeps things light, by reducing all beliefs and experiences to the surface: treating everything that appears (to happen or to be true) equally as appearance. Yet by paying close attention, one may begin to notice cracks in the surface. The Pyrrhonists observed that phenomenological attention or description of our impressions often runs into inconsistencies, paradox, or contradiction.

In the context of twentieth-century phenomenology, Edmund Husserl develops 'the suspension of belief and disbelief' as a method that frees the phenomenologist to attend to the sensation of her experience. Husserl's *epochē* is a method or mode employed at the beginning of phenomenological reduction. Pyrrhonian phenomenology, in contrast, originally positioned *epochē* as an experience that happens at 'the end' when our impressions are disoriented. We experience *epochē*

---

11   On the paradox of 'the laying down of nothing': Diogenes Laertius, *Lives of Eminent Philosophers*, ix.74.

through deep attention to the surface, by fully immersing ourselves in the sensation of our impressions.[12]

Just as multiple impressions fall into contradiction with each other so does one impression fall into conflict with itself. When one divides into two, our relationship to another is disrupted. We reach an impasse, the experience of *aporia*, which equally challenges the dogmatist's fidelity to one and the sceptic's neutrality to all, because it is our own orientation in the world that is called into question.

The Pyrrhonists called the sensation of being split between two and into two *equipollence* (*isostheneia*). Equipollence is sometimes framed as two equally compelling but incompatible propositions. In itself, each dogmatic reduction is equally convincing. However, since they are irreducible and incompatible with each other, and since they appear equally true, neither can be true. We are split between two positive reductions. We are also split between double affirmation and double negation, between both/and and neither/nor [R++−−]. Because both appear to be equally true, and they are incompatible, the validity of both sides must be doubted.

Experience reveals that equipollence is not a mere thought experiment belonging to the philosopher who indifferently gazes at the back of his hand. It can be found in sensuous experiences that fundamentally disorient us in the world. Equipollence is the experience of split sensation in response to a single stimulus: an increased sense of pleasure in the intensification of pain.[13] Equipollence is a singular *haptic marvel* that calls everything I know to be true into question: the first kiss of a woman that throws my commitment to God and my religious community into chaos. It is the experience of violence at the hands of someone we love. It is in the way we long for healing from the same hands that harm. It is in the way someone who I long to care for and protect shrinks in distrust from my touch.

---

12   Dialectical questioning, commonly associated with Socrates, is a form of supporting an interlocutor's attention toward their own impressions. The question requests deeper attention to the surface in the phenomenological description of one's impressions. By questioning his companion, he coaxes them to look closer at their own impressions than they were willing. Reduction as immersion is a process of pushing limits and overstepping.

13   On sensation as subjective and situational: Sextus Empiricus, *Outlines of Scepticism*, I.56, 80–87, 109, 210–11; II.52; on sensation as contradictory or paradoxical: I.91–94; III.194–97.

Equipollence is in my conflicting ethical convictions concerning how to touch and how not to touch. During a period of mandated lockdown, I was fully convinced of my responsibility to withhold my touch, isolating myself during pandemic. Yet I was equally convinced — in the same moment — of my responsibility to join thousands of strangers on the streets to protest against police brutality against Black lives. Each of my convictions concerning the rightness of touch is found guilty according the logic of another ethical conviction. The question of touch splits me in two.

Suspension can be pleasurable like floating in a saltwater pool. But the disorientation of how we grasp ourselves and the world can also be uncomfortable and exhausting. The necessity to make decisions, to move forward, without clear answers can be excruciating.

Pyrrhonism, according to Sextus Empiricus, recommends finding release from the personal crisis of undecidability, by 'going along with' societal laws and norms.[14] As I have mentioned, there are many modes of avoidance that shield one from being called into question when reduction bites the hand that first employed it on another. Withdrawal immerses itself in doubt to protect itself at the beginning before things can get messy. Immersion pushes its luck, taking a calculated risk, before withdrawing in the last moment.

Modes of avoidance allow us to carry on as usual during periods of crisis, to insist on normalcy, to justify one's desires without acknowledging the risk of these desires for others. The ancient sceptic, for example, calls everything into question but withdraws when the crisis of uncertainty threatens to call the sceptic himself into question. This moment in scepticism is a kind of dogmatism. Reduction as a one-directional touch does not allow itself to be touched back by its method.

I search for a kind of sceptical comportment that allows itself to be touched by doubt, vulnerability, uncertainty, and the unknown.

---

14   By following societal norms, one may feel momentarily released from the burden of choice and personal responsibility. However, when a society's customs and values prove to be inconsistent or in conflict with themselves, the individual is once again split by equipollence (as we see through the tragedy of *Antigone*). On conforming to norms in the absence of ethical judgement: Sextus Empiricus, *Outlines of Scepticism*, 1.21–41.

Equipollence	Two movements in one: leaning in/pulling back.
Paralysis	I stand on my toes with closed eyes. Keeping my hips sta-
Oscillation	tionary, I lean my heart slightly forward and back and then from side to side, finding balance in instability.
Vacillation	With movement so slow and so subtle, I may not appear to be moving at all.
	A caress that questions. I move my fingers across her skin. A transgression. A hesitation. A risk. A request.

Table 3. Suspension / *Epochē* [R++−−].

Rather than finding relief by backing away from the discomfort of having oneself called into question, I search for a practice of pausing with the crisis of suspension, allowing oneself to be disrupted by both phenomenological fullness and deprivation.

EXPERIENTIAL REDUCTION: OSCILLATION-IN-SUSPENSION

Epochē, as an event that happens to us, also demands a response. The end leads us back to a moment of deciding how to begin again.[15] Borrowing the sceptical slogan 'no more', we may say: *epochē* is no more a beginning than an end, no more a way forward than paralysis, no more method than an experience.[16] What is to be done in response to the disorientation of being suspended?

I initially describe two different models of the sceptic as represent- ing different kinds of methodological reductions: one based in subtrac- tion and provisional denial, one in accumulation and immersion.[17] I draw on these models to offer a phenomenological description of two poles of experience that have become intensified during the pandemic:

---

15 Husserl's *epochē* leads us to Pyrrho's *epochē*, which leads us to Husserl's *epochē*. We oscillate indefinitely between two kinds of *epochē*, that are found in the same moment. Hegel's sceptical phenomenology explicitly struggles with beginning/ends.

16 On the slogan 'no more': Diogenes Laertius, *Lives of Eminent Philosophers*, IX.75–76; Sextus Empiricus, *Outlines of Scepticism*, 1.188–90

17 On the refutation of subtraction and addition: Sextus Empiricus, *Outlines of Scepticism*, III.85–95.

the experience of reduced engagement and isolation, on one side, and the experience of exposure and being-together again, on the other. I now imagine the contrary impulses of withdrawal-and-immersion as the oscillating movement of an individual in suspension, whether suspension is itself experienced in isolation or being-together.

Many of us have had the experience over the last few years of being pulled back and forth between two extremes. In periods of quarantine during the shortest days of winter, I have had the experience of withdrawing from the 'outside world'. Suddenly, summer arrives, infection numbers dwindle, I'm sitting in the middle of a sunny park surrounded by, what feels like, swarms of bodies. Oscillating between these extremes of being-in-isolation and being-together is itself disorienting: withdrawing into a reduced social existence, immersing myself amongst others, withdrawing into reduction, re-immersion.

How do these two opposed experiences mirror each other? We can question how they are similar even in their opposition. But we may also question how they are incompatible, both equally valid and necessary, while demanding contrary courses of action. What happens to our subjectivity and relations when we are caught in-between isolation and immersion? Can the experience of being suspended — whether in isolation and or in a crowd — teach us a new kind of movement?

Reduction as modes of withdrawal is the creation of a negative space. This negative space becomes the very shape of desire, subjectivity, and relationality. Reduction as modes of immersion is the experience of overwhelming fullness, which leads us into the experience of *too many* impressions (beliefs, desires, and sensations).

Epochē is the sensation of shapelessness when my life is slowed to a standstill. *Epochē* is equally the experience of being suspended within a phenomenal bath. In withdrawal, my suspicion of the other led me to doubt myself. In immersion, I affirm myself with each new encounter. With every 'yes' to otherness, I say, 'this too is self.' But where do I stand in all this? What is my stance? To be suspended in fullness. To be suspended in nothingness. Through these two modes of sceptical reduction, we witness the mirroring of Being and Nothingness, of affirmation and negation, of self-definition and self-doubt.

How does one navigate embodied relations from a space of uncertainty and disorientation? I am split between opposing impulses and desires. During the pandemic, I've had to teach myself to withdraw: to treat others as a potential contagion, to hold the other at an arm's length, to draw boundaries, to avoid 'unnecessary' touching. And yet, at the same time, I long to pull my loved ones near, to dance with strangers, to expose myself to risk, to risk exposing others to my risk.

Against the backdrop of global disruption, each instance of coming-in-touch is thrown into question. Two awkward bodies fumble as they negotiate how to greet one another. Each one leans in to embrace, pulling away, hesitating, leaning in, pulling away. The brief moment of hesitation — of bodies oscillating between proximity and withdrawal — is the embodied practice of suspension, of holding open a question: the question of another's uncertain desire, of my own undetermined desire, of uncertain risk and reward.

Is the suspension of touch merely paralysis? Or can we find movement in suspension? Is suspension itself a kind of movement that generates new kinds of haptic desires, pleasures, and relations?

The disruption of everyday touch is an event that knocks us off our feet, disorienting our grasp on the world. Yet as Simone de Beauvoir argues in *The Ethics of Ambiguity*, allowing ourselves to fully experience the shock of crisis is the condition for ethical responsiveness to the unique demands of our present moment.[18] Pyrrhonian scepticism ultimately seeks tranquillity by relieving us from the responsibility of decision in the face of uncertainty. In contrast, de Beauvoir locates the call for responsibility and risk in the sceptical crisis of undecidability. In the experience of crisis, we are split by two equally powerful realizations: the uncertainty of the situation in which we find ourselves and the urgent imperative to respond to this moment.

The paralysis of uncertainty combined with a sense of urgency allows us to recognize our responsibility to the historical moment that constitutes our individual experience. Although we are free to respond as we please, every response or refusal to respond involves risk. Despite our good intentions, careful reasoning, or commitments to remaining neutral, we are nevertheless fully responsible for inevitable good and harm that results from our action and inaction.

---

18   Simone de Beauvoir, *The Ethics of Ambiguity*, trans. by Bernard Frechtman (Los Angeles: Open Road, 2015), p. 83.

The transformative potential of disruption depends on our response to having our way of life called into question. Although the
Pyrrhonists withdrew from ethical commitments, I find ethical value
in their slogan 'perhaps', which challenges us to dwell with the crisis of uncertainty regarding the rightness of our action.[19] 'Perhaps'
holds open the space of a question, demanding ongoing self-reflection.
Can we dwell with the discomfort and vulnerability of being held responsible for others? Can we resist the temptation of shutting down
the question with new forms of dogmatism? As de Beauvoir argues,
'[M]orality resides in the painfulness of an indefinite questioning.'[20]

HAPTIC SCEPTICISM FOR AN AGE OF UNCERTAINTY

Locating an embodied ethical responsiveness in scepticism may seem
counterintuitive in face of the international rise of conspiracy theories
and science denialism during the pandemic. But the danger of this
popular variety of cultural scepticism is that it tends to betray itself,
collapsing into radical dogmatism. The activity of doubting or questioning what is presented as truth, gives rise to a theory, which itself
becomes the new dogma that cannot be questioned.[21]

There is value in allowing oneself to question the most fundamental beliefs of one's society: How do we know the Earth is round? Are
vaccines dangerous? Can we trust the government? Conspiracy theories often begin with a moment of genuine critical enquiry that almost
immediately collapses into a new dogma: the earth is flat; vaccines in
all forms are unnatural and toxic; every government regulation is an
infringement on my freedom. The question is how to hold open an
initial space of questioning. How do we dwell in a space of ambiguity
without becoming totally paralysed by self-doubt?

On one hand, we might identify cultural scepticism as the problem. On the other hand, I'm interested in how a deepening of scepti-

---

19   The slogan 'perhaps': Sextus Empiricus, *Outlines of Scepticism*, 1.194.

20   Beauvoir, *The Ethics of Ambiguity*, p. 144.

21   On dogmatic-scepticism in response to the pandemic: Bara Kolenc, 'Skepticism's Cure
       for the Plague of Mind', *Women in Philosophy, Blog of the American Philosophical Asso-
       ciation* (9 September 2020) <https://blog.apaonline.org/2020/09/09/skepticisms-
       cure-for-the-plague-of-mind/> [accessed 11 June 2022].

cism can disrupt a kind of contemporary dogmatic-scepticism that is itself a pandemic.

Everyone has had different experiences of the pandemic and different responses toward pandemic restrictions. But one thing most of us have had to face is the experience of radical uncertainty. An experiential *epochē* of global proportions disrupts our being in a fundamental way. What are different responses to this disruption? How do our individual and collective responses make all the difference?

Uncertainty toward our personal and global situation gives rise to different kinds of self-doubt. Doubt expresses itself in very real anxieties about one's purpose. What am I doing with my life? How do I persist in my existence when everything has been suspended? Uncertainty is also the inability to envision one's future, whether that future is in the next few months, years, or that belongs to the next generations. Self-doubt is a temporary falling out of relationship to time both in relation to the present and future.

There are those who flee the experience of self-doubt by carrying on as if nothing has happened, clinging to their specific habits and traditions. Business-as-usual holds self-doubt at a distance.

Yet I would argue that living ethically-with-others demands *a touch of self-doubt*. Ethics demands a moment of suspension in which one questions, 'Is this action or choice right?' 'Is this responsible and caring?' It's precisely a lack of ethical clarity that prompts us to continue to question ourselves. The recognition of the inability to know if our choices are truly ethical, in some ways, is what makes us ethical. Ethics has a sceptical drive in this way. It drives forward in its unfulfillment. To be ethical is to continually question what it means to be ethical in each instance without arriving at any definite certainty.

The crisis of pandemic specially requires us to question the way we touch and the way we come into touch. The opportunity to doubt our touch in each instance ('Is this safe, responsible, caring') is also an opportunity for new ethical relations of touch. We learn that touching is not just a personal or private matter. The ethical imperative to question the way we touch has global reach.

There are unconscious and conscious layers to belief. We might associate dogma with our professed convictions that make up our identities (for example, our religious, political, or sexual orientations).

But the unconscious layer of belief is on the surface, impressed into our skin. I use the term 'haptic dogmatism' to highlight the way beliefs belong to our body. Every instance of touch, even touching that takes place in private and in solitude, is inherently social. Touch is shaped by a social and cultural backdrop. At infancy, our personality and belief structure are already being shaped by the touch of our caregivers. Our very sense of self is formed by touch before we are even aware of ourselves and others.

Haptic dogma is found in the way one's body is accustomed to come into touch with itself, with others, and with the world. The way I grasp myself (as self) through my grasp of the world. Haptic dogmatism is belief in the form of personal and cultural habits and practices involving touching and not touching. Dogma is not in itself destructive, but necessary. It's the possibility of stability through the orientation of a world view. But what happens when belief does not allow itself to be questioned?

Because beliefs are inscribed in our everyday movements and sensations, they are often invisible to us. We only become aware of them when our embodied orientation is disrupted. Disruption requires us to take a conscious stance in response to something that was formerly unconscious.

There is currently a global phenomenon of people who dogmatically cling to their right to come into contact as they please. This dogmatic certainty is an insistence on one's rights and on one's rightness. More specifically, it is an insistence on one's right to touch and on the rightness of one's touch.[22] Often this conscious haptic dogmatism is entangled with cultural scepticism, directed at science and the government. Many people have very good reasons to distrust their governments and 'the science' that they receive through the lens of economic interest. But this combination of dogmatism and scepticism also gives rise to conspiracy theories, reckless activity, and violence.

---

22   Initially, the resistance toward pandemic regulations or vaccination recommendations appeared to belong to a politically right leaning orientation, especially in countries like the United States that are political and socially structured by a two-party system. But the crisis of touch also throws the categories of 'left' and 'right' into question, as the dogmatic resistance to altered practices expresses itself across many cultural and political orientations.

The more extreme forms of cultural scepticism seem to correlate with more extreme forms of dogmatism.

Because belief exists in the body, the disruption of belief also takes place in the body and between bodies. Sceptical disruption through different kinds of reduction occurs beneath our fingertips and on the surface of our skin. Haptic scepticism attends to the embodied experience of *epochē*.

Haptic scepticism is the disruption of encounters and experiences that destabilize our bodily orientations and relationships. On a personal level, for example, an experience of illness, injury, or violation can shake our way of moving through the world. An experience of unexpected pleasure — a new kind of sexual encounter — might shake our basic understanding of who we are and what we desire.

The crisis of pandemic reveals the experience of haptic scepticism on a register that is extremely personal and global. As the disruption of the way we come into touch shakes our political and economic structures, we see how thoroughly our lives are structured by haptic dogma.

Haptic scepticism refers to experiences that disrupt our habitualization. In this sense both dogmatism and scepticism are passive experiences. But our active and conscious response to being disrupted can also be dogmatic or sceptical. A dogmatic response to disruption clings tighter to one's way of being, one's way of being-with-others. A sceptical response pauses and questions and even experiments with new forms of coming-into-touch and withdrawal. Both hesitation and experimentation are not only ethically necessary, but can result in new kinds of enjoyment and intimacies. Whereas the dogmatic response to the crisis of touch closes the possibility for transformed relations, desire, and pleasure, the sceptical practice of dwelling with the experience of uncertainty is where both the ethics and the enjoyment of touch begins.

CONCLUSION: TOUCH AND REDUCTION

The structure of touch teaches us something about the structure of reduction, which methodology conceals. Both are reciprocal relations that do not allow for objectivity or ethical neutrality.

Touch shows us that we are always already immersed in complex affective relationships. We are already in touch with more bodies than we can recognize. Touch throws us into a space of contradiction. And this contradiction is a tactile sensation, which exposes us to the tension between epistemology and ethics. On one hand, we can never know the reach of our touch. On the other hand, we are nevertheless responsible for our touching.

Unlike the other senses, touching offers us no rest from touch. We can close our eyes, plug our nose, cover our ears, refuse to open our mouths. But we can't turn off touch. Not only are we always on duty, but touch demands that we play two roles at once. With each touch, I am subject and object, both the toucher and the touched. Touch is reciprocal. The reciprocity of touch is a contradiction that can't fully be grasped at once, but nevertheless informs our existence. Whenever I touch another to convey a message or leave my mark, I am also touched back by this other who is touched by me.[23]

There is no such thing as a one-directional touch; there is no such thing as a one-directional reduction, although the history of philosophy is plagued by the fantasy of both. The two fantasies are not unrelated. Both reflect the desire for demonstration, for domination, for being beyond accountability and vulnerability. Theoretical reductions of the other enable violent touch. Violence further reduces the other to an extension of one's desire for power.

By bringing together haptic experience and sceptical reductions, I demonstrate how every touch, like every reduction, is a matter of relationality and thus ethics. Here, I make an even stronger claim. The qualities that make touch distinct — sensation as relationality and reciprocity — guide us toward more ethical relations, heightening our sensation and responsiveness toward the knowable and unknowable relations that comprise our existence.

---

23   Husserl's emphasis on the reciprocity and relationality of touch (the subject's dual role as the toucher-touched) drives debates in twentieth-century phenomenology of touch: see for example, Edmund Husserl, *Ideas Pertaining to a Pure Phenomenology and to a Phenomenological Philosophy, Second Book: Studies in the Phenomenology of Constitution*, trans. by Richard Rojcewicz and André Schuwer (Dordrecht: Kluwer, 1989); Maurice Merleau-Ponty, *The Visible and the Invisible*, trans. by Alphonso Lingis (Evanston, IL: Northwestern University Press, 1968); Jacques Derrida, *On Touching — Jean-Luc Nancy*, trans. by Christine Irizarry (Stanford, CA: Stanford University Press, 2005); Jean-Luc Nancy, *Noli me tangere: On the Raising of the Body*, trans. by Sarah Clift, Pascale-Anne Brault, and Michael Naas (New York: Fordham University Press, 2008).

Disalienation and Structuralism
Fanon with Lévi-Strauss
CHRISTOPHER CHAMBERLIN

INTRODUCTION

Frantz Fanon accepted his first medical assignment to the Blida-Joinville Psychiatric Hospital in Algeria in 1954, which he headed as director for two tumultuous years until resigning in 1956. Upon arrival, Fanon quickly initiated a reorganization of the hospital in accordance with the tenets of 'institutional psychiatry', a reform movement and new approach to collective psychotherapy pioneered in the 1940s by Fanon's supervisor and mentor, the French-Catalan communist and psychiatrist François Tosquelles.[1] Fanon's initial reform effort was remarkable primarily for how quickly it fell apart, having had next to no beneficial effect on the Algerian patients (all of them men) under his care. Fanon blamed that failure not on institutional psychiatry per se, but on neglecting to properly correspond its practice to the totality of its social situation. Fanon explains:

> It was necessary to try to grasp the North African social fact.
> It was necessary to demand that 'totality' in which Mauss saw

---

1   Camille Robcis, *Disalienation: Politics, Philosophy, and Radical Psychiatry in Postwar France* (New York: Columbia University Press, 2021).

the guarantee of an authentic sociological study. A leap had to
be performed, a transmutation of values to be achieved. Let's
say it: it was essential to go from the biological level to the
institutional one, from natural existence to cultural existence.[2]

The 'totality' of the 'social fact' cited here bears Marcel Mauss's un-
mistakable signature. This is the same notion that will be transformed
by Claude Lévi-Strauss into the kernel of the structuralist method.
In the method of its construction, Lévi-Strauss credited Mauss with
drawing a highly serviceable equivalence between the *social* and *reality*,
albeit one whose conceptual development he argues was prematurely
interrupted. Lévi-Strauss thus comes to define social reality as the articulation, or the disjunctive synthesis, between each discontinuous
dimension of human existence. The construction of a total social fact
— or social structure — had to account for what Lévi-Strauss defined
as the 'three dimensions' of social reality: (1) the symbolic or structural systems of a given society, (2) its history or transformations, and
finally, (3) the psycho-physiological level. 'Only in individuals', writes
Lévi-Strauss, 'can these three dimensions be brought together.'[3]

Fanon and his colleague Jacques Azoulay invoke this very tripar-
tite schema when concluding the summary of their failure at Blida-
Joinville:

> The biological, the psychological and the sociological were
> separated only by an aberration of the mind. In fact, they were
> tied indistinctly together. It is for want of not having integrated
> the notion of Gestalt and the elements of contemporary an-
> thropology into our daily practice that our failures were so
> harsh.[4]

An exploration of structuralism's role in Fanon's theory and practice,
through which the method and transformations of his psychotherapy
can be illuminated, thus seems to be overdue. This structuralist method

---

2   Frantz Fanon and Jacques Azoulay, 'Social Therapy in a Ward of Muslim Men: Meth-
     odological Difficulties', in Frantz Fanon, *Alienation and Freedom*, ed. by Jean Khalfa
     and Robert J. C. Young, trans. by Steve Corcoran (London: Bloomsbury, 2018), pp.
     353–72 (p. 363).

3   Claude Lévi-Strauss, *Introduction to the Work of Marcel Mauss*, trans. by Felicity Baker
     (London: Routledge, 1950), p. 26.

4   Fanon and Azoulay, 'Social Therapy', p. 363.

— which is characterized by a conceptual reduction to certain irreducible filaments of the experience of the human as a 'symbol-using'
species, and which for our purposes will be practically synonymous
with the anthropology of Lévi-Strauss — shapes Fanon's understanding of the relationship between mental illness and the cure, and further
on, his understanding of the relationship between psychotherapy and
politics. Owing no doubt to the occulted nature of its references in
Fanon's work (not to mention the long-running stigma that 'structuralism' bears as a supposedly superseded and politically moribund
project), structural anthropology's influence on Fanon's thinking remains an unopened secret, and part of the intention of this chapter
is to track the way that Fanon translates structuralist insights into the
nature of human 'sociality' into a simultaneously therapeutic and political program. In this way I seek to contribute to far more developed
mappings of the impact on Fanon's work (and his reciprocal reworking
and advancement) of the intellectual traditions of, for instance, radical
psychiatry, existential phenomenology, and psychoanalysis.[5]

For Fanon, structuralism didn't just improve psychoanalysis, it
made it possible, just as his understanding of the interlinked notions
of freedom and madness enabled him to transform structuralism into
a praxis in which not only the psychic wellbeing of the individual, but
the very renewal of social relations are at stake.

But the traffic of influence between anthropology and
psychoanalysis was not simply unidirectional: as his privileging
of the 'psycho-physiological' suggests, Lévi-Strauss embarked on
his own account of what he variously describes as 'mental illness',
'mental disturbance', or 'psychopathology', all rough synonyms for
what a long tradition of Western discourse calls 'madness'. That effort
did not just attempt to replace a medical model of mental illness
with a social or anthropological (much less genealogical) one, but,
more consequentially, and like Fanon in a different context, intended
to eliminate an unjustifiable separation between physiological and
mental explanations of psychopathological aetiology, between the

---

5   Cf. the aforementioned: Robcis, *Disalienation*; Lewis Gordon, *What Fanon Said: A
     Philosophical Introduction to his Life and Thought* (New York: Fordham University
     Press, 2015); David S. Marriott, *Lacan Noir: Lacan and Afro-pessimism* (New York:
     Palgrave Macmillan, 2021).

fate of the individual and that of collectives (and therefore between the disciplines of anthropology and psychoanalysis, as we will see shortly). While Mauss may have first systematized a link between these realms, Lévi-Strauss would derive new implications made possible by a theory of the symbolic function (as worked over from contemporaneous developments in modern linguistics) that was, at best, only rigorously intuited by Freud and Mauss in their time, but that was already a part of Fanon's wildly interdisciplinary outlook by the beginning of his work at the midcentury.

This chapter begins with a 'crash course' on Lévi-Strauss's understanding of the symbolic status of social life (and an abbreviated synthesis of the terminology he uses to describe it), particularly as it emerges out of the anthropologist's attempt to triangulate the causes of mental disturbance. Thereafter I will hint at some points of convergence between his theoretical principles and Fanon's radicalized psychoanalysis. 'Reduction', as both a method intrinsic to the dialectic and an object of theoretical deduction, is as essential to structuralism as it is a scientific precept in Fanon's simultaneously political and therapeutic program.

But my overarching aim in what follows, despite remaining mostly implicit, is to place on new footing one of the most controversial concepts in Fanon's oeuvre: *sociogenesis* (and his related development of a 'sociodiagnostic' method of analysis).[6] This notion was designed by the French-Martinican psychiatrist to retheorize the cause of mental illness and to go 'beyond' the impasses presented by desocialized and depoliticized theories on psychopathology that have tried to answer the same question through the concepts of ontogenesis/phylogenesis (the dialectic between individual and species elaborated by the late Freud), organogenesis (the dialectic between the psyche and body elaborated by postwar French psychiatry), and psychogenesis (the dialectic between the real and imaginary elaborated by the early Lacan).

---

6   See for instance: Sylvia Wynter, 'Towards the Sociogenic Principle: Fanon, Identity, the Puzzle of Conscious Experience, and What it is Like to Be "Black"', in *National Identities and Sociopolitical Changes in Latin America*, ed. by Mercedes F. Durán-Cogan and Antonio Gómez-Moriana (London: Routledge, 2001), pp. 30–66; David Marriott, 'Inventions of Existence: Sylvia Wynter, Frantz Fanon, Sociogeny, and "the Damned"', *CR: The New Centennial Review*, 11 (2012), pp. 45–89.

The larger, second half of this paper therefore examines how Fanon offered, as an alternative that nevertheless manages to carry along an account of the various dialectical poles that precede it (individual, body, imaginary, and so on), a sociogenic hypothesis — one that pivots on locating mental illness in the dialectic between symbolic structure and history that is intrinsic to a notion of 'the social' as *pharmakon,* as both source (alienation) and solution (disalienation) to psychic suffering. I will specifically look at how this principle is put to work in the clinical practice he founded at the Neuropsychiatric Day Centre of Tunis at the end of his life, in the late 1950s and early 1960s.

Fanon's dialectical style of reasoning is well established, being perhaps nowhere more impressively presented than in Ato Sekyi-Otu's opus, *Fanon and the Dialectic of Experience,* a work that nevertheless suffers from a fatal flaw: that of refusing to acknowledge that Fanon had any serious interest in the ethics of psychoanalysis. In focussing so narrowly on Fanon's method of ceaselessly disintegrating metaphysical truths or metalinguistic axioms through the solvent of the narrative of experience, Sekyi-Otu misses precisely how Fanon located the political and ethical valence of the symptom in the lived experience of the dialectic's arrest.[7] If, for Fredric Jameson, structuralism is not heterogenous to such a tradition of dialectical thinking but marked instead a breakthrough in which 'dialectical thought was able to reinvent itself in our time',[8] then it remains to be seen how Fanon reinvented this breakthrough in his own time and place.

LÉVI-STRAUSS: REDUCTION OF THE SOCIAL TO REALITY

In his magisterial survey of the collected works of Marcel Mauss, Lévi-Strauss boils the essence of culture down to 'a combination of symbolic systems headed by language, the matrimonial rules, the economic relations, art, science and religion',[9] to which he also adds its aesthetic forms and juridical systems. Despite the huge variety of their expression and their very different courses of historical development, these

---

7 Ato Sekyi-Otu, *Fanon's Dialectic of Experience* (Cambridge, MA: Harvard University Press, 1996).

8 Fredric Jameson, *Valences of the Dialectic* (London: Verso, 2009), p. 17.

9 Lévi-Strauss, *Introduction,* p. 16.

systems are inherently symbolic, meaning that they organize customs and institutions that 'unconsciously' provide an interpretation of physical reality, social reality, and the immanent links between them. To the extent that it is symbolic — a concept introduced by Lévi-Strauss and not found in Mauss — the social determines collective reality. The function of the symbolic is to express to its members a specific image of the social world that prescribes certain patterns of behaviour and modes of relation. That the symbolic is total (in the sense of having no external boundary or 'outside') means that no dimension of social exchange is not symbolically organized. When Lévi-Strauss refers to the 'social', then, he is referring to a *general* characteristic of human existence that is irreducible to any *particular* culture, namely the formative power of the symbolic function: human collectives, unlike animals, are not organized around natural needs but are founded on — and constitutively denaturalized by — the unconscious rules and activities of symbolic exchange. A schematization of the various terms I will be elaborating here is sketched out in Figure 1 below.

But the symbolic systems that any one culture is composed of are themselves mutually incommensurable and thus irreducible to each other. This is due in the first instance to their historicity: a particular culture is not an abstract entity but always a 'spatial-temporal given'[10] with its own material history; each culture is and has been impacted through interactions or exchanges with symbolic forms from 'adjacent' societies. Various symbolic systems — their combination in any single place, if mapped out by an observer, constituting what Mauss would have called a 'total social fact' — therefore have a history defined by their transformations; and those transformations, insofar as they indicate mutations in social reality caused by contact from the 'outside', betoken a non-relationality between symbolic systems, revealing in turn a porosity or inconsistency 'within' the symbolic field that fates its inability to exhaust all the meanings of reality. After all, were any social reality complete and self-sufficient, outside contact with 'foreign realities' would be foreclosed *ab initio* and historically inconsequential. Social reality is not airtight but riddled with gaps. As Mauss similarly insisted, cultures are not stable but exist in a 'state of perpetual

---

10   Ibid., p. 17.

aberration'[11] or a 'perpetual state of becoming'.[12] Put in a Lacanian vocabulary, one deeply influenced by Lévi-Strauss's equation between the symbolic and the Freudian unconscious, we could say that the record of cultures' constant transformation reveals how the symbolic bears within it an ontological discrepancy between 'the real' and the signifier, one that renders the real available for an expression that is always incommensurate to its sign.

We can provisionally conclude that the social, insofar as it always expresses itself symbolically, comprises an 'autonomous reality'.[13] But reality — and this is crucial — is at the same time not reducible to the social. While social life is *totally* symbolic, insofar as it leaves no aspect of collective relations untouched, 'no society is ever wholly or completely symbolic'.[14] Society cannot be reduced to the ensemble of social relations that it symbolically organizes. A social totality includes the symbolic and something more, a gap or excess in collective meaning produced by the ontological discrepancy between the real and the signifier.[15] That which the symbolic cannot assimilate is precisely concrete or lived experience, or the 'psychic reality' of the subject, that is irreducible to social reality.

Lévi-Strauss's understanding of reality in fact emerges out of his early focus on the social roots of the lived experience of psychopathology (this alternative 'origin' of his research itinerary providing a parallax view from which to reassess the entire array of structural anthropology's concerns). Lévi-Strauss glosses mental disturbances as 'abnormal modes of behaviour' — statistically abnormal, that is, strictly from the perspective of symbolically institutionalized practices — that have been 'desocialised and in some way left to their own devices'.[16] These symptoms are lived by the subject as a reality

11   Marcel Mauss, *A General Theory of Magic*, trans. by Robert Brain (New York: Routledge, 2001), p. 163.

12   Marcel Mauss, *Techniques, Technology and Civilisation*, ed. by Nathan Schlanger (New York: Berghahn Books, 2006), p. 142.

13   Lévi-Strauss, *Introduction*, p. 37.

14   Ibid., p. 17.

15   See especially: Shanna de la Torre, 'Madness and the Sensitive Anthropologist: Lévi-Strauss's New Structuralism', in de la Torre, *Sex for Structuralists: The Non-Oedipal Logics of Femininity and Psychosis* (New York: Palgrave Macmillan, 2018), pp. 39–59.

16   Lévi-Strauss, *Introduction*, p. 12.

Symbolic

- How human societies express social reality, unconsciously instituting shared meanings, collective relations, and modes of behaviour
- Composed of symbolic systems (economic, political, legal, kinship, religious, et al.)

Culture

- A 'spatio-temporal' given (i.e., an 'historicized' or particular configuration of symbolic systems)
- Mapping of the relations between symbolic systems yields a culture's 'structure' or 'total social fact'

History

- Cultural change; its condition of possibility is the incommensurability between symbolic systems; history is 'driven' by (a) outside contact from other cultures and/or (b) a breakdown of symptoms within a culture

Symptom (i.e., 'mental illness')

- The 'lived experience' of a psychic reality inassimilable to and 'desocialized' by social reality
  - Psychotic ('mad') symptom: delusion/hallucination (embodiment of incommensurability of symbolic systems)
  - Neurotic ('sane') symptom: discontent (imaginary reduction of incommensurability of symbolic systems)

Figure 1. Guiding terms for structural anthropology.

incommensurate or incommunicable to social reality. Nevertheless, Lévi-Strauss holds that the 'total [social] fact does not emerge as total simply by reintegrating the discontinuous aspects [i.e., the symbolic systems]. It must be embodied in an individual experience.'[17] That is to say that the lived experience of the symptom embodies the 'truth' of the total social fact precisely at a site in which the integration of its symbolic systems into a whole is revealed to be impossible. If Freudian psychoanalysis dignified such a symptom (that of the hysteric or obsessive, for instance) as an unconscious perspective on the frustrations civilization imposes on the individual's drive satisfactions, for Lévi-Strauss, mental illness is furthermore desocialized *because* the symbolic cannot 'write' it into the very reality it attempts to constitute. And in contrast to the 'average' mental illness of the 'sane' individual, the 'severely mentally disturbed' have a special structural status, insofar as they enact a wholesale refusal of the translation of their lived experience to the symbolically instituted field of meaning.

> [...] strictly speaking, the person whom we call sane is the one who is capable of alienating himself, since he consents to an existence in a world definable only by the self-other relationship. The saneness of the individual mind implies participation in social life, just as the refusal to enter into it (but most importantly, the refusal to do so in the ways that it imposes) corresponds to the onset of mental disturbance.[18]

An equivalence is drawn here between alienation, social participation, and 'sanity' — or what can also be called *neurosis* as the statistically 'normal' or 'average' state of subjectivity. It describes a state of incomplete symbolization, or an inability (or refusal) to reconcile one's lived experience with the (social and physical) reality expressed symbolically by culture. Neurosis is caused by that within the symbolic field that exceeds it: namely the real that the symbolic cannot fully capture, reconcile, or express. The 'sane' ultimately settle for an imaginary solution to this impasse in symbolic formalization — a 'self-other relation' bedevilled by frustration, aggression, and alienation. 'Discontent' is how Freud generally characterizes this symptom of the

---

17   Ibid., p. 26.
18   Ibid., p. 18.

neurotic in capitalist civilization.[19] In contrast, 'madness' — or what can also be called *psychosis* — describes a condition lived by 'individuals who find themselves placed "off system", so to speak, or between two or more irreducible [symbolic] systems'.[20] Unlike the sane, the mad are *alienated from social alienation itself*, rejecting even an imaginary reduction of lived experience — of their suffering, their enjoyment, their jouissance. Unlike neurotics, who reconcile their refusal of social reality through the surplus enjoyment of their discontent, psychotics fully realize the 'contradictions and gaps of the social structure' by embodying them physiologically, mentally, and socially in a psychotic delusion/hallucination (the difference between those terms being now insignificant).

It follows that the 'desocialization' or suppression of psychosis — whether through ostracization or internment, medicalization or extermination, or more broadly, the institution of a system of norms that trivializes madness as a cultural externality, individual idiosyncrasy, or illusory social construct — is how a culture represses its own inherent instabilities, its own irreconcilable, non-whole-yet-more-than-symbolic nature, and is thus how a culture disavows its inability to satisfactorily inscribe any of the subjects that constitute it.

Here I want to move on to 'The Effectiveness of Symbols', an early 1949 essay by Lévi-Strauss that will be a critical reference point for Lacan's return to Freud, and through it for Fanon's engagement with Lacanian psychoanalysis. Its main importance for our purposes lies in the distinction it begins to make between 'modern' and 'premodern' cultures, and thus in how it understands the different status of (and forms of treating) mental illness as structural anthropology would understand it. In this essay, Lévi-Strauss explores the parallels and divergences between a 'native' shamanistic cure and the 'modern' psychoanalytic cure, both of which involve a manipulation of the symbolic function to effect a transformation in the 'real' of the patient.

Myth, as a symbolic system, is reducible in the structuralist definition to a narrative organization of language whose function is to

---

19   Sigmund Freud, *Civilization and its Discontents*, trans. by James Strachey (London: Hogarth Press, 1930).

20   Lévi-Strauss, *Introduction*, p. 18.

constitute social reality and render an image of the universe — its past, present, and future; its internal reason and external limits; and the place of the subject in relation to others within a meaningful social whole. Myths tell stories that give substance to lived experience by recognizing and resolving (in variously satisfactory or unsatisfactory way) the universal crises of subjectivity and the real contradictions of social relations. For his part, Lacan defines myth as it operates in neurosis as

> a certain objectified representation of an epos or as a chronicle expressing in an imaginary way the fundamental relationships characteristic of a certain mode of being human at a specific period, if we understand it as the social manifestation — latent or patent, virtual or actual, full or void of meaning — of this mode of being.[21]

Lévi-Strauss, who provided Lacan the means to construct this formulation, situates the shamanistic and psychoanalytic cures at the interface between subject and myth. That is because mental illness emerges from this same interface, as the outcome of a traumatic incompatibility between the 'mythical time' of social reality and the temporality of lived experience.

The shaman of so-called primitive society, argues Lévi-Strauss, provides the sick a bridging language through which to incorporate a traumatically incommunicable experience into collective myth. This cure makes it possible to 'undergo in an ordered and intelligible form a real experience that would otherwise be chaotic and inexpressible', dialecticizing a conflict that previously had no meaning.[22] In effect, psychic reality is thus resorbed into social reality. But psychoanalysis, insists Lévi-Strauss, operates in a paradigmatically distinct context. 'The modern version of shamanistic technique called psychoanalysis thus derives its specific characteristics from the fact that in *industrial civilization* there is no longer any room for mythical time, except within

---

21 Jacques Lacan, 'The Neurotic's Individual Myth', *Psychoanalytic Quarterly*, 48 (1974), pp. 405–25 (p. 408).

22 Claude Lévi-Strauss, 'The Effectiveness of Symbols', in Lévi-Strauss, *Structural Anthropology*, trans. by Claire Jacobson and Brooke Grundfest Schoepf (New York: Basic Books, 1963), pp. 186–205 (p. 193).

man himself'.[23] Whereas the shaman's patient 'believes in the myth and belongs to a society which believes in it',[24] making integration an effective cure, the neurotic of Western capitalism belongs to a society that no longer furnishes collective myths capable of imbuing lived experience with signifying consistency — an absence secured, I would add, by the ascendance of scientific knowledge, which objectifies an image of the universe *without* subjective meaning and its attendant cosmic purposes, and which for that reason neither solicits nor secures belief (we will soon further complicate this evaluation of myth's status in modernity).

While operating at the same interface between the subject and myth, psychoanalysis inverts the shamanistic cure: it is not integration into a collective myth that is its goal, but the elaboration and abolition of an individual myth through a transference with the Other — specifically the Other of the analyst, who incarnates the signifier as a meaningless cause of desire. If the pre-modern cure integrates the symptom through signification, the modern cure reduces the meaning of an individual myth in order to construct a symptom, or produce new signifiers, that bring the subject into a novel relation to social reality.

In a lively 1963 exchange with Paul Ricœur and several sceptics in his circle that was reproduced in *The New Left Review*, Lévi-Strauss was interrogated about structuralism's programme and ambitions, where the question of his anthropology's propinquity to psychoanalysis and hermeneutics stood as a central issue. In marking a distance between them, Lévi-Strauss attempts to clarify that structuralism shares with contemporary hermeneutics (and the psychoanalysis to which both fields are indebted) an interest in the process of the generation of meaning, but that unlike Ricœur's program, he does not pursue a search for a 'meaning of meaning' because meaning as such arises by his count out of the play and combination of signifiers that are themselves, when isolated from each other, insignificant: 'meaning is always reducible', because 'behind all meaning there is non-meaning, while the reverse is not the case'.[25] It is here that Lévi-Strauss surveys the modesty of his enterprise, indicating that the ethnographer shares with

---

23 Lévi-Strauss, 'Effectiveness', p. 200.
24 Ibid., p. 192.
25 Claude Lévi-Strauss, 'A Confrontation', *New Left Review*, 62 (1970), pp. 57–74 (p. 64).

psychoanalysis only one of its aims: to elaborate the properties and limits of the human mind on the basis of a critique of the production of meaning. Structuralism repeats the Freudian discovery, distinguishing itself only in its scale: 'the ethnologist does the same thing for collective ensembles that the psycho-analyst does for individuals'.[26] In response to a follow up question from one of his interlocutors, who inquires whether structuralism would then attempt to constitute a 'collective psychoanalysis', Lévi-Strauss hesitates, noting that the second aspect of psychoanalysis — its elaboration and implementation of a theory of the cure — is one which 'he has left completely alone'.[27] Does Lévi-Strauss abandon this aspect of psychoanalysis for a lack of time and interest or out of a real limit to any anthropological undertaking? Of course, if we consider the example above, the ethnographer testifies only to the effectivity of the use of symbols in the shamanistic and psychoanalytic healing processes, and does not herself participate in its facilitation, with anthropology limiting itself to the scientific task of *explaining* the cure — particularly the social conditions of its potency — wherever it finds it in operation. If Lévi-Strauss thus casts structuralism as psychoanalysis' handmaiden in the human sciences, this nevertheless raises the question of whether a similar scaling of the theory and practice of treatment is possible, regardless of the profession, existent or not, that would take the responsibility for discharging it. In any event, we can see here that structuralism avowedly interprets the world to mark out the very limits of its interpretation, but it does not try to change it.

But another matter we have begun to thematize seems to be closely related to this one and deserves further attention, provoked by the fact that Lévi-Strauss primarily limited the object of his study to non-Western cultures, particularly their mythical systems. This self-recusal he outlines, albeit without justification, through an historical hypothesis: for Lévi-Strauss, modern societies have replaced myths with politics or political ideology. He cites the French Revolution as a prime example in European culture, even its paradigm.[28] If such polit-

---

26   Ibid., p. 71.
27   Ibid.
28   Claude Lévi-Strauss, 'The Structural Study of Myth', in Lévi-Strauss, *Structural Anthropology*, pp. 206–31 (p. 209).

ical ideologies supplement, on a collective rather than individual level, science's evisceration of subjective meaning on a cosmological level by giving narrative substance of a national or racial nature to the otherwise contingent and traumatic events of contemporary experience (now irreducibly coloured by the uneven development of capitalist culture on whose wings that same science rose), politics' distance from 'primitive' myths would solely be a matter of scale. To put it otherwise, the difference between myth and politics is historical and not structural, insofar as the political ideology of Nazism, to give yet another one of Lévi-Strauss's examples, is no different than any historical interpretation of its significance, since each of these hermeneutic 'disciplines', which each in their own way seek to establish one or several final meanings of history, are for Lévi-Strauss themselves 'variants of that mythology', and those in turn, he adds, perhaps only permutations of Biblical mythology.[29] But since modern politics, unlike the Bible, does not provide a total ideology — it being incapable of providing anything more than an incomplete image of the universe (notwithstanding various historical exceptions to this rule, both progressive and reactionary) — then we can see how the individual myth (which also 'historicizes' memories, the past of childhood, and the like) described by psychoanalysis comes to supplement an ideologically incomplete modern politics alongside which it historically arises. The gap or irreducibility between these two scales of mythical reality (i.e., individual and political) would then reaffirm, now in a new place, what we previously established above: that no culture is wholly symbolic.

This brings us back to Fanon's first failed reform effort at Blida-Joinville, where these two themes are conjoined in the problem of grounding a 'collective psychoanalysis' in the psychiatric hospital and of formulating a cure that must operate upon both individual myths (as expressed in symptoms) and collective myths (as expressed in culture and politics), and all of that in a setting and for a mixed patient population — in colonial North Africa — that embody an active and ongoing clash between 'modern' and 'traditional' cultural systems. This problematic is condensed, again, in this question: why did the European women under his care benefit from his therapeutic reforms and the

---

29   Lévi-Strauss, 'A Confrontation', p. 68.

Algerian men languish?[30] The answer provided by Fanon has by now been well summarized,[31] and without rehearsing the finer details of the principles underlying Fanon's social therapy (which we will do later), it must be noted that Fanon and the institutional psychiatry movement, in addition to utilizing traditional psychoanalysis and group therapy, assigned a vital therapeutic value to symbolic activity in the broadest sense of the term, which it was hoped would serve as 'a veritable social cement' among the patients and hospital staff.[32] Recreational and occupational activities — the establishment of a hospital journal and weaving workshops, the celebration of national holidays and the organization of patient-run planning committees, the screening of movies and even the playing of hide-and-seek, all of it conducted in French — were designed, as Fanon and his co-author admitted, to evoke the interest and participation of those familiar with these referents and mainstays of French (and to a different degree European) cultural life, and were for that very same reason absolutely foreign to Algerian (and to a different degree North African) cultural life. This meant that for the latter, the symbolic activity or 'unconscious' of the hospital remained insignificant, its narrative structure and temporality alien to their lived experience (including that of their mental illness), and thus incapable of soliciting their desire.

Without comprehending and integrating the North African total social fact — its myths, kinship structure, and other symbolic systems that give personal and collective significance to the temporality of lived experience — social therapy will have no therapeutic value. It is not a matter of assimilating the patient (whether French or North African) to their 'native' cultural milieu, but of instituting activities that articulate and reshuffle its constituent symbolic elements, whatever they are, so as to provide a space for the patient to manipulate, recombine, and live them differently. The hospital's symbolic activity must

---

30   While a sexual difference conspicuously coincides with the divergent fates of his European and North African patients, Fanon, unlike in his other writings in which sexual identity becomes relevant, does not indicate that gender is a factor in the specific nature of the ineffectiveness of his initial treatment.

31   Nigel C. Gibson and Roberto Beneduce, 'Further Steps toward a Critical Ethnopsychiatry Sociotherapy: Its Strengths and Weaknesses', in Gibson and Beneduce, *Frantz Fanon, Psychiatry and Politics* (London: Rowman & Littlefield, 2017), pp. 131–64.

32   Fanon and Azoulay, 'Social Therapy', p. 360.

incorporate a certain ethnopsychoanalytic orientation still missing at Blida-Joinville so that the symptom, which both speaks and is meaningless precisely within the specific cultural context of its emergence, has the symbolic scaffolding required to begin a chain reaction of mutual transformations between the personal (symptom) and collective (culture).

Now, hospital staff quickly corrected this mistake at Blida-Joinville, but the rapidly changing historical circumstances that led Fanon to submit his resignation in 1956 would also catalyse Fanon to tackle theoretically and clinically harder problems, precisely those that pertain to the question of the relationship between mental health and the political. In his resignation letter, we get a sense of the direness of the situation and the enormity of this task:

> If psychiatry is the medical technique that sets out to enable individuals no longer to be foreign to their environment, I owe it to myself to state that the Arab, permanently alienated in his own country, lives in a state of absolute depersonalization.
>
> [...]
>
> The function of a social structure is to set up institutions that are traversed by a concern for humankind. A society that forces its members into desperate solutions is a non-viable society, a society that needs replacing.[33]

Fanon's and his patients' experience of a particular non-viable society — unique to the colonial situation but by no means limited to this time and place in Algeria — creates an epistemological vantage that affords new insights into the universal structure of *all* societies. This will require radicalizing the project of a collective psychoanalysis, one that will henceforward be impossible to divorce from a program for society's political transformation.

FANON: REDUCTION OF THE SOCIAL TO THE DIALECTIC

Lévi-Strauss's reading of the psychoanalytic cure as a modern anti-assimilationist device, which we just saw was a formulation that was both derived from and gestative of his structuralist research, reverberates throughout Fanon's therapeutic approach. As stated before,

---

33   Frantz Fanon, 'Letter to the Resident Minister', in Fanon, *Alienation and Freedom*, pp. 433–36 (pp. 434–35).

institutional psychiatry makes disalienation its objective, a notion of healing that first and foremost rejects the asylum system and its carceral objective of treating the mentally ill as a danger who must be segregated from society and themselves. At the same time institutional psychiatry does not strive to adapt the patient to social reality as such an adaptation is impossible, and the disavowal of that fact the wellspring of mental illness. Mental illness, states Fanon, afflicts 'precisely those who do not manage to neutralize or distance the existence of the surrounding world.'[34] Such an illness will be all the more dire when the surrounding world — its public life, social bonds, and the institutions that guarantee them — is in a state of active disintegration. In any event, these conceptions of illness and disalienation rely on a notion of the symbolic nature of society that Fanon inherited and reworked from the human sciences.

In a sense, what Fanon advocates under the name of 'social therapy' is redundant: socialization is already therapeutic, and psychotherapy only the institutionalization of the social as its own end. The social is what Fanon, like Mauss and Lévi-Strauss, and to a critical extent Durkheim before them, will designate as the warp and woof of reality: not in any empiricist sense as 'that which is', but as one that is structured through the symbolic and the relations it mediates. Fanon simultaneously reduces the structural dynamics of social reality to the dialectic, that unceasing movement of the negative that he snapshots in various ways through its forms of appearance: as a fundamental tension, conflict, or capacity for transformation within the symbolic, whether frozen or in vivo. 'To be socializable', writes Fanon, 'is to be able to maintain a constant tension between ego and society',[35] a tension that the dialectic spans into a relation at every scale of existence, and in which the subject is born and develops in its fundamental alienation. Social existence is for Fanon, as with Lévi-Strauss, an experience of productive alienation. That is not in the least because the unconscious — comprising what Lévi-Strauss calls the 'fundamental

---

34   Frantz Fanon and Slimane Asselah, 'The Phenomenon of Agitation in the Psychiatric Milieu: General Considerations, Psychopathological Meaning', in Fanon, *Alienation and Freedom*, pp. 437–48 (p. 444).

35   Frantz Fanon, 'The Meeting Between Society and Psychiatry', in Fanon, *Alienation and Freedom*, pp. 511–30 (p. 521).

phenomena of mental life [...] that condition it and determine its most general forms' and acting as 'the mediating term between self and other'[36] — marks a definitive limit to both relationality and shared experience.

While Fanon's citations of structuralism and structural anthropology remain far sparser than those we find pointing in his work to psychoanalysis, psychiatry, and phenomenology, Jean Khalfa and Robert Young have inventoried the French-Martinican doctor's bibliography to reconstruct several essential referents, none of which may be more illustrative of Fanon's tacit understanding than a passage from Mauss that they suggest italicizes Fanon's grasp of the 'living' (i.e., dialectical) aspect of socialization and his strong aversion to any scientific project that would submit it to the 'corpse' of metaphysical abstraction. It is here, in a passage Khalfa and Young extract from the *Essay on the Gift*, that Mauss summarizes the object of the 'total social fact' that he insists the theorist must construct against any armchair taxonomization of cultural features.

> We have looked at societies in their dynamic or physiological state. We have not studied them as if they were motionless, in a static state, or as if they were corpses. Even less have we decomposed and dissected them, producing rules of law, myths, values, and prices. It is by considering the whole entity that we could perceive what is essential, the way everything moves, the living aspect, the fleeting moment when society, or men, become sentimentally aware of themselves and of their situation in relation to others.[37]

One of the possible definitions of ideology is this spontaneous experience of social life in a dehistoricized state. Alternatively, we may designate 'norms', or the self-justifying representation of a society, as the flaw of immediate experience that structuralism amends through its construction of models of the unconscious, the very same ones — at this point under the name of the 'social fact' — that Fanon admitted he had failed to incorporate into the planning and execution of his clinical program at Blida-Joinville. '[S]ome kind of model [of society],

---

36   Lévi-Strauss, *Introduction*, p. 35.
37   Marcel Mauss, *The Gift: The Form and Reason for Exchange in Archaic Societies*, trans. by W. D. Halls (London: Routledge, 1990), p. 102.

standing as a screen to hide it, will exist in the collective consciousness', writes Lévi-Strauss. 'For conscious models, which are usually known as "norms", are by definition very poor ones, since they are not intended to explain the phenomena but to perpetuate them.'[38] Structuralism is a highway that leads from justification (conscious models) to explanation (models of the unconscious), but for Fanon, going beyond the human sciences, the latter can only be a pitstop on a journey that makes disalienation its endpoint.

Translating this notion of structure into practice motivates Fanon's transformation of the psychiatric ward into a 'neo-society' in which patients would be able to repeat or enact certain conflicts or 'neurotic attitudes' that lie at the root of their afflictions.[39] Now, these conflicts are, at least initially, repressed, mortified, inhibited in their expression, or otherwise sublimated in the service of productive activity — across familial, industrial, educational, political, and other disciplinary institutions that had consolidated in Europe and, to a very different and uneven extent, in its colonial satellites by the mid-twentieth century. Mental illness is in this understanding caused, sustained, and nurtured *through* the disciplinary repression of conflict, not by the conflicts themselves. A notion of the Fanonian subject of the unconscious emerges here: 'the conflict is the patient', where conflict, this experience of the incommensurability of and maladaption to the symbolic, is precisely 'one of the most essential elements in the genesis of a personality'.[40] Where such conflict is foreclosed the illness is objectified and the subject fades. The cure does not lie in its resolution but in the activation and working-over of this conflict. To understand his therapeutic method, we must therefore grasp Fanon's understanding of mental illness: the mode of illness will indicate the mode of the cure. The ambivalent capacities of the social, its interpretation adopted and adapted from French anthropology and radical psychiatry, holds the key to both.

---

38   Claude Lévi-Strauss, 'Social Structure', in Lévi-Strauss, *Structural Anthropology*, pp. 277–323 (p. 281).

39   Frantz Fanon, 'Day Hospitalization in Psychiatry: Value and Limits', in Fanon, *Alienation and Freedom*, pp. 473–94 (p. 475).

40   Frantz Fanon, 'Day Hospitalization in Psychiatry: Value and Limits, Part Two — Doctrinal Considerations', in Fanon, *Alienation and Freedom*, pp. 495–510 (p. 504).

Fanon was clear concerning the insufficiency of a mechanistic understanding of causality for ascertaining the aetiology of mental disturbances: symptoms, he contends, cannot be determined by endogenous (organic or biochemical) or by exogenous (social or historical) factors, nor even by some combination thereof (in the Lacanian theory of psychogenesis, for instance), but must be examined as the outcome of a dialectic that has been rendered inoperative: that 'tension' or negativity between the self and other, between the body and history, both structured by the hallmark of social life, the 'uninterrupted dialectic of the subject and world'.[41] Mental disturbances follow a breakdown in relationality and arise when the possibility of their mediation is suppressed. The symptom, in turn, emerges as a displacement of this impasse, standing as both a memorialization of the repression of the dialectic and a 'privatization' of its conflict that restricts the orbit of its movement to a closed loop between the patient and a symptom that the dominant postwar psychiatric ideology impugns as a sickness beyond the patient's control (i.e., divorced from subjective intention) for which they (whether as an individual or so-called race) are nevertheless also held morally culpable.

To illustrate this notion of the arrested dialectic of the symptom, take Fanon's explanation of 'hallucination' and its transformation, in punitive hospital psychiatric settings, into the clinical phenomenon of 'agitation'. Hallucination begins as a regression to an earlier, oral stage of relationality.[42] It responds to the dissolution of the spatial and temporal coordinates that grant a given 'reality' its consistency (a dissolution triggered especially by war, torture, and other catastrophes). 'Systems of reference' always structure social reality; there are always 'lines of force that order culture'.[43] Both of these Fanonian idioms are conceptions that Alice Cherki suggests we translate into the structuralist notion of the symbolic in its function as a 'third element' that mediates between subject and world.[44] Under 'normal' circumstances

---

41   Ibid.

42   Fanon and Asselah, 'The Phenomenon of Agitation', p. 441.

43   Frantz Fanon, 'Racism and Culture', in Fanon, *Toward the African Revolution: Political Essays*, trans. by Haakon Chevalier (New York: Grove Press, 1967), pp. 29–44 (p. 33).

44   Alice Cherki, *Frantz Fanon: A Portrait*, trans. by Nadia Benabid (Ithaca, NY: Cornell University Press, 2006), p. 216.

these references and lines of force conflict with each other, leaving holes in reality that create spaces for the subject to invest with personal meanings; but colonial violence and racism, especially, lead to a radical disintegration of reality, eliminating even those productive gaps of meaning. In desperation, the patient replaces this non-viable reality with the 'pseudo world' of their own private hallucination ('pseudo' not in the sense of being fake or inauthentic, but as a desocialized image of social reality). Stripped of their 'natural' sociality — with its alienating powers of symbolization and mediation — the subject depends on a hallucination that crystallizes 'the apparent significance of his troubles', infusing them with 'new relations and meanings'.[45] Delusion, as Fanon describes it in his doctoral thesis, thus 'becomes the intentional equivalent of an insufficiently socialized, aggressive drive'.[46] What reality renders inexpressible returns in the speech of the symptom as an epistemological rupture with the social.

A simple opposition between cure and illness already loses its cogency: the 'individual's' psychopathology emerges as a cure to an 'outside' disintegration of social reality. The symptom is neither some aberration of a social norm nor some purely intrapsychic defect but a reaction to the Other. The asylum not only misrecognizes the dialectical nature of the symptom but redoubles its mystification, reinforcing a reification initiated in the social milieu. It is the meaningful character of the hallucination, then, — the fact that it speaks, has meaning, and functions as a compensation to the symbolic that has lost its living aspect — that dominant psychiatry silences by isolating the patient from others, cutting them off from the dialectic of speech, and refusing to recognize the symptom's status as a veritable 'modality of existence, a type of actualization, an expressive style'.[47] The hallucinatory symptom, as a final defence against subjective disintegration, is thereby transformed from a lived illness into a dead state of 'agitation', the latter a sickness strictly native to the psychiatric context. In denying

---

45   Fanon and Asselah, 'The Phenomenon of Agitation', p. 443.

46   Frantz Fanon, 'Mental Alterations, Character Modifications, Psychic Disorders and Intellectual Deficit in Spinocerebellar Heredodegeneration: A Case of Friedreich's Ataxia with Delusions of Possession', in Fanon, *Alienation and Freedom*, pp. 203–76 (p. 266).

47   Fanon and Asselah, 'The Phenomenon of Agitation', p. 447.

the patient's 'pseudo-reality', the psychiatric hospital denies the defect in 'reality' to which that hallucination responds. This 'opens the way to phantasms of bodily fragmentation or the crumbling of the ego'.[48] The punitive hospital effectively perfects the illness, objectifies it and makes it chronic, alienating the subject from their social alienation. 'Asylum putrefaction': this is what Fanon called this induced psychosis that plagues the psychiatric institution. Where the repression of conflict triggers the patient's mental disturbance, an iatrogenic factor reifies — thingifies, dehistoricizes, personifies — it into an absolute pathology.

Despite strongly qualifying the social field as the soil of psychopathology — whether described under the heading of 'sociogenesis' in *Black Skin, White Masks* at the beginning of his writings[49] or in his later clinical lectures as 'social psychopathology' — Fanon also insists on its irreplaceability as a therapeutic medium: 'the veritable social-therapeutic milieu is and remains concrete society itself'.[50] How to account for this double character of the social, its pathogenic and therapeutic potentiality?

In his radicalization of institutional psychotherapy, borne out of his later work at the Neuropsychiatric Day Centre of Tunis (CNPJ) at the Charles Nicolle Hospital (1958–60), Fanon outlines his theoretical and political justification for transforming the institution into an artifice capable of facilitating the spontaneously therapeutic — dialectical, conflictual, living — dimension of the social. The need to create, under artificial conditions, what is otherwise affirmed as a datum of human nature can only be understood as a response to an historical and political outcome: the living or symbolic nature of social life, and in turn the sociality of subjectivity, is not reliably or consistently nurtured in modern disciplinary societies (and does not fare well under any sign of capitalist culture), and even more, enters an unprecedented state of decomposition in the colonial situation and the antiblack racism with which it conjugates.

---

48   Fanon, 'Day Hospitalization, Part Two', p. 503.
49   Frantz Fanon, *Black Skin, White Masks*, trans. by Charles Lam Markmann, forewords by Ziauddin Sardar and Homi K. Bhabha (London: Pluto Press, 2008), p. 4.
50   Ibid., p. 500.

> In reality the nations that undertake a colonial war have no concern for the confrontation of cultures. War is a gigantic business and every approach must be governed by this datum. The enslavement, in the strictest sense, of the native population is the prime necessity.
>
> For this its systems of reference have to be broken. Expropriation, spoliation, raids, objective murder, are matched by the sacking of cultural patterns, or at least condition such sacking. The social panorama is destructured; values are flaunted, crushed, emptied.
>
> The lines of force, having crumbled, no longer give direction. In their stead a new system of values is imposed, not proposed but affirmed, by the heavy weight of cannons and sabers.[51]

There is no confrontation of cultures, no conflict of meanings between the realities of disparate symbolic systems, when it is the very unconscious 'third terms' or 'lines of force' themselves — those empty signifiers whose combinations produce meanings and demarcate its limits — that are eviscerated in the total transposition that replaces wholesale 'native' culture with a European one. Perhaps more accurately (or maybe as just the flip side of this phenomenon), all 'native' signifiers become empty ones, turned into hieroglyphs of a dead language that no longer constellate any significance but collectively refer to a void of meaning.

Hallucination — or any symptom for that matter — is reunderstood in this context as the sign of the faltering of the social field. But for that reason, it also emerges for Fanon as the most promising lever to press in the service of its renewal. Instead of eliminating the hallucination or eradicating conflict, the goal of disalienation becomes that of dialectizing the symptom: to facilitate its 'style' or 'modality of existence', indexical of an individual and collective crisis, through various means of symbolic mediation, including by investing in the curative capacities of art, work, writing, and collaborative processes of creative expression, all of which require taking responsibility for one's desire vis-à-vis others.

Fanon's aim is thus to socialize — first within the institution but then, ultimately, beyond it (see below) — a conflict that has been

---

51   Fanon, 'Racism and Culture', p. 32.

desocialized or 'placed off system' (as Lévi-Strauss put it). The goal, we might say, is to resocialize a symptom that society has privatized. Fanon therefore reimagined the psychiatric hospital as a place for preserving the therapeutic powers of socialization within the very society that was seeking to suppress it.

DISALIENATION: REDUCTION OF THE DIALECTIC TO THE POLITICAL

At this point, Fanon's understanding of mental illness looks very much like a theory of the 'social symptom' — in which one's seemingly most intimate suffering marks only the 'point of emergence of the truth of social relations'.[52] The symptom is political. Fanon's understanding of the cure likewise anticipates a Lacanian ethical orientation, one that directs the treatment to enable the subject to assume the cause of their desire in a field alien to their person, in the social Other.[53] Disalienation requires the subject to take responsibility for the truth of social relations: to expand the symptom beyond its stagnating self-reference and to create a space of mediation between the subject and its extimate (i.e., both inside and outside) cause.

> If the hospital setting forms a knot of social relations, of ambiguous encounters, then agitation loses its resonance as an entity, as irresponsible behaviour, as something incomprehensible. From a dialectical viewpoint, agitation then enters into the primordial cycle of the reflecting-reflected mirror: you give to me, I receive, I assimilate, I transform, I render to you.[54]

Social therapy starts by reaching down into the riveted dialectic of the mirror — in those frustrated imaginary relations that the eradication of symbolic references has turned into a cul-de-sac of destructive agitation — but only to immediately go beyond it. New signs must be introduced to curve its tunnel of reflections into a progressive architecture. Through participation in the hospital's collective activities, patients invent 'lines of force' that structure a new reality beyond the

---

52   Slavoj Žižek, *The Sublime Object of Ideology* (London: Verso, 1989), p. 22.

53   See Calum Neill, *Lacanian Ethics and the Assumption of Subjectivity* (New York: Palgrave Macmillan, 2011).

54   Fanon and Asselah, 'The Phenomenon of Agitation', p. 444.

play of projections. Articulating the symptom to its social truth, rather than immersing the subject in the time and space of actually existing society, returns to the social field the very disruptive supplement it has effaced.

A final but essential aspect that Fanon's final clinical experiment at Tunis demonstrates is how his new social therapy required inventing something we might call an 'open and closed institution' that, in mimicking the dialectical movement of the unconscious, subverts the 'enclosure' model of disciplinary institutions (and asylums in particular) without therefore producing that 'open' model definitive of systems in a society of continuous control (management, training, surveillance, etc.) that was, at the time, yet to come.[55] The day hospital at the Charles-Nicoll hospital was an attempt to put the political and theoretical principles of a 'late Fanon' into practice. It consummates his break with the 'neo-society' of the Tosquellean hospital, insofar as the latter, according to Fanon, hamstrings the therapeutic potential of 'concrete society itself' by retaining for itself the power to prevent patients from leaving the hospital, to prohibit their voluntary discharge. While Tosquelles's reforms of the hospital space — breaking from its disciplinary measures, segregationist practices, and hierarchical relations — had empirically therapeutic effects, this attempt at erecting a neo-society always fell short of realizing the cure. So Fanon:

> It is necessary, however, to acknowledge that with [Tosquelles's] institutional-therapy [sic], we create fixed institutions, strict and rigid settings, and schemas that are rapidly stereotyped. In the neo-society, there are no inventions; there is no creative, innovative dynamic. There is no veritable shake-up, no crises. The institution remains that 'corpse-like cement' of which Mauss speaks.[56]

Mortification, fixity, mummification, rigidity, stereotypy, cementation, tetanization, ankylosis, reification, corpsing: these are the metaphors Fanon deploys here and across his oeuvre to designate those moments in which the dialectic is arrested, those failures of socialization that

---

55   See Gilles Deleuze, 'Postscript on the Societies of Control', *October* 59, trans. by Martin Joughin (1992), pp. 3–7.

56   Fanon, 'Day Hospitalization, Part Two', p. 499.

he blames in this instance on the elimination of the patient's radical freedom to leave the hospital, to meet and refuse the doctor on a plane of unqualified equality. Even more importantly, the abrogation of the subject's final freedom prevents the patient from participating in *and transforming* social life outside of the psychiatric system, from engaging the daily rhythms and trivial exchanges of family, work, and cultural life, where they can create something new in the field of relations. When and only when this freedom is restored, then

> The patient no longer experiences his possible discharge as the product of the doctor's benevolence. The *a minima* master/slave, prisoner/gaoler dialectic created in internment, or in the threat thereof, is radically broken. In the setting of the day hospital, the doctor-patient encounter forever remains an encounter between two freedoms.[57]

If we can describe as *temporal* the dialectical movement that is catalysed through various symbolic activities that introduce a dynamic, lived quality to the experience of illness within the hospital, Fanon seems to establish, through the institutional ethics of what he calls 'semi-hospitalization', a supplementary and crucial *spatial dialectic* — namely, that between the hospital and society itself — that ultimately reconnects the therapeutic space to concrete society and its interleaved institutions. Together, this makes possible, for the first time, an unencumbered dialectic between the temporal and spatial coordinates of embodied experience that Tosquelles's closed institution forecloses through its amputation of the subject's freedom to refuse treatment (and by implication, their freedom to assume full responsibility for their subjectivity).

It is precisely in restoring this freedom that the hospital bears political implications that go beyond its healing effects, or more accurately, that inscribes the political within the marrow of its therapeutic program: the psychiatric hospital is henceforward designed to relate to, or establish a dialectical conduit between, its artificial instantiation of the lived, dynamic, dialectical dimension of the symbolic and the actually existing society in which that diachronic dimension of reality has been (politically and imaginarily) effaced in favour of an ideological

---

57   Ibid., p. 497.

affirmation of its synchronicity. This dialectical conduit is achieved not between some sort of alliance among various institutions, but through the mediating function of the *nomadic patient* who is free to travel between them, who recovers their living illness in the hospital and transfers the conflict of their symptom, in a further step in its dialectical rehabilitation, into the very social field that had disarticulated it. Nancy Luxon figures this final transformation of the Fanonian hospital as its reconstruction into a 'waystation' — a 'buffer zone' or 'transient support' — between a colonized world as it actually exists (i.e., in its disturbances and disintegrations of reality that both fertilize and disavow psychopathology) and a decolonized conjuncture that is yet to come (i.e., where those psychopathologies can be assumed as lived realities and articulated into something new).[58] No longer is the 'social' simply instrumentalized (or synthetically restored) to mediate the relationship between patient and their symptom in the closed space of the wards, but the hospital itself becomes a *heterotopia* with a centrifugal force that scatters a conflict first revived in the subject into the very spaces that had previously maligned its symptomatic condensation into a private illness. Only through this final, disjunctive connection between the hospital and its cultural context can the former, as a space of mediation between the dialectic and its negation, reintroduce into a colonized terrain the temporality of an antagonism that the latter has flattened. The reformed hospital therefore creates an unprecedented social space, a radically transferential milieu — between self and symptom, patient and other, and ultimately, among social institutions themselves.

Even beyond its mere 'implications' for politics, this conceptualization of the radical psychiatric hospital has its own, immanent conception of the *political* that seems to me to be vigorously opposed to what might otherwise be called *politics*,[59] to the extent that the latter encompasses, and also inevitably leads to, the stagnated slave/master dialectic, of which the doctor/patient is just a version — and which is always the symptom of an institutional putrefaction, of a desocial-

---

58   Nancy Luxon, 'Fanon's Psychiatric Hospital as a Waystation to Freedom', *Theory, Culture & Society*, 38 (2021), pp. 93–113.

59   For one formulation of this distinction see: Mladen Dolar, 'Freud and the Political', *Unbound*, 4 (2008), pp. 15–29.

ization, of a restriction of the dialectic that pivots on the banning of the radical freedom to act on another scene. Translated into a social context, such a radical freedom travels under the sign of revolution or a revolutionary struggle, in which the battle of the master/slave dialectic may be its first, but never its final, moment. Could this notion of the dislocative force of the political be related to a maxim that regularly appears in Fanon's texts, one in which it is asserted that the symptomatic fixations of madness constitute a 'veritable pathology of freedom'? Borrowed from the French psychiatrist Henri Ey, who himself inherited it from the German writer Günther Anders (in an essay later recited in Deleuze's *Logic of Sense*), this phrase denotes madness not as a utopian escape from the strictures of reason nor a universal human condition that needs to be recovered but a restriction of emancipatory action to the inertia of an imaginary opposition — the limitation of revolt, in other words, to a fight against a figment of fantasy, most immediately a master (authority, doctor, the enemy) that reproduces the social tie of this 'unhappy couple' and cultivates an identity encumbered by ressentiment and the inhibitions of slave morality, all of which contributes to a type of 'subversion [of authority] that serves the cause of oppression', as Jean Khalfa has put it.[60] 'Madness', as restated by Fanon in his 1956 letter of resignation, 'is one of the ways that humans have of losing their freedom'.[61] Against the sacrifice of freedom to an endless opposition, the new Fanonian psychiatric institution, once divested of its powers of control and retention, would make possible, or enable the subject to assume full responsibility for, their radical freedom to act, to effect a dislocation of the social link and the economy of values that reduce the subject to an identity: a freedom that would finally be fully conducive to the movement of the dialectic that does not stop in the encounter between the subject and symptom, in some confrontation between patient and the doctor or others in the ward, but that would ceaselessly socialize (and thus self-subjectivize) itself, all of which entails the disintegration of previous social ties and the institutions that invest their imaginary positions and relations.

---

60   Jean Khalfa, 'A Theory of Subversion that Could Not Also Serve the Cause of Oppression?', *Interventions*, 23 (2021), pp. 417–31.

61   Fanon, 'Letter', p. 434.

Here, at last, the terms of the psychopathological seem to be perfectly reversible into those of the sociopolitical, in which it is colonized society itself that appears to rely on the creation of its own 'pseudo world', its own hallucinatory reality, to maintain its ideological consistency, a hallucination that, in standing in for the actual disintegration of the social field that it replaces while blocking any progressive development of conflict that could achieve an authentic reality of dialectical relations, reifies extant bonds of association into immutable identities and imaginary relations (both personal and political). The 'patient' of such a colonized society must therefore ingest the *disintegrative* pill of the negative force of the political before the *integrative* chemistry of politics can begin. It is not the job of the psychiatric hospital to establish this work or determine the outcome of any politics to come, but to safeguard an ethical space in which a political act would be possible.

Black Box Allegories of Gulf Futurism
The Irreducible Other of Computational Capital
ÖZGÜN EYLÜL İŞCEN

INTRODUCTION

On the first day of October 2021, Expo 2020 Dubai, delayed by one year due to the COVID-19 pandemic, opened its doors. Until its closing at the end of March 2022, it hosted more than twenty-four million people, boosting the country's economy and tourism while fulfilling its goal of becoming a global hub for emerging technologies.[1] Constructed around the themes of opportunity, mobility, and sustainability, the one hundred ninety-two countries participating in the Expo showcased their competing futuristic narratives and innovations. In this respect, the Expo took place in the background of the shifting centres of global accumulation and the UAE's efforts to expand its regional footprint within this fast-changing international order.

Integrated with the Expo site was a permanent public art exhibition, curated by Tarek Abou El Fetouh, where Kuwaiti, Berlin-based artist Monira Al Qadiri attended with *Chimera* (2021) — a gigantic

1   Neil Halligan, 'Expo 2020 Dubai Records More than 24 Million Visits after Late Surge', *The National*, 2 April 2022 <https://www.thenationalnews.com/uae/expo-2020/2022/04/02/expo-2020-dubai-records-more-than-24-million-visits-after-late-surge-in-numbers/> [accessed 17 May 2022].

Figure 1. Monira Al Qadiri, *Chimera*, 2021, permanent aluminium
sculpture with iridescent automotive paint, 450 × 470 × 490 cm, Expo
2020 Dubai. Courtesy of the artist. Photo credit: Roman Mensing in
cooperation with Thorsten Arendt.

iridescent coloured sculpture based on the shape of an oil drill head
(see Figure 1).[2] With its size and colour, the artist intended to produce
a presence of a futuristic creature from outer space, mesmerizing and
unsettling the viewers at once. The Greek mythology-inspired title of
the work, *Chimera*, brings forth a figure of a mythical creature composed of incongruous parts gathered from multiple animals. In the
artist's iteration, the pre-oil times and post-oil futures merge within the
body of the sculpture. The iridescent quality of its surface hints at the
visual complexity of both oil and pearl, thereby recalling the centuries-
old pearl industry, which was replaced by the oil industry that has been
on the rise since the 1930s.

---

2 'Expo 2020 Dubai unveils first permanent public artwork by Kuwaiti creative', *Arab
News*, 4 July 2021 <https://www.arabnews.com/node/1888116/lifestyle> [accessed
17 May 2022]. The work was commissioned by Expo 2020 Dubai and is part of its
collection. See also the artist's website <https://www.moniraalqadiri.com/chimera/>
[accessed 30 May 2022].

Chimera makes multi-layered connections between pearl and oil, spanning from physical and symbolic qualities to thick layers of history and ecology (for example, oil as a geological phenomenon). In this respect, the shape of the oil drill head brings to the surface the materiality of extraction alongside the spectacles led by oil wealth. Its iridescent surface mirrors back the surrounding site full of those spectacles constituting Gulf Futurism, condensed within the glamorous, high-tech architecture of the Expo site.

Indeed, the Expo site demonstrates how contemporary Gulf Futurism builds upon profit-driven, technocratic premises, which adopt the prevailing neoliberal ethos of turning crises into opportunities. In opposition, the artists Sophia Al-Maria and Fatima Al Qadiri coined the term 'Gulf Futurism' in the early 2010s to attend to the socio-cultural contradictions inherent in the accelerated urban and technological development in the Arabian Gulf, especially since the 1970s oil boom. These contradictions often derive from the contrast between those high-tech architectural spectacles and what lies behind them, ranging from the destruction of desert ecosystems and Bedouin lifestyles to the segregation of socio-economic groups through extreme wealth disparities and securitized everyday life in the city.[3]

Nonetheless, the ongoing urban struggles and artistic practices in the larger Middle East and North Africa region enact what Jussi Parikka calls counterfuturisms to contest the material implications of Gulf Futurism in the present and imagine alternatives to the risks and hopes that it preemptively imposes in the region and beyond.[4] In resonance with futurisms that embrace a critical and emancipatory agenda, such as Afrofuturism, artists like Monira Al Qadiri intervene in the hegemonic uses and imaginaries of a given technology.[5] In this

---

3 'Al Qadiri and Al-Maria on Gulf Futurism', *Dazed Digital*, 14 November 2012, <https://www.dazeddigital.com/music/article/15037/1/alqadiri-al-maria-on-gulf-futurism> [accessed 15 October 2020].

4 Jussi Parikka, 'Middle East and Other Futurisms: Imaginary Temporalities in Contemporary Art and Visual Culture', *Culture, Theory and Critique*, 59.1 (2018), pp. 40–58. See also: Jussi Parikka, 'Counter-Futuring', *Counter-N*, ed. by Özgün Eylül İşcen and Shintaro Miyazaki, 12 April 2022 <https://doi.org/10.18452/24451>.

5 It is beyond the scope of this paper to sketch out these different futurisms with conflicting tendencies, which requires a further historical context. See: *Ethnofuturismen*, ed. by Armen Avanessian and Mahan Moalemi (Berlin: Merve Verlag, 2018); Bahar Noorizadeh, 'Weird-Futuring', *Counter-N*, ed. by Özgün Eylül İşcen and Shintaro Miyazaki,

regard, her work offers not merely a critique of Gulf Futurism but also a reflection on its material history with the aim of opening up a path for reimagining post-oil futures otherwise.

Al Qadiri's critical intervention should be understood against the background of the global trend of the smartness mandate.[6] Given the economic instability that followed the 2008–09 global financial crisis and the prospect of post-oil futures on the side, Gulf Futurism has taken the shape of the smartness mandate. This mandate aims at finding market-led and technology-enabled solutions to ever-growing economic and ecological crises that have a planetary scale. According to Orit Halpern, Robert Mitchell, and Bernard Dionysius Geoghegan, the growth of smart technology, characterized by datafication, optimization, and sustainability, has motivated a new model of managing and governing cities and the global supply chain. Yet, most of these technocratic premises address the recurring crises of capitalist modernity by investing in 'smarter' infrastructures to absorb them rather than by introducing structural changes.[7]

Indeed, these spectacles have material implications, such as how the city of Dubai has grown as a logistical hub via state-owned conglomerates (e.g., Dubai World) operating worldwide. These architectural spectacles exemplify what Kelly Easterling calls 'extrastatecraft', which she defines as a set of zones, devices, and narratives materializing an infrastructural space.[8] Accordingly, I argue that contemporary Gulf Futurism expresses the aesthetic regime of Dubai as a logistical city, which builds upon — while obscuring — the pairing of smart technology with a racialized labour regime via the Kafala (sponsorship) system.[9]

12 April 2022 <https://doi.org/10.18452/24452>. See also: Kodwo Eshun, 'Further Considerations of Afrofuturism', *CR: The New Centennial Review*, 3.2 (Summer 2003), pp. 287–302 <https://doi.org/10.1353/ncr.2003.0021>.

6   Orit Halpern, Robert Mitchell, and Bernard Dionysius Geoghegan, 'The Smartness Mandate: Notes Toward a Critique', *Grey Room*, 68 (2017), pp. 106–29 <https://doi. org/10.1162/GREY_a_00221>. Please note that here and in the remaining chapter 'Al Qadiri' is used to refer to Monira.

7   Ibid., p. 121. See also: Gökçe Günel, *Spaceship in the Desert: Energy, Climate Change, and Urban Design in Abu Dhabi* (Durham, NC: Duke University Press, 2019).

8   Kelly Easterling, *Extrastatecraft: The Power of Infrastructure Space* (London: Verso, 2014).

9   I elaborate on this point regarding the racial politics of smart urbanism within the context of contemporary Gulf Futurism, developing a transnational perspective span-

Situated within the realm of logistical worlding, the high-tech spectacles of sustainable futures constitute a larger space where the abstract logics of capital and data clash with the material and social conditions that animate them. In this regard, Al Qadiri's sculptural works, inspired by the industrial oil drill heads, link the extraction of geological layers (oil) to its impacts on the material and symbolic culture through aesthetic forms based on plastic (made up of fossil fuel) and 3D technology.[10] Thus, Al Qadiri situates their presence and medium within the geopolitical context of contemporary Gulf Futurism.

Al Qadiri's work thereby enacts a cognitive mapping that connects the convoluted geographies and systems ranging from the technological to the aesthetic. For Fredric Jameson, who coined the term, 'cognitive mapping' refers to an ongoing aesthetic inquiry, if not a struggle with political implications, that renders one's situatedness within the global networks of capitalism tangible.[11] Yet, cognitive mapping often designates an allegorical form since it mainly addresses the dialectical nature of mediation between different scales, such as the local and the global, or realms, such as the economic and the cultural. The inexhaustible gap integral to its process keeps the mediation operating through frictions. In other words, the allegorical model of cognitive mapping reconfigures it as a practice both material and speculative.

To develop these ideas further, I expand upon Al Qadiri's sculpture series to demonstrate how the figure of a black box constitutes an allegory of computational capital, of which Dubai's smartness mandate is a spectacular manifestation.[12] Here, I will underline the cybernetic

ning from Dubai to Beirut, in: Özgün Eylül İşcen, 'The Racial Politics of Smartness Urbanism: Dubai and Beirut as Two Sides of the Same Coin', *Ethnic and Racial Studies*, 44.12 (2021), pp. 2282–2303 <https://doi.org/10.1080/01419870.2021.1921233>.

10 This chapter focuses on Al Qadiri's series of works aligned together since the mid-2010s. These works, made up of different sizes, materials, and mechanisms, often engage with 3D technology in some capacity, whether design or printing, with oil drill heads as a figural inspiration and the iridescent tone connecting the physical qualities of oil and pearl. Given their larger sizes, *Chimera*, made of aluminum, and *Alien Technology*, made of fiberglass, are not 3D-printed.

11 Fredric Jameson, 'Cognitive Mapping', in *Marxism and the Interpretation of Culture*, ed. by Cary Nelson and Lawrence Grossberg (Champaign: University of Illinois Press, 1988), pp. 347–60.

12 I borrow the term computational capital from Jonathan Beller since it highlights the historical entanglements between computational and capitalist rationality, especially their rootedness in colonial history and imperial logic. In this sense, the term also

genealogy of the black box, often blamed for its exclusive, reductive modelling of the world with the aim of prediction and control, as in the case of the logistical worlding that underlies smart urbanism. Yet, the composite surface colours and shapes of Al Qadiri's sculptures manifest the complexity of a cybernetic black box, which makes them irreducible to a specific object. They condense both material history and imagination, thereby expressing the very limits of imperial aspirations, whether cybernetic or logistical, for total control and visibility. Ultimately, the historical trajectories of the black box and oil intermingle within Dubai's smartness mandate. This intermingling demonstrates how computational capital operates through 'frictions', in Anna Tsing's terms, where the possibilities of contestation and transformation arise.[13]

THE BLACK BOX AS AN AESTHETIC PHENOMENON

Since originating in the 1940s as part of military research (to which I will come back soon), the black box has gained multiple connotations, which require us to understand it as something more nuanced than a mere technical object. In this chapter, I briefly overview its cybernetic conception, focusing on its aesthetic regime due to the relevance of this regime to today's smartness mandate and to computational capital in general. The figure of the black box often designates a matter of opacity by implying the presence of structures and operations that constitute the realm of visuality while staying hidden. In other words, it refers to a system that one can know only through its inputs and outputs without accessing its internal functioning. Various purpose-oriented, system-like entities can fit this description, such as a computer, an institution, or the human mind.

---

marks the historical period of post-World War II, since when capitalist operations have increasingly relied on computational systems as a totalizing system, such as platform capitalism. See: Jonathan Beller, *The Message is Murder: Substrates of Computational Capital* (London: Pluto Press, 2018) <https://doi.org/10.2307/j.ctt1x07z9t>.

13   With her emphasis on frictions, Tsing connects the supposedly frictionless 'just-in-time' supply chains to the differential material conditions and social relations that animate them. I will come back to this idea later in the chapter. Anna Tsing, 'Supply Chains and the Human Condition', *Rethinking Marxism*, 21.2 (2009), pp. 148–76. See also: Anna Tsing, *Friction: An Ethnography of Global Connection* (Princeton, NJ: Princeton University Press, 2004).

For example, the black box speaks to the current condition in which humans use social media platforms while unaware of the algorithmic processes underlying the interfaces they interact through. In this sense, the software acts like ideology, constituting the fabric of social life yet operating beneath.[14] Therefore, the black box holds an interesting position regarding the mediation between invisible structures and the realm of the visible and often provokes an aesthetic gesture that renders those hidden structures tangible.

Nonetheless, this gesture of unveiling is much more complicated than it first appears. Continuing with the example of software: until it breaks down, or the hardware does, the user won't necessarily realize what lies behind their screen, spanning from the material infrastructure to the human labour that maintains the media. As Bruno Latour famously puts it, 'scientific and technical work is made invisible by its own success.'[15] In other words, when a machine runs efficiently, one can skip the internal complexity while focusing on its inputs and outputs. In turn, 'paradoxically, the more science and technology succeed, the more opaque and obscure they become.'[16] Computational systems absorb this pattern within their architectures and thus render it even harder to open the box. With today's machine learning systems and ubiquitous computing, the operating system lies beyond the perceptual threshold and direct control of the user and even the coder.

In this sense, I broaden Latour's idea of 'black-boxing', obscuring while functioning, to address abstractions through which computational capital works. Indeed, computational systems expand extractive operations of global capital by turning social behaviour (e.g., interacting with friends, playing games) into monetizable labour. Due to the shifting patterns of capitalist accumulation via computational media, it is complicated to unpack the 'rational kernel' and 'mystical shell' of the commodity, to use Marx's terms, to reveal the totality (history, rationality) enclosed within; one cannot merely 'descend into the hid-

---

14   Wendy H. K. Chun, *Programmed Visions: Software and Memory* (Cambridge, MA:
      MIT Press, 2011).

15   Bruno Latour, *Pandora's Hope: Essays on the Reality of Science Studies* (Cambridge,
      MA: Harvard University Press, 1999), p. 304.

16   Ibid.

den abode of production.'[17] The point here is that capitalist extraction has expanded its usual sites and mechanisms by varying scale and granularity (e.g., data mining) while intensifying the reproduction of social hierarchies predicated on race, gender, and geopolitics. Those abstractions occur within machines, via statistical models, databases, etc., under the guise of value-neutrality, i.e., in black boxes that obscure their own functioning and historicity.

To delve into that history, I will situate the cybernetic model of the black box, which shapes the dominant conception of computational systems today, within the cybernetic and logistical implications of the smartness mandate. According to Tung-Hui Hu, the figure of the black box demonstrates how infrastructure is foremost a speculative medium, more than it is a technical one, translating future capacity into the present while promoting fantasies of sustainability: 'Infrastructure requires not just maintenance, but also an imagination of its collapse so as to pre-empt and avoid that collapse; indeed, infrastructure is a way of designing the everyday to bear the load of emergency.'[18]

In this respect, today's rhetorics of crisis and sustainability intermingle within the smartness mandate, thereby highlighting its embeddedness within the development of a cybernetic and logistical model of the world in the aftermath of World War II. As this historical period and the context of the Arabian Gulf demonstrate, these coalescent developments constituted the rise of US imperialism and its dominance within the oil-centred economy, the military and financial sectors, as well as the global supply chain.

As mentioned above, the black box came into being during World War II alongside the development of radio, radar, and electronic navigational systems in British and Allied military research. Those measures later on motivated epistemological presuppositions, which marked the cybernetic turn in the 1940s.[19] As Peter Galison has

---

17　Alexander R. Galloway, '"Black Box, Black Bloc": A Lecture Given at the New School in New York City on April 12, 2010', p. 3 <http://cultureandcommunication.org/galloway/pdf/Galloway_Black_Box_Black_Bloc.pdf> [accessed 13 March 2022]. Galloway here cites: Karl Marx, *Capital: A Critique of Political Economy*, trans. by Ben Fowkes, 3 vols (London: Penguin, 1976), I, pp. 103 and 279.

18　Tung-Hui Hu, 'Black Boxes and Green Lights: Media, Infrastructure, and the Future At Any Cost', *English Language Notes*, 55.1–2 (Spring/Fall 2017), pp. 81–88 (p. 83).

19　Philipp von Hilgers, 'The History of the Black Box: The Clash of a Thing and Its Concept', *Cultural Politics*, 7.1 (2011), pp. 41–58.

shown, cybernetics evolved as a war science since it came out of military research on anti-aircraft defence systems, which aimed to track and predict the flight patterns of enemy pilots based on mechanisms of information feedback.[20] For Galison, in other words, cybernetic thought rose upon the premise of the opacity of the Other.

For example, the efforts of founding cybernetician Norbert Wiener and his compatriots to predict the future moves of enemy airplanes became an aspiration to compute human action and, ultimately, an aspiration to develop communication between a range of entities — humans, animals, and machines. Cybernetics fundamentally reconfigured the world as a series of interconnected systems or 'black boxes' — devices into which inputs (messages, information) feed and from which outputs proceed in coordination with the regulated behaviour of the given system towards a desired goal.[21]

Indeed, early cybernetics after World War II sought to create order out of chaos by utilizing communication and prediction as in information processing and systems thinking. The Cold War and the accompanying threat of nuclear annihilation situated computers as powerful tools and as metaphors promising 'total oversight, exacting standards of control, and technical-rational solutions to a myriad of complex problems'.[22] Rather than describing the world as it is, the interest of cyberneticians was predicting what it would become and fostering homogeneity instead of difference.[23] According to Orit Hal-

---

20 Peter Galison, 'The Ontology of the Enemy: Norbert Wiener and the Cybernetic Vision', *Critical Inquiry*, 21.1 (1994), pp. 228–66 <https://doi.org/10.1086/448747>. As Peter Galison details, cybernetics, which has roots in military research, was already shaped around racialized discourses since enemies were not all alike. On one hand, there was the Japanese soldier who was barely human in the eyes of the Allied Forces. On the other hand, there was a more enduring enemy, a 'cold-blooded and machine-like opponent' (p. 231) composed of the hybridized German pilot and his aircraft. Galison calls this enemy the 'cybernetic Other' (p. 264), arguing that it led the Allied Forces to develop a new science of communication and control in line with the fantasies of omniscience and automation.

21 Megan Archer, 'Logistics as Rationality: Excavating the Coloniality of Contemporary Logistical Formations' (Doctoral Dissertation, University of Brighton, 2020) <https://cris.brighton.ac.uk/ws/portalfiles/portal/22372242/Archer_Thesis_2020.pdf> [accessed 16 March 2022].

22 Antoine Bousquet, *The Scientific Way of Warfare: Order and Chaos on the Battlefields of Modernity* (New York: Columbia University Press, 2009), p. 124.

23 Orit Halpern, *Beautiful Data: A History of Vision and Reason since 1945* (Durham, NC: Duke University Press, 2015), p. 46.

pern, early cybernetics, as well as the information theory it inspired, relied on a 'not-yet-realized aspiration to transform a world of ontology, description, and materiality to one of communication, prediction, and virtuality'.[24]

Furthermore, Megan Archer situates such cybernetic aspirations for systemic standardization within the rise of logistical capitalism since the 1960s and its imperial order of expansion and control.[25] Logistics requiring the detailed organization and implementation of complex operations themselves have become a site of capitalist accumulation. I will highlight three historical trajectories in which these two fields, both rooted in military science, come into close contact.

First, the technical systems led by cybernetic research have transformed the scope and form of logistical operations since the 1960s. On the one hand, the black box obscured the extracting mechanisms involved in logistical operations, such as their reliance on material resources and human labour. On the other hand, there is a hypervisibility on the side of management/administration that tracks and surveils the work at the site (e.g., port) to decrease friction.[26] Thus, the figure of the black box has appeared in the form of shipping containers — uniformly sized boxes — that render logistical reorganization space- and time-efficient.

Second, Archer coins the term 'logistical rationality' to underscore that, like cybernetics, logistics aspires to filter out heterogeneity or noise and is rooted in the imperial order following World War II.[27] For Katherine Hayles, 'The power of the black box does not lie in concealing a knowable answer, but rather in its symbolization of the limits of knowledge.'[28] Yet, the impossibility of seeing inside the black box did not produce an epistemological limit for early cyberneticians. On the contrary, the cybernetic rhetoric of the time animated an epistemological object based on 'secured incalculability'.[29] As Philipp von

---

24   Ibid., p. 40.

25   Archer, 'Logistics as Rationality', p. 24.

26   Laleh Khalili, *Sinews of War and Trade: Shipping and Capitalism in the Arabian Peninsula* (London: Verso, 2021), p. 176.

27   Archer, 'Logistics as Rationality', p. 12.

28   Katherine Hayles, *Unthought: The Power of the Cognitive Non-Conscious* (Chicago: University of Chicago Press, 2017), p. 189.

29   Hilgers, 'The History of the Black Box', p. 43.

Hilgers notes, by way of black-boxing it was no longer necessary to know everything about individuals in order to manage and govern them.[30] Thus, cybernetic research invested in facilitating and maximizing communication and control between humans, animals, and machine systems, which eventually reduced the human being to a reified model of an interchangeable, information-processing entity.

The third and last trajectory lays out an aesthetic problem that the black box allegory poses: Its opacity cannot be undone merely by a gesture of unveiling. In other words, it is impossible to open the black box in terms of transparency because what lies beneath are the spatial-temporal regimes underlying the global supply chain as well as the colonial histories and social hierarchies they operate through. Hence, these regimes exceed the individual's immediate perception. In other words, the dialectical nature of mediation between different scales and realms comes forth again, which brings us back to Jameson's idea of cognitive mapping.

REVISITING JAMESON'S ALLEGORICAL MODE OF COGNITIVE MAPPING

The increasingly complex and abstract, algorithmically mediated operations of global capital have only deepened their extractive capacity while obscuring their operations, as the black box allegory implies. Given this condition, several scholars argue that the act of cognitive mapping, a term Jameson coined in the late 1980s, is no longer viable. For instance, for Wendy H. K. Chun, cognitive mapping has become an imperialist tool of network science itself, which seeks to link a local experience to global systems by flattening the subject into a functional category.[31] Noting that '[w]e are now constantly called on to map and to value mapping in order to experience power/agency', she asks: 'to what extent is the desire to map not contrary to capitalism but rather integral to its current form, especially since it is through our mappings that we ourselves are mapped?'.[32]

---

30   Ibid.
31   Chun, *Programmed Visions*.
32   Ibid., pp. 74 and 75.

In response to such concerns regarding the relevance of cognitive mapping today, Alexander Galloway reworks Chun's idea of software as ideology, operating beneath the surface but not without frictions, with Jameson's dialectical model of allegory.[33] Galloway argues that software corresponds to an allegory of the social, as it exacerbates or ridicules the tension within itself across the material (hardware) and symbolic (software) layers it operates through. For instance, social relations formerly outside the accumulative regime of capitalism are incorporated into its operation, indicating a process of real subsumption in Marxist terms via computational media, thereby expanding new frontiers of extraction like data mining. Nonetheless, with the term 'intraface', Galloway indicates the implicit presence of an outside — the socio-historical context — within the inside. In other words, the intraface affords a dialectical mapping of the relation between the aesthetic mediation (e.g., a digital image/object) and the larger context in which it has come into being.

In this respect, I still find Jameson's dialectical model of cognitive mapping helpful for attending to the local instantiations of global capital, where capitalism's differential impacts are strongly felt and negotiated. Indeed, Jameson's notion of cognitive mapping refers to a geopolitical aesthetic that enables individuals and collectives to render intelligible their positions in the capitalist world system and its historicity. Jameson closely ties the term to the historical condition of late capitalism,[34] 'in which the truth of our social life as a whole — in György Lukács' terms, as a totality — is increasingly irreconcilable with the possibilities of aesthetic expression or articulation available to us'.[35] Thus, cognitive mapping refers to the capacity for 'a situational

---

33   Alexander R. Galloway, *The Interface Effect* (Cambridge: Polity Press, 2012).

34   Cognitive mapping has been a significant part of Jameson's entire critical endeavour since the late 1980s, coupled with his other renowned concepts such as political unconscious, utopia, and geopolitical aesthetic.

35   Fredric Jameson, 'Class and Allegory in Contemporary Mass Culture: Dog Day Afternoon as a Political Film', in Jameson, *Signatures of the Visible* (New York: Routledge, 1992), pp. 35–54 (p. 54). For cognitive mapping, Jameson combines Kevin Lynch's empirical problems of city space with Louis Althusser's Lacanian redefinition of ideology as 'the representation of the subject's Imaginary relationship to his or her Real conditions of existence' (Louis Althusser, 'Ideology and Ideological State Apparatuses', in Althusser, *Lenin and Philosophy*, trans. by Ben Brewster (New York: Monthly Review Press, 1972), pp. 127–86 (p. 162), cited in Jameson, *Postmodernism, or, The Cultural Logic of Late Capitalism* (Durham, NC: Duke University Press, 1991), p. 51.

representation on the part of the individual subject to that vaster and properly unrepresentable totality which is the ensemble of society's structures as a whole'.[36]

Jameson's emphasis on totality is often criticized for replicating the totalizing, abstracting gaze of imperial visuality. Jameson himself, however, drawing upon Jean-Paul Sartre's concept of totalization (as distinct from totality), repudiates a bird's eye view of the whole. Thus, he affirms a project that 'takes as its premise the impossibility for individual and biological human subjects to conceive of such a position, let alone to adopt or achieve it'.[37] For Jameson, the act of cognitive mapping depends on praxis, which is to say, on the individual's active negotiation of (urban) space. Consequently, Jameson frames cognitive mapping as an aesthetic problem — a problem of mediation. Despite Jameson's romanticization of the Third World setting back in the 1980s, on the verge of what would be called the neoliberal turn, there is no privileged method and subject of cognitive mapping.[38]

Engaging with feminist and queer thought, postcolonial and critical race studies, Sandro Mezzadra and Brett Neilson underscore the possibility of observing systematic qualities across varied operations of capital without necessarily attributing to them a priori coherence. From this perspective, the extractive mechanisms of capitalism are 'tendential' rather than totalizing, constantly producing and reworking the hierarchies predicated on race, gender, sexuality, citizenship, and geopolitics.[39] These 'multiple outsides' do not constitute an outside of the capitalist system but refer to resources, natural or human, that capital cannot produce itself but ultimately operates through.[40]

Kevin Lynch's well-known book *The Image of the City* (Cambridge, MA: MIT Press, 1960) came out of his MIT-based research on 'the Perceptual Form of the City', in collaboration with György Kepes, which has become one of the predominant references in the field of cybernetic urbanism.

36 Jameson, *Postmodernism*, p. 51.

37 Ibid., p. 331.

38 Please see Jameson's highly discussed text on third world literature as a national allegory: Fredric Jameson, 'Political: National Allegory', in Jameson, *Allegory and Ideology* (London: Verso, 2019), pp. 159–216. See also: Imre Szeman, 'Who's Afraid of National Allegory? Jameson, Literary Criticism, Globalization', *South Atlantic Quarterly*, 100.3 (2001), pp. 803–27 <https://doi.org/10.1215/00382876-100-3-803>.

39 Sandro Mezzadra and Brett Neilson, *The Politics of Operations: Excavating Contemporary Capitalism* (Durham, NC: Duke University Press, 2019), p. 33.

40 Ibid., pp. 4–7.

These multiple outsides are operative but not reducible to the
unifying logic of capitalist system. They thrive on economic and political vulnerabilities produced by intersecting histories of colonialism,
racism, and patriarchy while they operate through contested human
encounters and power relations that not only maintain but also hold
the capacity to disrupt the global supply chain.[41] As Charmaine Chua
argues, 'Despite its gargantuan architecture and powerful imperial
reach, the world of logistics is constantly undermined by its own
contingencies and contradictions: precisely because of its aspirations
toward omnipotence, logistics is itself a deeply vulnerable entity, ultimately an "ideology (and fantasy)" of "full visibility as integral flexibility."'[42]

Within the scope of this chapter, the figure of the black box as
described above indicates the presence of what might be called the
Irreducible Other of computational capital. The realm of the Irreducible Other, which computational capital cannot fully assimilate into
its logic, designates a site of struggle for demystifying and transforming
the social relations of production, which is to say in Marxist terms, social reproduction. Therefore cognitive mapping, which foremost refers
to the totality of class relations on a global scale, takes the form of what
Nicholas Mirzoeff terms 'countervisuality', as it starts by inverting the
imperial regime of visuality underlying capitalist operations.[43] In other
words, countervisuality is never merely about seeing but rather about
claiming what Mirzoeff terms 'the right to look' and restoring one's
relationship to material reality and history. The opposite of the right
to look, in return, is not censorship, but visuality.

As Mirzoeff conceives it, visuality refers to a set of techniques for
classifying, segregating, and aestheticizing that are used to represent
the world in a way that legitimizes the authority of established power.

---

41   Tsing, 'Supply Chains and the Human Condition', p. 151.

42   Charmaine Chua, 'Logistics', in *The Sage Handbook of Marxism*, ed. by Beverley
      Skeggs, Sara R. Farris, Alberto Toscano, and Svenja Bromberg, 3 vols (Los An-
      geles: Sage, 2022), III, pp. 1444–62 (p. 1458). Here, Chua cites: Alberto Toscano,
      'Lineaments of the Logistical State', *Viewpoint Magazine*, 4, 28 September 2014
      <https://viewpointmag.com/2014/09/28/lineaments-of-the-logistical-state/> [ac-
      cessed 28 May 2022].

43   Nicholas Mirzoeff, *The Right to Look: A Counterhistory of Visuality* (Durham, NC:
      Duke University Press, 2011), p. 22.

Indeed, Mirzoeff speaks to the military roots of logistics when he connects the task of visualizing to the rising need of military theorists in the eighteenth century to grasp the increasingly complex and expansive battlefield.[44] Furthermore, the development of techniques of visuality has been entangled with the modern idea of Man's superiority and has rendered all other categories, such as colonized, invisible:

> This ability to assemble a visualization manifests the authority of the visualizer. In turn, the authorizing of authority requires permanent renewal in order to win consent as the 'normal' or every day because it is always already contested. The autonomy claimed by the right to look is thus opposed by the authority of visuality. But the right to look came first, and we should not forget it.[45]

Within the scope of this chapter, I situate the black box as an imperial imaginary as such, which imposes a specific, historically situated regime of aesthetics (as explained in the previous section). Yet, visuality is a site of constant negotiation rather than complete domination. Likewise, my resituating the black box as an allegory of computational capital is a gesture toward demonstrating its dialectical nature and understanding the complex entanglements of life forms, capital, and computation.

Accordingly, cognitive mapping necessarily involves reworking the imperial modes of visuality that are integral to capitalist logic but not reducible to it. Here, I take up Stefano Harney and Fred Moten's reconfiguration of the idea of 'logisticality' against the racial violence and coloniality inherent in logistical capitalism. By inverting the connotations of the term, they enact a social capacity to 'take apart, dismantle, tear down the structure that, right now, limits our ability to find each other, to see beyond it and to access the places we know lie beyond its walls'.[46] Under the contemporary smartness

---

44 Nicholas Mirzoeff, 'Visualizing the Anthropocene', *Public Culture*, 26.2 (2014), pp. 213–32 (p. 216) <https://doi.org/10.1215/08992363-2392039>.

45 Mirzoeff, *The Right to Look*, p. 2.

46 Stefano Harney and Fred Moten, *The Undercommons: Fugitive Planning and Black Study* (New York: Autonomedia, 2013), p. 2. As Harney and Moten highlight, the current scope and form of logistical operations via computational systems are rooted in the 16th century — the beginning of the long-distance imperial trade and the Atlantic Slave Trade.

mandate, countervisuality encompasses more than the visual field and unsettles the spatial and temporal regimes underlying the convergence of extraction, finance, and logistics that takes place via computational systems.

Ultimately, cognitive mapping is a diagnostic practice posing an aesthetic problem — a problem of mediation between separate yet entangled spheres, such as the global and the local, the economic (base) and the cultural (superstructure), or the psychic and the social. There is no one-to-one correspondence between these realms; instead, capital operates through these disjunctions, or what Tsing calls frictions. Therefore, Jamesonian cognitive mapping calls for an allegorical method or style which is more than a mere issue of transparency or a gesture of unveiling and mapping. In Jameson's terms, the allegorical does not resolve but heightens the very existence of these gaps, which characterize the Irreducible Other of (computational) capital.

MONIRA AL QADIRI'S SCULPTURAL SERIES AS BLACK BOX ALLEGORY

Reconfiguring Jameson's cognitive mapping via an allegorical model underscores the processual, constantly self-transforming nature of both capitalism and cultural analysis. As Jameson notes:

> the allegorical spirit is profoundly discontinuous, a matter of breaks and heterogeneities, of the multiple polysemia of the dream rather than the homogeneous representation of the symbol. Our traditional conception of allegory — based, for instance, on stereotypes of Bunyan — is that of an elaborate set of figures and personifications to be read against some one-to-one table of equivalences: this is, so to speak, a one-dimensional view of this signifying process, which might only be set in motion and complexified were we willing to entertain the more alarming notion that such equivalences are themselves in constant change and transformation at each perpetual present of the text.[47]

Accordingly, cognitive mapping seeks to evoke connections between seemingly unrelated sites, events, subjects, and narratives that underlie

---

47   Fredric Jameson, 'Political: National Allegory', p. 170.

capitalist operations, and that are constantly reworking their own conditions — like the colour of the light-reflective surface of Al Qadiri's
Chimera that changes with the daylight.[48] As Seb Franklin argues, the
expanded capacity of capital for the subsumption of communication
and aesthetics via computational media requires an allegorical (rather
than objective) representation of a system, for allegory allows the user
to grasp the otherwise unimaginable relation between multiple scales,
such as local and global.[49]

For instance, *Alien Technology* (2014–19) is a series of large-scale,
publicly displayed sculptures made of fiberglass plastic and coated with
the iridescent tone of automotive paint. Their iridescent colour resonates with the black gold of both oil and pearl, thereby offering a
complex visuality. Indeed, the sculptures speak to the artist's investment in making 'aesthetic connections between pearls and oil, through
their colour, materiality, symbolism, ecology and economy, as a way of
reimagining the past, present and future of the wider Gulf region'.[50] For
instance, Al Qadiri first displayed the series as a public sculpture in the
Shindagha Heritage Village in Dubai alongside the material residues
of local maritime history (see Figure 2).[51] That history, spanning centuries, involved trade routes and pearl diving that sustained economic
activities in pre-oil times, the times before oil arrived like an alien
visitor.

The most apparent connection occurs at the level of the medium
itself, as in the case of Galloway's intraface — the material presence
of historical context within the medium of the artwork itself. *Chimera*
and the series *Alien Technology* have developed alongside Al Qadiri's
other projects. These projects, which were exhibited at various venues,

---

48   Melissa Gronlund, 'What Monira Al Qadiri's Otherworldly Expo 2020
      Dubai Sculpture Says about the UAE', *The National*, 4 July 2021 <https:
      //www.thenationalnews.com/arts-culture/art/2021/07/04/what-monira-al-
      qadiris-otherworldly-expo-2020-dubai-sculpture-says-about-the-uae/> [accessed 3
      June 2022].

49   Seb Franklin, *Digitality as Cultural Logic* (Cambridge, MA: MIT Press, 2015), p. 96.

50   The quote is taken from the artist statement on her website <https://www.
      moniraalqadiri.com/chimera/> [accessed 16 May 2022].

51   This first iteration of Alien Technology was produced in Dubai in 2014 as part of
      AFAC's public arts program curated by Amanda Abi Khalil. Please see the artist's
      website: <https://www.moniraalqadiri.com/alien-technology/> [accessed 30 May
      2022].

Figure 2. Monira Al Qadiri, *Alien Technology*, 2014, public sculpture,
fiberglass, automotive paint, 3 × 3 × 3 m, Shindagha Heritage Village,
Dubai. Courtesy of the artist.

consist of small-scale, 3D-printed, alien-like sculptural objects made
up of plastic with iridescent colour, such as *Spectrum* (2016) and
OR-BIT (2016–18).[52] Plastic becomes a narrative tool encompassing
a process that runs from the extraction of geological layers of the
earth (oil) to the production of a fossil-fuel-based object (plastic),
whose shapes derive from industrial oil drill heads. Thus, the iridescent
surface of these alien-like figures is key to the temporal depth of the
work, which connects the pre-oil and post-oil times, which will arrive
when the oil reserves dry up or when oil loses its current value.

Plastic and car paint, which provides the iridescent tone, speak
to the fact that oil-centred, imperial, capitalist expansion has shaped
the history of the Arabian Gulf and the Middle East since the second
half of the twentieth century. Indeed, the so-called logistical revolution

---

52   While writing this chapter, the most recent iteration of Al Qadiri's series *Orbital* is on
      display at *The Milk of Dreams*, 59th Venice Art Biennale, 2022. They are 3D-printed
      plastic sculptures coated with automotive paint and integrated within a rotation ma-
      chine.

and its regime of visuality in Mirzoeff's sense coincide with the rise of an oil-centred economy that accompanied the dominance of US imperialism in the region. The availability of fossil fuels promoted just-in-time production and container shipping, and the transport of oil triggered the development of maritime logistics in return.[53] Indeed, oil's lubricant, sleek appearance provoked sociotechnical imaginaries, such as frictionless flow. Accordingly, the oil trade has created new spaces, structures, and infrastructures that reconfigure the shores of the Arabian peninsula while building upon colonial legacies such as the trade routes and bureaucratic structures of the British Mandate.

Hence, oil (and gas) pipelines do not only have the significant material function of connecting the sites of extraction and consumption. They also have aesthetic and political implications: Pipelines render oil invisible, which is to say, black-boxed, naturalizing its presence in people's lives.[54] At the same time, they hide the environmental impacts of extraction in a manner similar to how computational media hides their extraction sites, such as the rare earth and other resources used for their production and maintenance. The pipelines also bring about the fragmentation of the labour force because they require workers to be far away from one another rather than in close contact at the extraction site (as with coal mining). This makes it more difficult for workers to socialize and mobilize around collective demands.[55] In the meantime, oil wealth shapes the democratic politics within and beyond the oil-rich countries by sustaining the local elites and authoritarian regimes at a regional scale while imperial, foreign powers refashion democratic ideals for their own interests, mostly justifying their ongoing violence in the region.[56]

---

53   Khalili, *Sinews of War and Trade*.

54   Timothy Mitchell, *Carbon Democracy: Political Power in the Age of Oil* (London: Verso, 2013).

55   In another iteration, the artist publicly displayed two rotating sculptures titled *Future Past* at the abandoned Schwarzkaue (black changing room) at the General Blumenthal Coal Mine in Germany. With this work, she intended to highlight the historical resonance between different extractive industries and sites while shifting the registers of envisioning the post-oil future through its pasts. Please see <https://www.moniraalqadiri.com/future-past/> [accessed 25 May 2022].

56   Mitchell, *Carbon Democracy*, p. 31.

Indeed, the reserves of oil and gas in the Gulf and the larger Middle East region have been consequential to the rise of the United States as a global power in the post-World War II period. For instance, the establishment of the Gulf Cooperation Council (GCC) in 1981 as a regional bloc of the six oil-rich Arab monarchies — Bahrain, Kuwait, Oman, Qatar, Saudi Arabia, and the UAE — has been closely entangled with the US's dominant role in the oil-centred economy, the financial and military sectors, and the global supply chain.[57] Thus, a fuller analysis of the growth of Gulf cities as a logistical space requires attention to their regional dominance, which polarizes wealth accumulation and sharpens social hierarchies in the larger region.

In this respect, Dubai constitutes a fruitful setting to unpack such historically situated mechanisms integral to the current trend of the smartness mandate in the Gulf. Due to its limited oil reserves, Dubai's long-term success has relied on economic diversification, accompanied by various branding strategies. The region formed a strategic node within the wider circulatory networks of British colonialism since the late nineteenth century. Following the founding of the country in 1971, the UAE's logistical space advanced via Dubai's multimodal platforms (ports, airports, free trade zones, and logistics corridors).[58] Writing about the state-controlled portfolio of diverse corporations referred to as Dubai Inc., Rafeef Ziadah highlights the role of port infrastructures in linking diverse moments that underpin the logistics industry: capital accumulation, state-owned conglomerates promoting the internationalization of capital, and repressive labour regimes.[59]

Adam Hanieh identifies a capitalist class of 'Khaleeji capital', dominated by a few massive conglomerates around a Saudi-Emirati axis, which complicates the rentier state framework. This local capitalist class, promoting capitalist expansion with a public-private hybrid

57   Adam Hanieh, *Money, Markets, and Monarchies: The Gulf Cooperation Council and the Political Economy of the Contemporary Middle East* (Cambridge: Cambridge University Press, 2018), p. 23.

58   Following the withdrawal of the British forces, the United Arab Emirates was founded as a federation on 2 December 1971. It is formed of seven emirates — Abu Dhabi, Dubai, Sharjah, Ajman, Umm Al Quwain, Fujairah, and Ras Al Khaimah.

59   Rafeef Ziadah, 'Transport Infrastructure & Logistics in the Making of Dubai Inc.', *International Journal of Urban and Regional Research*, 42.2 (2018), pp. 182–97 (p. 183) <https://doi.org/10.1111/1468-2427.12570>.

model, draws profits from the regional and international export of capital and the deep exploitation of non-citizen labour via the Kafala system.[60] The Kafala, which is currently active in the GCC countries, Lebanon, and Jordan, stratifies the labour force across class, race, gender, ethnicity, and citizenship.

On the same trajectory, the accelerated urban growth in the Gulf has also led to the destruction of Bedouin/tribal forms of life and desert ecosystems, and to the segregation of socio-economic groups, such as low-class, non-citizen workers. Despite the confined spaces of the Gulf and the deprivation of some basic civil and labour rights, dozens of impactful strikes have swept across Dubai and other UAE cities since the early 2000s. There have been transnational mobilizations for fair labour standards for non-citizen workers, whose ultimate demand is dismantling the Kafala system as an industrial complex.[61] Given the regional dominance of Gulf capital, the Arab uprising of 2011 (and its so-called second waves since 2018) ultimately contested the hierarchies of the regional system by claiming people's right to shape their future paths. These mobilized communities reclaim their right to look and they contest the univocal futuristic projections prescribed by Gulf Futurism, thereby constituting the Irreducible Other of computational capital.[62]

Given this historical urgency, one of the most striking aspects of Al Qadiri's sculptures as a form of 'intraface' is the *temporal plane* it widens. Al Qadiri's work puts into practice Donna J. Haraway's idea

---

60 Hanieh, *Money, Markets, and Monarchies*, pp. 23–24. See also: Adam Hanieh, *Capitalism and Class in the Gulf Arab States* (New York: Palgrave MacMillan, 2011).

61 It is more accurate to frame the Kafala as the 'Kafala industrial complex', which involves a set of labour legislation, migration policies, border enforcement, privatization of services, and supremacist entitlement. See: Gemma Justo and Ghiwa Sayegh, 'Whose Home Is It? The Workplace of Migrant Domestic Workers Under Kafala', *Funambulist*, 19 February 2021 <https://thefunambulist.net/magazine/spaces-of-labor/whose-home-is-it-the-workplace-of-migrant-domestic-workers-under-kafala> [accessed 1 March 2022].

62 However, the later phase of the uprisings saw a determined effort by Arab ruling elites and foreign imperial powers to fight for regional domination in economic and political terms. Accordingly, the GCC has emerged as one of the main protagonists in suppressing the unrest and extending regional domination. Indeed, the UAE in particular has even become a commercial, military, and humanitarian nexus in the region. See: Rafeef Ziadah, 'Circulating Power: Humanitarian Logistics, Militarism, and the United Arab Emirates', *Antipode*, 51.5 (2019), pp. 1684–1702.

of conjoining imagination with material reality to construct the possibility of historical transformation.[63] My framing of cognitive mapping through the Jamesonian dialectical model of allegory acts on a similar plane of aesthetics, marking its utopian quality, characterized by its longing for an alternative:

> The Utopian moment is indeed in one sense quite impossible for us to imagine, except as the unimaginable; thus a kind of allegorical structure is built into the very forward movement of the Utopian impulse itself, which always points to something other, which can never reveal itself directly but must always speak in figures, which always calls out structurally for completion and exegesis.[64]

Expanding upon the Greek etymology of allegory, 'Allos (another, different) and agoreuein (speaking openly, in the assembly, in the agora)', Alberto Toscano demonstrates how allegory resonates with the idea of utopia where its ultimate iterations range from 'speaking otherwise in public' to 'speaking in public about otherness'.[65] Thus, the unsettling nature of allegory derives from its pointing out the dialectical nature of totalizing, determining forces such as capital rather than offering any stable meaning or positionality, thereby opening a crack within the present.

Through its presence at the Expo site, Al Qadiri's alien-like sculpture *Chimera* reflects the context that constitutes it — what lies beneath and beyond the spectacles of Gulf Futurism. Indeed, her connecting of pearl and oil imaginaries also offers a conception of historical continuity that grasps alternative possibilities within the present moment. For instance, through Al Qadiri's work, one can recall how contemporary urban struggles build upon the long histories of

---

63   Donna J. Haraway, 'A Cyborg Manifesto: Science, Technology, and Socialist-Feminism in the Late Twentieth Century', in Haraway, *Simians, Cyborgs and Natures: The Re-Invention of Nature* (New York: Routledge, 1991), pp. 149–83. See also: Morehshin Allahyari and Daniel Rouke, *The 3D Additivist Manifesto*, 2015 <https://additivism. org/manifesto> [accessed 24 February 2021].

64   Fredric Jameson, *Marxism and Form: Twentieth-Century Dialectical Theories of Literature* (Princeton, NJ: Princeton University Press, 2017), p. 142.

65   Alberto Toscano, 'Elsewhere and Otherwise: Introduction to a Symposium on Fredric Jameson's "Allegory and Ideology"', *Historical Materialism*, 29.1 (2021), pp. 113–22 (p. 118).

various waves of workers' mobilizations in the Gulf since the 1920s — spanning over time the diverse oil, pearl, and shipping industries — that have protested against racially segregated wage structures and housing.[66] Consequently, the artist simultaneously maps the black-boxed operations of capital, ranging from the extraction of oil to the fragmentation of the labour force, and generates an alternative narration that renders another collectivity and futurity possible.

CONCLUSION: REDUCTION AS EXPANSION

In my concluding remarks, I will briefly reflect on the idea of reduction as an expansion, which underlies some threads I have developed throughout the chapter. The first thread underscores the utopian potential of the allegorical nature of cognitive mapping. The seemingly reductive operation underlying the gesture of mapping becomes expansive since cognitive mapping expresses the incomplete, processual dynamics of totalizing systems, which is to say, of mediation itself. In this sense, a totalizing system such as capitalism never constitutes a full circle — a total capture. Here, the role of allegory is to demonstrate an inherent contradiction within a symbolic or aesthetic form, which reveals how the underlying structure (e.g., ideology) involves utopian and repressive tendencies at once. The efforts of cognitive mapping can take the shape of different methods and styles since it is as incomplete as the totalizing force that it tackles. In this respect, cognitive mapping becomes a struggle to reclaim the right to look, which simultaneously involves mapping the material reality and engendering a political collectivity that renders an alternative possible.

Cognitive mapping ultimately seeks to construct a global class consciousness that is not pre-given in the present moment. As discussed before, the increasingly complex and abstract, algorithmically mediated operations of global capital have only deepened the gap between the social order and its lived experience. Still, one can reaffirm Jameson's cognitive mapping at the very moment that it seems no

---

66 Alex Boodrookas and Arang Keshavarzian, 'Giving the Transnational a History: Gulf Cities Across Time and Space', in *The New Arab Urban: Gulf Cities of Wealth, Ambition, and Distress*, ed. by Harvey Molotch and Davide Ponzini (New York: New York University Press, 2019), pp. 35–57.

longer pertinent or viable. For Jameson, it is not despite but *because of their subsumption by the logic of the market* that cultural forms become a frontline of our struggles. They not only contest the extensive structures of capital and power but also express 'the nature of social life, both as we live it now, and as we feel in our bones it rather ought to be lived'.[67]

This point brings forth the other thread I want to highlight, which speaks to the aesthetic intervention the artist Monira Al Qadiri makes while working with computational media. Alongside a critical perspective on the tokenization of the post-oil futures in the region, she tackles complex historical and symbolic layers that constitute Gulf Futurism within an aesthetic form itself. Thus, she underscores the processual, expansive nature of signification and reclaims the medium of 3D rendering, which is often dominated by profit-driven spectacles of computational capital. Her spatial-temporal intervention claims a space for narrating the past and future of the Gulf that opens up alternative possibilities for post-oil futures in the present.

In this regard, the interpretation of Al Qadiri's work, such as *Chimera* at the Expo 2020 Dubai site, necessitates a reflection on the dialectical nature of Gulf Futurism and its countervisuality, which can evolve into one of its own spectacles. Yet, as Jameson demonstrates, cultural forms embrace contradictory tendencies, which speak to inherent contradictions of the cultural politics of capitalism itself (discussed above at length). Therefore, the spatial-temporal situatedness of each display transforms the meaning and impact of the countervisual gestures. For instance, the act of recalling the shifting patterns of labour and trade in the Arabian Gulf through Al Qadiri's *Chimera* cannot be isolated from the ongoing exploitation of the non-citizen workforce who have built spectacles such as the Expo site itself.[68]

Thus, cognitive mapping ultimately deals with reclaiming the right to speculate and imagine otherwise, which is to say, it operates tempor-

---

67   Fredric Jameson, 'Reification and Utopia in Mass Culture', in *Signatures of the Visible*, pp. 9–34 (p. 34).

68   Isabel Debre and Malak Harb, 'Expo 2020's Workers Face Hardships despite Dubai's Promises', *Associated Press News*, 5 December 2021 <https://apnews.com/article/coronavirus-pandemic-business-health-middle-east-africa-386c8ee45123e7bea212e14cc106adc2> [accessed 4 June 2022].

ally as much as spatially. In this respect, as I have shown throughout the chapter, the black box becomes an allegory of computational capital and the Irreducible Other that contests and resists capitalism's extractive mechanisms. The ongoing struggles for enacting alternative futures beyond the reach of what is prescribed by Gulf Futurism always cut across material and imaginative realms — where artistic practice and its public interventions can play a constitutive role.

Lines that Reduce
Biography, Palms, Borders
SAM DOLBEAR

PART ONE: BIOGRAPHY AS REDUCTION

Or, reduction as condensation,
reification, containment, truncation,
abbreviation, accumulation.[1]

The cover of Bronez Purnell's semi-autobiographical *100 Boyfriends* (2021) features a hand on its cover, etched on a dark background. Symbols for waves, like those on a weather map, appear outside the hand's outer reach, transforming it into a land mass: its fingers into peninsulas or jetties, its crease lines into roads or district boundaries. Gold objects and numbers are scattered in the spaces on the hand, to

---

*   This essay traverses a number of canons and permits some anachronisms in the spirit
    of the conversations that have taken place between staff and fellows at the ICI Berlin
    over the time of this core project.
1   These interludes are drawn from a shared document assembled in June 2020 by the ICI
    Fellows and Staff around the motif of 'reduction *as* X'.

evoke something of the contents of the novel: a heart, a safety pin, a bottle of poppers, a pentagram star, an outline of the Golden Gate Bridge. I wrote to Purnell to ask him about the cover and he replied that the designer Na Kim 'obvs knew I was a witchy Lady'.[2]

Towards the end of the novel, after a hookup, Purnell writes:

> I put my clothes on and walked out the door and turned to see him standing in the doorway waving at me. I looked at him and saw the same thing I saw when I looked at my right hand: a lifeline, running strong and clear through the center.[3]

Known as the 'lower transverse line' in palmistry, the lifeline curves around from the upper base of the thumb, down towards the wrist, and relates to health, constitution, and longevity. On the hand, the lifeline is something to be traced, examined, or glanced over. On the cover of *100 Boyfriends*, it is part of the city, something to be traversed, navigated, or passed over.

Robert Glück's 1994 novel *Margery Kempe* interweaves four lives split between a number of centuries. Partly set in San Francisco (one of the settings for Purnell's novel), Glück's own life during the height of the HIV/AIDS crisis, and his love and encounters with L. are interwoven with the life and work of the fifteenth-century mystic Margery Kempe, who recorded what is thought to be the first autobiography in English, *The Book of Margery Kempe* (1501). Glück concludes his novel with the lines:

> A failed saint turns to autobiography.

Then:

> I want to contain my rambling story in a few words.
>   *exult, exasperate, abandon, amaze*[4]

Authorship in Glück's *Margery Kempe* is forever slipping. The 'my' of 'my rambling story' that demands containment in four words, could

---

2   Personal correspondence from January 2022.

3   Bronez Purnell, *100 Boyfriends* (New York: MCD x FSG Originals, 2021), p. 115. Thank you to Ben Nichols for pointing me to this book.

4   Robert Glück, *Margery Kempe* [1994] (New York: NYRB Classics, 2020), p. 162.

be Glück's or Kempe's along with their many companions and inter-locutors. For authorship, as something that might denote singularity, separation, or autonomy, had already slipped in *The Book of Margery Kempe*, or had not yet formed as a subjective or artistic possibility.[5] The book might be named as the first autobiography but it also defines the impossibility of that form. In the introductory poem, Kempe writes:

> Thys boke is not wretyn in ordyr, every thyng aftyr other as it wer don, but lych as the mater cam to the creatur *in mend* whan it schuld be wretyn, for it was so long er it was wretyn that sche had forgetyn the tyme and the ordyr whan thyngys befellyn.[6]

This is rendered by Anthony Bale, Kempe's most recent translator, as:

> This book is not written in order, each thing after another as it was done, but just as the story came to the creature *in her mind* when it was to be written down, for it was so long before it was written that she had forgotten the timing and the order of when things happened. Therefore she wrote nothing other than that which she knew full well to be the whole truth.[7]

This *creature in her mind* is a possession, given the text, according to Bale, is constructed of visions that are divinely ordained, and ultim-ately authored by God, from Kempe's perspective.[8] The creature is a divine possession or occupation of Kempe's mind or else a displaced or estranged form of it, crouched before and possessed by a larger totality: the divine.[9] For Carolyn Dinshaw, there is another degree of

5   Walter Benjamin claims the novel to be the moment when authorship congeals in the bourgeois age. In *One Way Street* [1928], trans. by Edmund Jephcott, in *Walter Benjamin: Selected Writings*, ed. by Michael Jennings and others, 4 vols (Cambridge, MA: Harvard University Press, 2004–06), I (2004), pp. 444–88 (p. 444), he writes of the 'archaic stillness' of the book and the 'pretentious universal gestures' it carries. The novel isolates not just the writer but the reader, creating not just a reader but a sitter, in a library, in an armchair, in silence, not to be disturbed.

6   Margery Kempe, *The Book of Margery Kempe* [1501], ed. by Barry Windeatt (Cam-bridge: D. S. Brewer, 2004), p. 49. Emphasis mine.

7   Margery Kempe, *The Book of Margery Kempe* [1501], ed. and trans. by Anthony Bale (Oxford: Oxford University Press, 2015), p. 6. Emphasis mine.

8   Ibid., p. xvii.

9   A parallel with this understanding of the creature can be drawn with Benjamin and Kafka. See Carlo Salzani's 'Kafka's Creaturely Life', in *Kafka: Organisation, Recht, und Schrift*, ed. by Marianne Schuller and Günther Ortmann (Weilerswist Metternich: Velbrück Wissenschaft, 2019), pp. 396–407.

possession: Kempe is a creature not just in another time but a creature 'with another time *in* her'.[10]

In addition to this divine mode of possession, of creatureliness, *The Book of Margery Kempe* has other figures written within or between its lines. Kempe had scribes and 'listeners', who, according to Bale, would transcribe Kempe's dictation. The first of these figures was an acquaintance, possibly her son, who had lived in Germany, who died before they could complete the work. A priest then looked at the manuscript but found it 'ill-written' and incomprehensible. As the 'Proem', or introduction states:

> When the priest first began to write this book his eyesight failed
> so much that he could not see to form his letters, and he could
> not see to mend his pen. He was able to see all other things
> well enough. He set a pair of spectacles on his nose but then
> it was much worse than it was before. He complained to the
> creature about his illness. She said that his enemy envied his
> good deed and would hinder him if he could, and she urged
> him to do as well as God would give him grace and to not leave
> off. When the priest came back to this book, he could see as
> well (he thought) as he ever had before, both by daylight and
> by candlelight.[11]

Though the priest had stalled for four years and eventually told Kempe to seek other help from another person, who became the third person in the equation, the priest prayed for assistance, and found the text easier to comprehend as a result. This returns the question of possession to the divine: for prayer delivers coherence or permission that transform the priest's vision and cognition. It gives, according to Bale, the book a 'godly seal of approval', suggesting a divine, as much as a human, authorship.[12]

Biography forever holds onto this tension: how to write an account of a life when that life is forever displaced, estranged, and multiple, when it can easily not be written, or even comprehended, when authorship is forever murky. The 'my' of 'my rambling story' is a possessive

---

10   Carolyn Dinshaw, 'Temporalities', in *Oxford Twenty-First Century Approaches to Literature: Middle English*, ed. by Paul Strohm (Oxford: Oxford University Press), pp. 107–23 (p. 108). Dinshaw extends her reading to an argument about queerness, historical method, anachronism, and temporality in relation to Margery Kempe. Thank you to Virgil B/G Taylor for alerting me to this piece.

11   *The Book of Margery Kempe*, ed. and trans. by Bale, p. 6.

12   Ibid., p. xix.

pronoun that is already multiple: it could be Glück, Kempe, Kempe's first helper (perhaps her son), the priest, Kempe's second helper, the creature inside her head, God, Glück's lover, or the son of God. And this cast of characters is redacted, or condensed, into a single possessive pronoun: the 'my' of 'my rambling story'.

Glück's account too is reduced to a 'few' words: *'exult, exasperate, abandon, amaze'*. The omission of a final punctuation mark at the novel's close leaves open that which was interwoven, accumulating, rambling. The finite form of the book, the demand to contain its writing between a front and a back cover, forces this moment of condensation or containment. Just as the priest gets up, unable to process the work in front of him, so too Glück might have done the same, without even leaving a punctuation mark.

The demand of containment is made in and of film as much as in relation to the book. In *The White Dress* (2018), Nathalie Léger recounts a story in which her mother evokes an exercise developed by the director Claire Simon, when she works with students: to tell an entire story contained in one minute, like the film made by the Lumière brothers at the factory gates in 1895. Léger follows this reference with a number of questions:

> Where are you going to position yourself to look, what story are you going to tell, how are you going to tell it? One minute for the battle of Bordino, one minute for the closing of the Dubigeon shipyard in Nantes, one minute for a woman's life. I ask her [Léger's mother] what she would say, in one minute, how she would tell her story, her life, in what place, along what axis, beginning with what image?[13]

Can the act of biography, or autobiography, ever escape the tension between that which is rambling and that which is truncated, between four words, one minute, or a duration exact to the length of life itself? As Dilip Menon put it, how to write about everything when the act of writing is also an act of reduction?[14] How to address totality when our tools are always sabotaging that address? Can the category of biography be held on to, and if so, what is the point, if not to enact its failure?

---

13 Nathalie Léger, *The White Dress* [2018], trans. by Natasha Lehrer (New York: Dorothy, 2020), pp. 21–22. Thank you to Andrew Witt for pointing me towards this reference.

14 This was something said by Dilip Menon in our seminar in early 2022.

~

I first encountered the name 'Lotte Wolff' in the apparatus to Walter Benjamin's autobiographical work 'Berlin Chronicle' (1932), an attempt he made, of many, to condense an account of his life. He begins the text: 'I have long, indeed for years, played with the idea of setting out the sphere of life [Raum des Lebens] — *bios* — graphically on a map [Karte].'[15] This impulse first plays out figuratively: he channels a number of memories of the city and recalls a number of guides who widened its experience. About half way through the manuscript the mapping becomes more literal. He recalls a moment, a number of years prior, sitting at the *Café des Deux Magots* in *Saint-Germain-des-Prés*:

> Suddenly, and with compelling force, I was struck by the idea of drawing a diagram of my life [graphisches Schema meines Lebens].[16]

And he adds:

> With a very simple question I interrogated my past life, and the answers were inscribed, as if of their own accord, on a sheet of paper that I had with me.[17]

Benjamin goes on to lose this sheet of paper and with it the diagram. 'I was inconsolable [untröstlich]. I have never since been able to restore it as it arose before me then.' He tries to reproduce it, within the translucent pages of the *Pergamentheft*, the parchment notebook.[18] This reconstructed map, the one that survives, is made of forty-eight names, connected to each other by lines, dashes, and splodges.

Benjamin describes those named on the diagram as his 'Urbe-kanntschaften' (primal acquaintances): people he met not *through*

---

15   Walter Benjamin, 'Berlin Chronicle' [1932], trans. by Edmund Jephcott, in *Selected Writings*, ed. by Michael Jennings and others, II.2 (2005), pp. 595–637 (p. 596); 'Berliner Chronik', in *Kritische Gesamtausgabe*, ed. by Christoph Gödde and Henri Lonitz, 21 vols (2008–), XI.1: *Berliner Chronik / Berliner Kindheit um neunzehnhundert*, ed. by Burkhardt Lindner and Nadine Werner (2019), pp. 7–102 (p. 10).

16   Benjamin, 'Berlin Chronicle', p. 614; 'Berliner Chronik', p. 41.

17   Ibid.

18   For more on this notebook see: Ursula Marx and Erdmut Wizisla, 'Zarteste Quartiere: Walter Benjamins Notizbücher. Mit einem Blick in das Jerusalemer "Pergamentheft"', *Yearbook for European Jewish Literature Studies*, 6.1 (2019), pp. 147–69.

others, but in their own right, by chance encounter or circumstance: 'through neighbourhood, family relationships, school comradeship, mistaken identity, companionship on travels, or other such hardly numerous-situations'.[19] The account of the diagram breaks off with its retelling. He gets distracted, turns to a recollection of a story of a number of rings bought and exchanged by a number of figures on the diagram prior to the First World War, that also breaks off, again, without punctuation: 'To your finger constantly encircled'.[20] To write a life is to also get distracted, overwhelmed, derailed.

'Lotte Wolff' is a name that extends to 'Charlotte Wolff' and Charlotte Wolff was an early friend of Benjamin's — first, she was a doctor of reproductive medicine and electro-therapies in Berlin, later a hand reader and writer in Paris, and later still a sexologist and psychiatrist in London.[21] Wolff sits on Benjamin's reconstructed diagram between the radio producer and composer Ernst Schoen and the fashion journalist Helen Grund (whose hand Wolff read).

Alongside work on hands and sexuality,[22] Wolff wrote a number of works related to the narration of life: *On the Way to Myself: Communications to a Friend* (1969) and *Hindsight: An Autobiography* (1980).[23] She produced a *Lebenslauf* (literally a curriculum vitae, or 'life-course') in 1957 in her attempt to gain compensation from the post-war German state for what happened to her at the start of the previous German state.[24] She was also a biographer. In 1986, the year of her death, she published a vast work *Magnus Hirschfeld: A Portrait of a Pioneer in Sexology* in English.[25]

---

19   Benjamin, 'Berlin Chronicle', p. 614; 'Berliner Chronik', p. 42.
20   Benjamin, 'Berlin Chronicle', p. 616; 'Deinem Finger, dem sie sich vertraut', in 'Berliner Chronik', p. 45.
21   See Charlotte Wolff, *Hindsight: An Autobiography* (London: Quartet Books, 1980), p. 69.
22   On sexuality/gender: Charlotte Wolff, *Bisexuality: A Study* (London: Quartet Books, 1977); *Love Between Women* (London: Duckworth, 1971). On hands: *Studies in Hand-reading* (London: Chatto & Windus, 1936); *The Hand in Psychological Diagnosis* (London: Methuen, 1951); *The Human Hand* (London: Methuen, 1942).
23   See Charlotte Wolff, *On the Way to Myself: Communications to a Friend* (London: Methuen, 1969), and *Hindsight*.
24   See Wolff's compensation file in the office of the Entschädigungsamt Berlin: 341.655.
25   Charlotte Wolff, *Magnus Hirschfeld: A Portrait of a Pioneer in Sexology* (London: Quartet Books, 1986).

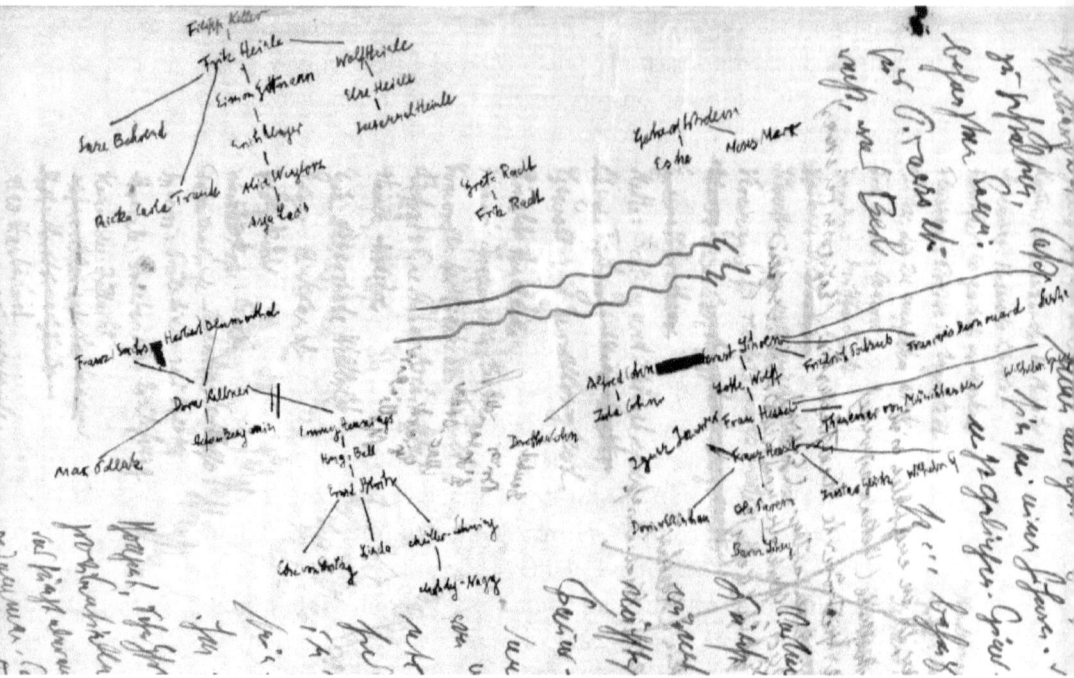

Figure 1. Walter Benjamin, Parchment Notebook (*Pergamentheft*):
National Library of Israel, ARC. 4, 1598/75 (detail).

When I eventually got hold of the manuscript of Benjamin's diagram rather than its transcription,[26] I was able to better think through
the diagram as a form, and the lines in particular: their shapes and sizes,
textures and speeds. I was able to better think of it as a 'form' that could
carry over into other 'forms' — in line with the Latinate root of 're-
ducere', to bring something back to something else.[27]

---

26   The transcribed forms exist currently in three places, though all with errors: Wal-
     ter Benjamin, *Berliner Chronik / Berliner Kindheit um neunzehnhundert*, in *Kritische
     Gesamtausgabe*, XI.1, pp. 390–91; Rolf Tiedemann and Hermann Schweppenhäuser,
     'Anmerkungen der Herausgeber', in Walter Benjamin, *Gesammelte Schriften*, ed. by
     Tiedemann and Schweppenhäuser, 7 vols (Frankfurt a.M.: Suhrkamp, 1972–91), VI
     (1991), pp. 623–828 (p. 804); Frederic Schwartz, *Blind Spots* (New Haven, CT: Yale
     University Press, 2005), p. 43.

27   I take this notion from the ICI's original statement on the topic of reduction: ICI
     Focus, Reduction, 2020–22 <https://www.ici-berlin.org/projects/reduction-2020-
     22> [accessed 1 March 2022].

Benjamin identifies a number of associations within the text around the diagram, as metaphors and analogies that also slip and transform. 'First', he writes, 'I envisaged an ordinary map, but now I would incline to a general staff's map [Generalstabskarte] of a city centre, if such a thing existed.'[28] The personal names slip into place names, to be navigated, constellated, traversed. The lines become lines of encounter, routing, and diversion. Benjamin then calls it a series of 'family trees' (Stammbäumen), where the lines between their names become lines of ascent or descent, branch and stem, within an ontogenetic or phylogenetic schema.[29] But the sentence goes on: He says it no longer resembles 'a series of family trees' but, in its reconstructed form, he writes that he 'would instead speak of a labyrinth [Labyrinth].'[30] He adds: 'I am concerned here not with what is installed in the chamber at its enigmatic centre, ego or fate, but all the more with the many entrances leading into the interior.'[31]

Other forms of association can easily be found or formed. For instance, Benjamin's diagram can be transposed into a table of elective or chemical affinities, following the schema of Torbern Olof Bergman's dissertation from 1775, which became the basis for Goethe's novel *Die Wahlverwandtschaften* (*Elective Affinities*) (1809), about which Benjamin wrote an essay, where people are drawn to or repelled from each other as much as substances are.[32] In the novel this is between Eduard, Charlotte, the Captain, and Ottilie, and Benjamin had his own love triangles as much as squares on the diagram.[33]

---

28   Benjamin, 'Berlin Chronicle', p. 596; 'Berliner Chronik', p. 10.

29   Ibid., p. 614; p. 42.

30   Ibid.

31   Ibid.

32   Torbern Olof Bergman, *A Dissertation on Elective Attractions* [Disquisitio de Attrac-tionibus Electivis, 1775] (London: Routledge, 2014); Johann Wolfgang von Goethe, *Elective Affinities* [1809], trans. by David Constantine (Oxford: Oxford University Press, 2008); Walter Benjamin, 'Goethe's Elective Affinities' [1924–25], trans. by Stanley Corngold, in *Selected Writings*, ed. by Michael W. Jennings and others, I, pp, 297–360. Bergman's text was first published in English in 1785 after being translated from the original Latin in 1785 by Thomas Beddoes. It is possible that Goethe read the *Dissertation* in the original Latin, but also from Heinrich Tabor's German translation, which appeared in the same year as the English, in 1785.

33   For an account of this see Howard Eiland and Michael Jennings, *Walter Benjamin: A Critical Life* (Cambridge, MA: Harvard University Press, 2014), pp. 117–76.

One might also add a maps of the stars — constellations abound, as they do throughout Benjamin's writings on astrology, but in his 'epistemological' frameworks too: 'Ideas are to objects as constellations to stars', he writes in the 'Epistemo-Critical Prologue' to his book on German mourning plays, or *Trauerspiel*.[34] In the constellation, for Benjamin, truth arises not from its reduction to the single and isolated thing, but through a whole mediated by an image that might appear suddenly, in a flash, that also transforms.[35]

One could add another form: the diagram as a piece of radio infrastructure; a network, or circuit, perhaps familiar to Ernst Schoen, Wolff's neighbour on the diagram, with wires, switches, resistors, all occupying the space between the names.[36] And perhaps there's a further transposition of the diagram that can be developed *via* Wolff: the diagram as a handprint. My question here: what would happen if a palm reader read the diagram in a naive manner, if they were to mistake it for a hand? If the etymology of 'biography' points to a writing (*-graphia*) of life (*bios*), then can the hand (if not the body) be understood as such a record or ledger of accrued experience? Can the hand reader therefore be granted, even if too literally, the category of a biographer?

Within the account of the diagram, Benjamin posed questions in relation to fate and character that are also of interest to the palmist:

> Whether cross-connections are finally established between these systems also depends on the intertwinements of our path through life [Verflechtungen unseres Lebenslaufes]. More important, however, are the astonishing insights that a study of this plan [the diagram] provides into the differences among individual lives.[37]

Then a number of questions follow:

> What part is played in the primal acquaintanceships [Urbe-kanntschaften] of different people's lives by profession and

---

34   See Walter Benjamin, *Origin of the German Trauerspiel*, trans. by Howard Eiland (Cambridge, MA: Harvard University Press, 2019), p. 10.

35   See Andrea Krauß, 'Constellations: A Brief Introduction', *MLN*, 126.3 (2011), pp. 439–45.

36   These claims are explored further in Sam Dolbear and Esther Leslie, *Dissonant Waves: Ernst Schoen and Experimental Sound in the Twentieth Century* (London: Goldsmiths Press, forthcoming 2023).

37   Benjamin, 'Berlin Chronicle', p. 615; 'Berliner Chronik', p. 42.

school, family and travel? And above all: Is the formation of
the many offshoots governed in individual existence by hidden
laws? Which ones start early in life, and which ones start late?
Which are continued to the end of life, and which peter out?
'If a man has character,' says Nietzsche, 'he will have the same
experience over and over again.'[38]

This Nietzsche quote appears in Benjamin's essay 'Fate and Character'
(published in 1921): "'If a man has character, he has an experience
[Erlebnis] that constantly recurs." This means: if a man has character,
his fate is essentially constant.'[39] The movement is circular: if one has
fate, one has character; if one has character, one has fate. One's chance
encounters at certain moments in one's life, in the formation of 'primal
acquaintances', establish hidden laws that mark out certain passages, or
paths of experience. The diagram, then, like the palm, is a mapping of
those paths, those laws that direct and define the course of one's life.

Through a process of determination and overdetermination, I will
build a number of instances of reduction in relation to lines *via* Wolff's
Studies in Hand-reading (1936) and *The Human Hand* (1942).

The first mode of reduction can be called *internal reduction*, in
which the constitution of the body or the psyche is visible and/or
interpretable on the hand. Cheiro's *Palmistry for All*, a classic instruc-
tion manual from 1916, claims that the hand, through nerves, is in
direct contact with the brain.[40] The publisher's preface to *The Human
Hand* quotes Wolff on a similar point: 'The hand is a visible part of
the brain.'[41] This leads to the second form of reduction, a *diagnostic
reduction*. In *Studies in Hand-reading*, Wolff traces particular lines on
the hand to diagnose various conditions, constitutions, and dispos-
itions of the body and psyche. For example, the director of a large
fashion house has a number of 'lines of influence' springing from the
Heart Line to indicate 'a passionate nature.'[42] This method of *diagnostic
reduction* of the entire body (or person) congeals into a judgement or

38   Ibid.
39   Walter Benjamin, 'Fate and Character' [1919/1921], trans. by Edmund Jephcott, in
     Selected Writings, ed. by Michael Jennings and others, I (2004), pp. 201–06 (p. 202).
40   Cheiro, *Palmistry for All* [1916] (London: Corgi Book, 1975), p. 15.
41   Wolff, *The Human Hand*, p. xii.
42   Examples could be more numerous throughout *Studies in Hand-reading*, but this case
     is listed on pp. 21–22.

name or label. For example, some of the cases in Wolff's book are listed not by profession, initials, or personal name, but via a physiological characteristic: one case she names simply as 'Lack of Head Line'.[43]

In later work, particularly her book *A Psychology of Gesture* (1945), some of Wolff's techniques enter a more acute setting: psychiatric hospitals on the outskirts of London, which she visited for a number of years, observing patients as they ate and interacted with each other. She reduces a whole set of behaviours to a term. For example, she identifies two hysterics and two people with 'persecution mania' (another term for acute paranoia) just from observing their gestures whilst they eat.[44] For Wolff this is another case of *internal reduction*, given that it is an example of the visible condition of an interior state, as if there was an internal state untouched by the outside, untouched by history. Benjamin outlines these dialectical movements in 'Fate and Character' where 'the external world [...] can also in principle be reduced [zurückgeführt], to any desired degree, to his inner world, and his inner world similarly to his outer world.'[45]

Opposed to this revelation of interior moments is an *external reduction*, the third mode, whereby the hand can be read as a displaced or transposed map of something outside: a longer totality, whether it be the world and/or the cosmos. On the hand of the fashion journalist Helen Grund, for example, Wolff identifies a prominent Ring of Saturn, a line that loops below the middle finger, which indicates a tendency to depression.[46] In this judgement a whole history collapses: the history of Saturn within a history of those born under its influence, tied to it a whole temperament and disposition.[47] Other such examples appear throughout Wolff's *Studies*.

---

43   Ibid., p. 145.

44   Charlotte Wolff, *A Psychology of Gesture* (London: Methuen, 1945), pp. 162–63. This method also culminates in Wolff's book, *The Hand in Psychological Diagnosis*.

45   Benjamin, 'Fate and Character', p. 202. Note that Benjamin is referring at this point in the essay to the 'active man', which has been translated from both 'handelnde Mensch' and 'wirkenden Menschen'. See Walter Benjamin, 'Schicksal und Charakter', in Benjamin, *Gesammelte Schriften*, II (1977), pp. 171–79 (p. 173).

46   Wolff, *Studies in Hand-reading*, p. 68.

47   See Raymond Klibansky, Erwin Panofsky, and Fritz Saxl, *Saturn and Melancholy: Studies in the History of Natural Philosophy, Religion, and Art* (Montreal: McGill-Queen's University Press, 2019).

A temporal reduction follows from here, the fourth instance: *the reduction of the future in the form of lines of fate or destiny*. If you are the poet Paul Éluard, according to Wolff, your Line of Fate is cut by four clear Lines of Influence at very specific ages: fifteen, twenty-four, twenty-eight, and thirty-four, which indicate significant shifts in character and circumstance in those years.[48] Those shifts transform your future, your destiny. Other people, according to Wolff and the manuals of hand reading, don't have much fate, and so they are less subject to its governance or power. This is something Benjamin addresses in 'Fate and Character' in proximity to the Nietzsche quotation also found in 'Berlin Chronicle': 'If a man has character, his fate is essentially constant. Admittedly, it also means: he has no fate — a conclusion drawn by the Stoics.'[49]

Another form of temporal reduction, the fifth, is past oriented: where past movement or a past event congeals as something legible on the body or hand. In *The Human Hand* (1942), Wolff claims that during the First World War, doctors developed a technique to date war trauma from the position and placement of certain marks on nails. Named after the French physician Joseph Honoré Simon Beau (1806–65), these marks, named 'beau lines', are said to appear at the root of the nail at the moment of trauma and, given the nail takes a specific amount of time to grow out (one hundred and sixty days), a physician could date, or measure the time of a trauma, by the position of the line on the nail.[50]

Graphology — the study of handwriting, a concurrent fascination of the period (about which Benjamin also wrote) — is a significant parallel here, in that it saw past movement crystallized on the page in the form of lines. As such, to read handwriting is to read gestures frozen or transformed on the page.[51] The same could be said of the 'wrinkle' on the body, a particular form of the line that has its own interpretive history.[52]

---

48   Wolff, *Studies in Hand-reading*, p. 71. Fate, it should be said, is here not taken in the Benjaminian sense that relates more guilt, debt, and law.

49   Benjamin, 'Fate and Character', p. 202.

50   Wolff, *The Human Hand*, p. 82.

51   See Wolff, *A Psychology of Gesture*, p. 5. See also Eric Downing, 'Divining Benjamin: Reading Fate, Graphology, Gambling', *MLN*, 126.3 (2011), pp. 561–80.

52   See Sam Dolbear, 'Reading Wrinkles', 19 May 2021 <https://raeblodmas.substack.com/p/reading-wrinkles> [accessed 1 March 2022].

One might add a *hereditary reduction*, as a kind of temporal reduction, which holds that certain lines on the hand are inherited or even fixed at birth. Julius Spier, whom Wolff studied with in Berlin prior to developing her own hand-reading methodology,[53] held that the right hand is the ancestral hand, inherited and fixed on the hand of the child, whereas the left hand is transformed and marked over time.[54] Elsewhere, Wolff says that the left hand resembles the hand of the mother, the right corresponds to the hand of the father.[55]

Wolff carries over some notions of heredity into *Studies* when she discusses the hand of the composer Armande de Polignac:

> Her tendency to suffer from nervous disorders is the natural accompaniment of the astonishing intensity of her emotions and the extent of her intellectual range. It is probable that heredity plays some part in this last named characteristic, for on her mother's side Armande de Polignac is descended from the Goethe family. Her talents as a philosopher and a musician are bound up with a deep feeling of unrest and of dissatisfaction with reality, which inspires her efforts to create another and symbolic world.[56]

This nervous disposition is evidenced through the way in which the heart line comes to an end between the fingers of Jupiter and Saturn.

The final reduction might be called an *identitarian reduction*, whereby the so-called 'complexity' and uniqueness of the hand and its print is used as a signature *of* the body or the person. For instance, one might think of the example of the fashion director and designer Madeleine Vionnet, who stamped her garments with a print of her finger to stop the counterfeiting of her wares.[57] Only her fingerprint

---

53   Wolff writes: 'I was inspired to continue my studies in hand-reading not only by the discoveries which had been made in the field of graphology, but also by the psycho-analytical works of Sigismund Freud and C. G. Jung. I tried to apply to hand reading the newly found knowledge of the unconscious with the light it threw on dreams, imagination and art. I found an excellent teacher in Julius Spier, and later on, when I began to study the French literature on the subject, I discovered that M. Mangin-Balchasar had made several important attempts to apply modern knowledge of psychology to chiromancy' (*Studies in Hand-reading*, p. 6).

54   See Wolff, *The Human Hand*, p. 24. Also Julius Spier, *The Hands Of Children: An Introduction to Psycho-Chirology* [1955] (London: Routledge, 1999), p. 48.

55   See Wolff, *The Human Hand*, p. 24.

56   Wolff, *Studies in Hand-reading*, pp. 105–06.

57   See Dolbear, 'Reading Wrinkles'.

was her fingerprint. The palm reader also engages with this notion of identitarian reduction: as they read the lines, they read them on the basis that they are singular to the person sitting. They define that person's life, that person's fate. And the final instance of this identitarian reduction is by the state, which also collects hand prints and stores them in its archives.[58] The question here is how the state comes to recognize or not recognize those who fall within its fold.

PART TWO: LINES AS BORDER AS REDUCTION

> Or, reduction as collapse,
> transgression, demand[59]

Charlotte Wolff was arrested (or almost arrested) in 1933 on the platform of Hasenheide U-Bahn (now Südstern), suspected as a spy for dressing androgynously. The day after, she renewed her passport and left for Paris on the train, to escape a regime newly hostile to her, for her gender-identity, her sexuality, her politics, her religion.[60] Many of the others on the diagram also escaped on train lines out, along lines of friendship and infrastructure, disseminating from their names — and, as they travelled, they would pass over other lines of property, of states (themselves shifting), to places potentially of greater if not total safety. Another 'transposition' of the diagram comes into view at this point as a series of train-tracks, the names perhaps stations along lines of movement, lines of escape.

When Avery Gordon ran a workshop at the ICI Berlin in November 2021, she spoke briefly of the artist Bouchra Khalili's *Mapping Journey Project*, produced between 2008 and 2011. For the work, Khalili

---

58   For this history see Allan Sekula, 'The Body and the Archive', *October*, 39 (1986), pp. 3–64.

59   Again, this interlude is quoted from a shared document assembled in June 2020 by fellows and members of staff around the motif of 'reduction *as* X'.

60   See Wolff, *Hindsight: An Autobiography*, pp. 108–10. This account varies slightly in Wolff's 'Lebenslauf' held in her legal papers prepared for compensation against the German state: Entschädigungsamt Berlin: 341.655.

recorded oral testimonies of the journeys of eight people who had been forced to make 'illegal' journeys of escape or migration. As the audio is playing, videos show the speaker's hand as they mark out the route in permanent marker on a map. The permanence of the marker is intentional, to cut through existing state boundaries and leave a permanent record. These videos were then all placed in the same space together. As hands mark, a voice can be heard:

> When I arrived in Skopje [North Macedonia]
> They told me that my papers looked a little fake
> They told me 'You cannot enter the country.'
> And they called the police
> And I was jailed for 8 months and 20 days, something like that
> Afterwards they sent me to Bangladesh ... The man I paid to go to Italy
> said 'Wait a few months, we'll find another road.'[61]

Echoing Robert Glück's intention to contain the story in a few words, Tobi Haslett has written, in relation to Khalili's work, that 'An appalling five-year gauntlet collapses into eleven minutes'.[62] Time that was once stretched out, experienced within something close to real time, is condensed into memory and testament, through the voice and hand.

In 2011, at the end of the project, Khalili converted the tracings into a series of screen printed constellations, each point a city, or a place of punctuation, whether a pause, derailment, diversion, departure, imprisonment, release. In these maps, the world is abstracted out of its striations: the lines that mark the world (as state boundaries) become background. The sky is profaned, constellated again.

The border, as a line, demarcates: it places you on either side of something, even if it is itself displaced, into ports and airports but also into classrooms or employment or housing law. If and when you are on it (the physical border), you wait to pass (to a different regime of law and enforcement), and this is one of the moments of precarity, when someone else decides your fate according to a mixture of law and discretion. The border agent, in this sense, is like a governmental palm reader: they read or

---

61   Quoted in Tobi Haslett, 'A Philosophy of the Cauterized Wound: Tobi Haslett on the Art of Bouchra Khalili', *Art Forum*, March 2019 <https://www.artforum.com/print/201903/tobi-haslett-on-the-art-of-bouchra-khalili-78669> [accessed 1 March 2022].

62   Ibid.

they let a machine read your destiny, they read or they let a machine read your fingerprints to see if you may pass.

One way I have come to understand reduction over the last year or so is through the *coarsening* of political demands. As Manuele Gragnolati put it: 'reduction as concentration, condensation, synthesis (getting to the essence and to what is at stake)'.[63] What could be necessary for this gesture if not a coarsening of demands as a call for abolitions of various kinds: of borders, of fear, of suffering.[64] The essence of the matter is perhaps: who cares what the lines on the hand mean in relation to the cosmos if this world renders those meanings superfluous anyway, when the most active palm reader remains the guard at the border, when fate does not function even to prescribe banal paths, but commands, through contingencies of nature and law, violence for those it so unevenly targets.[65] As György Lukács wrote at the start of *Theory of the Novel* (1914–15): 'Blessed are those times when the starry sky is the map of all possible paths — ages whose paths are illuminated by the light of the stars.'[66] To re-constellate the sky would be to reconstitute the lines not only between but upon ourselves.

63   This is a quotation from the shared document 'reduction *as* X' assembled in June 2021.

64   Examples of this movement accumulated in my head over the years. In *Minima Moralia*, Theodor W. Adorno writes 'There is tenderness only in the coarsest demand, that no-one shall go hungry any more' (Zart wäre einzig das Gröbste: daß keiner mehr hungern soll). See Adorno, *Minima Moralia: Reflections on a Damaged Life*, trans. by Edmund F. N. Jephcott (London: Verso, 2005), p. 156, and Adorno, *Minima Moralia: Reflexionen aus dem beschädigten Leben* [1951] (Frankfurt a.M.: Suhrkamp, 1970), p. 206. Other examples could be added.

65   M. Ty explores this question in the essay 'Benjamin on the Border', *Critical Times*, 2.2 (2019), pp. 306–19 (p. 315): 'Through a strike of fate, a contingent movement becomes a decisive misstep; and the border produces this misfortune.' Their paper 'To Break with Fate' at the conference *Walter Benjamins 'Zur Kritik der Gewalt'* of the Humboldt-Universität zu Berlin on 12 February 2021 expands on these questions. See the online video recording on <https://symposiumtheoriederpolitik.wordpress.com/programm/> [accessed 26 June 2022].

66   György Lukács, *Theory of the Novel* [1914–15], trans. by Anna Bostock (Cambridge, MA: MIT Press, 1971), p. 29. Translation slightly altered.

Post-anti-identitarianism
The Forms of Contemporary Gender and Sexuality
BEN NICHOLS

I recently came across an item in my local queer bookshop that struck me as both trivial and intriguing. With a cover in the colours of the progress pride flag, *The Queens' English* (2021) styles itself as a 'dictionary' of queer life.[1] A publication aimed squarely at a popular audience, it nonetheless mimes this somewhat standardizing, technical, and specialist (as I will explore, we might even say reductive) reference form. Across its over 800 entries, this dictionary offers its readers a digest of a whole host of gender and sexual identities: demigender, graysexual, aromantic, heteroflexible, polysexual, neutrois are just a handful of terms. These identities complement the lengthening initialism that commonly stands in for non-cis-hetero culture and life: LGBTQIA+, or lesbian, gay, bisexual, trans, queer/questioning, intersex, asexual, with a 'plus' that implies inevitable expansion. Whether we live in an era of more intensely proliferating gender and sexual identities, or whether this proliferation has always characterized gender and sexuality more generally is open to debate. But whatever the answer, the interest in identity now complements how social identity looms large across life in many Anglophone contexts, where social and political

---

1   Chloe O. Davis, *The Queens' English: The LGBTQIA+ Dictionary of Lingo and Colloquial Phrases* (London: Square Peg, 2021).

emergencies continue to make the work of identity-based thought and movements urgent and necessary, even as many commentators on both the left and the right still decry the apparent dominance of 'identity politics', as they have done for decades.[2]

How are the academic fields of feminist, queer, and trans studies to respond to this identitarian moment, influenced as they are by anti-identitarian thought? Through conceptual frameworks rooted in post-structuralism and psychoanalysis, or through critiques of the framework of liberal rights, representation, and recognition that identitarian positions seem to require, these fields have been defined in prominent ways by their scepticism towards *identity*. Identity *reduces*: it reduces us to vectors of knowledge-power, or it reduces the errancy of desire, or the instability of language, or opportunities for coalitional struggle. Within the most prominent frameworks of gender and sexuality studies, identity still tends to seem either theoretically and conceptually impossible, politically problematic and exclusionary, or just aesthetically uninteresting. My main question in this chapter is whether this framework of anti-identitarianism remains adequate or helpful for theorizing gender and sexual life now, where it seems that identities are only proliferating. If anything, gender and sexual life is becoming more identitarian than ever before. One response to this is to say that we therefore have an acute need for anti-identitarian thought. Another would be to use this moment to reflect on whether all forms of attachment to identity are problematic in the way that anti-identitarian thought has tended to imagine. Are all forms of attachment to identity identical?

There are a number of ways in which we can read forms of reduction at the heart of this identitarian proliferation. For one thing, in conceptual terms, as I hint above and as we will see more below, identity has been strongly associated with reduction. But equally, a prominent form of response to the new complexity of the terrain of

---

2   For a recent left-liberal critique of identity politics see Mark Lilla, *The Once and Future Liberal: After Identity Politics* (New York: HarperCollins, 2017). For a similar argument from a neoconservative perspective see Francis Fukuyama, *Identity: Contemporary Identity Politics and the Struggle for Recognition* (London: Profile Books, 2018). Suzanna Danuta Walters summarizes many of the historical debates on identity politics in her 'In Defense of Identity Politics', *Signs*, 43.2 (2018), pp. 473–88.

gender and sexual identity has been to turn to genres or forms that help schematize it — that is, to reductive or reducing genres. One example is 'the list' as a form, as in the initialism LGBTQIA+ cited above that substantializes each identity in the list and also formalizes them as more or less equivalent. Across popular print publishing and social media, a range of guides, such as *The Queens' English*, have similarly taken the form of what are essentially lists: dictionaries, A-Zs, and ABCs-style guides. To give them a name, I call these 'information genres' and they take their place in much broader histories of the importance of such forms to queer and other forms of minoritized life for whom the issue of access to information has been particularly important. The point in the context of this chapter is to highlight the close relation between expansion and reduction: the expansion of sexual and gendered life seems also to generate an attachment to genres and forms that are schematic, formalizing, reductive. This is not to claim that there is any conceptual necessity to the link between expansion and reduction, but to register the context of these guides where the two phenomena seem to have gone hand in hand.

At the same time, these new genres which seek to list, catalogue, and enumerate gender and sexual identities also encourage us to look back at the histories of feminist, queer, and trans studies for alternative non-anti-identitarian genealogies. Doing this, we can see that there have been significant seams within these fields that have not sought to do away with identity altogether, but rather have sought to historicize it, or else looked to foreground the versions of identity that may be obscured by more prominent or institutionalized forms. Rather than a wholesale rejection of identity, this work was often grounded in a rejection or problematization of a specific range of identities: prominently, woman, lesbian, gay, transgender. Perhaps we can see the proliferation of identities now as part of the continuation of a basic project to decentre this specific range of identities. The point then, particularly towards the end of the sections that follow, is to dwell on how forms of social identity bear the *rhetorical burden of identity* and its seeming reductiveness differently.

TRACING ANTI-IDENTITARIANISM

There have of course been good reasons why some of the most important and defining formulations in feminist, queer, and trans theory
have been anti-identitarian ones. Amongst other things, these formulations have helped us to interrogate a stable and exclusionary idea
of 'woman'.[3] They have encouraged us to see heteronormativity as a
structure whose influence operates well beyond the direct treatment of
self-identified lesbian, gay, or bisexual people.[4] And they have taught
us about the sometimes neo-colonial travels of the category 'transgender' when it is exported around the world.[5] Identitarianism has also
been seen as inadequate for producing ethical projects based on self-
abandonment as exemplary non-violence,[6] inadequate as the basis for
the broadest visions of social justice and transformation,[7] and inadequate for the practical provision of healthcare interventions, such as
in the contexts of HIV/AIDS.[8] The list could likely go on. The many
important reservations about identity that have been articulated in
gender and sexuality studies, particularly since, and most prominently
within, queer theory, have resulted in a situation in which identity has
come to have something of a political essence. If asked to characterize
these fields, and particularly the field of queer theory, would anyone
with a real familiarity with them ever say that their main concern is
with identity?

Some conceptual roots of anti-identitarianism can be traced to
the influence of post-structuralism and psychoanalysis in formulations
that have characterized queer thought. A touchstone text in this regard
would of course be Judith Butler's *Gender Trouble: Feminism and the*

3   Judith Butler, *Gender Trouble: Feminism and the Subversion of Identity* [1990] (Lon-
     don: Routledge, 1999).

4   Michael Warner, 'Introduction', in *Fear of a Queer Planet: Queer Politics and Social
     Theory*, ed. by Michael Warner (Minneapolis: University of Minnesota Press, 1993),
     pp. vii–xxxi.

5   Aniruddha Dutta and Raina Roy, 'Decolonizing Transgender in India: Some Reflec-
     tions', *TSQ*, 1.3 (2014), pp. 320–37.

6   Leo Bersani, *Homos* (Cambridge, MA: Harvard University Press, 1995).

7   Wendy Brown, *States of Injury: Power and Freedom in Late Modernity* (Princeton, NJ:
     Princeton University Press, 1995).

8   Simon Watney, 'Emergent Sexual Identities and HIV/AIDS', in *Imagine Hope: AIDS
     and Gay Identity* (London: Routledge, 2000), pp. 63–80.

Subversion of Identity (1990), where Butler argues through largely Foucauldian terms that the stable identity of 'woman' that they imagine
some feminist work to have been attached to is in fact the outcome or
product of regulatory and exclusionary practices that, amongst other
problems, uphold the dominance of heterosexuality. Butler also draws
on a wide range of other thinkers to question the 'metaphysics of substance' on which they imagine this stable notion of *woman* to rely.[9]
This notion of a stable being is problematized not only because of
its construction within discourse/power, but also via recourse to the
destabilizing effects of the unconscious and of language, which both
reveal the 'foundational illusions of identity' and unsettle its 'reductive efforts of univocal signification'.[10] Butler's later work in the 1990s
similarly problematized sexual as well as gender identity categories. In
the 1999 Preface to the tenth anniversary edition of *Gender Trouble*,
Butler hopes for 'a coalition of sexual minorities that will transcend
the simple categories of identity' and that 'would be based on the irreducible complexity of sexuality and its implication in various dynamics
of discursive and institutional power'.[11] While there is an irreducibility
that identity categories misrepresent here, Butler also corrects a mis-
understanding of *Gender Trouble*, clarifying that its critique of identity
'is no reason not to use, and be used, by identity'.[12] Despite the conceptual problems with certain formulations of identity that were raised
in Butler's work, as they clarified, this did not mean that they thought
it could, or should, be escaped entirely.

But beyond Butler, other influential figures within queer theory
continue to be drawn to conceptual frameworks that have tended to
imagine 'identity' as an impossibility. Prominent voices in the field
keeping this more thoroughgoing strain of anti-identitarianism alive
include Jasbir Puar, who has problematized the framework of intersectional identities using models of affect and assemblage derived from
Deleuzian thought, and, from a quite different perspective, Lee Edelman, committed as his work remains to a model of queerness as a

---

9   Butler, *Gender Trouble*, p. 14.
10   Ibid., pp. 44 and 132.
11   Ibid., p. xxvi.
12   Ibid.

kind of Lacanian Real that confounds all identity. For Edelman, 'queer-ness can never define an identity; it can only ever disturb one.'[13] For Puar, 'intersectional identities are the byproducts of attempts to still and quell the perpetual motion of assemblages, to capture and reduce them, to harness their threatening mobility.'[14] In her more recent work, Puar similarly roots her analysis of international disability politics in a concept of affect as 'ontological irreducibilities that transform the fantasy of discreteness of categories not through their disruption but, rather, through their dissolution via multiplicity'.[15] The theoretical commitments in both Puar and Edelman make the complete impos-sibility of identity and categories a much more central concern than it had been in Butler.

As the mention of Puar perhaps begins to indicate, a prominent way of critiquing identitarianism now is to attach it to or fold it into a critique of Western liberalism. That is, in queer theoretical writing now, one is arguably less likely to encounter a post-structuralist de-construction of identity as the most pressing scholarly project, but the spirit of this deconstruction continues in critiques of identity for being part of an implicitly Western liberal rights project that seems to demand stable subjects for representation. For example, in a special issue of the US-based journal *Social Text*, titled 'Left of Queer' (2020), Puar and David Eng have continued their individual projects of cri-tiquing the conceptual bases of minority rights claims. What Puar has called 'homonationalism' and what Eng has called 'queer liberalism' both name structures in which the identities of formerly marginalized people (or, more specifically, of lesbians and gay people) are folded into modern liberal states rooted, both in terms of their histories and contemporary orientations, in racism and colonialism.[16] The claims of these formerly marginalized people to be recognized within the terms

---

13   Lee Edelman, *No Future: Queer Theory and the Death Drive* (Durham, NC: Duke University Press, 2004), p. 17.

14   Jasbir K. Puar, *Terrorist Assemblages: Homonationalism in Queer Times* (Durham, NC: Duke University Press, 2007), p. 213.

15   Jasbir K. Puar, *The Right to Maim: Debility, Capacity, Disability* (Durham, NC: Duke University Press, 2017), p. 36.

16   See Puar, *Terrorist Assemblages*; David L. Eng, *The Feeling of Kinship: Queer Liberalism and the Racialization of Intimacy* (Durham, NC: Duke University Press, 2010).

of those nation states serve therefore only to bolster these racist and colonialist projects.

In the more recent incarnation of this argument that they have offered together, Eng and Puar also fold into their account the ever-increasing range of sexual identities vying for recognition, or what they call 'the evolution of LGBTQ+ in US identity politics'.[17] They argue that this evolution leads to the continued formation of liberal subjects as bearers of rights, which rests on the 'sublation' of three main concepts that exceed the bounds of identity and the liberal subject: '*debility, indigeneity,* and *trans*'.[18] They therefore make the case for what they call both a 'subjectless' and 'objectless' critique that, they argue, avoids these negations.[19] Interestingly, while they directly critique what they see as the way in which queer studies has become reduced to a version of US area studies, their critique of liberal inclusion has originated from, and speaks most prominently to, the context of the contemporary United States. It is also clear that the paradigm of the liberal state that they employ is the US. Moreover, as they implicitly suggest by citing a wide range of US-based scholarship that does this, articulating the desire to set the sights of queer studies beyond the US nation-state now so thoroughly marks scholarship coming from the US that the demand only positions one even more strongly in that geopolitical location.[20] The exact extent to which their critique of liberal inclusion remains true in other locations is perhaps to be determined. Are all forms of liberal inclusion the same?

Or perhaps another question would be, where exactly is this liberal inclusion happening? At one less frequently cited moment in her famous essay on paranoid and reparative reading, Eve Kosofsky Sedgwick asks what I take to be a similar question. To rehearse the overall argument briefly: Sedgwick argues that modern Anglophone critical theory has mostly been characterized by a 'paranoid' mode which seeks to uncover hidden violences and oppressions in whatever it attends to. This mode has an important role to play, but also deserves to be seen

---

17   David L. Eng and Jasbir K. Puar, 'Introduction: Left of Queer', *Social Text*, 38.4 (2020), pp. 1–23 (p. 7).
18   Ibid., p. 2, original italics.
19   Ibid., p. 16.
20   Ibid., p. 19 n. 9.

as just one among many possible approaches. The approach she calls 'reparative' is focused just as much, for example, on what is enabled or made possible by the inevitably adulterated, imperfect, or even violent phenomena of the world: it is about finding sustenance or pleasure in the objects that we study. One of the hallmarks of one version of paranoid thought, she argues, is that it relies on the 'prestige of a single, overarching narrative: exposing and problematizing hidden violences in the genealogy of the modern liberal subject'.[21] She continues:

> Where are all these supposed modern liberal subjects? I daily encounter graduate students who are dab hands at unveiling the hidden historical violences that underlie a secular, universalist liberal humanism. Yet these students' sentient years, unlike the formative years of their teachers, have been spent entirely in a xenophobic Reagan-Bush-Clinton-Bush America where 'liberal' is, if anything, a taboo category and where 'secular humanism' is routinely treated as a marginal religious sect, while a vast majority of the population claims to engage in direct intercourse with multiple invisible entities such as angels, Satan, and God.[22]

While the version of the essay I cite here was published in 2003, in 2022, when I write this, we might similarly ask if the formation of a liberal subject who bears rights is really the most acute violence we can imagine when, as Eng and Puar themselves write, 'far Right and ultra-nationalist governments have been (re)elected and/or strengthened in both democratic and authoritarian states.'[23]

Will all versions of appeals to liberal personhood, to a subject who is the bearer of an identity and of rights, always mean the same thing? I do not ask this to defend what has been critiqued as universal liberal humanism. For one thing, this would mean taking on decades of theorizing within critical theory that has sought to dislodge or otherwise trouble the modern liberal subject. Moreover, important renewed critiques of humanism have been offered in recent years by a range of scholars who have explored the variously abject positions afforded

---

21   Eve Kosofsky Sedgwick, *Touching Feeling: Affect, Pedagogy, Performativity* (Durham, NC: Duke University Press, 2003), p. 139.

22   Ibid., pp. 139–40.

23   Eng and Puar, 'Introduction: Left of Queer', p. 3.

to Blackness within the 'universal liberal human project'.[24] Instead, I point to a conceptual knot: if the problem with universalist liberal humanism is its *universal* concept of the human, then is there a problem with claiming that liberal humanism is itself universally always one thing? This conceptual knot does not go unremarked in scholarship that takes on universal liberal humanism. In her recent book *Becoming Human* (2020), Zakiyyah Iman Jackson similarly recognizes that the Enlightenment humanism that she takes to be the paradigm of liberal humanist thinking is itself 'a multivocality with contradiction and moving parts, and thus not reducible to its more infamous ideas', whilst remaining ringingly clear on its place in the history of anti-Blackness.[25]

INFORMATION GENRES

The scholarly consensus that I have briefly traced, however, contrasts somewhat with how gender and sexuality are increasingly lived in less academic contexts. For example, the fiercely anti-identitarian energies of queerness as articulated by some queer theorists have been given identitarian form, as I would not be the first to observe, by being folded into the lengthening initialism that names non-cis-heterosexual identities. This continues to expand from LGBT, or LGBTQ, to LGBTQIA+, or to cite one particularly full recent version: 'LGBT-QQIP2SAA' (lesbian, gay, bisexual, transgender, queer, questioning, intersex, pansexual, two-spirit, androgynous, asexual).[26] Facebook, of course, now famously offers users more than 70 gender categories to choose from.[27] As I mentioned above, this context is liable to make us

---

24   Zakiyyah Iman Jackson, *Becoming Human: Matter and Meaning in an Antiblack World* (New York: New York University Press, 2020), p. 28. Jackson references a very wide range of scholars related to her project: Frantz Fanon, Lewis Gordon, Saidiya Hartman, Hortense Spillers, Fred Moten, Aimé Césaire, Sylvia Wynter, Frank Wilderson III, Katherine McKittrick, Christina Sharpe, Denise Ferreira da Silva, Achille Mbembe, and Alexander G. Weheliye (p. 19).

25   Ibid., p. 23.

26   Guy Davidson, 'Queer Literary Studies and the Question of Identity Categories', *Literature Compass*, 17 (2020), e12561 (p. 12n2) <https://doi.org/10.1111/lic3.12561>.

27   For a discussion of this and a list of the gender options available on the US and UK versions of the site see Patricia Gherovici, *Transgender Psychoanalysis: A Lacanian Perspective on Sexual Difference* (London: Routledge, 2017), p. 29.

think either that we need anti-identitarian thought more than ever, or else that clinging on to it is a losing battle.

To test out how to view this contemporary expansion of gender and sexual identities in light of the history of anti-identitarianism in the fields of gender and sexuality studies, I would like to look to some genres of writing in which this proliferation and expansion is registered in some specific ways. For the purposes of this volume, I am interested in the link between identitarian proliferation and certain genres or styles or forms that we might imagine as quite reductive. Over the last few years, across popular publishing and social media in Anglophone contexts, we have seen the appearance of a number of queer genres of writing that take the form of, essentially, lists and style themselves after forms that schematize and formalize information: dictionaries, A-Zs, 'ABCs' guides, or even, in one case, the periodic table. To give examples of a few titles here: *The Queens' English: The LGBTQIA+ Dictionary of Lingo and Colloquial Phrases* (2021), *The Queeriodic Table: A Celebration of LGBTQ+ Culture* (2019), *From Ace to Ze: The Little Book of LGBT Terms* (2018), or *The A-Z of Gender and Sexuality: From Ace to Ze* (2018).[28] While we could look to many places to see the expansion of gender and sexual identity categories recorded, these kinds of texts, on the one hand, give us a useful overview of the terrain, and, at the same time, introduce formal questions about reduction.

Moreover, these works take their place in a much broader history in which what we might call 'information genres' have been central to queer and many other forms of minoritized life: guidebooks, bibliographies, event listings, personal ads, safer sex education manuals, coming out guides, young adult advice books. These kinds of genres have a greater significance for minoritized people whose lives depend on access to information that is often not available within mainstream and readily accessible genres of cultural reproduction and dissemination. As the media studies scholar Cait McKinney writes, 'groups marginalized because of gender, sexuality, and race have the most to

---

28   Davis, *The Queens' English*; Harriet Dyer, *The Queeriodic Table: A Celebration of LG-BTQ+ Culture* (London: Summersdale, 2019); Harriet Dyer, *From Ace to Ze: The Little Book of LGBT Terms* (London: Summersdale, 2018); Morgan Potts, *The A-Z of Gender and Sexuality: From Ace to Ze* (London: Jessica Kingsley Publishers, 2018).

tell us about how, when, and for whom information matters.'[29] What interests me about the titles I cite above though is their relation to cultural forms that are particularly reductive, standardizing, and schematizing. Dictionaries collect, catalogue, and define language usage. A-Z guides provide lists that comprehensively present and schematize the significant features of a given phenomenon. In the UK, A-Z Maps are a well-known brand of map that since 1936 has provided comprehensive roadmaps of the UK. Maps, of course, translate the complexity of three-dimensional life into a flat, modularized formal representation. The proliferation and expansion of new forms of gender and sexual life seems to have gone hand-in-hand with highly reductive cultural forms.

The hitherto unmentioned 'information genre' that has a key role to play here is the contemporary Internet. Indeed, it would be difficult not to relate any proliferation in gender and sexual identities to the new media forms that we now live with. Many platforms from YouTube to Reddit have become places for sharing information and guidance that refines, breaks down, and reformulates the increasing complexities of contemporary gender and sexual life. One popular YouTuber — who now goes by the name of Ash Hardell and at the time of writing is on temporary hiatus from producing videos — also published a book in 2016 called *The ABC's of LGBT+* (2016). The book starts with a 'cheat sheet' aimed at an 'LGBTQIA+ terminology novice' and includes 105 terms including: 'Abrosexual/romantic: Someone who experiences a fluid and/or changing orientation'; 'Aporagender: Both a specific gender identity and an umbrella term for being a non-binary gender separate from man, woman, and anything in between while still having a very strong and specific gendered feeling'; 'Diamoric': a term for describing the sexual and romantic orientation towards non-binary people.[30] Mardell suggests that the book is explicitly for any LGBTQIA+ person who is 'looking for their label'.[31]

---

29   Cait McKinney, *Information Activism: A Queer History of Lesbian Media Technologies* (Durham, NC: Duke University Press, 2020), p. 3.

30   Ashley Mardell, *The ABC's of LGBT+* (Coral Gables, FL: Mango Media Inc, 2016), pp. 7, 8, 9, and 12. Apple ebook.

31   Ibid., p. 46.

There might be a set of easy academic critiques of the project of this book. For one thing, the belief that any category could be sufficient for transparently capturing a lived reality is of course an idea that we are inclined to think of as naive. According to some dominant conceptual frameworks that I briefly addressed earlier, any identity is simply impossible because of the inevitably corrosive force of the unconscious or because of our distribution as subjects across 'ontological irreducibilities' of affect. Moreover, the proliferation of identities or labels does not escape the overarching reductive logic of identity and labels itself. From Michel Foucault, we know that modern power works not through restricting sexual identity, but through the 'proliferation of specific pleasures and the multiplication of disparate sexualities' in what he dubbed 'the perverse implantation'.[32] From Marxist scholars, we are familiar with parallels that we might draw between neoliberal consumerist logics based on infinite choice and the seemingly infinite options for sexual and gendered life similarly out there to 'choose'.[33] But all of this said, it is hard to simply dismiss Hardell's project. Hardell has over 600,000 subscribers on YouTube, which is a far greater reach than any queer theorist. The book is an interesting phenomenon for how it lays out many fine-grained distinctions and names them: it is a digest of a range of careful taxonomies of sexual and gendered life.

Nevertheless, in some ways, the examples in the previous paragraphs perfectly exemplify the politics of liberal inclusion that Puar and Eng critique. For them, the expanding list of identities laying claim to liberal rights is 'predicated on a signifying chain of identity as analogy and the awarding of legal rights and entitlements through a politics of incremental recognition'.[34] The problem with 'identity as analogy' is that new forms of identity still rely on the unproblematized and recognizable liberal subject of rights. For Eng and Puar, it seems that no form of identity could escape this. The works cited above demonstrate

---

32   Michel Foucault, *The History of Sexuality*, trans. by Robert Hurley, 4 vols (London: Penguin, 1978–2021), I: *The Will to Knowledge* [1976] (1998), pp. 49 and 36.

33   See for example Rosemary Hennessy, *Profit and Pleasure: Sexual Identities in Late Capitalism* (London: Routledge, 2000); Donald Morton, 'Changing the Terms: (Virtual) Desire and (Actual) Reality', in *The Material Queer: A LesBiGay Cultural Studies Reader*, ed. by Donald Morton (Boulder, CO: Westview, 1996), pp. 1–33.

34   Eng and Puar, 'Introduction: Left of Queer', p. 5.

Eng and Puar's point rather perfectly via their formal organization. *The ABCs of LGBT+*, for example, could not do any more to invite us to see the identities that it describes as analogous: they are presented as an alphabetical list of basically similar and equivalent entries. In the other volumes cited above, too, the identities and terminology that they lay out for us are presented in lists of alphabetical entries. In formal terms, each identity is rendered the same, even if the content may differ. Moreover, these texts are likely to seem thoroughly to be about a 'politics of incremental recognition'. They are for those who are 'looking for their label' or for the category within which they might demand recognition. This resonates with a distinction between recognition and redistribution often discussed by Nancy Fraser, amongst others, where the former is about extending recognition within the basic political terms of the status quo and the latter is about a more thoroughgoing reorganization of political life with social justice in mind.[35]

At the same time, the information genres I have briefly addressed may offer some challenges to this narrative. For one thing, Puar and Eng are clear that the main aspect of the 'recognition' that they problematize is legal recognition. It is claims for 'legal rights and entitlements' that problematically seek the validation of the state. By contrast, these guides make no claims on the law. Indeed, in their very forms they cite and perform themselves specifically as, as I have said, *information genres* (the dictionary, the A-Z, and so on). The guides I have cited make it clear that what is at stake is *information* rather than legal redress or recognition. That is, as these guides make clear, there may be uses and deployments of identitarian expansion that are not fully explained within the terms of either recognition or redistribution. Arguably, it is through embodying reductive forms — through reducing the identitarian expansion to nothing more than more information — that these guides might encourage us to think in these terms.

Moreover, to my mind, there are also some conceptual confusions in how Puar and Eng use the concept of 'liberal'. They would not be alone in using 'liberal' to evoke a catch-all evil which condenses prob-

---

35   Nancy Fraser, 'Social Justice in the Age of Identity Politics: Redistribution, Recognition, and Participation', in Fraser and Axel Honneth, *Redistribution or Recognition?: A Political-Philosophical Exchange* (London: Verso, 2003), pp. 7–109.

lematic political and economic orientations, as well as a specific theory of the subject. For them, the 'evolution of LGBTQ+ in US identity politics' is a specifically liberal phenomenon — they use the terms 'liberal', '(neo)liberal', and 'neoliberal'.[36] Yet, liberalism as a political and social orientation, at least in some of its articulations, actually stands in tension with the recognition of non-dominant social identities. One high-profile instance that articulates this is Mark Lilla's popular book *The Once and Future Liberal: After Identity Politics* (2017). Lilla calls for moving away from identity politics approaches by arguing that such approaches fractured the liberal left in the US and therefore led to the election of Donald Trump in 2016.[37] Moreover, the many decades' worth of critiques that have been levelled at the 'liberal humanist subject' by conceptual work in the Euro-American humanities have made it clear that the problem with the conceptualization of this subject is that it conceives of a universal humanity unmarked by specific social identities. Of course, Puar and Eng might suggest that their point is that many social differences are now folded into conceptions of the universal human within contemporary multiculturalist liberalism. Therefore the meaning of the liberal subject has shifted and established social differences have lost their potential to anchor any radical politics. But nevertheless their critique of the 'evolution of LGBTQ+ in US identity politics' puts them actually *on the side* of liberals.

Moreover, while we would be hard-pushed to find scholars celebrating this for its relation to liberal inclusion, there have nevertheless been prominent strains of queer thought that have been interested in the categorial expansion that Eng and Puar malign. There have always been strands of queer thought that have been interested in enumerating, listing, or cataloguing forms of gender and sexual identity. To take one widely-cited and canonical example, Jack Halberstam's *Female Masculinity* (1998), even as it works to distance itself from a naïve belief in categorization, is also all about bringing new forms of masculinity into wider view. Halberstam argues for the 'production of new taxonomies', as well as for more precision in gender categories: 'The human potential for incredibly precise classification has been

---

36   See e.g. Eng and Puar, 'Introduction: Left of Queer', pp. 3–4.
37   Lilla, *The Once and Future Liberal*.

demonstrated in multiple arenas: why then do we settle for a paucity of classifications when it comes to gender?'[38] To take another canonical and widely-cited example, David Valentine's *Imagining Transgender: An Ethnography of a Category* (2007) is a critique of the forced use of the category of 'transgender' in some non-profit discourse but also an attempt to capture a wide-ranging and complex system of gender and sexual classification amongst Black and Brown sex workers in New York in the late 1990s that stands in tension with this category. The sex workers who Valentine works with cannot be assimilated to a position that just wants to celebrate exceeding identity categories though: they still adhere to 'a system of categorical orderings' even though it is organized differently to 'mainstream identity politics'.[39]

Equally, in more recent work than Halberstam's and Valentine's, scholars working on the history of sexuality have continued to be interested in narrating the emergence of apparently new forms of sexual identity. Benjamin Kahan's recent book *The Book of Minor Perverts* (2019), for example, looks back to the heterogeneous classifications and categorizations of sexology to draw parallels with how the hold of the homo/hetero binary on sexual definition has begun to erode in recent decades. Historians have conventionally dated the emergence of the homo/hetero binary that has organized dominant understandings of sexuality in the twentieth century to the end of the nineteenth century, but Kahan argues that it did not actually come to have true dominance until the 1980s and 90s, particularly after the AIDS crisis did so much work to catapult homosexuality into public consciousness. No sooner did this binary achieve this dominance than it began to erode, which Kahan credits to the emergence of queer cultures and theoretical paradigms from the 1990s, which explicitly situated themselves as being about something *more than* this binary. He lists some examples of the 'proliferation of sexual and gender identities and bodily morphologies' that have happened since the 1990s: 'trans, down low, genderqueer, asexual, etc.'[40]

---

38   Jack Halberstam, *Female Masculinity* (Durham, NC: Duke University Press, 1998), pp. 8 and 27.

39   David Valentine, *Imagining Transgender: An Ethnography of Category* (Durham, NC: Duke University Press, 2007), p. 136.

40   Benjamin Kahan, *The Book of Minor Perverts: Sexology, Etiology, and the Emergences of Sexuality* (Chicago: University of Chicago Press, 2019), p. 136.

If we wanted to look for it, there is a yet more extensive minor history of scholarship in the field that has resisted its anti-identitarianism. For example, Heather Love's *Feeling Backward* (2007) argues for holding onto rather than jettisoning apparently spoiled identities: 'We need an account of identity that allows us to think through its contradictions and to trace its effects.'[41] In his recent book *Categorically Famous* (2019), Guy Davidson recovers some of the importance of identity categories to queer life, citing work by Rita Felski, Michael Snediker, Jeff Solomon, Christopher Reed, and Christopher Castiglia that indicates a 'disenchantment with anti-identitarianism' in the process.[42] In my own recently published writing, I have noted how, throughout the 1990s and early 2000s, a range of scholars in lesbian studies, Black studies, and cultural materialism pushed back against what was perceived as the postmodern anti-identitarianism of queer thought.[43] Despite this minor history, and, indeed, as the continued existence of work in this vein implies, the dominant image of the field that endures is an anti-identitarian one. As I indicated above, I think it is a fair claim to say that no one with a real familiarity with the field would argue that its primary orientation was in fact *towards* identity. Standing against identity remains a powerful norm in the field.

But perhaps we can also specify this claim further, as it seems from the summary above that not all forms of identity have been seen as equally problematic. Rather than completely rejecting identity, foundational anti-identitarian work in queer theory was formed in relation to a specific range of identity categories. To return to the work of Judith Butler, for example, we are reminded of how it is the category 'woman' that is the foil for their problematization of identity in *Gender Trouble*. Contemporaneous work by Butler turned to the categories of *gay* and, more prominently, *lesbian* to argue that these identities run the risk of reproducing the activity of 'regulatory regimes'.[44] These categories

---

41   Heather Love, *Feeling Backward: Loss and the Politics of Queer History* (Cambridge, MA: Harvard University Press, 2007), p. 44.

42   Guy Davidson, *Categorically Famous: Literary Celebrity and Sexual Liberation in 1960s America* (Stanford, CA: Stanford University Press, 2019), pp. 15–16.

43   Ben Nichols, 'Library Fever: Lesbian Memoir and the Sexual Politics of Order', *Textual Practice*, early online publication (2022), p. 3 <https://doi.org/10.1080/0950236X.2022.2032303>.

44   Judith Butler, 'Imitation and Gender Insubordination', in *Inside/Out: Lesbian Theories, Gay Theories*, ed. by Diana Fuss (London: Routledge, 1991), pp. 13–31.   .

should therefore be the 'very rallying points for a certain resistance to classification and to identity as such'.[45] At the same time, Butler puts forward a view of identity as inherently unstable: the repetition necessary to perform stable identity also results in inevitable instability. For Butler, the non-negotiable fact of this instability is also the source of political and ethical value. If this instability is so intrinsic to identity then we might ask whether we really should have been resisting identity all these years, or actually embracing it more strongly. That is, there seems to be some confusion between the account of what identity is (namely, inherently unstable) and the need to object to it. While, as above, Butler later clarifies that she sees no reason not to use identity, in this influential moment the notion of stable lesbian and gay identities comes to seem perhaps like a foil or rhetorical move — a set of straw categories. Indeed, as far as I am aware, no other area of study focused on social identity has been founded in this way on displacing what might be seen as its organizing identities. Where anti-identitarianism endures in queer thought now, is it the continuing legacy of a foundational move to problematize a very specific set of categories?

To conclude in a yet more speculative and also anecdotal register, I see a similar dynamic also in experiences of teaching in gender and sexuality studies. In this context, there seem to me to be some inconsistencies in what is recognized as *identity*. On the one hand, the critiques of identity categories and labels that have been made in gender and sexuality studies fields are popular and readily understood. Students will happily critique apparently shallow 'identity politics'. And yet they also frequently make identitarian claims — say, in the name of genderqueer asexual people, or neurodivergent pansexuals — that they do not recognize as such. I have no investment in critiquing these students, but I am interested in how they do not see these kinds of claims in relation to 'identity' or as representing the kind of identitarianism that they also critique. Perhaps there is even something about the rhetorical charge of the word 'identity' that makes it a concept one cannot see oneself in relation to.

What gets imagined as an identity and what does not? It seems easy to critique 'woman', 'lesbian', 'gay', 'transgender' as identities, but

---

45   Ibid., p. 16.

genderqueer asexual, neurodivergent pansexual, or other forms of identity do not register as such. These are surely only *not* identities if you imagine that only a specific range of categories should bear the burden of being identities. In her recent essay 'In Defense of Identity Politics' (2018), Suzanna Danuta Walters notes what I take to be a related dynamic at work in critiques of 'identity politics'. She argues that critics of 'identity politics' approaches (who in Walters's account are mostly straight white men) often imagine that only those who are marginalized due to race, class, gender, or sexuality actually have an identity. In making this move, Walters argues, these straight white men somehow get to imagine themselves as not having an identity and as being free from its confines.[46] But in my speculative and anecdotal take on the fate of 'identity' in gender and sexuality fields here, it is by no means always just white, cis, straight males who get to not have an identity, or who can imagine themselves as being free from its restrictions.

POST-ANTI-IDENTITARIANISM?

If at one moment in the early 1990s in Anglophone (and primarily US-based) academia, it seemed particularly urgent to step outside of identity categories, then this does not seem to have become the dominant way of understanding in contemporary gender and sexual life. Part of the critique of identity categories in queer scholarship has been that they in some sense *reduce* something more properly considered irreducible. The proliferation of identity options that I have surveyed in this short piece would not seem to contradict this: indeed, a curious genre that has emerged in relation to this proliferation is that of the *information genre* that mimes prominent reductive, standardizing information forms, such as dictionaries and A-Zs. The expansion or proliferation of gender and sexual categories seems to have drawn the popular queer imagination towards genres that, I have suggested, are reductive. The point has not been to try to disprove this reductiveness, but rather to stage it as a notable area to think about in making, to cite the title of this volume, *The Case for Reduction.*

Moreover, my claim has been that considering ways of living gender and sexual life now prompts us to reconsider the prominent

---

46   Suzanna Danuta Walters, 'In Defense of Identity Politics', pp. 476–77.

anti-identitarianism of gender and sexuality studies as a field. Even if identity categories reduce, they do not seem to be going away. I have used the current proliferation of identities as the ground for considering the significant seam of anti-identitarianism in queer theory in particular and to ask whether such a theory remains adequate. The proliferation of identity categories has also been an occasion to look back at the history of the field for non-anti-identitarian histories. In light of theoretical models that foregrounded the inherent and necessary instability of all identity, it can perhaps be difficult to recover who exactly is supposed to have had a fixed identity anyway. Through historicizing anti-identitarianism, we can also see that it is specific identity categories that formed the crucibles for anti-identitarian thought or that were presented or styled as performing a greater fixity and reductiveness. In this history of the field, it was particular identities that were implanted with this fixity to form the foils for the anti-identitarian moves of early queer thought.

If we are not necessarily 'post' anti-identitarianism, as if we had experienced some great paradigm shift, then it could nevertheless at least be time to think of the 'post' in my title as a gesture of historicization, or rethinking and reflection. Perhaps the identitarianism of queer life now might encourage us to pause and shift attention from an opposition to identity, to continue to think about the manifold attachments to identity that might exist and what they each might mean. To cite the words of Heather Love again, 'We need an account of identity that allows us to think through its contradictions and to trace its effects.' In some ways, the lists of new identities that I have surveyed prompt us to do this. In the mixture of proliferation and reduction that they put into play, in confronting us with a sheer variety of categories, they encourage us to do the work of figuring out the 'effects' of each one. If there have been good reasons to be sceptical about the use of identity in certain contexts, does this mean that this scepticism should be applied unilaterally? Perhaps our current moment encourages us to ask or return to this question. In the process, we get a new perspective not just on the expanding contemporary forms of gender and sexuality, but also on those historical categories of identity that have been so vexed and contested in the history of the field.

Nothing Beyond the Name
Towards an Eclipse of Listening in the Psychotherapeutic Enterprise

SARATH JAKKA

A theory, in its quest to name, disclose, explain, resolve, or reduce, is suspended between a wish and a promise. The wishes, desires, and dreams that anticipate a particular theory are neither made fully explicit at its outset nor do they need to bear an agreeable relation with what that theoretical enterprise promises in terms of the visions that are conjured, or the consequences that are enabled. This disjunction, between the wishes that give rise to a particular theoretical reduction and the horizons of wish-fulfilment they chart out, anticipates other disjunctions to come. When these reductions and narratives participate in their milieus, their fate becomes uncertain as they are often appropriated, misappropriated, reappropriated, or even de-appropriated in ways that could never be fully anticipated. In their attempts to defend themselves, whether in disputes with the interrogators that surround them, or the ever-looming possibility of obsolescence, most theoretical projects are haunted by dreams for an enduring relevance, for posterity, a need for either permanence, objectivity, invulnerability, or inscrutability. This haunting is all the more the case for theories that lay claim to being sciences of the will, of fear, of dreams or desires.

FREUD'S TABLET, RUMPELSTILTSKIN'S BARTER: DREAMING SENSE, NAMING NONSENSE

In a letter dated 16 August 1895 to Wilhelm Fliess, Sigmund Freud recalls with amusement his son Oliver's trait for 'concentrating on what is immediately ahead'.[1] Freud recounts: 'An enthusiastic aunt asked him, "Oli, what do you want to become?" He replied, "Aunt, five years, in February."'[2] Oli's aspirations might be said to carry the unwitting humility of tautology, an ambition with neither project nor object, a satisfaction with being itself. In that very year, however, Freud the father harboured theories and ambitions of a very different sort. In another letter to Fliess dated 12 June 1900, Freud shares this dream:

> Do you suppose that someday one will read on a marble tablet on this house:
>
> > Here, on July 24, 1895,
> > the secret of the dream
> > revealed itself to Dr. Sigm. Freud[3]

Five years after the epiphany regarding the nature of dreams had first visited him, Freud was dreaming grand visions of the reputation and legacy that would be attached to his theories. He had a strong sense that through his insight into dreams, he would be able to formulate a theory that would address questions fundamental to all of psychology such as the nature of defences, wishes, needs, memory, repetition, symptoms, etc. But the intensities that set in motion the elaboration of his theory of dreams were not merely governed by the wish to discover and explain that which had not yet been named. His professional and social location, the status that might accrue to the victor who furnishes explanations to certain concerns, and the contests that framed such a quest played important roles in brewing the dreams that in turn fuelled Freud's theory of dreams.

---

1   Sigmund Freud, 'Letter to Wilhelm Fliess, Bellevue, August 16, 1895', in *The Complete Letters of Sigmund Freud to Wilhelm Fliess, 1887–1904*, ed. and trans. by Jeffrey Moussaieft Masson (London: Belknap Press, 1985), p. 136.

2   Ibid.

3   Freud, 'Letter to Wilhelm Fliess, June 12, 1900', in *The Complete Letters*, p. 417.

The atmosphere of competition, collaboration (and condescension) can be sensed in an earlier letter to Fliess dated 16 May 1897, in which Freud admits:

> After all, we do not want to be the only intelligent people in the world; what makes sense to us must also be to the liking of a few capable fellows [...] I spared myself informing you of two miserable critiques that have come to my knowledge since Nuremberg — one of them by an assistant of Chrobak. You can calmly put up with it.[4]

In both this letter and the one written three years later — when he imagines being commemorated in a tablet — Freud can barely contain his excitement over the novelty and certainty of his conclusions on dreams, especially in contrast with the existing psychological literature. In both letters, Freud expresses his glee for possessing the secrets of the psyche, of knowing that which no else knows, by equating himself with another bearer of secrets from German folklore, the imp Rumpelstiltskin.

In the 1897 letter, Freud writes: 'Now I have finished and am thinking about the dream [book] again. I have been looking into the literature and feel like the Celtic imp: "Oh, how glad I am that no one, no one knows ..." No one even suspects that the dream is not nonsense but wish fulfillment.'[5] In the 1900 letter, Freud is concerned about not having enough cases for the elaboration and proof of his theory, but remains excited over the main thesis regarding dreams and the process of wish fulfilment, repeating his allusion to the gleeful imp while specifying the existing literature on dreams, over which his own theory would be a definite improvement:

> So far there is little prospect of it. But when I read the more recent psychological books (Mach's *Analyse der Empfindungen*, 2nd ed., Kroell's *Aufbau der Seele*, and the likes), all of which have a direction similar to my work, and see what they have to say about the dream, I am indeed pleased, like the dwarf in the fairy tale, because 'the princess does not know'.[6]

---

4   Freud, 'Letter to Wilhelm Fliess, May 16, 1897', in *The Complete Letters*, p. 243.
5   Ibid.
6   Ibid., p. 417.

The value of revealing 'the secret of the dream' would command the attention it did precisely because dreams are ambivalent interlopers that trouble any assumption of transparency that might accompany wakeful memory and knowledge. Dreams are perennially tantalizing in the depths they generate but never fully disclose. It is only fitting then that accompanying Freud's attempt to map dreamwork, to name and make sense of what the prevailing science considered nonsense, are allusions to the ambivalence and tensions that are native to theoretical ambitions. Like Rumpelstiltskin who had the secret talent to spin straw into gold, Freud pursued his talents to spin the nonsense of dreams into sense. Like the imp he references, he too seeks a reward in order to make sense of his own work, in this case imagining a marble tablet as symbolic recompense.

One of the ironic aspects of dreams is that in their very moment-ariness, they sometimes present a *total* clarity or resolution. A similar irony can be said to haunt Freud's case of dreaming a tablet, in which he imagines a horizon of permanence for his theory of dreams — phe-nomena that are dynamic, ambivalent, and unpredictable. Inscribed in the imaginary tablet, the labour of Freud's thought was underwritten as a property that was to be attached to the reputation accompanying his proper name. In this proprietary impulse — seeking for oneself that which belongs to no one else — we see other resonances between the wish for property that undergirds Freud's theoretical impulse and Rumpelstiltskin's mischievous barter.

Rumpelstiltskin's barter involves the secrecy of his name, which 'the princess does not know'. If the princess were able to discover and state his name, she would not have to give her child up to the imp's ownership. Rumpelstiltskin delights in his anonymity and sets up a game through which he exercises his obscurity as a form of power over the other more sovereign forms of power, such as that represented by the princess. Freud too delights in the obscure status of his insights, only grudgingly allowing for the possibility that others too were worthy enough to participate in his commerce of ideas, that Fliess and he were not 'the only intelligent people in the world', that 'what makes sense to us must also be to the liking of a few capable fellows'. Here we can sense a fundamental ambiguity involved in protecting (or producing) a secret whose value was tied to its transactions with the larger world. Disclosing the secret, it seems, could simultaneously increase one's weight or position in the world (this weight and location in the guise of a tablet) and do away with the secret's exclusivity — thus the anxiety around one's symbolic property becoming common knowledge. It's perhaps this volatility entailed in keeping secrets that leads Rumpelstiltskin, leaping and hopping on one leg, to cry:

> Still no one knows it just the same,
> That Rumpelstiltskin is my name.[7]

The imp is singing and dancing outside his home in the back of beyond, between the far end of a forest and a mountain, delighting in having released his secret aloud, safe in the assumption that there is no one to overhear it. But unknown to him, his rhyme is overheard by a name-seeking informant dispatched by the princess. Enraged that he has lost the game and the reward, Rumpelstiltskin, in a violent tantrum, stamps himself deep into the earth, seizing one of his feet to tear himself right down the middle into two. This act of splitting is the consequence of the whimsical risk to announce an unascertained name and the unanticipated listening that renders its secrecy untenable. Can we take this split that concludes the tale as being about the mutually constitutive yet agonistic relation between naming and listening? If Freud associated this tale with his own theoretical ambitions, can this casual reference also be revealing of a more fundamental, disagreeable yet generative tension between two modes of reduction — naming and listening — that frame the practice and theory of psychotherapy as a whole? In its trafficking of names, a psychology wishes to listen to and reveal the workings of the mind and its location in the social world, to trace the origins of mental disorders while promising programs for the recovery of mental and social health. To what extent then does a psychology's reductive regime of naming impinge upon or distance itself from a listening defined by neither wish nor project, a listening intrinsic to psychotherapeutic praxis, which might even need to actively subtract, unname, de-educate, or decreate from the proprietorial impulse of naming?

---

7   Brothers Grimm, 'The Fairytale of Rumpelstiltskin', *Guardian*, trans. by Joyce Crick, 13 October 2009 <https://www.theguardian.com/books/2009/oct/13/fairytales-rumpelstiltskin-brothers-grimm> [accessed 12 Jan 2022].

CRYSTALS, PRECIPITATES, FLAMES: POWERS OF NAMING AND
LISTENING

Fania Pascal recounts an episode in which Ludwig Wittgenstein, pick-
ing up a volume of Grimm's fairy tales, reads out

> with awe in his voice: 'Ach, wie gut ist dass niemand weiss
> | Dass ich Rumpelstilzchen heiss.' [Oh, how good it is that
> nobody knows | That I am called Rumpelstiltskin] 'Profound.
> Profound,' he said. I liked 'Rumpelstiltskin', understood that
> the strength of the dwarf lay in his name being unknown to
> humans.[8]

If Pascal understood the imp's strength to reside in his name not
being known, what might these powers be? Since the subject of such
a question is negative in character, perhaps it is better addressed by
an inverse query, by first asking what underlies the power of naming.
Do the powers of naming or listening consist in the different types
of reduction that are peculiar to them? In *The Psychoanalysis of Fire*,
Gaston Bachelard writes: 'In the field of psychoanalysis the naming of
things is often sufficient to cause a precipitate; before the name, there
was only an amorphous, troubled, disturbed solution; after the name,
crystals are seen at the bottom of the liquid.'[9] For Bachelard, psychoanalytic naming is imagined as a process of reduction, the forming of
a precipitate where before there was only a troubled medium. Adding
elements of symmetry, clarity, and reflectivity to the gravitational pull
of the name, he further specifies the psychoanalytic name as reducing
amorphous matter into crystals. In the related images of the precipitate and the crystal, a transaction is carried out where something that
is 'amorphous, troubled, disturbed' is transformed into a thing with
gravity and clarity, the latter seeming to be a more desirable good than
the former.[10] But are there hidden costs to such a transaction? Does
the sovereign act of naming displace or violate the obscure powers of
the imp?

---

8   Fania Pascal, 'Wittgenstein: A Personal Memoir', in *Wittgenstein: Personal Recollec-
     tions*, ed. by Norman Malcolm and Rush Rhees (Oxford: Oxford University Press,
     1984), pp. 12–50 (pp. 19–20).
9   Gaston Bachelard, *The Psychoanalysis of Fire*, trans. by Alan C. M. Ross (London:
     Routledge and Kegan Paul, 1964), pp. 39–40.
10   Ibid., p. 40.

In his 'Introduction' to *Language and Learning: The Debate Between Jean Piaget and Noam Chomsky*, Massimo Piattelli-Palmarini visualizes the two prevailing ontological commitments to how biological life emerges, as 'the *crystal* on the one side (invariance of specific structures) and the *flame* on the other (constancy of external forms in spite of relentless internal agitation)'.[11] Piattelli-Palmarini identifies the drive for 'invariance' as stemming from a crystal ontology in the history of science (and its related extrapolations as they carry over to the psychological and social sciences). If we were to restrict ourselves to the crystallization or reduction involved in naming as necessarily involving invariance, even if only in the preliminary act of the assignation of a specific symbol, it would be adequate to understand how naming tends towards the foreclosure of listening. Here, the different senses of the word precipitate — such as the act of transforming what Bachelard terms 'amorphous, troubled, disturbed' into the crystals that gather in the bottom of the solution — can illuminate the hidden costs of naming's intolerance to variance.[12] If to name is to precipitate, and to precipitate is to 'cause (an event or series of events) to happen quickly, suddenly, or unexpectedly', 'to plunge; to descend steeply or vertically', or 'to fall suddenly or violently *into* a particular state or condition', then naming is an event which contains within it violence, haste, and the violence of haste.[13] How does the name engage in violent haste? Naming's invariance need not refer to what Piattelli-Palmarini identifies as the microscopic crystalline underworld 'that dictates its laws to the macroscopic' nor need it be an unchanging referent or meaning, given the flux and transformations that define the fate of a name.[14] In the names instituted by a discipline like psychology that seeks to preserve its expertise, invariance is to be seen in the desire for property relations, the desire to foreclose in advance who gets to interpret and operate upon a certain set of concerns.

---

11   Massimo Piattelli-Palmarini, 'Introduction', in *Language and Learning: The Debate between Jean Piaget and Noam Chomsky*, ed. by Piattelli-Palmarini (Cambridge, MA: Harvard University Press, 1980), pp. 1–20 (p. 6).

12   Bachelard, *The Psychoanalysis of Fire*, p. 40.

13   'Precipitate, v.', in *OED Online* (Oxford: Oxford University Press, 2020) <https://www.oed.com/view/Entry/149643> [accessed 2 January 2022].

14   Piattelli-Palmarini, 'Introduction', p. 7.

In the institutionalization of a psychology, its shield-bearers enter into a contract by which what is 'amorphous, troubled, disturbed' is prone to being plunged violently into the rules that govern the keeping of its names. Naming's invariance then is not so much a matter of meaning but one of sovereignty.

THE DOUBLE-EDGED MAGIC OF NAMING AND THE FATE OF LISTENING

In his *Brown Book* Wittgenstein remarks that 'one could almost imagine that naming was done by a sacramental act and that this produced some magic relation between the name and the thing'.[15] The magic of the name is in line with the magic that characterizes the instituting powers of the law or of property, an announcement of control that comes to fundamentally determine or create our social worlds.

Another aspect of naming's magic consists in providing visibility, form, and consistency to what previously was either non-existent or only fleetingly and obscurely registered, a basin of attraction around which the surrounding realities it invokes can congregate and interact. In this act of focusing, naming provides affordances for listening, an initial step in the concatenating or patterning of sequences, of bringing crystalline order to what might have seemed chaotic. Naming as an act of theorization could also be viewed as an interstitial event which in turn was precipitated by acts of patient observation and listening.

Describing the process of arriving at descriptions of the basic fixed action patterns — or IRMs (Innate Releasing Mechanisms) — that constitute instinctive behaviour in the discipline of ethology, the neuroscientist John Duncan tells us that,

> As we watch bees humming in the flowers, seagulls squabbling over scraps, or clouds of fish over a reef, the chaos of our first, casual impression is replaced by the new ethologists' vision. Now we see stable structures of behaviour elicited by consistent sensory events, and complex, ever-changing wholes built up through assembly of these fixed, constantly recurring fragments.[16]

---

15   Ludwig Wittgenstein, *The Blue and Brown Books* (Oxford: Blackwell, 1998), p. 172.
16   John Duncan, *How Intelligence Happens* (New Haven, CT: Yale University Press, 2010), p. 5.

Naming's agonistic relation with listening consists in privileging certain forms of listening while obscuring or actively excluding or destroying others. Carefully observing and watching insects and animals to draw conclusions about their essential character might involve simultaneously participating in a larger paradigm whose confidence and commitment to identifying fundamental patterns help create technologies, industries, and economies that are involved in the elimination of insect and animal populations.

How are we to reckon then with the double-edged power of naming and the challenges it presents to listening? It might be useful to consider here the epistemology of early Chinese thought that takes pains to avoid a thorough commitment to naming's relation to a referential reality. In his careful elaboration of coherence (or *Li*) in *Ironies of Oneness and Difference*, Brook Ziporyn observes that early Chinese philosophy invoked an epistemology that 'functions on the basis of only names and stuffs; no other entities, such as properties, attributes, essences, ideas, universals, or particulars, are necessary'.[17] What Ziporyn indicates through the term 'stuffs' is the manner in which the coherence conveyed by a name emerges simultaneously in the backdrop of its incoherence, of that which is nameless. As he explains:

> The valued and disvalued, the intelligible and its own undermining, emerge simultaneously, come forth together (同出 tongchu): when we name something, we implicitly also name with the name 'namelessness' that to which it is contrasted, from which it emerges, against which it is nameable. The positing of any valued coherence is also the positing of its own prior and surrounding incoherence (its indiscernibility prior to its emergence, and its undiscoverability in the contrasted background around it), which is what grounds it and makes its presence possible. The emergence of the coherence and the incoherence, these opposites, are aspects of a single event. Every coherence (name, value) has a double meaning: it names both the coherence and the ultimate incoherence with which it is coherent, and it is this coherence (togetherness) of the coherence and the incoherence that alone makes any coherence coherent (intelligible).[18]

---

17   Brook Ziporyn, *Ironies of Oneness and Difference: Coherence in Early Chinese Thought; Prolegomena to the Study of Li* (Albany: State University of New York Press, 2012), p. 51.

18   Ibid., p. 145.

Of value in an epistemological attitude that practises according primacy to the simultaneous emergence of names *and* the namelessness that serves as its backdrop, is the constant tending to the *ways* in which the former produces the latter and the ironic recognition that the latter is prefigured in the former.

It can be argued that the label 'namelessness' itself is a name, subject to all the problems associated with naming. Ziporyn explains that the horizons indicated by the Daoist notions of namelessness, incoherence, and the disvalued 'are simultaneously both within and without the system of names, simultaneously named and unnamed'.[19] As he elaborates:

> They are surds, which, in attempting to mean what is no part of the whole system of names, actually end up meaning both (a) 'the unvalued part' of the whole, the background that is left over after the named part has been picked out, and also (b) 'the entire whole, which is subsequently divided into named and unnamed'.[20]

Were it to be merely an abstract concern, then the named namelessness could be seen as an act of bracketing away a noise, or an inconvenience that interrupts the coherence being sought. In the context of a psychotherapeutic paradigm, however, it could indicate a realm of suspense that is to be actively embraced and nurtured in the various dimensions of living praxis that come to define it. In his lecture 'Psychoanalysis and Cybernetics, or on the Nature of Language', Jacques Lacan is alive to these ironies involved in naming and meaning, and to their intimations for the directions of psychoanalytic technique. For Lacan the backdrop of the symbolic is not one of incoherence, rather it is one of repression. He concludes his lecture by stating:

> No doubt something which isn't expressed doesn't exist. But the repressed is always there, insisting, and demanding to be. The fundamental relation of man to this symbolic order is very precisely what founds the symbolic order itself — the relation of non-being to being.

---

19   Ibid.
20   Ibid.

What insists on being satisfied can only be satisfied in recognition. The end of the symbolic process is that non-being come to be, because it has spoken.[21]

For Lacan, the ironic suspense that comes to bear between the expressed and the repressed, between the symbolic and non-being, is an attempt to answer a question he poses earlier on in the lecture: 'What is the meaning of meaning?'.[22] Such a meaning is not enclosed in a predetermined circuit where 'whatever doesn't come on time simply falls by the wayside and makes no claim on anything. This is not true for man, the scansion is alive, and whatever doesn't come on time remains in suspense. That is what is involved in repression'.[23] By foregrounding this suspense, Lacan conceives the psychoanalytic enterprise not as consisting in the imaginary horizons of 'coaptation', 'normalisation', or 'rectification' but as invested in 'following' the 'here and now'.[24] The meaning of psychoanalytic work then is not prefigured in advance, rather it's a scansion in suspense, a liveliness that is yet to arrive. If scansion here indicates a step or stress that is yet to happen, it also indicates an encounter that necessitates listening, a listening that is far from beholden to what is familiar, learnt, named, or prescribed. Listening is an organ characterized by limits and openings, at once an instrument for hearing that which is named or remembered and for seeking to reach beyond.

THE IRONIC DISCIPLINE OF LISTENING: FREUD'S EVENLY-SUSPENDED ATTENTION, THE DRONE IN HINDUSTANI CLASSICAL MUSIC

In his meditation, *Listening*, Jean-Luc Nancy makes a distinction between hearing and listening:

> If 'to hear' is to understand the sense (either in the so-called figurative sense, or in the so-called proper sense: to hear a siren,

---

21 Jacques Lacan, 'Psychoanalysis and Cybernetics, or on the Nature of Language', in *The Seminar of Jacques Lacan*, ed. by Jacques-Alain Miller (New York: Norton, 1988–), II: *The Ego in Freud's Theory and in the Technique of Psychoanalysis, 1954–1955*, trans. by Sylvana Tomaselli (1988), pp. 294–308 (p. 308).

22 Ibid., p. 307.

23 Ibid., pp. 307–08.

24 Ibid., p. 307.

a bird, or a drum is already each time to understand at least the rough outline of a situation, a context if not a text), to listen is to be straining toward a possible meaning, and consequently one that is not immediately accessible.[25]

Listening recedes where a regime of hearing dominates. The manner in which hearing for names comes to dominate a praxis of listening would in turn depend on the extent to which a paradigm of naming seeks to totalize or eclipse the backdrop of namelessness from which it issues. Listening is an ironic discipline in that it values, anticipates, and awaits what lies outside its disciplinary bounds. Regimes of expertise on the other hand are oriented towards exclusion and erasure, disciplines that either bracket away what lies outside them or are in a haste to incorporate encounters with novelty within the names that have been designated to signal its boundaries. Can we read Freud's practical recommendation of the dyadic relation between the analysand's free association and the analyst's evenly-suspended attention in the light of the struggle between naming and listening? In Freud's plain outline of the technique of evenly-suspended attention, he cautions against the dangers of what we can redescribe here as the reductive aspect of deliberate attention as might be exercised by a listener or an analyst:

> It consists simply in not directing one's notice to anything in particular and in maintaining the same 'evenly-suspended attention' (as I have called it) in the face of all that one hears. In this way we spare ourselves a strain on our attention which could not in any case be kept up for several hours daily, and we avoid a danger which is inseparable from the exercise of deliberate attention. For as soon as anyone deliberately concentrates his attention to a certain degree, he begins to select from the material before him; one point will be fixed in his mind with particular clearness and some other will be correspondingly disregarded, and in making this selection he will be following his expectations or inclinations. This, however, is precisely what must not be done. In making the selection, if he follows his expectations he is in danger of never finding anything but

---

25   Jean-Luc Nancy, *Listening*, trans. by Charlotte Mandell (New York: Fordham University Press, 2007), p. 6.

what he already knows; and if he follows his inclinations he will certainly falsify what he may perceive.[26]

Freud identifies two dangers: First, in this narrowing that characterizes listening via deliberate attention, the absorption and movement that comes with tracking one object, pursuing one line of enquiry over others, leads to the occlusion of other details and paths which we are then not in a position to evaluate. Second, if we were to keenly follow only what we deliberately attend to, we might be occupying ourselves mainly with our reflexes, or what we started out knowing or assuming, as opposed to the possibilities that lie outside our immediate reflexes and expectations.

The reduction involved in following a name then is to be supplemented or breached by another kind of reduction, the holding space of free association and evenly-suspended attention. Here, the moment of suspended attention seems to pose the question: What would it mean to listen beyond knowledge or certainty, to listen without actively assuming separability, without actively seeking to name? In this temporal imperative of psychoanalytic technique, listening becomes a mode of attunement, deconditioning, or deindividuation. The hum of awareness maintained by the analyst is conceived as not being monopolized by directed attention. Such a conception shares some of the concerns that shape the drone as conceived and encountered in Hindustani classical music. In Hindustani classical music, an instrument such as a tanpura is tasked solely with the purpose of continuously sounding a drone. Music theorists usually relate the place and function of the drone to sonic concerns in Indian philosophy. In *Music and Musical Thought in Early India*, Lewis Rowell states that the continuous drone is 'a symbolic representation of the continuum of unmanifest sound' as well as a 'subconscious attempt to externalise the universal continuum of unmanifest sound — and to imply thereby that each individual performance arises from, and returns to, the substratum of

---

26   Sigmund Freud, 'Recommendations to Physicians Practicing Psychoanalysis (1912)', in *The Standard Edition of the Complete Psychological Works of Sigmund Freud*, ed. and trans. by James Strachey and others, 24 vols (London: Hogarth, 1953-74), XVIII (1955), pp. 109–20 (pp. 111–12).

undifferentiated vital sound'.[27] By carrying over this sonic image to
the psychoanalytic setting, we can regard Freud's recommendations to
analysts as concerned with attending to manifest, conscious content
as it arises without departing from the substratum of undifferentiated
unconscious content. The dangers and tensions of directed attention
do not merely involve the limits of the bodies that participate in a
psychotherapy session, they also involve the social and cultural limits
imposed by the names and practices of psychotherapeutic disciplines
at large.

The theories, cases, and names of psychoanalytic theory (and
psychology more generally) thus occupy a perverse status by restricting the lines of inquiry it sought to open. In this perverse preoccupa-
tion with finitude, disciplinary naming strains to perpetually summon
itself with a commitment to exhaust the unthought at some future
point. Michel Foucault sees the convoluted role of finitude in the sciences of the psyche as consisting in the Icarian relation between the
cogito and the unthought. Hubert Dreyfus brings together Foucault's
insight in the following manner:

> Since he is an opaque object in the world, man's own men-
> tal content is foreign and obscure to him, yet, as source
> of all meaning, he is 'perpetually summoned towards self-
> knowledge'. If man is to be intelligible to himself, the unthought
> must ultimately be accessible to thought and dominated in ac-
> tion, yet insofar as this unthought, in its obscurity, is precisely
> the condition of possibility of thought and action it can never
> be fully absorbed into the cogito.[28]

Here naming takes on an impossible responsibility, a ceaseless obliga-
tion to summon into finitude, to keep naming so that no remainder
remains. Foucault locates this relentlessness in the Kantian injunction
for the 'limits of knowledge to provide a positive foundation for the
possibility of knowing'.[29] If naming is obsessed with the possibility of

---

27   Lewis Rowell, *Music and Musical Thought in Early India* (Chicago and London: Uni-
      versity of Chicago Press, 1992), p. 53.

28   Hubert Dreyfus, 'Foreword to the California Edition', in Michel Foucault, *Mental
      Illness and Psychology*, trans. by Alan Sheridan (Berkeley: University of California
      Press, 1987), pp. vii–xliii (p. xvii).

29   Michel Foucault, *The Order of Things: An Archaeology of the Human Sciences* [trans. by
      Alan Sheridan?] (London: Routledge, 2002), p. 345.

knowing, listening seeks the limits and effects of knowledge to provide a foundation for exploring the possibilities of not knowing. For Nancy, to listen:

> [i]s always to be on the edge of meaning, or in an edgy meaning of extremity, and as if the sound were precisely nothing else than this edge, this fringe, this margin — at least the sound that is musically listened to, that is gathered and scrutinized for itself, not, however, as an acoustic phenomenon (or not merely as one) but as a resonant meaning, a meaning whose sense is supposed to be found in resonance, and only in resonance.[30]

The dangers of reduction in disciplinary naming consist not merely in its finite character, rather its violence is contained in the desire to *totalize* its finitude. This totalizing impulse moves beyond the mere construction and elaboration of psychological theories and extends to the practices and institutions that govern a discipline at large.

LISTENING: THE UNREMARKABLE CASUALTY OF CONSILIENCE

If Freud inaugurated his work on dreams with the dream of a tablet that would cement his legacy, his wish was posthumously fulfilled. A plaque was placed in the very location he desired on 6 May 1977. By the time the tablet was installed, Aaron T. Beck had already developed the therapeutic protocol of evidence-based Cognitive Behavioural Therapy, the paradigm that would over the following decades supplant psychoanalysis as the most extensively recognized therapeutic method. A new series of names and theories now bearing the tag of science even more insistently would contend for validation, authority, and legal exclusivity. In the modern psychological sciences, a positive pursuit of finitude is set up to enact what Viktor Frankl terms a 'nothing-but-ness'.[31] The exclusionary conditions such as 'nothing-but-psychiatric drugs might be legally permitted' or 'nothing-but-empirical evidence might guide an expert diagnosis', while not being stated in such stark terms, visit those seeking relief from mental health services with stark regularity. Therapists belonging to different disciplines recognize

---

30   Nancy, *Listening*, p. 7.
31   Viktor Frankl, *The Will to Meaning: Foundations and Applications of Logotherapy* (New York: Penguin, 1988), p. 21.

these ravages of naming and have to work out idiosyncratic strategies for a listening that avoids the glare of disciplinary projects. The ravages of naming are especially seen in the pressure to arrive at a quick diagnosis. In a chapter titled 'Avoid Diagnosis (Except for Insurance Companies)', Irvin Yalom notes the current over-emphasis on diagnostic efficiency, in which 'managed-care administrators demand that therapists arrive quickly at a precise diagnosis and then proceed upon a course of brief, focused therapy that matches that particular diagnosis'.[32] As Yalom notes, diagnosis — as with any naming — often becomes a 'self-fulfilling prophecy'.[33] Yalom questions this perplexing haste, going onto wonder: 'and what therapist has not been struck by how much easier it is to make a DSM-IV diagnosis following the first interview than much later, let us say, after the tenth session, when we know a great deal more about the individual? Is this not a strange kind of science?'.[34]

What is the larger backdrop in which names are allowed to proliferate but the radical task of listening is orphaned? Could we venture a speculation into the ways in which contemporary regimes of psychological naming exile listening? These horizons are of course constructed and performed differently for the various disciplines and subdisciplines that come to identify with the name of psychology and psychotherapy. The present-day economies of interaction between the different psychological sciences are so complex that it would be difficult to construct a synthesis. Yet, the different disciplines are united in certain fundamental assumptions which may or may not be made explicit. Aside from shared methodological assumptions, such as the belief that objective psychological facts can be obtained through evidence-gathering and verification techniques, there are shared visions about how the different disciplines are related to each other as they participate in the advancement of knowledge about psychological truths, and reinforce a commitment to progress and the promise of social betterment coded in it.

---

32 Irvin D. Yalom, *The Gift of Therapy: An Open Letter to a New Generation of Therapists and their Patients* (London: HarperCollins, 2002), p. 4. Ebook.

33 Ibid., p. 5

34 Ibid.

We can find definitive statements of such shared visions in the scientific polemic of Steven Pinker. In *The Blank Slate*, Pinker counters views critical of the inherently reductionist nature of the psychological sciences by stating that a distinction needs to be made between good and bad (or as he terms it, 'greedy') forms of psychological reductionism. For Pinker, 'greedy' or 'destructive' reductionism consists in 'trying to explain a phenomenon in terms of its smallest or simplest constituents', such as the beliefs or narratives served to research grant agencies that 'breakthroughs in education, conflict resolution, and other social concerns' can be obtained 'by studying the biophysics of neural membranes or the molecular structure of the synapse'.[35] To be insisted on and defended is the good or 'hierarchical' reductionism which 'consists not of replacing one field of knowledge with another but of *connecting* or *unifying* them. The building blocks used by one field are put under a microscope by another. The black boxes get opened; the promissory notes get cashed'.[36] Pinker provides examples from geography and linguistics to evoke this grand vision of consilience where 'an isolated geographer would have to invoke magic to move the continents, and an isolated physicist could not have predicted the shape of South America'.[37] For Pinker, mental life, given its location between the realms of culture and biology, also 'has to be understood at several levels of analysis, not just the lowest one'.[38] The insights from various levels of psychology — neural, evolutionary, cultural, social, and clinical — are imagined for the most part as mutually coherent, comprehensible, and cooperative. Pinker's view of cooperative and coordinating scientific knowledge systems is a utopian vision that foregrounds consilience. Such a view is better understood as a desire for a total resolution that sustains the purposiveness of scientific actors rather than an account of the way in which psychological and scientific disciplines have come to operate.

In an interview for a science magazine, the neuroscientist Eve Marder provides a more credible articulation of the ways in which the

35   Steven Pinker, *The Blank Slate: Modern Denial of Human Nature* (New York: Penguin, 2003), pp. 69–70.
36   Pinker, *The Blank Slate*, p. 70.
37   Ibid.
38   Ibid.

various levels and sub-disciplines of psychological enquiry are placed in relation to each other. Marder's account of the relations between different scientific levels emphasizes ambiguity and opacity rather than the transparency that might be promised by the ambitions of a panoramic view. Unlike Pinker, who sees the hierarchies of various levels of psychological reduction as based on connection and unification, Marder conceives of the multiple levels as arranged on an 'ambiguity hierarchy' where each level forms around 'how much ambiguity you can tolerate in the data, or the kind of data, or the kind of questions you can ask'.[39] For Marder, the total picture of psychology is imagined as one where 'individual sciences layer themselves into that increasing web of ambiguity, as you get further from the structure with single ion channels and closer to human language'.[40] Scientific actors employ different versions of these visions of scientific totality depending on what makes for good research practice or what gives their activities a sense of larger social purpose. Deftly handling ambiguity is a necessity for crafting and adapting to the intricacies of an experiment while certitude and juridical rectitude allows one to maintain either a sense of a higher purpose or a position of epistemic authority.

In this fog between opacity and transparency, the burgeoning names and explanations that make up the various psychological sciences are allowed to expand unfettered, maintaining flexibility where the cyclical production of the research industry is concerned but developing rigidity at the legal, vocational, and scientific gates of states and corporations. If scientific-psychological authority is amassed around exclusionary mechanisms that act as gatekeepers for what counts as a legitimate psychotherapeutic insight or intervention, then the radical unknowing and waiting that is listening is either neglected or domesticated. The dominance of the psychological sciences in determining what counts for therapeutic care are mainly guaranteed by the concrescence of contradictions rather than a total consensus regarding consilience. Funding bodies, national health systems, and insurance companies are incentivized to

---

39   Steven Strogatz, Interview, 'Eve Marder on the Crucial Resilience of Neurons', *Quanta Magazine*, 17 May 2021 <https://www.quantamagazine.org/eve-marder-on-the-crucial-resilience-of-neurons-20210517/> [accessed 13 April 2022].

40   Ibid.

prefer therapeutic models that emphasize quantitative proof and outcomes. Meanwhile the psychological scientific establishments are able to regard their dominance as being due not so much to the diktats of administrative managerialism as to the objective rigour of their truths. In this concrescent wound that is opened up by bureaucratic indifference and psychology's physics-envy, listening lingers unnurtured. Listening in the psychotherapeutic enterprise is in many respects a subterranean activity, one that has to carry on despite the evidentiary injunctions of a particular disciplinary assemblage. Listening occupies a condition of exile and like any exilic condition is allowed to continue obscurely, timidly, until even this interstitial dwelling is threatened with further violence.

Reduction in Computer Music
Bodies, Temporalities, and Generative Computation
FEDERICA BUONGIORNO

PREMISE

'I think most musicians working with electronics are probably not very satisfied with the state of electronic music today, and the crucial missing element is the body'.[1] Bob Ostertag made this observation in his 2002 article 'Human Bodies, Computer Music', and to some extent, twenty years later we are still facing the very same problem. As a result of this 'crucial missing element', the concept or idea of composition has gained priority over execution, so 'virtuosity has been out of fashion' for some time now: all those steps between the artist's body and the final outcome, mediated by computers and digital technologies, tend to render invisible what musicians physically do onstage.[2]

In the age of codes and pervasive computing, the way our body interacts with reality needs to be reconceptualized: As Mark B. N. Hansen puts it, the body can be referred to as a 'body-in-code', meaning 'a

---

1   Bob Ostertag, 'Human Bodies, Computer Music', *Leonardo Music Journal*, 12 (2002), pp. 11–14 (p. 11).

2   Ibid. As Dani Deahl notes, performing electronic music live basically means having two options: 'stand behind a table with a bunch of gear and knobs and faders, or play a backing track and sing on top'. See Dani Deahl, 'Electronic Music Has a Performance Problem, and This Artist is Trying to Solve It', *The Verge*, 5 April 2019 <https://www.theverge.com/2019/4/5/18277345/chagall-van-den-berg-performance-sensors-gloves-motion-tracking-suit> [accessed 9 November

body whose (still primary) constructive and creative power is expanded through new interactional possibilities offered by the coded programs of "artificial reality".[3] Thus, the body-in-code is 'submitted to *and consti-tuted by* an unavoidable and empowering technical deterritorialization — [it is] a body whose embodiment is realized, *and can only be realized*, in conjunction with technics'.[4] The modes of this type of embodiment are particularly clear in contemporary electronic music, which heavily relies on different kinds of (digital) technology in order to be produced and performed and which, as we shall see, can also employ genera-tive computation for sound production. Computer music represents an interesting field to reflect on the problems related to human-machine interaction: 'the twentieth century sets the stage for a new intensified kind of musical inquiry, which contributes to a new techno-embodied form of artistic inquiry and creativity.'[5] It is precisely this 'new techno-embodied form' that I wish to explore in this contribution.

2021]. For some artists neither of these options is acceptable. For instance, Chagall van den Berg (a musician and performer from the Netherlands) claims that: 'Either it was going to be real and live, but boring to watch and distant from the audience, or I'd play a recording and be able to dance around onstage. Dancing around and being one with the audience was way more appealing, but the musician in me really didn't like the idea of singing along to a track. So I had a dilemma' (quoted by Deahl). Deahl comments: 'This dilemma van den Berg faced is a problem many DIY and electronic artists encounter — how do you incorporate movement and expressiveness when you essentially perform standing at a desk, using an interface the audience will likely never see? And then make it interesting?'. One might furthermore ask how to involve the audience in a counter-intuitive set based on acousmatic listening, where the audience has no intuition of the source of sound and cannot correlate the movements to the sonic outcome. Van den Berg proposed a high-tech solution: she 'performs wearing motion-tracking gloves and a full-body suit covered in sensors, which, during this [...] performance, not only control a projection of a digital avatar that appears behind her, but also control nearly every instrument and effect in the music and her voice. As she moves across the stage, her avatar, floating in space, moves in sync. [...] Every hand and body movement has cause and effect, crafting a pop-infused dreamscape that's mesmerizing to watch' (ibid.).

3   Mark B. N. Hansen, *Bodies in Code: Interfaces with Digital Media* (London: Routledge, 2006), p. 38.

4   Ibid, p. 20; emphasis in the original.

5   Joshua B. Mailman, 'Cybernetic Phenomenology of Music, Embodied Speculative Realism, and Aesthetics-Driven Techné for Spontaneous Audio-Visual Expression', *Perspectives of New Music*, 54.1 (2016), pp. 5–95 (p. 7). The technology of any era tends to expand the instrumentalism of music, as observed by Pauline Oliveros with her remark that 'every instrument is a prosthesis' — Oliveros also coined the term 'deep listening' in 1989, to describe the practice of radical attentiveness in listening to experimental compositions. See the record by Pauline Oliveros, Stuart Dempster, Panaiotis, *Deep Listening* (Important, 473, 2020: reissue).

1. BODIES, INSTRUMENTS, AND TECHNOLOGIES

Before computer music, compositions could never be perfectly timed due to the limits of human accuracy. It was part of virtuosity to work around these limits, around imperfections that made each piece and each execution something unique. With the advent of digital technology, processes that up until then had been physically executed with analog synthesizers could be translated into a mathematical, exact computer language. This meant an unprecedented precision in timing beats. As Ostertag noted, composing now means pre-setting and organizing the connections and parameters of synths, while performing a composition means executing these pre-arranged sets of parameters by intervening in the evolution of the musical process and altering those parameters while performing live. But if one plays by operating on automatic processes, the performer's input is radically *reduced* because her body barely moves and virtuosity is not necessarily a requirement.[6] However, there is something fundamental that computer music still shares with traditional music: the negotiation with instruments, which is pretty much a physical — meaning embodied — process, even if those instruments are now computers.

In a 2013 article, Mark Fell tells an interesting story, which dates back to 1987. In that year, Spanky and DJ Pierre — a duo of producers also known as Phuture — purchased a Roland TB303, 'a more or less ignored little synthesizer known for its astonishingly bad imitation of bass guitar'.[7] They had no idea of how to use the instrument, which came without a manual. They experimented with the synth, simply starting 'to turn the knobs', and the result of this process was the making of 'Acid Tracks', i.e. the first Acid House record in the history of music. It turns out that Phuture reversed the process of composition: there was no priority of the concept over the execution, it was all

---

6   Ostertag, 'Human Bodies, Computer Music', p. 13. Of course, this is not always true, as Ostertag observes: in 1919 Leon Theremin created the 'theremin', an instrument capable of producing sound by employing two oscillators at non-audible radio frequencies, so as to create a differential tone controlled through changes of the electric capacitance (ibid., p. 13). This allows for virtuosity, though the instrument remains very limited, since it can play only one timbre.

7   Mark Fell, 'Collateral Damage', *The Wire*, January 2013 <https://www.thewire.co.uk/in-writing/essays/collateral-damage-mark-fell> [accessed 2 November 2021].

about using the instrument with no *idea* of how to do it, engaging in a physical and practical relationship with it. In a way, they became synth 'virtuosi'. In his article, Fell contrasts this way of proceeding with that of Thomas Dolby, a supporter of a completely different conception of composing — one that prioritizes, again, the idea over the execution. In an interview for British television back in the 1980s he was asked to describe his ideal synthesizer, and he replied: 'I sit at the synthesizer, I imagine any sound, the synthesizer makes the sound and then I play it.'[8] This is quite a demiurgic way of conceiving the relation with the instrument, which is just a passive tool that executes the musician's ideas — no embodied negotiation here, but rather a matter of pure imagination.

As Fell notes, technology should not be seen just as a form of mediation or even as an obstacle for creativity and expression: it should be considered 'part of a wider context within which creative activity happens.'[9] I would argue that there are two mutually related conditions here that are phenomenologically relevant to fully understanding the potential of embodied negotiation with instrumentation. The first condition was already mentioned (albeit not developed) by Fell in his 2013 article — it is the notion of 'structural coupling', which comes from Humberto Maturana and Francisco Varela's theory of autopoiesis. The second condition is the radical relativization of passivity and activity theorized by Edmund Husserl in his late writings (in the 1920s) on passive syntheses.

2. PHENOMENOLOGICAL EXPLANATIONS: STRUCTURAL COUPLING AND PASSIVE SYNTHESES

In a 2018 interview, Italian producer and musician Caterina Barbieri described her own musical composition process in these terms:

> You are immersed in the sound and the sound is at the same time inside and outside of you. And you cannot tell the difference, because you become that sound and that sound becomes you [...]. I really appreciate the music that involves me not only as a cultural subject. The music that forces me to leave

8   Ibid.
9   Ibid.

behind my subjectivity and become an object myself, fused together with the sound — the music that makes me surrender to the power of sound and makes my ego die a little.[10]

What Barbieri is describing here is precisely a form of 'structural coupling'. In their 1972 book *Autopoiesis and Cognition*, Maturana and Varela argued that, in order to continue living, organisms must be structurally coupled to (some elements of) their environments: in the case of human beings, eating food, for example, or breathing air or drinking water.[11] Living systems engage in a two-way, mutually triggering interaction with their environment. Clearly, this model is based on the principle of treating 'cognition as a biological phenomenon'.[12] However, the authors were fully aware of the fact that even artificial systems can become autopoietic unities: 'if living systems were machines, they could be made by man', they write. If we refuse to prioritize ideas over their execution and begin to seriously value the idea of a negotiation with instruments that, as Barbieri puts it, 'makes my ego die a little', we enter a situation of structural coupling with instruments and the audience: we have one extended, living system made up of the composer, the instrument, and the sonic environment (which also includes the audience in a live performance, as we shall see) that can be conceived as an autopoietic system in which the musician's intervention triggers effects in the environment that in turn have feedback effects on the musician's activity. This implies a first methodological *reduction*, i.e. giving up Dolby's idea that everything happens in the head of a demiurgic performer who creates sounds by exploiting passive and inert instrumentation: the artist / performer reduces her role as a creator, ruler, and subject of knowledge. This leads us to Husserl's theory of passive syntheses.

Husserl's phenomenological understanding of activity and passivity rests upon a (second methodological) *reduction* of their difference, which perfectly aligns with Barbieri's concept of the creative process:

---

10   See Scott Wilson, 'Caterina Barbieri on Synthesis, Minimalism and Creating Living Organisms out of Sound', *Fact*, July 2018 <https://www.factmag.com/2018/07/08/caterina-barbieri-signal-path/> [accessed 2 November 2021].

11   Humberto R. Maturana and Francisco J. Varela, *Autopoiesis and Cognition: The Realization of the Living* (Dordrecht: Reidel, 1972).

12   Ibid., p. xvi.

Today it seems that the focus of music industry is very much
on the simplification of music interfaces, to make the creative
process faster and accessible, at least in the digital world. But I
think that this approach to technology is problematic and mis-
leading, because the creative process needs *limits* to overcome
and esoteric interfaces to explore. In my experience, music always comes out of a process of *negotiation* between the design
of the technology and the human imagination, rather than a
simple *imposition* of an idea upon *passive* matter.[13]

Husserl's notion of passivity evokes an apparent paradox: how can
syntheses be *passive*? In the history of philosophy, and especially in
the Kantian idealistic account, syntheses are conceived of as those
acts performed by consciousness in order to bind together the contents that appear to it in such a way as to disclose objective unities,
which subjects can subsequently know; i.e., syntheses are activities
performed by the ego. So how can they be *passive*? Passivity does
not only provide the (aesthetic) material for synthetic activities. 'The
synthetic activity of consciousness', writes Victor Biceaga, does not
'consist in the application of a priori rules to a collection of isolated,
simple and passively registered sense data':[14] sensory material is never
simply 'passive'. Passive genesis is 'active' in a way, to the extent that
it also discloses synthetic articulations of meanings, which are not the
result of egoic activity, even though they are not totally independent
of it. History, sedimentations, habitus: as noticed by Merleau-Ponty in
his critique of Husserl's concept of *Sinngebung*, subjective constitution
of meaning is never absolute, since it is affected by sedimentations
(bodily schema, habitus) that provide the passively instituted horizon
of our experience.[15] The tactile, embedded, physical memory that the
musician has of the instrument belongs precisely to this dimension.
This passivity enters seamlessly into the performer's conscious activity
and predelineates its possibilities, leaving them open — at the same
time — to continuous creative reconfigurations.[16] In Merleau-Ponty's

---

13   See Wilson, 'Caterina Barbieri' (my emphasis).

14   Victor Biceaga, *The Concept of Passivity in Husserl's Phenomenology* (Dordrecht: Sprin-
      ger, 2010), p. xii.

15   See Maurice Merleau-Ponty, *Institution and Passivity: Course Notes from the Collège
      de France (1954–1955)*, trans. by Leonard Lawlor and Heath Massey (Evanston, IL:
      Northwestern University Press, 2010).

16   Couldn't this be a possible description of improvisation?

words: 'consciousness [is not] the flux of *Erlebnisse*, but consciousness of lacks, of open situations':[17] it is unstable by definition and results from a permanent negotiation between active constitution of meaning and passive genesis. Metaphorizing the original meaning of Maturana and Varela's notion of 'structural coupling', I would say that the syntheses accomplished by the ego and passive syntheses are structurally coupled:

> If the ego is able to interpret the content of its present perceptual experience despite its actual incompleteness, it is because it has at its disposal an interpretative grid comprising latent or inactive meanings that can come either from sedimentations of previous acts or from the background horizon of the present perceptual experience.[18]

Knowing does not proceed *ex nihilo*: in Barbieri's terms, 'the idea of composing from silence by means of an additive design as well as the "start/stop" logic related to the digital practice are undermined.'[19] The structural coupling of activity and passivity implies the structural coupling of their respective temporalities, that of the concept (the idea) of the composition and that of its execution.

3. ARTICULATING NEW TEMPORALITIES: PIECE TIME AND GESTURAL TIME

As many researchers have observed, there is a difference — which is at the same time a correlation — between technology as a means of *construction* and technology as a means of *expression* (to put it in Fell's terms).[20] Construction is the formal, structural temporality of *writing* the piece, whereas *expression* is the temporality of its execution, of virtuosity, of the event. However, as we learned from the example of Phuture's 'Acid Tracks', the boundaries between the two sides are far from being clear-cut. In an article written in 1996, Jonathan D. Kramer analysed three classical compositions by Beethoven, Mahler,

---

17   Merleau-Ponty, *Institution and Passivity*, p. 131.

18   Biceaga, *The Concept of Passivity in Husserl's Phenomenology*, p. xv.

19   See Will Betts, 'Interview: Minimalist Electronic Artist Caterina Barbieri', *Sound of Sound*, 31 July 2017 <https://www.soundonsound.com/news/interview-minimalist-electronic-artist-caterina-barbieri> [accessed 2 November 2021].

20   Fell, 'Collateral Damage'.

and Ives in order to emphasize a distinction (already theorized by Judy Lochhead) between the 'piece time' and the 'gestural time' of a composition: while piece time is 'strictly tied to temporal place-context' independently of the content, gestural time 'can be separated from its original and defining temporal place-context while still retaining part of its original significance'.[21] What does this mean exactly?

Again, we have two temporal orders: 'one order depends on the succession of musical events as heard in performance' (i.e. as executed: gestural time), 'while the other depends on conventionally defined gestures that carry connotations of temporal function (beginning, ending, climax, transition, etc.) regardless of their immediate context' (piece time: the piece as it is written, thought, and structured).[22] It is precisely at this point, in this difference, that the audience's role turns out to be pivotal to the definition of gestural time: musical time as experienced by listeners does not only exist within the succession of moments defined by piece time, but also emerges in the listeners themselves. It turns out that, at least retrospectively, musical gestures imply virtual continuities that can be very different from those given in the piece time — 'virtual' meaning precisely that those gestures do not exist 'objectively' but in the mind of listeners.[23] In Kramer's words:

> My own personal narrative time as I listen does not simply coincide with this structural hearing, although the two are not unrelated either. Since my narrative depends in part on the emotions and memories that I associate with the various tunes quoted [the reference is to Ives's use of intertextuality] it is uniquely my own.[24]

---

21   Judy Lochhead, 'The Temporal in Beethoven's Opus 135: When Are Ends Beginning?', *Theory Only*, 4.7 (1979), pp. 3–30 (p. 4), cited in Jonathan D. Kramer, 'Postmodern Concepts of Musical Time', *Indiana Theory Review*, 17.2 (1996), pp. 21–62 (p. 28). Kramer shows that all three examples (Beethoven's *String Quartet in F Major, op. 135*, Mahler's *Seventh Symphony*, and Ives' *Putnam's Camp*) present postmodernist characteristics even though they were composed prior to the modernist period, thereby claiming that postmodern features can be also found — in principle — in works that chronologically don't belong to the postmodernist era, since postmodernism can be understood 'as an attitude more than as a historical period' (p. 22).

22   Kramer, 'Postmodern Concepts of Musical Time', p. 28.

23   Ibid., p. 30.

24   Ibid., p. 60.

Minimalist music resorts to this differential relation between these two temporalities in order to structure new perceptual articulations of time. In her 2012 MA dissertation on the construction of phenomenal 'space' in experimental music, Sarah Davachi describes the peculiar static, sustained temporality that arises from La Monte Young's minimalist use of techniques such as the reduction of sonic materiality, sustenance, and repetition, in the following terms:

> This phenomenal sense of totality is also characterized by a particular impression of the temporal 'whole' in that an entire duration is essentially truncated into one effectively 'irreal' moment; indeed, absolute time persists but what one tends to experience is something more like an extended sense of pure duration. [...] One could argue that what is felt is both the in-itself lived experience, and also the sense of existential discord that arises between subjective experience and the indifferent continuum of absolute time and objective materiality.[25]

The reference to pure duration reminds us of Henri Bergson's theory of time consciousness. Along with Husserl, Bergson is the philosopher who programmatically insisted the most on the difference between subjective, qualitative time perception and objective, quantitative time apprehension. In Bergson's account, 'pure duration' only emerges through a *reduction* of objective time to inner time perception, which represents the lived-experience of time as the continuity and permeation of states of mind that is characteristic of consciousness. Duration is contrasted by Bergson to objective time, the time measured by clocks, which consists of the succession of juxtaposed phases, external to each other, and which turns out to be a translation of inner duration into space — what the clock measures is not 'time' but the space conventionally established between the hands.[26] Therefore, we can identify a start-phase and an end-phase within objective, spatialized time, which is a linear time, whereas the same identifi-

---

25   Sarah Davachi, *Irreal Worlds: Constructions of Phenomenal 'Space' in Experimental Music, 1962–1978* (Master's Thesis, Fine Arts in Electronic Music and Recording Media, Mills College, 2012) <https://www.academia.edu/1961555/Irreal_Worlds_Constructions_of_Phenomenal_Space_in_Experimental_Music_1962-78> [accessed 3 November 2021].

26   See Henri Bergson, *Time and Free Will: An Essay on the Immediate Data of Consciousness* [1889], trans. by F. L. Pogson (Mineola, NY: Dover Publications, 2001).

cation does not hold for pure duration, which is a continuum and a cyclic time. Thus, we could also label the dimension of pure duration (time-continuum) as the *analog* dimension of time, whereas the discrete dimension of objective time could be labelled as the *digital* dimension of time. To return to Kramer's terminology, we could associate 'pure duration'/analog time with gestural time (the time of the musical event) and objective/digital time with the 'piece time' (the conventional time in which the piece is thought). Just like passivity and activity, and receptivity and synthesis, piece time and gestural time are also 'structurally coupled', i.e. in continuous mutual osmosis.

It is not by chance that, as Davachi observes, La Monte Young aims to turn the aesthetic experience inward in order to enter 'into' or, in some sense, to become closer to the essential qualities of the sound itself. Many elements central to his compositional approach were influenced (both stylistically and conceptually) by the traditional practices of Indian classical music with its cyclic temporality — a reference shared by Barbieri herself.[27] Her music evokes altered states of mind where perceptions of time and space are constantly distorted and challenged through minimalist techniques based on repetition and sustained attention — a journey, I would say, into (Bergson's) pure duration.[28]

This framework forms the background of Barbieri's second album *Ecstatic Computation*, released in 2019: the concept of 'ecstatic computation' revolves around the use of computation (i.e. sequencing techniques and pattern-based operations) to explore the modes of human perception and memory processes so as to ultimately induce a sense of ecstasy and contemplation. A *reduced* sequence of initial codes (algorithms) generatively produces a larger body of outputs. Of course — and this is the interesting point for us — resorting to computation complicates the relation between gestural time (analog

27   See Wilson, 'Caterina Barbieri'.

28   Here I understand 'sustained attention' as a form of 'deep listening' in Pauline Oliveros's sense: 'she considered sound not only to be the audible vibrations of the air around us, but the totality of many vibrational energies throughout the universe. To listen is to be aware of one's self in that collective whole' (Jonathan Williger, review of Oliveros, Dempster, Panaiotis, *Deep Listening, Pitchfork*, 10 February 2020 <https://pitchfork.com/reviews/albums/pauline-oliveros-stuart-dempster-pan-deep-listening/> [accessed 9 November 2021]).

time) and piece time (digital time) on two levels: as I will show in the next section, it seems to deepen the differentiation between the two orders of time. While it thereby apparently radicalizes the absence of the body, it also offers a possible solution to it.

4. FROM GENERATIVE COMPUTATION TO PSYCHEDELIA

Let's start with the first point, which concerns the temporal logic of computer music. As Curtis Roads explains,

> a computer translates every human gesture into a formal operation. This system is encoded in the logic of a programming language and executed according to the algebra of the machine hardware. A crucial question is this: At what level of musical structure do such formalisms operate?'[29]

In other words: if formal algorithms represent extremely powerful means of invention through which, as in Barbieri's case, the sonic universe can be enormously expanded, how do we ultimately translate them 'into the real world of acoustics, psychoacoustics, music cognition, and emotional response'?[30] As observed by Horacio Vaggione (quoted in Roads), 'the rigor of the generative process does not guarantee the musical coherence of the work', and this happens because 'music is not a purely formal system; rather, it is grounded in acoustics, auditory perception, and psychology'. In this sense, electronic music provides new examples of the opposition between music-making, 'the immediate spontaneity of improvised performance onstage', and 'the careful, reflective process of studio-based composition'.[31] Again, music as it is thought, programmed, or written is one thing, music as it is performed and heard quite another. In such cases as Barbieri's articulations of musical patterns from a reduced set of generative algorithms, how does the transition to embodied music take place?

---

29   Curtis Roads, *Composing Electronic Music: A New Aesthetic* (Oxford: Oxford University Press, 2015), p. 38.

30   Ibid.

31   Horacio Vaggione, 'Analysis and the Singularity of Music: The Locus of an Intersection', in *Analyse en Musique Électroacoustique, Acts de l'Académie Internationalde Musique Électroacoustique* (Bourges: Éditions Mnémosyne, 1996), pp. 268–74, quoted by Roads, *Composing Electronic Music*, p. 39.

Roads refers to the difference between *chronos* (measurable and objective time) and *tempus* (perceived or subjective time) as is theorized by Olivier Messiaen in his *Traité* (1994). This reference should remind us of Bergson's distinction between pure duration and objective time, which we have already discussed: subjective duration does not necessarily coincide with chronometric, objective time, since it can be influenced and altered by eminently subjective elements such as memories and expectations. But it is precisely this mismatch or misalignment that creates an ecstatic effect in works such as Barbieri's: the repetition and sustaining of algorithmically generated patterns does not produce a linear, digital temporality; rather, in the perception of listeners, it turns into a circular, cyclic movement of recursiveness and differential changes, with no real starting or stopping — 'a dynamic and living being able to develop its own organic laws, whose inner potential for growth and change is embedded in the initial instructions of the sequencer'.[32] As I showed above: despite their difference, or indeed *because* of their difference, gestural time and piece time work together to create an ecstatic sonic environment.

But the temporality formed by the combination of generative algorithms and their modulation through analog synthesizers, i.e. through actual voltages set according to predefined parameters, does more than just reconcile gestural time and piece time. Repetition — that is, the looping technique — 'constitutes a good deal of our everyday experience of contemporary capitalism's reliance on repetition, familiarity, and virality'.[33] As observed by David C. Jackson in his interpretation of William Basinski's pieces, 'the ability to loop and make time return using magnetic tape has an important history in the development of the avant-garde and runs through experimental music, films, and the increased commodity form of musical instrumentation'.[34] Loops, then, play an important part in ordering the everyday flow of our consciousness and assembling our temporal and rhythmic interactions with machines, culture, and the social environment.

---

32   I am quoting Caterina Barbieri from a conference presentation that Barbieri kindly shared with me.

33   David C. Jackson, 'Repetition, Feedback and Temporality in Two Compositions by William Basinski', *érudit*, 33 (2019), para. 1 <https://doi.org/10.7202/1065021ar>.

34   Ibid., para. 2.

I find Jackson's interpretation of Basinski's work interesting, for it can be applied to other experiments within minimalist, electronic music and especially to Barbieri's work. Jackson shows that Basinski's works are generally composed through 'the unspooling of various loops on magnetic tape, which he has collected and archived, and the real-time processing of these loops with delays and reverbs' — the latter (delay and reverb) being effects to which Barbieri also extensively resorts. Basinski has argued for an understanding of the loop and its repetition and duration as a critical component of memory and consciousness, stating that 'memories are loops, our memories are made of loops. We have loops that constantly go around and around'.[35] I am fascinated by this phenomenological analogy between musical techniques and everyday experience (how loops 'go around and around' as a 'form of memory or consciousness and how they connect to ideas about everyday events, duration, and the instant'), since the analogy opens up a musical (theory and) practice that employs loops and feedback in a critical direction, aimed at questioning the usual acoustic experience through experimentation and variations on its temporality.

> In Basinski's practice, producing, storing, and playing back a loop is an important part of transmitting and transforming the consciousness embedded in the technologies that record, store, and play back memories, the passage of time, and experiences. Magnetic tape, as well as other forms of time-based media, are part of our stream of consciousness and contribute to its construction and shaping, which in turn shapes our experiences through the processing of the flow of sensations and perceptions.[36]

If we assume, as suggested by Jackson/Basinski, that there is an analogy between the looping temporality of music and that of our everyday experience as it is shaped by the current capitalist regime, then employing looping (and other) techniques in order to shape new forms of sonic temporality — for instance, as in Barbieri's case, the cyclic temporality produced by emphasizing gestural time — means searching for ways to *transform* our collective, shared temporality: 'Entrained rhythms tie affective states, the experience of flow, to neurocapitalism

---

35   Ibid., para. 3.
36   Ibid.

through repetition and feedback that harness shared collective temporal experiences, which are synchronized to multiple industrialized temporalities of consumption, digital networks, and accelerated life in the twenty-first century.[37] I interpret Barbieri's music as such an attempt to resist the repetitions and synchronizations of collective entrainment by deploying sustained rhythmic forces through repetition, delay, and sustained attention.

It is through this intervention on the psycho-acoustic level that we can come back to the problem of the 'crucial missing element' that the body represents in computer music and suggest a possible solution. This tentative solution involves the creation of a musical environment that is shared with the listeners and is based on:

- the undoing of the artist as a creator (demiurgic force) who imposes her 'idea' on passive and raw sonic material;

- an emphasis on the machine as a creative and active force, i.e. the introduction of generative computing as a creative technique and the subsequent emphasis on the human-machine relationship as negotiation;[38]

- the articulation of different time-structures through techniques such as repetition, loop, and sustained attention, and the rejection of the standardized, commodified conception of musical time, thereby altering and challenging our 'normal' psychoacoustic experience.

This psycho-acoustic alteration can be framed as a deeper attentiveness on the listeners' part, an attention *reduced* to and focused on the

---

37   Ibid., para. 5.

38   Most computer music is composed without the actual involvement of any musicians playing instruments in real time: the composer is a 'controller' who defines what elements and parameters should be put into a timeline, and where (see Robert Henke, 'Live Performance in the Age of Supercomputing', 2007 <https://roberthenke.com/ interviews/supercomputing.html> [accessed 8 November 2021]). Even though the conception of the musician/composer as a mere 'controller' is somewhat reductive, it reinforces the idea of the composer as the 'mind' that decides which elements are relevant and which are not and treats the sonic material as a merely passive element within a design process that is the least embodied one possible, since it does not even involve any actual musician. This is a strong dualistic notion of music composition, which tends to reintroduce a sort of mind/body split, to put it with Descartes.

primary qualities of sound, i.e. as a form of 'deep listening' in Pauline Oliveros's sense: 'a practice that is intended to heighten and expand consciousness of sound in as many dimensions of awareness and attentional dynamics as humanly possible'. This technique also implies resistance to the mainstream's musical temporality, in that its

> salience resides in its contrast to mainstream culture's riptide trajectory towards distraction and saturation, towards siloed media and political environments. It also stands in opposition to the numbing listening habits encouraged by streaming, which positions music as a utilitarian tool for productivity, something to be ignored while your concentration rests elsewhere.[39]

The two concepts of *negotiation* and of the alteration of the psychoacoustic level (psychedelia) imply a strong reference to the body: it is the body of the artist, even more so than her mind, that has to 'struggle' with the machinery (the computer, the synths) and to acknowledge that it also produces living, sonic material; it's her body that is onstage and that plays around with the machinery so as to create something that is co-produced and co-designed. And it is the body of the listener as a psycho-physical unity that is affected by the alteration of the linear temporality we are used to in non-experimental, mainstream music. Even if we are unable to recognize what's happening onstage, to identify what the performer is actually doing and where the sound is actually coming from,[40] we do share with her the experience of a different temporality that we actually also help construct, since — as we have seen — gestural time implies the listeners' different narratives and subjective modes of perception.

---

39   Williger, review of Oliveros, Dempster, Panaiotis, *Deep Listening*.
40   'The audience looks at a laptop whilst listening to music. But what exactly creates the music and how the performer interacts with this tool is completely non-transparent. The laptop is not the instrument, the instrument is invisible. And to obscure things even more we have to realize that most of the time there is not one single instrument and it is not "played" by the performer': this is how Robert Henke's 'Live Performance in the Age of Supercomputing' describes the situation of 'acousmatic listening' in computer music, i.e. the type of listening experience a person has when she's unable to identify the source of the sound.

CONCLUSION

As noted by Bob Ostertag, before the advent of machines that could automate sophisticated processes, there was no performance without the body. In a sense, 'the entire problem is just one window into the tension residing at the very core of modern life — that between the human body and the machine.'[41] This tension is the hallmark of our time, and it is not a problem that can be 'solved' and made to disappear. We can only work around it through permanent negotiation. In this sense, to return to Mark Hansen, it is true that we are 'bodies-in-code' — yet, we are still 'bodies' that (in a kind of phenomenological circle) *create* something only insofar as they are *created* by something, are *active* only insofar they are practically *limited* by material, things, artefacts, machines, and everything that exceeds our subjectivity and — as Barbieri puts it — 'makes my ego die a little'.

---

41   Ostertag, 'Human Bodies, Computer Music', p. 14.

Reduction in Time
Kinaesthetic and Traumatic Experiences
of the Present in Literary Texts
ALBERICA BAZZONI

1. TOWARD AN AESTHETIC OF THE LIVING PRESENT

The living present is the home of temporality. It is a perceptive, cognitive, and affective disposition of the self, a kinaesthetic awareness of the flowing of life. In the living present, the self is the propulsive force on the edge of its own becoming. The living present is the constantly renewed discovery of the becoming of being.

In this chapter, I investigate the dimension of the living present as a form of temporal reduction, looking at its manifestation in literary texts. How is a temporal experience accessed and represented in language? What are the affordances of literary texts in relation to the living present? What does an aesthetic of the living present reveal about the culture and politics of a specific text and its context? First, I propose here a focus on the living present as different from an understanding of the present as a still moment that coincides with eternity, an instant outside of time, which is dominant in aesthetic reflections on temporality in literature. Second, I correlate the reduction at play in the experience of the living present to the reduction at play in trauma and begin to articulate the relationship between the two. In the final part,

I discuss the affective, ethical, and political dimensions of the temporality of the living present as a site of subjectivation, which effects a counter-reduction of normative discourses. Overall, I sketch here the coordinates of an aesthetic of the living present in literary texts, outlining the essential questions and variables regarding its configuration, its relationship with experience, and its philosophical and political implications. Such an aesthetic of the living present can serve to interrogate other texts, as a key lens to draw out the different relationships to the temporality, embodiment, and subjectivity they inhabit and exhibit.

In focusing on temporality, I frame reduction not as an idealistic method, a logical-epistemological device, a conceptual operation — such as when a theory is reduced to a more fundamental theory, or when inhomogeneous multiplicity is reduced to a coherent taxonomy/category/pattern/norm — but chiefly as an experiential practice: reduction as an experience of concentration in the present. From a phenomenological perspective, the constitution of temporality lies at the core of the constitution of experience — that is, the constitution of subjectivity in the co-constitutive encounter between self and world. Reduction — what Edmund Husserl defines as *epochē* or 'bracketing' — is that performative approach which seeks to grasp and express the embodied and emplaced experience of the world, which is essentially temporal.[1] As Francisco Varela explains in his essay 'Present-Time Consciousness', which brings together phenomenological, cognitive, and neurological studies, in 'any true phenomenological study, the exploration of time involves the gesture of reduction'.[2] Focusing on the living present is an exercise in reduction to the irreducible, the material and libidinal core of the self, the founding encounter with the world through sensation, the primary vital impulses before and beyond their organization into a coherent narrative of memory and projection, and before and beyond the constitutive effect of power on subjects.

A focus on the living present is congruent with multiple yet interrelated traditions of philosophical thought that, distinguished from the metaphysical and phallogocentric perspective predominant in modern

---

1   Edmund Husserl, *The Phenomenology of Internal Time Consciousness*, trans. by Nancy M. Paul and W. Scott Palmer (Bloomington: Indiana University Press, 1964).

2   Francisco Varela, 'Present-Time Consciousness', *Journal of Consciousness Studies*, 6.2–3 (1999), pp. 111–40 (p. 112).

Western philosophy, have maintained a keen interest in the embodied, historical, and affective dimensions of existence, and that extend from Baruch Spinoza to Henri Bergson and Edmund Husserl, continue into the theorizations of the body, experience, and subjectivity developed by Maurice Merleau-Ponty, Jean-Luc Nancy, Gilles Deleuze, and Félix Guattari, and arrive at the feminist, neomaterialist, and posthuman perspectives of Rosi Braidotti and Donna J. Haraway — among many others.[3] In dialogue with, and in response to, the linguistic paradigm of deconstruction, these strands of thought place embodied experience at the centre of a redefinition of subjectivity, agency, and political struggle through the nourishment of desire and openness to change that pertain to the dimension of the living present.

The *hic et nunc* of the living present is defined primarily as a kin-aesthetic experience — that is, a sensory awareness of embodiment and movement. Bergson, who plays a crucial role in the investigation of the lived experience of time, describes the experience of the present, the duration of time in its development, as a musical sequence of sounds, a continuous flow with no clearly demarcated beginnings and ends.[4] Similarly to Bergson's understanding of consciousness as duration through 'attention to life',[5] the practice of meditation follows the flow of inhale and exhale breathing to concentrate on the flowing present.[6] The experience of the present of a kinaesthetic body is what is found at the end of a phenomenological reduction, its precious discovery and its limit. Cognitive studies on the embodied mind by George Lakoff, Mark Johnson, Antonio Damasio, and Varela point in the same direction.[7] In Donald Winnicott's psychoanalytical perspec-

---

3   In tracing the multiple developments of this philosophical perspective, I am following Rosi Braidotti's own formulation in *Metamorphoses: Towards a Materialist Theory of Becoming* (Cambridge: Polity Press, 2002).

4   Henri Bergson, *Matter and Memory*, trans. by Nancy M. Paul and W. Scott Palmer (New York: Dover Publications, 2012).

5   Ibid., p. 12.

6   See Tullio Giraldi, *Psychotherapy, Mindfulness and Buddhist Meditation* (Cham: Palgrave Macmillan, 2019).

7   See Mark Johnson, *The Body in the Mind: The Bodily Basis of Meaning, Imagination, and Reason* (Chicago: University of Chicago Press, 1987); George Lakoff and Mark Johnson, *Philosophy in the Flesh: The Embodied Mind and its Challenge to Western Thought* (New York: Basic Books, 1999); Antonio Damasio, *Descartes' Error: Emotion, Reason, and the Human Brain* (New York: Putnam, 1994).

tive, the living body is the home of the 'true Self', the experience of a 'spontaneous impulse' and the expression of a 'spontaneous gesture'.[8]

What is reduced in the present, and how is this temporal reduction configured? In the living present, there is a reduction of temporal dimensions of memory and projection. In simple words, attention focuses on a reduced temporal dimension, which approximates the experience of the present in its constant flowing. Other temporal dimensions, consisting of retention of the past and protention towards the future, are always active within the present perception itself, as perception is already shaped by previous experiences (including how our senses have been trained and used before) and sustained by anticipation of what is to come. However, attention can be modulated to reduce the timespan on which it focuses and its direction, so that the longer arc of memory (past) and projection (future) recedes to the background and is only relevant insofar as it is contained within the present, which takes centre stage. Reduction to the present is a matter of attention: an intensified experience of the present comes to the foreground temporarily, and within a certain frame, revealing itself as the site of the embodied encounter with the world.

Varela analyses extensively the constitution of temporality in the present, bringing together a phenomenological frame and cognitive neurological studies. He writes:

> There is always a centre, the now moment. [...] This centre is bounded by a horizon or fringe that is already past (I still hold the beginning of the sentence I just wrote) and it projects towards an intended next moment. [...] These horizons are *mobile*: this very moment which was present (and hence was not merely described, but lived as such) slips towards an immediately past present. Then it plunges further out of view. [...] This moment of consciousness is inseparable from a flow. [...] Consciousness does not contain time [...]. Instead, temporal consciousness itself constitutes an ultimate substrate of consciousness where no further reduction can be accomplished.[9]

Varela stresses the mobile horizon of constitution of the present and the centrality of temporal consciousness in the constitution of sub-

---

8   Donald W. Winnicott, *The Maturational Processes and the Facilitating Environment* (London: Hogarth Press and the Institute of Psychoanalysis, 1965), p. 145.

9   Varela, 'Present-Time Consciousness', p. 113.

jectivity itself. The perceptive and affective unit of the body is able to last, that is, in Bergson's words, it is at the centre of an experience of duration. The flow of temporality has in the kinaesthetic present its point of encounter between the body and the world, and between past experiences and the yet unknown future.

When we reduce time to the living present, what does this type of reduction create space for? What energy and what affective disposition emerge from such a reduction? A related set of questions concerns how reduction to the present occurs, what 'the mode of access to the experience itself' is.[10] While the living present is experienced as a continuous flux, it only comes to the foreground intermittently. It is not part of the human experience to live continuously immersed in an unproblematic concentration in the present and sensorial enjoyment, for such a condition is not given in a continuum, nor is it given always in the same shape. Memory, projections, and overlapping temporal layers all interweave within the subject's experience of time, creating a discontinuous relationship with the present. An intensified experience of the living present can occur in different ways — through an intentional exercise, an individually or collectively ritualized practice, or as an emerging event, as the insurgence of sudden vitality. In fact, the practice of attention to the present itself opens up spaces for the emergence of the unknown to be heard and for vital energy to be mobilized. In the experience of the kinaesthetic present, there is a movement of expansion and intensification of the self.

When literary studies engage with the experience of the present, or philosophical studies draw on literary texts to reflect on the present, it is predominantly described in terms of a static experience, a fixed instant outside of time that coincides with eternity. I am interested instead in the experience of the moving of time in its happening, contingency, and embodiment. In other words, I am drawing a precise temporal distinction between concentration on the kinaesthetic present (embodied, flowing) and on the static present (disembodied, instant outside of time), the latter representing the atemporality of metaphysics. Here I foreground the notion of 'becoming', which em-

---

10   Ibid., p. 115.

phasizes processes, that is 'mutations, changes and transformations, rather than Being in its classical modes'.[11]

In drawing this distinction, I am in conversation with a body of philosophical work that seeks to re-shape the concept of presence. While the notion of 'presence' critiqued by Jacques Derrida refers to 'the fullness and permanence of the origin, the end or final purpose, speech, mind, and being', and is intrinsically logocentric and metaphysical, outside of the linguistic paradigm within which Derrida operates there opens a space for a radically different — and radically anti-metaphysical — understanding of presence.[12] In Braidotti's formulation, '[a]s models to account for the kind of subjects we have already become, representational thinking and the linguistic turn are outdated. I opt here instead for a neomaterialist, embodied, embedded approach.'[13] In this view, the living present is the temporality which discloses 'our nonhermeneutic apprehension of the world in all its sensuous materiality'.[14] 'The present of "presence" is a place of experience and unmediated contact with material things freed from the ambivalence and multiplicity of recollection, interpretation, and narration.'[15]

The distinction between living and static present works to undo the conflation of metaphysical instantaneity-eternity and anti-metaphysical embodied experience, which largely dominates studies on the present in literary works (and not only literary works). As temporal discontinuity has heightened with the advent of modernity, modernist writers such as Marcel Proust, Virginia Woolf, James Joyce, and Luigi Pirandello have brought a reflection on time and subjectivity to the fore. Epiphanies, revelatory instants beyond meaning, 'archaic mimesis' irrupt in narrative and poetic discourse.[16] Yet, such an in-

---

11   Braidotti, *Metamorphoses*, p. 2.

12   Vincent P. Pecora, 'Be Here Now: Mimesis and the History of Representation', in *Presence: Philosophy, History and Cultural Theory for the 21st Century*, ed. by Ranjan Ghosh and Ethan Kleinberg (Ithaca, NY: Cornell University Press, 2013), pp. 26–44 (p. 27).

13   Rosi Braidotti, 'The Politics of Life as Bios/Zoe', in *Bits of Life: Feminisms at the Intersections of Media, Bioscience, and Technology*, ed. by Anneke Smelik and Nina Lykke (Seattle: University of Washington Press, 2008), pp. 177–95 (p. 182).

14   Pecora, 'Be Here Now', p. 40.

15   Ethan Kleinberg, 'Presence *in Absentia*', in Ghosh and Kleinberg, *Presence*, pp. 8–25 (p. 10).

16   Pecora, 'Be Here Now', p. 31. Pecora refers here to Walter Benjamin's notion of the poetic.

tensified awareness of temporality and the emergence of 'present moments' can take up entirely different meanings depending on whether they are configured as a metaphysical instantaneity outside of time, on the one hand, or as the awareness of the constant becoming of an embodied being, prior to conceptualization and signification, on the other. Postmodernism has inherited an awareness of temporal discontinuity, further widening the rupture between signification and material ontology and neglecting the present as the temporality of the flowing of life.

However, from the nineteenth century to today, writers have engaged with an exploration of the kinaesthetic experience of the present, both representing it in texts and performing it through texts.[17] In the Italian context, in the works of a precursor of modernism such as Giacomo Leopardi and in those of full modernists Pirandello and Giuseppe Ungaretti, vitalistic drives, bodily presence, primary interactions with others, and nature coexist and contend with representations of the discontinuity and unattainability of presence. In the course of the twentieth century, it is especially women writers, such as Elsa Morante, Anna Maria Ortese, Goliarda Sapienza, and Fabrizia Ramondino, who delve into the dimension of the living present, using the text to deconstruct normative discourses and foster agency by expressing sensorial experiences, vitalistic impulses — including the erotic — and empathetic relationships with others and the environment. The distinction between the static present and the kinaesthetic present serves to disclose different poetics at work in different texts, shedding light on their conception of temporality and, through temporality, on embodiment and becoming.

The kinaesthetic present as the becoming of life in its happening can be contrasted with the entrapped temporality of trauma. To focus on the living present and to be stuck in the present are, in fact, in a rela-

---

17　Of course, temporality has always been an intrinsic element of literary expression as much as philosophical reflection. In 'Declensions of "Now"', for example, Manuele Gragnolati and Francesca Southerden analyse poems from the Middle Ages from a perspective that, although it does not resort to the vocabulary of the living present, is very much congruent with its conceptual ground. See Gragnolati and Southerden, *Possibilities of Lyric: Reading Petrarch in Dialogue* (Berlin: ICI Berlin Press, 2020), chapter 4: 'Declensions of "Now": Lyric Epiphanies in Cavalcanti, Dante, and Petrarch', pp. 85–108 <https://doi.org/10.37050/ci-18_04>.

tionship of mutual tension, as one state can morph into the other, the
dynamic flux of perceptions always at risk of stumbling into overlaps,
disjoints, and iterations. Phenomenological studies on the temporality
of trauma point out the ways in which trauma impacts on the primary experience of time. In 'Telling Time: Literature, Temporality and
Trauma', Wendy O'Brien observes:

> One of the most common qualities evidenced in trauma narra-
> tives is reference to the distortion of time. Time comes undone
> when experience makes clear [...] one's own death. [...] There
> is a collapse of all those psychological principles of organiza-
> tion that we rely on in order to structure experience.[18]

The impact of trauma on temporality affects our very cognitive structures, as it creates a breach to 'the cornerstones of lived experience:
perception, the body, memory, birth and death, culture'. It fundamentally disrupts 'perception of such basic phenomena as space (distance),
identity and time'.[19] In traumatized temporality, the continuous flow
of time is interrupted, and so are space and identity. The subject is
no longer working as a cognitive emplaced unit that brings together
perceptions, as described by Varela; instead, multiple dimensions fragment the subject herself.

In her fundamental reflections on the temporality of trauma and
narrative, developed in *Unclaimed Experience*, Cathy Caruth identifies
the specific nexus between trauma and time, characterized by inescap-
able iterations.[20] If the flow of temporality is what allows for a narrative
to develop and thereby make change possible, its interruption traps
subjects in an overwhelming paralysis. Caruth describes the stuck temporality of trauma as 'the encounter with death' and 'the ongoing
experience of having survived it'.[21] As time stops flowing, the vital process of becoming turns into entrapped iteration, the present turns into
the iterative re-enactment of the past, and the future is pre-empted

---

18   Wendy O'Brien, 'Telling Time: Literature, Temporality and Trauma', in *Temporality
      in Life as Seen through Literature*, ed. by Anna-Teresa Tymieniecka (=*Analecta Husser-
      liana*, 86 (2007)), pp. 209–21 (p. 209).

19   Ibid., p. 210.

20   Cathy Caruth, *Unclaimed Experience: Trauma, Narrative, and History* (Baltimore, MD:
      John Hopkins University Press, 1996).

21   Ibid., p. 7.

of any futurity. The present is taken over by an *over-presence* of other temporal-spatial dimensions that paralyse the subject. In trauma, it is the present that is reduced.

As the living present is the core, unmediated experience of temporality in its unfolding, how can language convey such an experience? How can embodiment be performed in and through language? O'Brien asks a similar question in relation to trauma narratives: '[h]ow can trauma be written? In giving words to trauma and its after effects, aren't all those aspects of such overwhelming encounters with unmediated life lost? The very act of writing requires one to structure and temporalize events.'[22] If writing arguably requires structure and temporalization, the way in which literary texts do it provides a different answer to this question, one that has less to do with   ex-perience than with performing it.

Literary texts, with their sophisticated organization of spatio-temporal coordinates, offer revealing insights into the human experience of time. They represent a variety of 'modes of access' to the experience of the present, both in their content and in their function. When looking at a text, we can interrogate specifically what means it employs to express kinaesthetic and traumatized experiences of the present, including its imagery, its manipulation of tenses and deictics, its construction of narrative and rhythmic patterns, its configuration of the speaking or narrating voice. Literary texts enable us to approach language and the question of representation from a different perspective, which does not limit language to its semantic function as a relationship between signifier and signified.

Literary texts are particularly suited to bring the non-representational dimension of language to the fore, *performing* temporalization. Phenomenology, with its focus on embodiment, provides insightful tools to understand the ways in which literary texts bridge the allegedly insurmountable gap between signified and signifier, between world and language. As Jean-Claude Coquet — a French linguist of phenomenological orientation — remarks, the linguistic 'I' is always and primarily a body, as written language is not disassociated from the corporeal dimension of oral speech: 'The body takes part as much in

---

22   O'Brien, 'Telling Time', p. 211.

reading as in writing. [...] Therefore, writing is inseparable from the voice.'[23] In the performative aspect of enunciation, language maintains a close relationship with somatic experience, through projective modalities that highlight continuity over alterity: 'there is no discontinuity between the event, the experience of the event [...] and the expression of the event. They complement each other.'[24] In this way, the textual performance of an experience of temporality expresses the very constitution of the self — and its disruption — as essentially temporal.

2. HERE AND NOW, EVERYWHERE AND ALL THE TIME, AGAIN AND AGAIN

Having outlined the theoretical and methodological coordinates of an aesthetic of the living present, let us look at some examples of temporal experiences in literary texts.

'L'infinito'

Sempre caro mi fu quest'ermo colle,
e questa siepe, che da tanta parte
dell'ultimo orizzonte il guardo esclude.
Ma sedendo e mirando, interminati
spazi di là da quella, e sovrumani
silenzi, e profondissima quïete
io nel pensier mi fingo; ove per poco
il cor non si spaura. E come il vento
odo stormir tra queste piante, io quello
infinito silenzio a questa voce
vo comparando: e mi sovvien l'eterno,
e le morte stagioni, e la presente
e viva, e il suon di lei. Così tra questa
immensità s'annega il pensier mio:
e il naufragar m'è dolce in questo mare.[25]

---

23   Jean-Claude Coquet, *Le istanze enuncianti. Fenomenologia e semiotica*, ed. by Paolo Fabbri (Milan: Bruno Mondadori, 2008), p. 68. Unless otherwise specified, all translations from Italian are mine.

24   Ibid., p. 40.

25   Giacomo Leopardi, *Canti* (Milan: Mondadori, 2016), p. 112

('Infinity'

This lonely hill was always dear to me,
and this hedgerow, which cuts off the view
of so much of the last horizon.
But sitting here and gazing, I can see
beyond, in my mind's eye, unending spaces,
and superhuman silences, and depthless calm,
till what I feel
is almost fear. And when I hear
the wind stir in these branches, I begin
comparing that endless stillness with this noise:
and the eternal comes to mind,
and the dead seasons, and the present
living one, and how it sounds.
So my mind sinks in this immensity:
and foundering is sweet in such a sea.)[26]

Giacomo Leopardi (1798–1837), poet, philosopher, narrator, erudite,
is attracting renewed interest (also outside of the Italian context) for
the compelling way in which he speaks to contemporary questions,
and specifically for his original understanding of the embodied mind,
his radically materialist thought, and his post-anthropocentric view
of a shared materiality among nature, humans, and nonhumans.[27]
Leopardi's 'L'infinito' (Infinity) is arguably one of the most known and
studied poems in the Italian literary tradition. In this context, I look at
it as an extremely rich and dynamic figuration of the living present.

The first element I want to draw attention to in this poem is the
image of the hedgerow, which contains the poet's experience as it
limits the view: 'da tanta parte | dell'ultimo orizzonte il guardo esclude'
(cuts off the view | of so much of the last horizon). The hedgerow
works effectively as an image of *reduction*: it performs an *epochē*, which
'brackets' the view outside and concentrates the poet's attention on the
experience taking place within the frame.

---

26   Giacomo Leopardi, *Canti*, trans. by Jonathan Galassi (London: Penguin, 2010), p. 107.

27   See *Mapping Leopardi: Poetic and Philosophical Intersections*, ed. by Emanuela Cervato,
     Mark Epstein, Giulia Santi, and Simona Wright (Newcastle upon Tyne: Cambridge
     Scholars Publishing, 2019). See also the recent English translation of *Zibaldone*, ed.
     by Michael Caesar and Franco D'Intino, trans. by Kathleen Baldwin and others (New
     York: Farrar, Straus and Giroux, 2013), which provides an invaluable tool for making
     Leopardi's philosophical work accessible to the English-speaking world.

Having set this bounded frame of experience, the poem sets into motion a dynamic relationship between the emplaced and embodied temporality of the experience in the present, and the imagination of other spaces and time. 'L'infinito' is generally interpreted by focusing on the dimension of infinity and eternity evoked by the poetic voice beyond the boundary of the hedgerow, which moves the poet's imagination because of its sensorial absence, its unattainability. The development of the poem however also elicits a focus on the *here* and *now* of the poet's experience, which is rooted in the living present. Through the frame provided by the hedgerow and then the sound of the branches, the poet's experience is anchored to its present centre. Acting as a powerfully perceptive and embodied unit, the poet inhabits temporality as much as he is inhabited by it. The expansive and intensified dimension of the living present enabled by reduction contains within itself the other temporal dimensions, which 'sovvengono' (come to mind) to the poet:[28] 'l'eterno' (the eternal), 'le morte stagioni' (the dead seasons), and 'la presente e viva' (the present | living one). The living present is here the embodied awareness of temporality. And it is in the very awareness of temporality — 'questa immensità' (this immensity), 'questo mare' (such a sea) — rather than in the absent and silent immensity beyond the reach of the senses that the poetic voice sweetly 'naufraga' (founders).[29]

In this temporal experience, the senses play a crucial role. In particular, the poem showcases the centrality of sound in the dimension of the living present: 'E come il vento | *odo stormir* tra queste piante, io quello | infinito silenzio a questa *voce* | vo comparando [...] e la presente | e viva, e il *suon* di lei' (And when I *hear* | the wind *stir* in these branches, I begin | comparing that endless stillness with this | *noise* [...] and the present | living one, and how it *sounds*). The poet's experience of the present is described through sound, an experience in listening to nature; significantly, the sound of the wind is

---

28   The verb 'sovvengono', unlike the translation 'come to mind', does not imply a mental activity, and can be interpreted as describing a movement of emergence to awareness, a presentification to the self.

29   Here the translated version, 'such a sea', is more ambiguous; '*questo* mare' literally means '*this* sea' (and not '*that* sea'), continuing the contrast between '*quello* infinito silenzio' ('*that* endless stillness'; literally '*that* infinite silence') and '*questa* voce' ('*this* noise'; literally '*this* voice') established earlier in the poem.

described as a voice, 'voce', thus reinforcing the shared dimension and interpenetration of human and non-human. In her philosophy of the voice, Adriana Cavarero mobilizes sound in an anti-metaphysical perspective, highlighting its embodied, contingent, and flowing feature: 'Sounds are not perceived simultaneously but in succession. It is this characteristic that prevents hearing from becoming the foundation of an unlikely acoustic metaphysics.'[30] The sound of the voice manifests 'the empirical contingency of the context' and it 'evokes a discontinuous becoming, characterized by the constantly renovated present of the "nows"'.[31] Similarly to Bergson, who resorts to the metaphor of a musical sequence in order to describe the constitution of temporality as duration, Leopardi expresses his intensified temporal awareness in the present in terms of sound, the auscultation of the voice of nature, pointing to a materialist and anti-metaphysical perspective.

Finally, a consideration on the structure of 'L'infinito'. The poem features mostly a paratactic structure, with sentences and syntagms following one another in a continuous flow: 'interminati | spazi di là da quella, e sovrumani | silenzi, e profondissima quïete' (unending spaces, | and superhuman silences, and depthless | calm); and again, in the second part: 'e mi sovvien l'eterno, | e le morte stagioni, e la presente | e viva, e il suon di lei' (and the eternal comes to mind, | and the dead seasons, and the present | living one, and how it sounds). The paratactic flow is reinforced by the use of repetition and variation, including the use of the same terms — silenzio, questo, pensier (silence, this, mind) — and of a web of semantically cohesive terms — infinito, immensità, interminati, sovrumani, profondissima (infinity, immensity, endless, superhuman, depthless), which alternate with specific elements from the natural world — colle, siepe, vento, piante, mare (hill, hedgerow, wind, branches, sea). Through repetition, variation, and parataxis the poem creates a dynamic rhythm that performs the flowing of the temporal experience it represents, ending on the image of the sea — unbounded and relentlessly becoming.

---

30   Adriana Cavarero, *A più voci. Filosofia dell'espressione vocale* (Milan: Feltrinelli, 2003), p. 49.
31   Ibid., p. 193.

The image of the sea and the sensorial interconnection with the
natural elements is also central in the following two passages, this time
from narrative texts, respectively by Ippolito Nievo and Goliarda Sapienza, which describe moments of intensified awareness of embodied
presence. Ippolito Nievo (1831–1861) is a Mazzinian revolutionary
who died at thirty-one shortly after fighting in Garibaldi's Exped-
ition of the Thousand. *Le confessioni d'un italiano* (*Confessions of an
Italian*) is a long historical novel tracing the development of the Italian Unification, but it is also a coming-of-age novel characterized by
contradictions and digressions, rich in moments of spontaneous vitality and strong sensations which delineate a radical and materialist
ethics.

> Oh la vita dell'universo nella solitudine è lo spettacolo più su-
> blime, più indescrivibile che ferisca l'occhio dell'uomo! Perciò
> ammiriamo il mare nella sua eterna battaglia, il cielo né suoi
> tempestosi annuvolamenti, la notte né suoi fecondi silenzi, nel-
> le sue estive fosforescenze. È una vita che si sente e sembra
> comunicare a noi il sentimento di un'esistenza più vasta più
> completa dell'umana. Allora non siamo più i critici e i legislato-
> ri, ma gli occhi, gli orecchi, i pensieri del mondo; l'intelligenza
> non è più un tutto, ma una parte; l'uomo non pretende più di
> comprendere e di dominar l'universo, ma sente, palpita, respira
> con esso.[32]

> (Oh yes, the life of the universe experienced in solitude is a
> majestic spectacle beyond all words! That is why we admire
> the sea in its eternal battles; the sky with its tempestuous array
> of clouds; the night in its fecund silences and in its summer
> luminescence. All this life makes us feel the presence of some
> existence vaster and deeper than our own. It means we human
> beings are no longer the critics and the lawmakers, but the eyes,
> the ears and the thoughts of the world; intelligence is no longer
> all, but a part; man no longer thinks he can understand and
> dominate the universe, but feels, palpitates and breathes with
> it.)[33]

The young protagonist's discovery of the sea narrated in this passage
exemplifies one of these moments, 'redemptive moments of release

---

32   Ippolito Nievo, *Le confessioni d'un italiano* (Milan: Mondadori, 1981), p. 417.
33   Ippolito Nievo, *Confessions of an Italian*, trans. by Frederika Randall (London: Pen-
      guin, 2014), p. 346.

from the Cartesian worldview that dominates modernity', where the ideological orientation of narration is put aside, and the protagonist finds himself immersed in the experience of the living present.[34]

Goliarda Sapienza (1924–1996) is a Sicilian queer radical writer and actress, increasingly regarded as one of the most original voices in twentieth-century Italy. Her major novel, *L'arte della gioia* (*The Art of Joy*), is also a combination of historical narrative and coming-of-age novel — Nievo actually being one of its literary models. Informed by an anarchist and Epicurean outlook, it tells the story of Modesta, born on the first day of 1900, and her pursuit of 'the art of joy' — the rejection of any normative imposition, the auscultation of the self, and the free enjoyment of the senses.

> Ora solo una pace profonda invade il suo corpo maturo a ogni emozione della pelle, delle vene, delle giunture. Corpo padrone di se stesso, reso sapiente dall'intelligenza della carne. Intelligenza profonda della materia ... del tatto, dello sguardo, del palato. Riversa sullo scoglio, Modesta osserva come i suoi sensi maturati possano contenere senza fragili paure d'infanzia tutto l'azzurro, il vento, la distanza. Stupita, scopre il significato dell'arte che il suo corpo s'è conquistato in quel lungo, breve tragitto dei suoi cinquant'anni. È come una seconda giovinezza, ma con in più la coscienza precisa d'essere giovani, la coscienza del come godere, toccare, guardare.[35]

> (Now, only a profound peace invades her mature body at each sensation of her skin, veins, joints. A body that is its own master, made wise by an understanding of the flesh. A profound awareness ... of touch, sight, taste. Lying on her back on the rocky ledge, Modesta observes how her developed senses can take in the entire blue expanse, the wind, the distance, without the fragile fears of childhood. Astonished, she discovers the meaning of the skill her body has acquired during the long, brief course of her fifty years. It's like a second childhood, but with a precise awareness of being young, an appreciation of how to touch, see, enjoy.)[36]

---

34   Pecora, 'Be Here Now', p. 41.

35   Goliarda Sapienza, *L'arte della gioia* (Turin: Einaudi, 2008), pp. 482–83.

36   Goliarda Sapienza, *The Art of Joy*, trans. by Anne Milano Appel (London: Penguin, 2013), p. 634.

In this passage, Modesta pauses to enjoy intensified sensations of aliveness — joy, characterized by the possibility to contain within herself the vastness of the sky, the wind, the horizon, entering into a resonant relationship with the environment without fear and without control, for the experience is both the result of a practice, the art of joy, and an always renovated surprise. Abandoning herself to the pleasure of the senses and the enjoyment of her body constitutes Modesta's achievement in the novel. This achieved freedom, however, does not coincide with a final and crystallized form of identity; rather, it is a profound awareness of temporality, where the living present functions as the heightened awareness of the temporal — embodied and mutable — constitution of the self: Maturity is a second childhood, an ongoing process of becoming. In both Nievo's and Sapienza's novels, passages such as these make explicit the materialist horizon that informs their works, as the experiences they represent encapsulate the protagonists' approach to existence, an approach that is performatively reflected in syncretic, dynamic, and non-teleological narrative structures.[37]

We can now contrast these figurations of the temporality of the living present with representations of traumatized time. The experience of trauma, an extreme awareness of vulnerability, causes an interruption in the flow of temporality. Trust that the next moment will come is suspended, the chain of memory and anticipation is disrupted, the dimension of the past irrupts and overlaps with the present, emptying it of its regenerative potential. While in the living present the subject is at the centre of perceptions, memory, and projections, interacting with the world as an embodied and emplaced unit with duration, trauma can impact on the cognitive ability to organize space and time. Experiences of traumatized temporality are pervasively present in writings by oppressed subjects, who are exposed both to intense forms of violence and to the cognitive dissonance deriving from the naturalization or mystification of the violence they undergo in dominant discourses.

Elena Ferrante's short novel *I giorni dell'abbandono* (*The Days of Abandonment*) centres on the loss of cognition, the disorienta-

---

37   On the performative relationship between narrative structure and materialist ethical
      worldview in *Le confessioni d'un italiano* and *L'arte della gioia*, see Alberica Bazzoni,
      'Nievo's Pisana and Sapienza's Modesta: Female Heroism as a Challenge to Gendered
      Configurations of the Nation', *The Italianist*, 39.3 (2019), pp. 332–46.

tion, the spatial and temporal entrapment experienced by a woman, Olga, whose husband's sudden abandonment triggers in her previous wounds.[38] While in the living present the frame — the performance of a reduction — concentrates attention by holding the experience, in *I giorni dell'abbandono* the protagonist is trapped in her apartment: an inexplicably locked door stops time from flowing, ghosts from the past invade the rooms, the body is an unruly and destructive force. In her collection of essays *Frantumaglia*, Ferrante describes the experience of traumatized time: 'The eruption of suffering cancels out linear time, breaks it, makes it into whirling squiggles.'[39] The collapse of temporality represented in the novel is the direct overturning of the kinaesthetic present:

> Non volevo correre, se correvo mi rompevo, già ogni gradino lasciato alle spalle si disfaceva subito dopo persino nella memoria, e la ringhiera, la parete giallina mi correvano di lato fluide, a cascata. [...] alle spalle mi sentivo una scia gassosa, ero una cometa. [...] Forse ero troppo stanca per trattenere il mondo dentro l'ordine consueto.[40]

> (I didn't want to run, if I ran I would break, every step left behind disintegrated immediately afterward, even in memory, and the banister, the yellow wall rushed by me fluidly, cascading. I saw only the flights of stairs, with their clear segments, behind me was a gassy wake, I was a comet. [...] Maybe I was too tired to maintain the usual order of the world.)[41]

The subject cannot retain perceptions and compose them into duration, spatial distinctions melt and vital movement is impeded. When trauma impacts on temporality, the present is overcrowded with other

---

38 On trauma in *I giorni dell'abbandono*, see Victor H. Zarour Zarzar, 'The Grammar of Abandonment in *I giorni dell'abbandono*', MLN, 135.1 (2020), pp. 327–44, and Alberica Bazzoni, 'Trauma, Sadomasochism, and the Female Body in Elena Ferrante's *I giorni dell'abbandono*', in *Italian Studies Across Disciplines: Interdisciplinarity, New Approaches and Future Directions*, ed. by Marco Ceravolo and Anna Finozzi (Rome: Aracne, 2022), pp. 165–201.

39 Elena Ferrante, *Frantumaglia*, trans. by Ann Goldstein (New York: Europa Editions, 2016), pp. 107–08.

40 Elena Ferrante, *I giorni dell'abbandono* (Rome: Edizioni e/o, 2002), pp. 105–06.

41 Elena Ferrante, *The Days of Abandonment*, trans. by Ann Goldstein (New York: Europa Editions, 2005), p. 118.

dimensions, in which the subject loses orientation and risks disintegration:

> se mi fossi abbandonata, sentivo che quel giorno e lo spazio
> stesso dell'appartamento si sarebbero aperti a tanti tempi di-
> versi, a una folla di ambienti e persone e cose e me stesse che
> avrebbero esibito tutte, simultaneamente presenti, eventi reali,
> sogni, incubi, fino a creare un labirinto così fitto da cui non sarei
> più uscita.[42]

> (if I were to abandon myself, I felt, then, that day and the very
> space of the apartment would be open to many different times,
> to a crowd of environments and persons and things and selves
> who, simultaneously present, would offer real events, dreams,
> nightmares, to the point of creating a labyrinth so dense that I
> would never get out of it.)[43]

Another fundamental element of traumatized time is that of iteration,
which blurs all distinctions between temporal dimensions. The narrative fragments that compose Sapienza's *Destino coatto* (Compulsory
Destiny), for example, articulate an experience of disrupted time and
self through the use of syncopated language, claustrophobic spaces,
hallucinations, and obsessions. In this brief prose, the speaking voice
'cries out' (to use Caruth's apt definition of narratives of trauma) a temporal block, a state of suspension which exhausts any sense of openness
and change:

> Vorrei tanto scordarmi di ieri ma non posso. Lavoro per casa,
> cucino, tengo in braccio Carluccio, ma non posso scordarmi di
> ieri. È lì, davanti a me. Ieri con quel sole che spaccava le pietre lì
> davanti dietro i vetri sporchi di pioggia. Domani li debbo lavare
> un'altra volta.[44]

> (I would really want to forget about yesterday but I can't. I
> work at home, I cook, I hold little Carluccio, but I can't forget
> about yesterday. It's there, in front of me. Yesterday, with that
> crushing sun right there behind the windowpanes, dirty with
> rain. Tomorrow I shall clean them again.)

---

42   Ferrante, *I giorni dell'abbandono*, p. 126.
43   Ferrante, *The Days of Abandonment*, p. 141.
44   Goliarda Sapienza, *Destino coatto* (Rome: Empiria, 2002), p. 110.

These texts provide contrary instances of figurations of the living present, representing the traumatized time of loss, depression, and anxiety. Sapienza's experimental collection, which consists of narrative fragments that do not recompose any narrative development, effectively represents the disrupted temporality of trauma. Past and present, perceptions and hallucinations, disconnected experiences and dreams all overlap, eroding the embodied relationship between self and world grounded in the sense of temporality:

> Mi sembra che stavo vomitando. Qualcuno mi teneva la testa e la tazza era grigia, sbeccata. Qualcuno mi teneva la fronte e mi frugava nella gola, in fondo. Mi faceva il solletico. Volevo ridere ma avevo freddo. Sempre ho sofferto il freddo ed il solletico. Carlo lo sapeva e sempre mi afferrava alla vita e mi faceva il solletico ma non vomitavo. Ridevo. Mentre adesso non posso ridere e vomito. Vomito delle palline bianche nel cesso dove ieri ho cercato di fare *la pupù, come dicevamo a Catania, ti ricordi, Carlo?* E non ci sono riuscita.[45]

> (I think I was vomiting. Somebody was holding my head and the toilet was grey and chipped. Somebody was holding my forehead and rummaging deep in my throat. It tickled me. I wanted to laugh but I was cold. I've always suffered from cold and tickle. Carlo knew it and he grabbed my waist all the time and tickled me but I didn't vomit. I laughed. But now I can't laugh and I vomit. I vomit white little balls in the toilet where yesterday I tried *to poo, like we used to say back then in Catania, do you remember, Carlo?* And I couldn't.)

In Ferrante's and Sapienza's texts, the process of becoming through the continuous flow of temporality is interrupted. While in experiences of the living present the subject feels a deep interconnection with the world, as scenes involve a relationship with the natural elements and especially the sea, these passages take place in the entrapped space of the house, with walls, doors, and dirty windows impeding connection — which is primarily a connection with the subject's own embodied self. As the present is reduced to other temporal dimensions, the unity and duration of the self disperses.

---

45   Ibid., p. 95.

3. AFFECT, DESIRE, POLITICS

What is at stake in a reduction to the living present? And what relationship exists between trauma and the living present? The focus on the living present, and its interruption in traumatized time, sheds light on the affect of temporality and interrogates specifically the question of vulnerability. As O'Brien observes, '[t]he term *trauma* has been used to describe a wide variety of experiences all of which share in common the individual's recognition of her/his own vulnerability.'[46] The affect that sustains the living present consists in a core sense of trust. In conditions of safety, time is experienced as continuous, the chain of temporality is sustained by trust that the next moment will come. Trauma — the experience of one's extreme vulnerability through violence and loss — renders the continuity of time unsafe. Trauma disrupts the subjects' belief that they will continue to exist through time, taking away the affective ground of trust and the flow of life that it sustains.

If the living present is rooted in an affect of trust, the importance of a reduction to the living present is related to an ethics and politics of becoming. The act of reduction consists in the creation of a holding frame, a safe context within which to practice trust and negotiate unsafety. Literature, and the arts in general, is one of these spaces. Writing and reading can be understood as acts of creating continuity through time, sustaining attention, performing the very encounter between self and world in its temporal happening. Through reduction, creating a holding frame, we learn to negotiate unsafety within a safe boundary. The frame, the 'hedgerow', also holds experience in theatrical and musical performances, in rituals, in the therapeutic session, in meditation. Practicing transitions between different states of attention, moving inside and outside of the frame of reduction, nourishes awareness of the temporal and embodied constitution of the self and sustains the ability to thread unsafety. Reduction to the living present is related to what Michel Foucault, reflecting on ancient philosophy as a practice, defines as 'techniques of the self' or 'arts of existence', and to the practices of the self that are central in Eastern traditions of thought, especially Buddhism and Taoism.[47]

---

46 O'Brien, 'Telling Time', p. 209.
47 Michel Foucault, *The History of Sexuality*, trans. by Robert Hurley, 4 vols (London: Penguin, 1978–2021), II: *The Use of Pleasure* [1984] (1992), pp. 10–11.

Finally, the experience of the kinaesthetic present is linked to processes of subjectivation and nourishment of desire which have a precise ethical and political connotation. The reconfiguration of the sovereign subject as a desiring, embodied, and relational subject is a core project of feminism, and of subaltern struggles more broadly. As the temporality of embodied becoming, the living present is a site of possibility of such a reconfiguration of the subject:

> This subject is psychologically embedded in the corporeal materiality of the self. The enfleshed intensive or nomadic subject is an in-between: a folding in of external influences, and a simultaneous folding out of affects. As a mobile entity — mobile in space and time — this subject is continually in process but is also capable of lasting through sets of discontinuous variations while remaining extraordinarily faithful to itself.[48]

As a temporal dimension that humans share with other animals and the natural environment, the living present is also the domain of relationality and environmental embeddedness, for it is the flow in which the encounter with the world is constantly produced, thus pointing to a posthuman, ecocritical ethics.[49] The living present nourishes openness to the unknown and the actualization of 'the endless vitality of life as a process of continuous becoming'.[50] It enables processes of dis-identification from normative identities and the re-appropriation of one's embodied subjectivity. As Braidotti claims,

> Positive metamorphosis can be seen as political passion. It endorses the kinds of becomings that destabilize dominant power relations and deterritorialize fixed identities and mainstream values. Such a metamorphosis infuses a joyful sense of empowerment into a subject that is always in the process of becoming.[51]

In this sense, subalterns' redeployments of reduction serve to counter normative and violent reductions of 'others' — women, Black people,

---

48   Braidotti, 'The Politics of Life', p. 187.
49   See for example Astrida Neimanis, *Bodies of Water: Posthuman Feminist Phenomenology* (London: Bloomsbury Academic, 2017) <https://doi.org/10.5040/9781474275415>.
50   Braidotti, 'The Politics of Life', p. 182.
51   Ibid., p. 192.

queer people, disabled people — to their bodies. Reduction is inherited as a practice of questioning dominant discourses, to which
the productive domain of experience is opposed.[52] Deeply inspired
by Audre Lorde's poetics and politics of the erotic, Black Buddhist
queer thinker and activist Lama Rod Owens summarizes with great
clarity the political stake of embodiment for subaltern struggles: 'I
noticed in my practice that internalized oppression continued as long
as I remained disembodied. The work of embodiment was the work of
reclaiming my body, healing and managing my trauma, and embracing
agency over my own body.'[53]

A focus on the living present activates processes of dis-identification and makes space for new beginnings and changes. Reduction
enables us to open to the unshaped, to put aside what we already know
and how we are constructed, enacting a movement of subtraction from
other temporalities which are connected to heteronomous, overdeter-
mining structures. In the living present, we practice how to unlock
traumatized structures of time, so that life can flow again.

---

52   See Sonia Kruks, *Retrieving Experience: Subjectivity and Recognition in Feminist Politics*
     (Ithaca, NY: Cornell University Press, 2001).
53   Lama Rod Owens, *Love and Rage: The Path of Liberation Through Anger* (Berkeley, CA:
     North Atlantic Books, 2020), pp. 80–81.

Seeking *Home*
Vignettes of Homes and Homing
AMINA ELHALAWANI

Leaving is always
like this. Years
of hours and days
ticked off like
a body count:
what's left but
shards of memory
smoothed and hoarded,
shrapnel griefs,
a few regrets?
It should be simple
[...]
But lines etched
into skin after years
of weather
chart boundaries
we cannot cross:
[...] lines of salt[1]

According to the World Migration Report 2020 of the International
Organization for Migration (IOM), the world saw yet another upsurge

---

1   Lisa Suhair Majaj, 'Departure', in Majaj, *Geographies of Light* (Washington, DC: Del
     Sol Press, 2009), pp. 43–44 (p. 43). Courtesy of the author.

in migration with around 272 million migrants in 2019.[2] For these migrants, the question of home is a complicated one, and one which needs careful examination beyond the dichotomous home and away, place of origin and place of residence, which often haunt postcolonial and diaspora studies. My endeavour in this chapter, thus, is to look at the concept of home, and attempt to identify some aspects of what constitutes and/or (re)creates it for displaced individuals, by considering how home manifests itself in two disparate projects: *Salt of this Sea*, a film by Palestinian director Annemarie Jacir and *The Idea of Home*, a collection of essays by Australian writer John Hughes.[3]

I begin my reflection by asking what really distinguishes home from any other space. 'Home', like any other place, is built on a two-way relationship between people and the space they inhabit, and this chapter seeks to understand what is home by examining how places shape and are in turn shaped by individuals, what Paolo Boccagni calls 'homing' (or home as a social/relational process).

> As a process, homing holds a relational, appropriative and future-oriented side which should not go unnoticed. Contrary to the static and irenic subtext of the notions of home and domesticity, homing is an open-ended matter of evolving strivings, claims-making and conflicts; hence, an ultimately political matter.
>
> While homing is played out at an individual level, it also points to a question of broader societal relevance.[4]

Making a claim on ownership and being allowed access to both the home and the homeland thus constitutes a big part of 'homing', which by default designates a bordered space whose inside is walled or bounded from the outside world, and yet whose borders remain porous as interaction with that world continues to happen on a day-to-day basis. What migration highlights is the degree of porosity or impene-

---

2   *World Migration Report 2020*, ed. by Marie McAuliffe and Binod Khadria (Geneva: International Organization for Migration, 2019), p. 2.

3   *Salt of this Sea*, dir. and written by Annemarie Jacir, performances by Suheir Hammad, Saleh Bakri, Marwan Riyad Ideis, and Sylvia Wetz (Trigon-film, 2008); John Hughes, *The Idea of Home: Autobiographical Essays* (Artarmon: Giramondo Publishing Company, 2004).

4   Paolo Boccagni, *Migration and the Search for Home: Mapping Domestic Space in Migrants' Everyday Lives* (New York: Palgrave Macmillan, 2017), p. 23.

trability spaces are made to perform. The (im)mobility of individuals across borders unmasks the inherent power relations within what constitutes home and its relation to the outside world. Moreover, it highlights the necessary relations between individuals and space in the production of the home structure, both literally and metaphorically.

Edward Said describes exile as '[an] unhealable rift forced between a human being and a native place, between the self and its true home'.[5] Addressing the issue of displacement and migration in general, Sara Ahmed also describes migrant journeys as involving 'a splitting of home as place of origin and home as the sensory world of everyday experience'.[6] One way to explain this is through Gilles Deleuze and Félix Guattari's concept of 'deterritorialization'.[7] When bodies which are mobile by nature move away (whether forcefully or voluntarily) from their original home this deterritorialization creates a complicated dynamic in the spatial representation of the homeland. And yet these works/narratives — themselves gestures for what lies 'beyond' like Martin Heidegger's famous invocation of the Heidelberg bridge — transpose their authors to these faraway *homes*.[8] The words in such transnational narratives of home house a reductive though complex version of the 'home' as 'deterritorialized'.[9] The condensation

5   Edward Said, *Reflections on Exile and Other Essays* (Cambridge, MA: Harvard University Press, 2000), p. 179.

6   Sara Ahmed, 'Home and Away: Narratives of Migration and Estrangement', in Ahmed, *Strange Encounters: Embodied Others in Postcoloniality* (London: Routledge, 2000), pp. 77–94 (p. 90).

7   Gilles Deleuze and Félix Guattari, *A Thousand Plateaus: Capitalism and Schizophrenia*, trans. by Brian Massumi (Minneapolis: University of Minnesota Press, 1987).

8   Martin Heidegger, 'Building Dwelling Thinking', in Heidegger, *Poetry, Language and Thought*, trans. by Albert Hofstadter (New York: Perennial Classics, 2001), pp. 141–59. In this essay, Heidegger brings up the idea of the bridge structure to contemplate the relation between 'location' and 'space' as well as that between 'man' and 'space'. In his discussion, he explains that thoughts are able to take us to distant places: 'We do not represent distant things merely in our mind — as the textbooks have it — so that only mental representations of distant things run through our minds and heads as substitutes for the things. If all of us now think, from where we are right here, of the old bridge in Heidelberg, this thinking toward that location is not a mere experience inside the persons present here; rather, it belongs to the nature of our thinking of that bridge that in itself thinking gets through, persists through, the distance to that location. From this spot right here, we are there at the bridge — we are by no means at some representational content in our consciousness. From right here we may even be much nearer to that bridge and to what it makes room for than someone who uses it daily as an indifferent river crossing' (p. 154).

9   Deleuze and Guattari, *A Thousand Plateaus*.

of different elements relating back to materiality, geography, memory, imagination, and affects in these works presents home as a translocality which traces its history back to multiple tangents of inherited and experiential points of origin beyond the materiality of its walls or spatiotemporal locality.

In other words, while home is experienced from a certain location, it bears within itself histories and affects beyond stone and mortar or even the very territory it claims. Such materiality and immateriality of the home go hand in hand, because being is an embodied practice. According to Edward Casey, 'to be in the world, to be situated at all, is to be in place.'[10] To be home, to feel home, or even to make home is thus also by default to be in place. In other words, the relationship between bodies and place is at the heart of defining what home means. As such, home remains for the most part within the realm of personal experience or rather endeavour. Hence it becomes imperative to conjure home through thinking in singular cases.

In this context, the trope of the vignette — which is not restricted to literature but also borrowed by ethnographers and sociologists — becomes not only a metaphor for home writing, but also a tool which helps me (as well as the reader) to unpack the emotions, thoughts, and affects in what the text perceives as the experience of home, and as such this 'reductive' tool (or the vignette) packs/condenses what often seems ineffable, overwhelming, or impossible to express.[11]

In a poem called 'Athens Airport', Mahmoud Darwish presents his readers with a group of people stuck in transit at Athens airport, having left their home, unable to reach another.

> *Where did you come from?* asks the customs' official.
> And we answer: *From the sea!*
> *Where are you going?*
> *To the sea*, we answer.
> What is your address?
> A woman of our group says: *My village is the bundle on my back.*[12]

---

10   Edward Casey, *Getting Back into Place: Toward a Renewed Understanding of the Place-World* (Bloomington: Indiana University Press, 1993), p. xv.

11   Boccagni starts his own book, *Migration and the Search for Home*, with vignettes from his fieldwork with migrants.

12   Mahmoud Darwish, 'Athens Airport', in Darwish, *Unfortunately, It was Paradise: Selected Poems*, trans. and ed. by Munir Akash and Carolyn Forché with Sinan Antoon and Amira El-Zein (Berkeley: University of California Press, 2003), p. 12; italics in the original.

The terse answer of the woman — how matter of fact her reply to the customs' official is, and how it relates to survival and ownership — raises urgent questions on the nature of 'home' beyond its territorial spatial presence. In an attempt to find dwelling elsewhere, this woman's home is reduced to a 'bundle' of whatever she could carry. To borrow Darwish's image, I choose to separate loaded moments in the texts under scrutiny, which I call vignettes of home and/or homing. And my fascination with this trope is a fascination with the double bind of *packing* and *unpacking* the encounters and experiences that these texts present, their meanings, the emotions that are attached to them and the consequences they entail.

In other words, refusing to reduce home to just a location, though understanding that comprehending the complexity of the concept can only happen through some form of reduction, I choose to perform a reductive trope not necessarily to arrive at home as a destination or trajectory by reaching a final or ultimate definition, but simply to move *homeward*, coming closer to what the concept might stand for or hold by multiplying its meanings. In this journey, certain keywords stand out: temporality, experience, embodiment, condensation, or intensification, since here the experience is somehow homing itself in time and space — both shifting, both fleeting, but also somehow fixing something at least partly in narrative.

In the following section I shall illustrate what I mean by these vignettes through discussing scenes from *Salt of this Sea* and excerpts from *The Idea of Home*.

VIGNETTE 1: SCENES FROM *SALT OF THIS SEA*[13]

Salt of this Sea is a film which poetically packages difficult questions of belonging, of home, of loss, of trauma in a series of reduced or concentrated images both beautiful and painful. Annemarie Jacir's film demonstrates the tension embedded in (re)visiting Palestine for those in the diaspora, and how one constructs an image of home, as well as how one faces a place of which one has no firsthand experience but through inherited narrative memory. Suheir Hammad, a Palestinian-

---

13   I'm grateful to the ICI Berlin and to my fellow colleagues for their conversations on *Salt of this Sea*, and their engagement with my research in general.

American poet, author, and political activist, plays the lead role in Jacir's film, Soraya, whose story in fact resembles very much Hammad's own.

The casting of Hammad in this role is significant. Hammad, who was born in Amman Jordan to Palestinian parents, travelled to Brooklyn, New York with her parents when she was five, and through the film both actress and character encounter their homeland firsthand for the first time.[14] It is an encounter, though, with a place they already know!

In one scene from *Salt of this Sea*, Soraya is sitting with Emad, the Palestinian she meets and becomes friends with in Ramallah, on top of a hill, The landscape sprawls beneath them while they look all the way towards Jaffa and the sea. As Emad gestures to Soraya where Jaffa is, she in turn accurately describes the city and her grandparents' daily routine:

> Soraya: My grandfather swam in that sea every morning, then he'd walk on Al Helwa Street to reach Al Tawfiqiya library, then on to Al Nuzha Street. Cars weren't allowed to pass on Al Nuzha. The orange traders — Jaffa oranges — met at Al Salahi market. My grandfather always talked about the Al Madfa Café: Umm Kulthum sang there, and Farid al-Atrash. My grandmother really loved Farid. Sometimes, my grandparents went to the cinema. The Hamra Cinema. When they were broke, they'd wait by the side door and the doorman would sneak everyone in. Have you ever been there?
>
> Emad: Are you sure you've never been?

Soraya's narrative of Jaffa is not one of a simple fixed place but rather of a lived space, full of movement, itineraries, and experiences. It reveals a complex understanding of space in practice, as constantly produced as it is being experienced or *lived*, a space in which the real and the symbolic intertwine and which is based on a 'trialectics of being': 'spatiality', 'historicality', and 'sociality'.[15] Soraya's grandfather's

---

14   Hammad wrote her poetry collection *breaking poems* (New York: Cypher Books) after this experience.

15   Edward W. Soja, *Thirdspace: Journeys to Los Angeles and Other Real-and-Imagined Spaces* (Cambridge, MA and Oxford: Blackwell Publishers, 1996), pp. 70–71. According to Henri Lefebvre, social space is made up of complex relations between three levels of experiencing it, which Soja identifies as: perceived space, conceived space, and

walks of Jaffa draw out the city, not as a concept, not from above, but as spatialized utterance. In comparing walking to speech acts, Michel de Certeau considers pedestrian activity as a three-fold 'enunciative act': 'a process of appropriation of the topographical system on the part of the pedestrian [...], it is a spatial acting-out of the place [...]; and it implies relations among differentiated positions, that is, among pragmatic "contracts" in the form of movements.'[16] Within this narrative, the freedom of movement of Saraya's grandfather was not only allowed, but a certain ownership of place was practiced.

On the other hand, as Carol Fadda-Conrey points out, Soraya draws for us 'a narrative map of her grandparents' Jaffa', one that 'link[s] her life to a history that she feels she has missed' even though she has not in fact experienced it except through 'ancestral memories and stories'.[17] It is exactly at that moment in the film that Emad recounts his confinement and frustration, his experience of borders creating a tension with the free uninterrupted landscape they are in. Emad is sitting on top of a hill, looking into the horizon all the way to Jaffa and the sea, and yet is unable to navigate this 'open' landscape due to the enforcement of checkpoints and restrictions based on his identity. This juxtaposition of the ability to travel through inherited memory to Jaffa (so in a way through imagination) and the inability to experience it firsthand, is an example of the characters' continuous active confrontation with the material conditions of what they consider to be home.

In this particular frame, however, the camera pans out and exposes the open landscape sprawling towards the sea, posing no real barriers, but rather positioning them at the edge, at a threshold, which, if surpassed, would reconcile them with their past and allow them to reclaim their freedom in the present, a quest they decide to subversively

---

lived space. Building on Lefebvre's triads, Edward Soja conceptualizes his idea of third space, as a space where '[e]*verything* comes together': 'subjectivity and objectivity, the abstract and concrete, the real and the imagined, the knowable and the unimaginable, the repetitive and the differential, structure and agency, mind and body, consciousness and the unconscious, the disciplined and the transdisciplinary, everyday life and unending history' (pp. 56–57).

16   Michel de Certeau, *The Practice of Everyday Life*, trans. by Steven Rendall (Berkeley: University of California Press, 1984), pp. 98–99.

17   Carol Fadda-Conrey, *Contemporary Arab-American Literature: Transnational Reconfigurations of Citizenship and Belonging* (New York: New York University Press, 2014), p. 96.

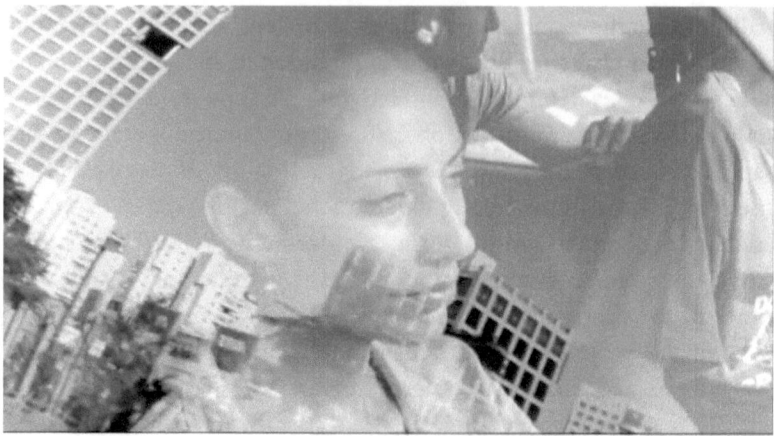

Figure 1. Still from *Salt of this Sea*, dir. by Jacir, 1:00:35. Photo Credit:
Philistine Films. Courtesy of the director.

undertake over the course of the film: to discover the land which they consider to be theirs but from which they are barred.

In this still frame from *Salt of this Sea* (Figure 1), the gaze of the camera through a car window, the refracted images and mirroring along with the close up on Soraya's face, bring us closer to understanding that what we are getting is a very personal, even visceral experience of the story. Soraya's face/body is made to merge with the territory it is trying to reclaim as its own. Over the course of this journey, the film plots out a map of traumas where Emad gets to visit whatever ruins are left of his village of Dawayima and Soraya gets to visit her grandparents' very house in Jaffa right by the sea.

Soraya's encounter with her ancestral home is overwhelming. The encounter is reminiscent of lines from a poem by Mahmoud Darwish dedicated to Edward Said. Set as a dialogue, the speaker, probably Darwish himself, asks Said what it was like to go back to his home in Jerusalem, while the voice of Said in the poem responds: 'I could not meet loss face | to face. I stood by the door like a beggar. | How could I ask permission from strangers sleeping in my own bed?'.[18] Likewise,

18   Mahmoud Darwish, 'Edward Said: A Contrapuntal Reading', trans. by Mona Anis, *Cultural Critique*, 67 (2007), pp. 175–82 (p. 180) <https://doi.org/10.1353/cul. 2007.0026>.

Figure 2. Stills from *Salt of this Sea*, dir. by Jacir, 01:25:00–01:31:00.
Photo Credit: Philistine Films. Courtesy of the director.

finding her grandparents' house already inhabited by someone else
makes Soraya sick. Though the current owner invites them in, Soraya
cannot make peace with the fact that her grandfather was never com-
pensated for the loss that he and his family had to endure, accusing
the current owner of the house of stealing her family's home as they
were forced to leave. In the following frame in the film Soraya breaks
down by the sea. And while the dream of capturing home diminishes
— as only memories survive in the form of waves which enact the
whispers of those who lived there, of those who left, memories that
are impossible to grasp because of their fluidity — the house itself
and its tiled floors stand witness to its original owners. Nonetheless,
the confrontation with the material structure of the house is only a
confirmation of Soraya's loss of what she identified as home. The imagined is lost with the encounter of the real and the narratives of her
grandfather's house are now complemented if not overwritten by her
own very painful encounter with its loss.

An equally moving scene is that in which Emad and Soraya embark
on a process of homemaking in Dawayima, the village that was razed to
the ground, and where Emad originally comes from. In this scene, an
attempt to reclaim what was lost is enacted through the simple actions
of spreading a bedcover to sleep on and hanging a picture on the wall
with the word home on it, almost akin to how a prop changes the

setting immediately and magically in theatre, even if for a moment.[19] The contrast between the act of homemaking and the violence inherent in the image of the ruins of the village provides a moving encounter with a past that intersects so viscerally with the present only to remind the characters of their perpetual loss (Figure 2). And yet it allows for that fleeting moment of homing to occur: in this moment, the past (they light a candle for the dead), the present (they hang a picture, make a bed, put up a curtain even, and plant something in the garden), and the future (where they sit and dream of what they would do if they lived there or rather what they would have done if the present was different) set home as a notion apart from time, as a place where temporalities converge.

These moments of homing are brief, however, vignette-like, real enough, and yet elusive in contrast to the reality in which they live.

VIGNETTE 2: FROM JOHN HUGHES'S *THE IDEA OF HOME*

John Hughes is an Australian writer whose maternal grandparents travelled from Ukraine to Australia fleeing the Second World War. And while his book *The Idea of Home: Autobiographical Essays* presents itself as a set of essays, its subtitle gives away its own subjective trajectory and reveals that these essays are in fact 'autobiographical' — hence, highly personal.

The depiction of houses in Hughes's text, especially his mother's obsession with the basement, sheds light on how houses *home* people and objects rather than just 'house' them:

> The basement is the memory of the house. It expands though its walls remain fixed. In truth, it makes a mockery of walls. [...] My mother has no time for walls. She refuses to allow them to get in the way.[20]

The basement walls in Hughes's text expand to accommodate objects that Hughes's mother either keeps collecting or refuses to throw away, so that the structure of the house explodes beyond the contours of its

---

19   I'd like to thank Manuele Gragnolati for the interesting conversations we had about this scene in particular.

20   Hughes, *The Idea of Home*, p. 52.

designated space because of the mother's act of compulsive accumulation of objects which outgrows the storage space.

According to Casey,

> Built places [...] are extensions of our bodies. They are not just places, as the Aristotelian model of place as a strict container implies, *in which* these bodies move and position themselves. Places built for residing are rather an enlargement of our already existing embodiment into *an entire life-world of dwelling*. Moreover, thanks to increasingly intimate relationships with their material structures, the longer we reside in places, the more bodylike they seem to be [...] they become places created in our own bodily image.[21]

The analogy between the basement and memory is central, thus, because it nods to a layering of narratives and a constant resurfacing of that which lies forgotten, perhaps repressed within the body of the house, which represents an extension of the bodies of its inhabitants.

For Hughes, the objects his mother hoards are a means of turning the house into a home, a means of creating belonging, a process of homing, despite having 'no interest in what she collects'.[22]

> Her collecting is an act of rescue: all the unwanted, unloved, broken, bargain, superseded things of the world are, if not redeemed by her keeping, at least given a home. They belong. And there can never be enough.[23]

Despite the process of boxing or repressing these items to lay forgotten, on a deeper level the mother's refusal to get rid of objects from their past, their childhood, etc., as well as her compulsion to continue homing 'other people's junk', may resemble a more complex desire to both remember and forget by burying these items indiscriminately in the basement, never to be disturbed.[24] 'Once the object is put in the basement it need never be visited again. Forgotten, it is at peace.'[25]

As Hughes points out, however, even though his mother never intended these objects to resemble a legacy, when she dies, someone

---

21   Casey, *Getting Back into Place*, p. 120.
22   Hughes, *The Idea of Home*, p. 67.
23   Ibid., pp. 67–68.
24   Ibid., p. 67.
25   Ibid., p. 70.

will have to sort through them, *remember* them, in a way *archive* them, as Hughes himself is now recalling all the stories of his grandfather in this very book upon the knowledge of his loss. 'That is the curse of objects, and their beauty I suppose: they keep the past alive and they guarantee the future, straddling the present like a bridge.'[26] The boxes his mother stores in the basement and beyond, like his grandmother's recipes which he received during his PhD years in England, 'bridge' temporalities and geographies. These recipes of home cooking link Hughes's present in England with his family's present in Australia and their past in Ukraine. They take him *home*, which like the basement defies walls, borders, and geographies, and is only graspable through association and affect.

I will not dwell on that further and would like to instead look at an episode in the book in which, unlike Soraya who could sketch a narrative map of Jaffa, Hughes confesses that he knows very little of his family history, beyond what his grandfather was willing to share. According to Hughes, a continual project of forgetting haunted his grandfather's life. Erasure was actively sought to cope with the inter-minable process of homemaking, which manifested in his grandfather's obsession with building houses.

Hughes's grandfather continuously built houses but 'he treated them like tents'.[27] As soon as he finished a building project, he would start the next to the extent that the family would not need to make a trek across town to move from the old house to the new one, because the new project would be housed on the plot of land next door.[28] Every time he finished a building project, he would start a new one, a relentless endeavour of starting anew, of becoming, of defying fixation and walls through creating structures that are continuously denied to house memory, constantly denied to become home.

> My family knew the houses themselves would last forever; knew, too, that each, for them, was just another transit camp. There could be no attachment. Before they'd even settled my grandfather would sit at the dining table drawing plans for the next move.[29]

---

26   Ibid., p. 59.
27   Ibid., p. 50.
28   Ibid., pp. 49–50.
29   Ibid., p. 50.

Hughes's grandfather's building endeavour is ultimately a continuous project of homemaking and unmaking, in which the family is not allowed to settle into a state of being but is constantly forced to move, and restart the process of appropriating their dwelling place and forming new relations to it. Home becomes a continuously moving trajectory in this context.

In continual search for a feeling of home, Hughes is fascinated by his family's almost mythical journey during the Second World War in which they walked from Kiev to Naples, where they boarded a ship to Australia. In an attempt to recreate their journey, he decides to retrace their route by train but this time from Naples to Kiev, as if through retracing his family's footsteps before their exile, he would be able to conjure something of that memory which was forever lost to him. His encounter with the city of Naples, in his hands a map drawn by his grandfather which he fails to follow because it does not concord with reality, makes him realize his own fascination with the imagined over the real space: 'I preferred maps to reality and words to actions.'[30] His family journey could only be relived in his imagination. He writes:

> When I returned to Naples the unreality of the city hit me with a force even stronger than my first experience of it. I realised then, as I should have realised two years before, that the journey could only ever be imaginary for me. My journey had nothing whatsoever to do with war, or exile, or survival. By retracing my family's steps I would erase them one by one until all I was left with would be a list of names [of cities and train stations] like the one I had outlined above.[31]

Hughes then decides to cancel his plan because '[He does not] want the past to change'.[32] The only means by which he could own these places would be to not encounter them at all. Without an encounter with the reality of those cities, Hughes would be able to keep intact his imagined construction of them, which otherwise would shatter in the face of experiencing such spaces firsthand. At another occasion in the book, for example, Hughes writes of how sharing the photographs of his visit to Kiev with his grandfather 'stung in a way [Hughes]

---

30   Ibid., p. 169.
31   Ibid., p. 171.
32   Ibid., p. 173.

never fully realised. They destroyed Kiev (for him) [his grandfather] as effectively as the Germans did.[33] For Hughes's grandfather, those stories destroyed the possibility of affectively reconstructing a memory of the place at the time when he left. In this view, to encounter the space anew would be to destroy its memory, and thus destroy the perpetual longing for what it represented or is constructed to represent.

GRASPING HOME

Home in these narratives is constructed not only out of places or houses but in the meanings that they carry. Home may be emplaced but is not spatially bound by its very walls. Bodies home houses as much as houses home people. As such, home in both cases signals to something that lies beyond its very structure. Grasping it is made both difficult and possible because of the fact that it is itself a reduction caught up in a complicated entanglement between the past, the present, and the future, which allows it to only be captured in fragments or vignettes, be they stories, objects, or lived moments of getting close or veering towards it but never really catching it. In other words, there is always something very elusive about home, and in these two works, we can never really be home or rather reach home, we can only get *almost* there…

---

33   Ibid., p. 24.

Law Is Other Wor(l)ds

XENIA CHIARAMONTE

> there is no single road per se to human improve-
> ment. There are many paths, each situated in the
> actual places, such as prairies, forests, deserts,
> and so forth, and environments where our tribal
> societies and cultures emerged. The experiences
> of time and history are shaped by places.
>
> Daniel R. Wildcat[1]

REDUCTION TO TEXT

The law, perfect stranger: a high-ranking stranger in front of which fear or reverence, gestures that recall the sacred, emerge and tend to prevent a deeper inquiry. As a matter of fact, the knowledge of law seems destined to belong to a restricted circle of people, and to remain an affair for specialists, the only ones able to understand its concocted and redundant language. As for the others: as long as they do not find themselves 'before the law' they can cautiously ignore that door.

---

1   Daniel R. Wildcat, 'Indigenizing the Future: Why We Must Think Spatially in the Twenty-first Century', *American Studies*, 46.3 (2005), pp. 417–40 (p. 434) <https://journals.ku.edu/amsj/article/view/2969> [accessed 1 June 2022], quoted in Karen Barad, 'Troubling Time/s and Ecologies of Nothingness: Re-turning, Re-membering, and Facing the Incalculable', *New Formations: A Journal of Culture/Theory/Politics*, 92 (2018), pp. 56–86 (p. 60) <https://doi.org/10.3898/NEWF:92.05.2017>.

In the genealogy of law, we already find this trace as it is a specialized class that deals with law: the jurists. It is a privileged class, of course, but it should be noted that it is not the one in power, and therefore to be confused with neither politics nor morality nor religion, as they have other social figures.

The word *jurist* is registered exclusively in the Latin language because in the nebula surrounding the origin of *ius*, at least one thing is certain: it was invented in Rome.[2]

Here a preliminary clarification is needed. The English language does not distinguish precisely between *ius* and *lex* and tends to use the word *law* indiscriminately. To clarify the distinction, in these opening lines we will employ 'law' to mean *lex* and 'right' to mean *ius*.

What does it mean that *ius* or *right* is a Roman invention? After all, have we not always known that laws were also issued in ancient Athens? Ancient Greece did not know the profession of the jurist. There were legislators — there is no doubt about that — but not jurists. The laws emanated from kings and bore their names. Those laws often died with them. There was a coincidence between ruling, or being the political head of Greek society, and being a legislator. The law always had a 'father'. One might say that psychoanalysis has remained attached to this Greek vision of the law: a law bearing the name of the father. Indeed, the Greek law was the law of the father.

The opposite is true about *right*, which qualifies as such precisely insofar as it is impersonal, acephalous, and in a state of perpetual transmission. Law and right are two apparently similar forms, and indeed are often confused with each other even though they carry different etymologies, thus inviting different archaeologies.

Lex, which derives from *legere*, refers to the action of publicly reading a text that contains an injunction to a person who is present, and doing so in the presence of the ordering magistrate. This is the form of law that existed in Greece. However, what was invented within the walls of the city of Rome was another form, which consisted in a depersonalized and apocryphal *reduction* of the law to a text. The text as such is *ius*. As Yan Thomas writes, following the effective distinction

---

2   Aldo Schiavone, *Ius: The Invention of Law in the West* (Cambridge, MA: Harvard University Press, 2012).

sketched by his mentor André Magdelain: 'Between *ius* and *lex* lies the whole difference between a prescription that has no origin and one that must be attributed to someone.'[3]

THE ARCHITECTURE OF THE CITY

What is the origin of this prescription without origin? From Thomas we know only one thing about the origin of *ius*, and we know it *de relato*: it emerged *ab urbe condita*, in a founded city. Only indirectly, therefore — that is, relying on the very space that brings *ius* into being — can one affirm that it originated.

Hence the genealogy of right — through this mediated and spatial origin — shows the traits of a form that is in fact always already a *relation*.

If right is first and foremost a relation (here within the space of the city), rather than detecting its identity — intended as its individual elementary structure — we would only have to explore its primal relationality, its always already *common* character. And from that, perhaps, we would be inclined to see in it a kind of architecture. Indeed, right could be described as the invisible and magical architecture of the city. But if, like architecture, it coincides with the space of the city, its relational nature can lead to more appropriate questions than those commonly asked of it. Instead of the classic moot question 'what is right?' such a genealogy proposes to look at *how* and *where* it acts, how its operations function, that is, what is implicated in this primal relation.

Once the distinction between *ius* and *lex* has been made and explained, one is permitted to use the more common English word 'law' (intended as *diritto, droit, derecho, direito, Recht*) with reference primarily to *ius*, that is, the legal technique and juridical science.

This piece aims to explain how law — in this precise sense of *ius* — works: the implication of its always already transmitted 'origin', the operations it performs, and the technique by which the objects of law are forged and transformed. The attempt is to show the making of these categories through an eminently casuistic approach. The case is indeed

---

3   Yan Thomas, 'Idées romaines sur l'origine et la transmission du droit', in Thomas, *Les opérations du droit* (Paris: EHESS-Seuil-Gallimard, 2011), pp. 69–84 (p. 72). Unless otherwise noted, all translations are mine.

the essential laboratory for the practice of law. Once the toolbox has been defined, a specific case, that of 'nature', will be tackled in order to test the categories of law and see its technique of reducing the 'real' world at work.

A COLLECTION TRANSMITTED

The Romans do not accord law any origin, nor even a founder. Instead, we possess foundational traces of the city. They are mythical but the intent is to establish a foundation. However, the founder of Rome never intended to give himself the title of demiurge of the law. According to the sources, the emphasis is placed not on the origin or invention of law but on its *transmission*: 'the *ius* is presented in a body of rules known under the sign of their collector' and 'the origin of the norms is erased under the eponym of the one who received and transmitted them.'[4] The emphasis is so clearly placed on the legal text that it purposely eclipses the role of its potential authors: neither in the singular nor in the plural do we have traces of a subject of the invention of law. There are certainly several compilers but no authors.

Law is first and foremost text. Who are its inventors? Agents — whose names are in oblivion — who *succeed* one another in the service of a continuous translation. Hence the juridical temporality we are describing is not really historical: 'Jurisprudence does not have a history, but a genealogy. The unity of the same collective subject runs through it.'[5]

In the words of Cornelia Vismann, one can say that 'the beginnings of law lie in the archive', which functions as a *receptacle*:[6]

> As an archive can never contain itself as its own beginning, it is a commencement in the strict sense, this initial point can only be archived as a blank. [...] [A]n archive archaeology [...] refers to that which does not speak, the space of the archive, the shelves, the dust. It mistrusts words and especially the word *arkhé* itself.[7]

---

4   Ibid., p. 71.

5   Ibid., p. 77.

6   Cornelia Vismann, 'The Archive and the Beginning of Law', in *Derrida and Legal Philosophy*, ed. by Peter Goodrich, Florian Hoffmann, Michel Rosenfeld, and Cornelia Vismann (London: Palgrave Macmillan, 2008), pp. 41–54 (p. 42).

7   Ibid., p. 51.

Such an emphasis on materiality in the approach to law is by no means common. In order to offer an idea of how law is commonly thought of, one might resort to Max Weber's words: 'An order will be called *law* [Recht] if it is externally guaranteed by the probability that coercion (physical or psychological), to bring about conformity or avenge violation, will be applied by a *staff* of people holding themselves specially ready for that purpose.'[8]

The debate over what is meant by 'staff' and whether such a translation is adequate is far from over. What is certain is that this view carries a certain idea of law and its constructs, i.e. its institutional inventions: law is seen as command and sanction and the coercive aspect — coming from a certain handful of people — is underlined.

While looking at the archive-form, or better, at law as receptacle, means focusing attention on 'things', on the materiality of legal sources, an approach such as Weber's is systematically centred on the person (whether juridical or physical).

And there is more: looking at the constructs of law as things means focusing on the technical aspect emancipated from this or that social actor, and on law as a *medium* that creates with words what it designates and pronounces. Thus, an approach based on the law as a text, on *ius*, can be detached from an approach centred on *lex*.

But let us proceed in order. We shall see, first of all, how law, as a language and a means of constructing forms, is better understood through *legal* ways.

LOST IN TRANSLATION

Trying to read the language of law and its technical operations means not allowing oneself to be deceived by perspectives that hope to 'unveil' something by superimposing other languages on the language of law. This is a problem common to jurists, too, who become attached to other branches of knowledge and end up turning to other forms of knowledge in order to decipher the law, with the dramatic result that they fail to grasp the main aspect: law is first and foremost a technique.

---

8   Max Weber, *On Law in Economy and Society*, trans. by Edward Shild and Max Rheinstein (New York: Simon & Schuster, 1954), p. 5.

The crucial suggestion that we take up, starting from the teaching of Thomas, is that of refining the gaze that we turn to law, precisely by focusing on the techniques and language that this same art has constructed to operate in the social world.

Let us start by seeing how the operations of the law should not be seen (and do not work), and what kind of 'other' knowledge is superimposed on them to the detriment of an understanding of what is at stake in legal technique.

First of all, the macroscopic approach, whether political or purely theoretical: 'in general legal theory or political theory [...] with the aim of considering everything, one ends up offering a general inter-pretation of the totality of the world, i.e. a meta-discourse, for which another can immediately take its place.'[9]

A commonly used phrase, at least among jurists, invites us to see the common functionality of philosophy and law but also to recognize their different spatialities: philosophy is to Athens as law is to Rome. These are two ways, two very different forms, but with a common function: organizing the world through categories. This shared func-tion, and the substantial difference between philosophy and law, is not easily understood. On the one hand, the analogies are certainly there: they are both languages. On the other hand, they order the world in different ways.

The problem with a philosophical approach to law is that it fails to grasp the most important thing about law, namely that it is an operative language. Its language is technical in the sense that it pronounces what it does and does what it 'promises' to do through its own uttered words. Legal language is performative: law builds things with and through 'its' words. This is why the words of law are not only concepts but first and foremost *tools*. That is, they are words that serve to operate.

---

9   Yan Thomas, 'Prefacio', in Thomas, *Los artificios de las instituciones. Estudios de derecho romano* (Buenos Aires: Eudeba, 1999), pp. 9–12 (p. 10). In such a manner that recalls the process of being 'lost in translation', here we follow — and translate into English — the Italian edition of the text as the original Spanish foreword cannot be located: Yan Thomas, 'Prefazione a *L'artificio delle istituzioni*', trans. and presented by Michele Spanò, in *Almanacco di Filosofia e Politica 2. Istituzione. Filosofia, politica, storia*, ed. by Mattia Di Pierro, Francesco Marchesi, and Elia Zaru (Macerata: Quodlibet, 2020), pp. 249–53 (p. 251).

Law almost never offers definitions; it does not clarify the meaning of the words it uses. Rarely do we find norms that offer the meaning of a notion and the rules of interpretation of the notion itself. It would be more correct to say that the language of law, rather than being made up of concepts, is made up of words that over time can also undergo variations, even very profound ones, in meaning. They are signifiers rather than meanings, so to speak.

That is why an approach that wants to see as errors the inconsistencies that can be found in the different meanings of legal names forgets the nature of legal lemmas, and takes words for coherent logical categories. Further on, with reference to the signifier 'nature', we will see how different if not contradictory meanings of the same word overlap.

At the same time, the millennial refinement of the words of law tends not to allow a 'casual' use of lemmas. Law is not a language full of synonyms. On the contrary, legal language tends to regard as an error the equivalence between names that can often be found in ordinary language. Possession, ownership, or property can, for example, be used indifferently in common usage, but for law they are different categories, whose equivalence would only be seen as an error, and even a serious one at that. The rule — known to linguists, and seemingly outlandish — that states that synonyms do not exist, or are very rare, since etymology is always different and thus refers to different linguistic nodes and potential associations, applies to legal language too. Law, therefore, is first and foremost a performative language whose signifiers are almost never synonyms. As a result of this sophistication, we have the plethoric and almost tautological nature of the legal language.[10]

Let us then proceed to ask ourselves again: What happens when the words of the law are superimposed by other categories, which are entirely valid but belong to another field of knowledge (in which and for which they function)? What happens is that we end up *lost in translation*. We dare to say that even the most critical approach to law is often radically flawed and inherently naïve.

---

10   Bruno Latour, 'Note brève sur l'écologie du droit saisie comme énonciation', *Cosmopolitique*, 8 (2004), pp. 34–40.

LEGAL ILLUSIONISM

Law is not a person as we all too often end up treating it — with a voluntarist approach, then — but a thing, or a multiplicity of things together with their instituting praxis, the form that gives shape to things.

While philosophy is linked to its great thinkers, the study of law is never a study of this or that author or even of this or that theory. Only rarely, and specifically in doctrine, can theories be put forward that prove useful for understanding certain legal operations.[11]

This point is relevant for clarifying the fallacy of another approach to law, the sociological one. On the one hand, the sociological approach cares about social actors, so once again it is not so much the operations that are seen, but those who act on them. One could say — using the abovementioned formula — that scholars have become attached to the law of the father and are unable to kill him: they see the father everywhere and, in the vein of what Michel Foucault said of sovereignty, they are unable to cut off the head to finally see, in all its material multiplicity, the molecular nature of legal operations on the social world.

More generally, it should be noted that the object of law is not the 'real' world as it can be immediately perceived. Sociologists would call it a construction. But there is an important difference to be noticed between the sociological approach to law and the one advanced here.

First, legal construction has a normative vocation, not an explanatory one — as it does for sociology. Second, those constructions described by sociologists aim at revealing something real: they seem to think that by explaining law with a series of social constructs they unveil the 'true' character of law; approximating the categories of law to those of common sense, understood as real, they claim to show that law is 'doxa', or falsehood.

Law, however, does not need anyone to notice that it is 'false', because it does not consider itself 'true' or real. And there is more: in its 'falseness' lies its power. A possibly convincing metaphor we can offer

---

11 Marie-Angèle Hermitte, 'Le droit est un autre monde', *Enquête*, 7 (1999), pp. 17–37 <https://doi.org/10.4000/enquete.1553>.

is that of illusionism. When one sees a show of illusions, does one go to see reality at work? We are quite certain that the spectator wants to be amazed by the magician's artfully constructed tricks. And if someone comes along and says 'I'll tell you the secret now', what would happen? Well, this would ruin the show and deactivate the logic that presides over sleight of hand; the techniques employed by the magician would no longer constitute a performance but, perhaps, a course for aspiring magicians taught by an envious and malevolent colleague. In other words, the spectator knows that the game is true insofar as it is false, or, to put it better, the game works due to the special performance of its fictional nature.

Law does not care at all to be 'revealed' for what it is. Paradoxical as it may seem, law works insofar as it neither desires truth nor mimics reality: 'it reinvents another world.'[12] Clearly this passage is difficult to understand. Let us try to assemble a few bricks of this architectural composition that designs and informs the social world while we also recognize its formidable distance and abstraction from the latter — knowing that such a disposition might sound paradoxical for a technique that concretely organizes social relations.

INSTITUTING PRAXIS

Let us see how the legal technique of reducing the social world works and explore its operations. In fact, what operations do jurists carry out? As Thomas notes,

> when jurists have to qualify, according to the categories of law, any data likely to enter the legal sphere — any object in the 'external world' being virtually subject to such a sphere of influence — they have to combine two fundamentally irreducible operations, a judgment of knowledge and a judgment of value.[13]

It could be said that in the case of law, knowing and deciding are two operations that occur together and cannot be separated except at the price of irreparably splitting in two the very *res* of law, that is, its

---

12   Ibid., para. 1 of 50.
13   Thomas, 'Présentation', *Enquête*, 7 (1999), pp. 13–15 <https://doi.org/10.4000/enquete.1543>, para. 1 of 4, my translation.

elementary matter that simultaneously constitutes the subject matter of the dispute and the dispute itself.

At the same time, one must be careful to see how the logical operations that law performs are set up: as counter-intuitive as it may seem, and as much as one may believe that objects are first of all there in the world, and then secondarily to be legally inscribed, the reverse is rather true: 'from the beginning, and even before the somehow pre-legal nature of the objects has been established, the "thing" in question is already legally predetermined.'[14]

The assumption that the things of the world are already there, offered, given, and that they become legally qualified only subsequently, through logical reasoning, is itself a construct. 'Constructivists by profession, jurists need [...] the assumption that the data on which they operate are primary with respect to them.'[15]

Let us see what this constructivism means through an example. When a jurist today — let us say a judge, for the sake of clarity — has to qualify the events that the case offers her in a civil, administrative, or criminal trial, she performs exactly this kind of operation: she possesses a code in which certain constructs have been collected, which in fact take the name of legal institutions, and she translates the events occurring in the world into legal names. The point is: those instituted 'things' are the ones which enable the disjunction necessary for the unravelling of the legal conflict itself. Without these names of the law, the very elementary unit of the instituting act, we would not know how to articulate, disjoin, know, and eventually decide the facts. Such are the operations that law still performs today.

The opposition Thomas sees is therefore between the given and the instituted. The legal performance par excellence is that of instituting. Therefore, law does not participate in any kind of naturalness; on the contrary, it corresponds to the instituting practice. As Thomas incisively writes, 'In the world of institutions nothing can have the status of a given.'[16]

---

14   Ibid., para. 2 of 4.
15   Ibid., para. 3 of 4.
16   Thomas, 'Prefazione a *L'artificio delle istituzioni*', p. 250.

And, from the point of view of institutions, there is no place for what sociology and anthropology call *social facts*. A fact that presents itself as social cannot do so immediately and spontaneously. A procedure is needed to qualify it as such, otherwise it is like saying that it is natural. And, if one starts from the notion of social facts, the need to distinguish between what is natural and what is social would not be comprehensible. More technically, if one wanted to frame the 'social fact' per se, one would only derive a set of interconnections without disjunctions or categories. The links would remain internal to an 'interminable chain of interdependencies'.[17] As such, they would not find any kind of separation, distinction, or qualification that would bring them into the sphere of the social.

Law 'produces only a social rationality, to which it fictionally confers the necessity that most cultures, beginning with our own, attribute to the order of nature'.[18]

According to Thomas, what we call social (not given) cannot possess any kind of (hypothetically given) transparency. What is social cannot be given but must be instituted. Without an art of instituting, we cannot give any shape to social objects and therefore to institutions.

As Thomas notes,

> In the long history of the West, law has been the means par excellence of institutional construction — of these montages made up of words, which, as long as they are uttered by those who have the power to do so, have the ability to promote the existence of what they enunciate.[19]

At the origin is language as an act: without this special language that is law, which does what it says while saying what it does, institutional constructs could not have taken place — hence the social objects, which, precisely because they are constructed by distinctions, can be said to be instituted, and therefore social. This instituting technique shapes reality through linguistic artifices. Its devices are made of words. Law is that human art which creates things through its own words.

---

17   Ibid., p. 251.
18   Thomas, 'Présentation', para. 4 of 4.
19   Thomas, 'Prefazione a *L'artificio delle istituzioni*', p. 250.

Law is that language which names and decides, that vocabulary which invents the words it uses to 'order' the social world.

> The scholastic tradition referred to the things of law precisely as 'names of law' or as 'incorporeal things'. There is only a nominal legal nature, and the world of tangible realities is apprehended by law only through its own entities, operations classified and treated in turn as objects.[20]

Hence the *ars iuris* creates categories that it then uses, and that present themselves precisely as the objects of law, not as 'reality', which they have not the slightest intention of mimicking, and which on the contrary they duplicate in order to multiply the potential of the social relations which they at the same time institute.

This is why the criticism often levelled at the law, according to which it does not reflect the social world with its 'unnatural' — at times irremediably plethoric — language, is inappropriate. It does not intend to reflect the world: 'law is another world'.[21] And indeed, in order to function, it cannot but separate, discern, and operate among the objects it has named.

Law is a technical and creative form that functions as an art of radically denying 'reality' and reducing it to its own categories. The essential legal performance is to institute, and the Roman tradition teaches us the extraordinary legal skill of 'tearing apart' reality: here fiction makes fun of the constraints of external truth to law.[22]

ABSTRACTION AND THE CASE

But then what does the law do — one might legitimately ask — with the 'outside' world? Thomas would answer that the predefinitions and external constructions of objects serve only to circumscribe certain points for the application of norms:

> The objects of law are only social objects: the genome, the animal, or death [...] are not here genetic entities, living beings,

---

20   Thomas, 'Présentation', para. 4 of 4.
21   As in the title of Hermitte, 'Le droit est un autre monde'.
22   Yan Thomas, 'Fictio legis. L'empire de la fiction romaine et ses limites médiévales', in Thomas, *Les opérations du droit*, pp. 133–86.

or biological events, legally binding by essence: they are only places where norms of unavailability (of the genome), of appropriation (of the animal), or of suspension of the prohibition to kill (a living human subject) are projected.[23]

Once again law, instead of producing identities, constitutes the very *place* that informs social forms. The architecture of the city of Rome can still be seen as the infrastructure of our societies.

Law gives more importance to what its operative names can allow one to do than to the primary meaning to which these names would bind social relations. We will see shortly how the word 'nature' was used to perform different operations without being a conceptual category with univocal meaning. As Thomas affirms,

> the objects that law constructs must always be suitable for operations of generalization, however narrow or singular they may be. This is why legal rules never envisage singular units, but always logical classes, abstractions in which singulars are included (the person, property, the thing that is the object of legal relations between persons, etc., with all the sub-entities into which these abstractions are divided and subdivided). The world of law is not only an entirely constructed world. It is also a world of necessarily abstract constructions.[24]

The potentiality of generalization and the singularity of the case are always essentially inseparable. Indeed, the *extreme* that the case offers to legal science is such precisely to the extent that its radical singularity can offer ground for its stabilization. Conversely, what is ordinary is presented as intrinsically unserviceable to the cause of legal change. This is above all a view of casuistry that comes from the ancient Roman world.[25]

For this reason, both the Foucauldian fascination with the case and the Deleuzian passion for radical singularity pose problems with regard

---

23 By 'social' here Thomas clearly means 'instituted', 'invented' as opposed to 'natural' or 'given'. Thomas, 'Présentation', para. 4 of 4.

24 Ibid., para. 4 of 4.

25 Yan Thomas, 'L'extrême et l'ordinaire. Remarques sur le cas médiéval de la communauté disparue', in *Penser par cas*, ed. by Jean-Claude Passeron and Jacques Revel (Paris: Éditions de l'École des hautes études en sciences sociales, 2005), pp. 45–73 <https://doi.org/10.4000/books.editionsehess.19926>. Now also in Thomas, *Les opérations du droit*, pp. 207–37.

to how the case plays a role in legal casuistry. We do not need to delve too deeply into this matter here, but two methodological caveats are needed.

Both authors make of the case something that it is not, or rather exalt a polarity of the case without seeing its other face. For instance, Foucault's recounting of the case of Pierre Rivière, which elevates the case by making it a paradigm of an extremely significant change in the history of psychiatric and judicial power,[26] should be read in the light of Carlo Ginzburg's critique:

> A long time ago I realized that the norm cannot foresee all anomalies, while every anomaly by definition implies the norm. Hence the cognitive richness of anomalies, which should not be confused with their ideological idolization (I am thinking of Michel Foucault's attitude towards the case of Pierre Rivière).[27]

In Gilles Deleuze's genuine passion for jurisprudence, the case is seen as the quintessential site of law, while the normalization and stabilization of the case is to be radically avoided. As is well known, Deleuze argues that 'Jurisprudence is the philosophy of law, and deals with singularities, it advances by working out from [or prolonging] singularities'.[28] One might say — borrowing the words of Laurent de Sutter and Kyle McGee — that, for Deleuze, 'As an immanent practice of the case, law (*droit*) is the incarnation of what philosophy has to achieve for herself in order to be able to leave the world of law (*loi*), judgment and debt, whose fascinated observation has caused her stagnation.'[29]

The case must be kept, according to Deleuze, for its radical singularity — as if the case could survive on its own or represent an extreme that, contrary to Thomas's view, should not be 'stabilized'.[30] However,

---

26   *Moi, Pierre Rivière, ayant égorgé ma mère, ma soeur et mon frère... Un cas de parricide au XIXe siècle*, presented by Michel Foucault (Paris: Éditions Gallimard, 2007).

27   Carlo Ginzburg, 'Il caso, I casi', *doppiozero*, 12 April 2019 <https://www.doppiozero. com/materiali/il-caso-i-casi> [accessed 2 June 2022], my translation. See also his introduction to *Il formaggio e i vermi. Il cosmo di un mugnaio del '500* [1976] (Turin: Einaudi, 2009), pp. xvi–xvii.

28   Gilles Deleuze, *Negotiations 1972–1990*, trans. by Martin Joughin (New York: Columbia University Press, 1995), p. 153.

29   Laurent de Sutter and Kyle McGee, 'Introduction', in *Deleuze and Law*, ed. by de Sutter and McGee (Edinburgh: Edinburgh University Press, 2012), pp. 1–14 (p. 4).

30   Thomas, 'L'extrême et l'ordinaire', in *Les opérations du droit*, p. 209.

legal technique, as we are trying to show here, can only contain and operate simultaneously with a radical abstraction and a concreteness of cases. The two aspects are not to be divided.

Keeping 'faith' with the radicality of the case would neither advance law nor multiply the potential of the social relations that law intends to institute. In the face of this historical or philosophical-legal passion for the case, one must therefore keep in mind that the case is all the more extreme insofar as it contains the characteristics that can be used for the stabilization of the solution that it provides. Therefore, it is not a question of giving primacy to the precedent, but on the contrary of seeing in the case the extraordinary potency of the events that challenge the categories of law and the solutions it has already found. Such an operation imposes the use of other fictions and names or of the same ones but changed in meaning, that is, interpreting those names that are signifiers in an original and innovative way.

THE QUESTION OF NATURE

Let us then take a case, that of the concept of nature; we have seen how the distance between natural/given and legal/instituted cannot be but sidereal. However, the concept of 'nature' today is taken up rather casually with reference mainly to the environment, particularly the natural environment.

In the face of climate breakdown, jurists are asked to dust off their complex and dangerous relationship with nature. Let us briefly recall the major events that connect law and nature.

In pagan Roman law, nature certainly existed, but it was never conceived as being in a conflictual position to juridical reason, whether as the source of law or as the ultimate, binding norm. For the Romans, only the laws and customs of the city were sources of law. Thomas shows the *making* of nature through the concrete operations of jurisprudential casuistry, which reaches a legal 'illusionism' that is unparalleled today. The Roman legal laboratory was so subversive with respect to the material 'fact' that through sleight of hand it institutes nature itself, each time enhancing its effects or cancelling its conditions, over and over again.

Casuistry demonstrates how nature meant at least three different things to Roman jurists. Here we follow the casuistic reconstruction and interpretation offered by Yan Thomas in 'Imago naturae. Note sur l'institutionnalité de la nature à Rome':[31] first, nature was undoubtedly the primeval wild world in which all original goods are found, which no one has (yet) appropriated: the *res communes* which, in the natural age, were common to all on the basis of a primitive indivision. Despite this apparently utopian vision, the law shows that it institutes nature by making it perform a series of purely technical operations: nature itself is a title to purchase, a reason for annulling, interrupting, or transmitting goods. In an apparently paradoxical way, nature seems to provide the strongest title (right) because it is original, and the weakest one because nature can always lapse. As if to underline its agency, for Roman jurists, nature gives what it could even regain one day or another, excluding the legitimate owner from enjoyment and returning *res nullius*, the good of everyone and no one. Second, nature can also be a kind of restored condition. Third, nature constitutes a reference that the law uses to extend legal relations.

Let us clarify the latter point by resorting to some examples of juridical reasoning and operations that Thomas provides. What Roman jurists postulate as 'nature' may be inferred from an analysis of procedures that use 'nature' itself as a reference point.

According to Roman law, in nature everyone is free, and slavery does not take place. This is the first assumption that law makes about 'nature' in relation to slavery: that slavery is not 'natural' but freedom is; this is a way of emphasizing that slavery cannot but be itself instituted by certain men, to the detriment of others, who are thus subjected *against* nature to the will of a master. However, it is at the same time

---

31   Yan Thomas, 'Imago naturae. Note sur l'institutionnalité de la nature à Rome', in
      *Théologie et droit dans la science politique de l'État moderne. Actes de la table ronde
      de Rome (12–14 novembre 1987)*, Publications de l'École française de Rome, 147
      (Rome: École Française de Rome, 1991), pp. 201–27 <https://www.persee.fr/doc/
      efr_0000-0000_1991_act_147_1_4171> [accessed 17 July 2022] (repr. in Thomas,
      Les opérations du droit, pp. 21–40). I also refer to the Italian edition in which Thomas
      is published together with Jacques Chiffoleau: Yan Thomas, 'Imago naturae. Nota
      sull'istituzionalità della natura a Roma', trans. by Giuseppe Lucchesini, in Yan Thomas
      and Jacques Chiffoleau, *L'istituzione della natura*, ed. by Michele Spanò (Macerata:
      Quodlibet, 2020), pp. 13–45.

clear that it is a matter of assuming the existence of a 'natural' freedom in order to actually be able to create freedom through an instituting dynamic.

In fact, once slavery was established, not by nature, but through law (first *fictio*), the *manumissio* — the formal emancipation from slavery — was established too (second *fictio*). In other words, freedom is constructed as natural, then abolished, and finally reconstructed. With the formal emancipation, law abolishes natural freedom through a legal operation and at the same time restores it. This restitution of rights can be partial as in the case of the person enslaved at birth, but also total as in the case of prisoners of war. Indeed, the latter would regain the freedom they had originally possessed. This would not be valid for the enslaved who did not originally enjoy it. Yet even this sharp distinction between two types of freedom — between the 'ingenui' who are born free and the 'liberti' (or 'libertini') who are 'manumitted from legal slavery'[32] — has ended up fading through a series of legal operations that sought to guarantee the natural freedom of the person enslaved at birth, that is, the freedom of one who, by status, had never enjoyed it. This case shows even more clearly that nature does not constitute an external limit at all, but that, on the contrary, it is instrumentalized: 'in any restitution of rights', Thomas writes, 'it is necessary to admit, thanks to fiction, that the legal act concluded by the incapable [in our case the enslaved] is non-existent: to cancel the effects retroactively, the magistrate restores the situation that existed prior to the act. Similarly, the *restitutio in natalibus* [restoration of original birth rights] [...] suggests that birth in servitude did not take place. The *ingenuitas* [to be born free] of the subject is presumed because it is necessary for the remedial action of the procedure.'[33] The freedom that nature would offer everyone thus becomes the outcome of an artifice modelled by legal art, which ridicules 'natural' reality just as it institutes it through fictions of fictions.

---

32   See the entry 'inge'nui, inge'nuitas' in William Smith, *A Dictionary of Greek and Roman Antiquities* (London: John Murray, 1875), p. 637 <https://penelope.uchicago.edu/Thayer/E/Roman/Texts/secondary/SMIGRA*/Ingenui.html> [accessed 19 July 2022].

33   Thomas, *'Imago naturae*. Note sur l'institutionnalité de la nature à Rome', p. 221.

CRIMES AGAINST NATURE

The peculiar Roman use of nature becomes clearer by contrasting it
to later understandings. It is in Justinian legislation that the so-called
crimes against nature, above all homosexuality and incest, first take
shape. Nature becomes a moral and universal norm, constituting an external limit to the law, one hitherto unknown to Roman jurists. Nature
is seen as divine creation and thus becomes the Law. In fact, in the elev-
enth century — as Jacques Chiffoleau tells us — heresy and sodomy
emerged as crimes against nature. Nature takes shape out of this division between appropriate sexuality and inadequate and unproductive
sexuality.[34] The issue of homosexuality was central in the medieval
discourse on nature. Nature and the limits it posed have contributed,
in a decisive way, to an order of 'natural' discourse, which, among the
many echoes it has scattered over the centuries, also reaches our contemporary ears in the Berlin speech given by Joseph Ratzinger in 2011,
where he references the 'language of nature' as objective reason, *natura
naturata* (understood as the order of the created world) derived from
natura naturans (understood as God).[35] Furthermore, as Chiffoleau
points out, there is another cardinal institutional formation that the
discourse on nature serves: sovereignty. Nature is depicted as omnipo-
tent, Mistress and Patron of the world; this understanding culminated
in the interpretation offered by Alain de Lille: the crime against nature
par excellence, sodomy, becomes an injury of the majesty of Nature,
one could say a *crimen leasae majestatis Naturae*. The conjunction of
majesty with nature, thus posed, grows new features and potential,
establishing the connection between the conception of nature and
forms of power. And there is more: it does not seem accidental that,
in the same historical period, the inquisitorial technique was formed

---

34   Jacques Chiffoleau, 'Contra naturam. Per un approccio casuistico e procedurale alla na-
     tura medievale', trans. by Davide Pettinicchio, in Thomas and Chiffoleau, *L'istituzione
     della natura*, pp. 47–102. The original article is Jacques Chiffoleau, 'Contra naturam.
     Pour une approche casuistique et procédurale de la nature médiévale', *Micrologus.
     Nature, Sciences and Medieval Societies*, 4 (1996), pp. 265–312.

35   Joseph Ratzinger, 'The Listening Heart: Reflections on the Foundations of Law',
     22 September 2011: <https://www.vatican.va/content/benedict-xvi/en/speeches/
     2011/september/documents/hf_ben-xvi_spe_20110922_reichstag-berlin.html>
     [accessed 22 June 2022]. See also Paolo Cappellini, Natalino Irti, Andrea Nicolussi,
     and Aldo Travi, 'Dopo Ratzinger al Bundestag', *Vita e pensiero*, 1 (2012), pp. 61–66.

and refined, aimed at extracting confessions through unspeakable acts of torture, and at finding the hidden truth in the souls of the unfortunate, heretics, sodomites, or 'witches'. Chiffoleau underlines that it is precisely the 'witch hunt, presented above all as a defense of human and divine majesty', that 'contributes in a powerful way, I believe, to the institution of modern sovereignty'.[36]

Nature became a limit to law, an external reality that shall be respected. Nature has been constructed as an essence that is external to things instituted by humans, such as law, and at the same time as a boundary that one must be careful not to cross. And this consideration should recall, by analogy, certain current ecological and juridical positions, according to which nature is a sort of untouchable Eden that needs strict protection, especially from the human, as if nature is something from which the human is excluded.

BEFORE GAIA: THE PLACE OF LEGAL IMAGINATION

The order of ecological discourse, widespread among scholars and activists alike, still seems to look at nature as a form of law. Nature would dictate something that has the features of a norm. It would then be up to the human being to intercept, decipher, translate, and interpret this (law of) nature. Nature is still seen as the Other that demands something. What does nature require? What would nature tell us if it had a language? What would it oblige us to?

One might say that not only are these somewhat naive assumptions — which presuppose that nature itself exists as such and can have a rationality, if only we pay it due attention — but that they evade the most important question that should be asked today: that of cohabitation and togetherness. This is because they end up isolating an entity, an identity that is distinctly separate from the human although the underlying project (and modern guilt) would reside precisely in this separation. So even though the purpose of contemporary ecological discourse would be to bring the two sides together, it is precisely to speak of nature as a separate entity that reconfirms the distance one would like to reduce.

---

36   Chiffoleau, 'Contra naturam. Per un approccio casuistico e procedurale', p. 92.

This order of discourse ends up being counterproductive from an ethical and political point of view. It refuses to acknowledge that we are now faced with an extremely more complex issue: the challenge that Isabelle Stengers has vividly named as 'the intrusion of Gaia'.[37] It is a question not of protecting a nature with a peaceful face and in the form of a national park, but of building spaces of survival and cooperation,[38] of finding a way to live in the time of catastrophes in which both the human and the more-than-human are active agents: 'in this new era, we are no longer only dealing with a nature to be "protected" from the damage caused by humans, but also with a nature capable of threatening our modes of thinking and of living for good'.[39]

Instead of new ontologies that prescribe divisions, we shall exercise our attitude of conceiving the assemblage of different species and the transindividual dimension of the living. Instead of our human externality with respect to the natural entities to be protected, we would see the inextricable entanglements of objects and subjects, things and people, finally appear before our eyes, testifying to their mutual interdependence.

Looking at things from this perspective, one would discover that a place for ethics and politics as well as law still exists, and indeed can only be redesigned. And it is precisely the approach that makes nature into something untouchable that opens the door to defeatism. It does not make sense to pose the question in terms of what this nature, hypothetically radically separate and distinct from the human, would require or oblige us to do or not to do. The post-naturalist question could rather be formulated in these terms: what kind of coexistences do we want to build?[40] How, once we recognize the social world as a world in which human and non-human have always coexisted, can we build a better common form-of-life?

---

37   Isabelle Stengers, *In Catastrophic Times: Resisting the Coming Barbarism*, trans. by Andrew Goffey (London: Open Humanity Press, 2015) <https://doi.org/10.14619/016>, pp. 43–50.

38   Anna Tsing, *The Mushroom at the End of the World: On the Possibility of Life in Capitalist Ruins* (Princeton, NJ: Princeton University Press, 2015).

39   Stengers, *In Catastrophic Times*, p. 20.

40   Steven Vogel, 'Environmental Philosophy after the End of Nature', *Environmental Ethics*, 24.1 (2002), pp. 23–39.

As Bruno Latour highlighted, our problem as moderns — who have never really been modern — is that we imagine worlds that do not exist: a natural world without subjects and a human world without objects.[41] We imagine a clear separation which does not represent the condition of the *place* where we live in.

We alter, therefore we are. Can we, then, avoid using the term 'nature' to develop a theory and practice aware of the outrageous dangers our technologies are capable of producing? Can we develop a post-naturalist environmental approach that starts from the question: what kind of biodiversity do we want to institute? And, in biodiversity, it would be crucial and pioneering to also include the multiple forms-of-life of the human.

Let us conclude by sketching the implications of such a position-ing in legal terms.

The dynamics of instituting provide a sure foothold. Through a view capable of seeing the process of instituting — clearly, a human one — we can finally say that the legal significance of 'nature' is neces-sarily instituted. There is no (hypothetical) spontaneity at work.

One cannot obtain legal protection effects, one cannot guarantee rights to nature — in whatever way one wishes to define them — without an institutive form, that is: there are no natural rights that can arise spontaneously without a process that institutes them as such. Nature will not obtain rights by itself. (It goes without saying that the whole tradition of natural law tends to return to the surface with the recent ecological turn in legal studies.)

At the centre of law are cases and forms of protections. What is important is that 'nature' —whatever this signifier refers to — becomes suitable for judgment, for the really relevant question is not whether 'nature' becomes a subject or not, but how non-human entities can act in court.[42]

To date the main option has been the personification of nature, as in the recognition of the rights of nature by the Ecuadorian con-stitution, by Bolivian laws, and more recently by Chile through a

---

41   Bruno Latour, *We Have Never Been Modern*, trans. by Catherine Porter (Cambridge, MA: Harvard University Press, 1993).

42   Christopher Stone, 'Should Trees Have Standing? Toward Legal Rights for Natural Objects', *Southern California Law Review*, 45 (1972), pp. 450–501.

constituent moment. These are extremely important transformative processes that pivot on the Andean cosmovision. Recourse to similar references in the Western world, however, risks constituting, instead of a process of rethinking habitation on this earth, further plunder. This is the case, at least, without a profound work of *transduction* as a 'model of translation' in which 'difference is [...] a condition of signification and not a hindrance'.[43]

Nature seen as substance poses many problems and, after all, does not challenge the main issue, which is the need to rethink forms of protection not so much of this or that subject but of the *places* in which the forms of assemblages cohabit.

Efforts should be made to think, and above all to rethink in a contemporary guise, the *rights of places* themselves, that is, to consider places as right-holders (which is quite different from places as subjects of rights) or, in other words, as the material form of inhabiting and being in common.[44]

Ecological damage shows that what is called into question is always more than one subject, human or non-human, because the damage affects both.[45] What is more, it can affect future generations, the inhabitants of the planet, as well as those closest to the affected area.

What is needed is a legal imagination that works toward lateral alternatives to subjectivation. A more technically equipped and historically grounded approach would lead us to grant value to proposals that are only apparently less politically expendable:

---

43   Eduardo Viveiros de Castro, 'Perspectival Anthropology and the Method of Controlled Equivocation', *Tipití: Journal of the Society for the Anthropology of Lowland South America*, 2.1 (2004), pp. 3–22 (p. 20) <http://digitalcommons.trinity.edu/tipiti/vol2/iss1/1> [accessed 1 June 2022]. The reference is to a concept employed by Gilbert Simondon, *L'Individu et sa génèse physico-biologique* (Paris: Millon, 1964).

44   For insight into the issue of rights of places in antiquity, see at least: Emanuele Conte, *Diritto comune. Storia e storiografia di un sistema dinamico* (Bologna: Il Mulino, 2009); Thomas, 'L'extrême et l'ordinaire'; Ennio Cortese, 'Per una storia dell'arcivescovo Mosé di Ravenna (m. 1154) sulla proprietà ecclesiastica', in *Proceedings of the Fifth International Congress of Medieval Canon Law: Salamanca 21–25 September 1976*, ed. by Stephan Kuttner and Kenneth Pennington (Vatican: Biblioteca Apostolica Vaticana, 1980), pp. 117–55.

45   See Michele Spanò, '"Perché non rendi poi quel che che prometti allor?". Tecniche e ideologie della giuridificazione della natura', in Thomas and Chiffoleau, *L'istituzione della natura*, pp. 103–24.

> To realise that the debate on personification has virtually ob-
> scured any alternative solution is a striking experience. Nature's
> objectification might have provided safer ground for building
> protection regimes, looking at western anthropology.[46]

Conducting an archaeology of things, without having to make them
persons — which, by the way, in law does not allow the acquisition of
a higher rank — would allow us to consider their value as such. A way
that is not naively naturalist, but consciously *instituent* would lead us
toward a more materialist approach.

A certain way of dealing with 'things', even the things of 'nature',
would steer us toward another course that would bring the category of
unavailability to the centre of the debate and shift the axis to the 'value
of things',[47] rather than to some sort of dignity of nature constructed in
the image and likeness of the human one. Especially since even human
dignity did not come from itself at all, and is once again the outcome of
an instituting praxis instead of a given of nature. This path would lead
to conceiving the so-called cultural heritage that generations transmit
to each other as a place where biodiversity must also be central. As-
signing a value to common things, and establishing a non-proprietary
belonging based on use rather than property is at the heart of the
current debate on the commons.[48] The *res communes*, excluded from
commerce, may be seen as its Roman forerunners.

The *forest* — etymologically what lies outside (of the city) —
claims to be protected and to be as much a part of our heritage as
human inventions.[49] The place where the interdependence between

---

46 Yan Thomas, 'The Subject of Right, the Person, Nature', in *Legal Artifices: Ten Essays
    on Roman Law in the Present Tense*, ed. by Thanos Zartaloudis and Cooper Francis,
    trans. by Anton Schütz and Chantal Schütz, intro. by Thanos Zartaloudis and Anton
    Schütz, afterword by Alain Pottage (Edinburgh: Edinburgh University Press, 2021),
    pp. 107–43 (p. 117).

47 Yan Thomas, 'La valeur des choses. Le droit romain hors la religion', *Annales.
    Histoire, Sciences Sociales*, 6 (2002), pp. 1431–62 <https://doi.org/10.3406/ahess.
    2002.280119>.

48 See Paolo Napoli, 'Indisponibilità, servizio pubblico, uso. Concetti orientativi su
    comune e beni comuni', *Politica & Società*, 3 (2013), pp. 403–26 <https://doi.org/
    10.4476/74759>.

49 There are two possible etymologies of 'forest': in Latin *foris* means 'outside' (as in
    'foreign') and *forestem silvam* are 'the outside woods'; another trace can be found in the
    Latin word *forestis*, 'forest preserve' from the legal lemma *forum*: 'court' or 'judgment',
    which might imply the concept of a wood subject to a ban.

humans and non-humans needs to be rethought and instituted is yet
to be created and shall start with the deposition of toxic human excep-
tionalism.

An important warning coming from Karen Barad should be
heeded as we begin this ongoing and collective labour:

> Not to privilege all other beings over the human, in some per-
> verse reversal, but to begin to come to terms with the infinite
> depths of our inhumanity, and out of the resulting devastation,
> to nourish the infinitely rich ground of possibilities for living
> and dying otherwise.[50]

---

50   Barad, 'Troubling Time/s', p. 86.

EXCURSUS

On the List

SAM DOLBEAR, BEN NICHOLS, AND CLAUDIA PEPPEL

> The list is not as innocent as it looks.
>
> Paul Tankard

In her essay 'First Things', Lauren Berlant describes a number of undertakings, routines, insights, and tasks that form first thing in the morning. Among breakfast habits, taking medicine, suicidal thoughts, and the walking of dogs, Berlant inconspicuously mentions that 'Lists get made', which raises the question not only of the form lists can take in order to be recognized as such, but of the circumstances in which they emerge.[1] Lists get made at difficult moments in life, when anxiety creeps in, when the day begins unstructured or ends unproductively. They get made when an overview is lost, when decisions have to be made, structure is needed, or instructions must be followed. Lists get made when we can't motivate ourselves, when we feel tired, when things get undone or don't happen the way we want them to. Lists get made when we fail to remember or lose our orientation, when we need to make plans for the future and expectations in real life, when wishful thinking does not eventuate.

---

1   Lauren Berlant and Kathleen Stewart, *The Hundreds* (Durham, NC: Duke University Press, 2019), 'First Things', p. 3.

Lists get made and proliferate. They compile, group, or rank ideas, ingredients, pieces, plans, procedures, details, desires, feelings, records, lovers, victims, or rather any kind of content in a reduced form. They can be written, spoken, or take a non-linguistic, even visual form. They hold various temporalities: Lists of things *to do* in the future, reminders from the past. Usually presented in a sequence and assembled according to some practical or conceptual necessity, they offer the promise, perhaps the illusion, of keeping track, of bringing control to the flux of things and thoughts, of putting confusion to a halt. They can be tentative, playful, and assertive, confident but provisional, imposing but suggestive, and ultimately futile. They might accumulate along a certain line or theme, but they also might fracture that accumulation, to work between levels and levities, tones and styles. Lists provide structure, they offer overview, the pleasure of erasing things one has accomplished. They promise effectivity, a certain productivity in the here and now, the hope to master one's life, to overcome procrastination. They offer the pleasure of continuity, of keeping track, of winning over inertia. According to Umberto Eco, lists are the struggle against and for the sheer superiority of infinity, a form of representation that 'suggests infinity almost *physically*, because in fact *it does not end*, nor does it conclude in form'.[2] He distinguishes between 'a poetics of everything included' and 'a poetics of the etcetera', between verbal and visual lists.[3]

'The list is not simply a means of collecting, but of sorting things out', writes Paul Tankard.[4] Lists are 'managerial devices',[5] but also, or even for that reason, aesthetic, pleasurable, and have a 'strong affective momentum'.[6] Lists can elicit 'frustration, feelings of control and security (the world in order), or, on the contrary, insecurity and fear (of that

---

2   Umberto Eco, *The Infinity of Lists: From Homer to Joyce*, trans. by Alistair McEwen (London: MacLehose Press, 2009), p. 17.

3   Ibid., introduction and p. 17.

4   Paul Tankard, 'Reading Lists', *Prose Studies*, 28.3 (December 2006), pp. 337–60 (p. 341).

5   Ibid., p. 344.

6   Eva von Contzen, 'Theorising Lists in Literature: Towards a Listology', in *Lists and Catalogues in Ancient Literature and Beyond: Towards a Poetics of Enumeration*, ed. by Rebecca Laemmle, Cédric Scheidegger Laemmle, and Katharina Wesselmann (Berlin: de Gruyter, 2021), pp. 35–54 (p. 50).

which we cannot grasp, in size and number); pleasure (derived from the appeal of the act of reading, the act of decoding, and the associative powers); disappointment (lack of explanation, narrative embedding); alienation from the text; awe in view of the poet's skills, etc.'[7] Lists 'delight and frustrate': they have an 'enormous appeal'.[8] They are self-perpetuating: because there is 'no such thing as a list of one'. Once one has started a list, 'a pressure is exerted for it to be continued.'[9] Though its essence is mainly a formal feature, something ritualized, magical, invocative emanates from the act of making a list. At the same time, lists are ordinary, banal, boring. One might even say that the best thing about them, their biggest promise or appeal, is that they do not have to be interesting (which of course is different to saying that they are not).

Scholars often reach for a certain simplicity when defining lists, though the etymology is varied and refers to a very heterogeneous use, deriving from the Germanic root *liston/lista*, meaning 'border, hem, edge, strip'.[10] 'At their most simple, lists are frameworks that hold separate and disparate items together.'[11] Eva von Contzen offers a reduced, or 'minimalist definition: the "list" is a set of items assembled under some principle in a formally distinctive unit'.[12] These units could be the sentences themselves, arranged in such a way as to make them appear separate, or they might utilize other forms: from dashes to numbers, letters, points, and other dividers. Within these units the list constitutes, as Tankard argues, an 'argument or assertion at the most minimal level of articulation possible'.[13] The reach towards the simple and the minimal reflects these qualities in lists themselves. Lists 'hold'

---

7   Ibid., p. 50.

8   Ibid.

9   Tankard, 'Reading Lists', p. 342.

10   See 'list', in *Online Etymology Dictionary* (2022), especially 'list (n.2): "a narrow strip," Old English *liste* "border, hem, edge, strip," from Proto-Germanic **liston* (source also of Old High German *lista* "strip, border, list," Old Norse *lista* "border, selvage," German *leiste*) [...]. The Germanic root also is the source of French *liste*, Italian *lista*. The word has had many technical senses in English, including "lobe of an ear" and "a stripe of color." This also is the *list* in archaic *lists* "place of combat" (late 14c.), from an earlier sense "boundary;" the fighting ground being originally at the boundary of fields' <https://www.etymonline.com/word/list> [accessed 20 July 2022].

11   Robert Belknap, *The List: The Uses and Pleasures of Cataloguing* (New Haven, CT: Yale University Press, 2004), p. 2.

12   Contzen, 'Theorising Lists in Literature', p. 36.

13   Tankard, 'Reading Lists', p. 339.

and 'assemble' rather than offer accounts of the relations between what is held or assembled. They are always a kind of montage, a cut-out, a part of a larger whole. They are arguments or assertions *reduced* to the lowest possible level, and merely show rather than explain themselves.

We encounter the same problem when trying to describe definitively how lists relate to reduction: because any attempt at definition tends towards expansion or complexity. But they have many reductive elements. In a basic sense they constitute a quantitative reduction: as the philosopher John Searle writes, 'any list you care to make about anything automatically creates two categories, those that are on the list and those that are not.'[14] Lists reduce things to what is there and present on the list. Yet, they arguably share this quality with pretty much any form of representation, which is always necessarily selective. Furthermore, in a qualitative sense, lists reduce chaos to order: they are a schematic form of representation. Whether this constitutes a 'reduction' seems up in the air. By clarifying 'states of affairs', schematics also increase understanding and make future thought and action possible. Then, in a similar way, lists reduce complexity to simplicity. They take a complex set of particularities and reduce it to a set of salient points or key principles without necessarily narrating the full relation of those points or principles to each other. In short: lists relate to reduction in two ways: first, as a quantitative reduction — as a form of making smaller, more concise; and second, as a qualitative reduction — as a form of condensation, in which the thing is grasped in a moment. Yet, they still accumulate, proliferate, *get made.*

What shape do lists have? When lists form vertically, they might use dots, indents, and space to create delineation and separateness. Lists in literary works are unusual, they not only introduce 'a sudden verticality into the horizontal flow of text',[15] but seem 'to represent an extra-literary discourse'.[16] Entries often stand loose and yet together,

---

14   John Searle, 'The Storm over the University', *The New York Review of Books*, 6 December 1990 <https://www.nybooks.com/articles/1990/12/06/the-storm-over-the-university/> [accessed 21 July 2022].

15   Michel Butor, 'The Book as Object' (1964), quoted in Brian Dillon, 'Why Literature Loves Lists: From Rabelais to Didion, an Incomplete List of Listmakers', *Literary Hub*, 14 September 2018 <https://lithub.com/why-literature-loves-lists/> [accessed 20 April 2022].

16   Tankard, 'Reading Lists', p. 337.

and are often employed in 'syntactic and conceptual coherence to both the other elements and the surrounding narrative material'.[17] One famous example is Joan Didion's packing list, taped inside her wardrobe door for years, part of her essay *The White Album*, a gripping though devastating journey through the decade of 1968–78.

TO PACK AND WEAR:
2 skirts
2 jerseys or leotards
1 pullover sweater
2 pair shoes
stockings
bra
nightgown, robe, slippers
cigarettes
bourbon

bag with:
shampoo
toothbrush and paste
Basis soap
razor, deodorant
aspirin, prescriptions, Tampax
face cream, powder, baby oil

TO CARRY:
mohair throw
typewriter
2 legal pads and pens
files
house key[18]

In her restless and sober style, Didion recalls all sorts of events in the outer world as well as in her private life. She writes about racism, hyper-violence, her visits to Eldridge Cleaver and his involvement in the Black Panther movement, the assassination of Robert Kennedy, Jim Morrison and The Doors, trials for murder like the Manson case, and the case of Betty Lansdown Fouquet, 'who put her five-year-old daughter out to die on the center divider of Interstate 5'.[19] Didion also writes about how she, as a reporter and successful writer, was

---

17   Contzen, 'Theorising Lists in Literature', p. 36.
18   Joan Didion, *The White Album* [1979] (London: HarperCollins, 2017), pp. 34–35.
19   Ibid., p. 11.

frequently on the road and confronted with many odd and terrible things, and about how these selective events tore her life apart. 'I began to doubt the premises of all the stories I had ever told myself.'[20] She continues:

> I was supposed to have a script, and I had mislaid it. I was supposed to hear cues, and no longer did. I was meant to know the plot, but all I knew was what I saw: flash pictures in variable sequence, images with no 'meaning' beyond their temporary arrangement, not a movie but a cutting-room experience.[21]

Didion describes an inability to give incompatible images a narrative contour, one of the many signs of the impending collapse she experienced in the summer of 1968, which is also featured in her essay as well as in the detailed psychiatric report that followed soon after. The packing list reveals how the formal simplicity of the list has a stabilizing function in the face of unremitting disorder: the banality of everyday objects as the remains of what might constitute a normal and repeatable life, reassuring oneself of oneself and of one's preparedness in case of travel or emergency whilst also offering a continuity into a possible future.

Another striking example is Susan Sontag's 'Notes of a Childhood', a twenty-three-page-long list of selective memories as part of her *Early Diaries 1947–1963*, dated from January 1957. Flashbacks to childhood scatter her diaries; written in a paratactic style and accentuating the fragmentary, they are reproduced without any reference to the age at which or circumstances in which they took place, interrupting or rather eliminating any further chronological context. They leave the reader at a loss yet captured by their suggestive nature. David Rieff comments that the style has a 'notational, almost stream-of-consciousness manner' and adds that this is 'the closest she came to straightforward autobiographical writing', even if unintentionally.[22] Here, another ability of the list is played out, namely to give cohesion to a plethora of loose details and at the same time to testify to a pause: The notes, from which

---

20   Ibid.
21   Ibid., pp. 12–13.
22   Susan Sontag, 'Notes of a Childhood', in *Reborn: Susan Sontag, Early Diaries 1947–1963*, published posthumously and ed. by her son David Rieff (New York: Farrar, Straus and Giroux, 2008), pp. 106–29 (p. 106).

we here quote one page only, appear strangely detached but at the same time — as the past's own present — everlasting:

> [...]
> Daddy telling me to eat the parsley, it's good, in the Fun Club
> The big white blister on my finger when some paper caught fire from the Bunsen burner (I had my chemistry equipment in the small roll-top desk).
> Thelma de Lara. The picture of Jesus in the basement. 'That's a picture of God.'
> (8) Mother telling me she was going to marry Nat.
> Sharing a room with Mother the first two years in Tuscon. (Nat recommended it.)
> Reading Ida Tarbell on the Duponts.
> Finding a Kosher restaurant for Grandma.
> The Normandy Isle School. Ida + Leo Huberman.
> Chemistry sets.
> Peter Haidu putting his hand on my thigh under the water (age fourteen).
> Getting home to a barbecue dinner.
> Crying in the movie For Whom the Bell Tolls—with Mother, in a big Manhattan theatre.
> Poison ivy. Dr. Stumpf.
> The ebony swinging doors (Chinese) that gave on to the living room in the house in Great Neck.
> The table Christmas tree in Florida: silver with blue lights.
> Wanting a sapphire.
> Capturing grasshoppers to put on the keys of a toy piano.
> [...][23]

The inherent reduction of the formal arrangement results as a framework and creates a context and cohesion, even as the memories are wildly disparate. As Belknap writes, 'This is to say that the list is simultaneously the sum of its parts and the individual parts themselves.'[24] Because of their dual nature, lists must therefore be looked at from two opposing viewpoints: the individual units that make up a list (what does it hold?) and the function or purpose of the list as a whole (how does it hold together?).[25]

---

23   Ibid., p. 107.
24   Belknap, The List, p. 15.
25   Ibid.

Another shape that lists can take is horizontal — formed as a block, separated by commas, which present less of a demand to be struck or scribbled out, completed — such as in Georges Perec's 'Notes on the Objects to Be Found on My Desk' (1976). A much longer enumeration seems to be necessary here than when the list is formally marked as such from the outset:

> A lamp, a cigarette-case, a bud-vase, a stone for striking matches, a cardboard box containing small filing cards of different colours, a large *papier-mâché* penholder with seashell inlays, a glass pencil-holder, several stones, three turned-wood boxes, an alarm clock, a push-button-calendar, a lump of lead, a big cigar-box full of knick-knacks (no cigars), a steel spiral device in which you can put pending mail, a polished stone dagger handle, ledgers, exercise books, loose leaves, various writing instruments and accessories, a big blotting stamp, several books, a glass full of pencils, a little gilded-wood box.[26]

The protagonist, who explores the elusive everyday and tries to make sense of his immediate surroundings, is obsessed with observing, compiling, and checking by means of enumerations and provisional lists, as well as with suffering from digression and the maelstrom of arbitrary classifications. Insofar as the list seeks to account for something present, it might also attempt to represent something absent or failed. Such examples can be found in Kafka's list of impossibilities:

> The impossibility of not writing, the impossibility of writing German, the impossibility of writing differently. One might add a fourth impossibility: the impossibility of writing.[27]

To write a list in the negative form, as something that refuses specific things, or even refuses the demand of the form itself, as an account of something absent or impossible, is to take a risk: either to come to terms with an impossibility, to cement it, or to break the link with this

---

26   Georges Perec, 'Notes on the Objects to Be Found on My Desk, An Attempt at Exhausting a Place in Paris', in Perec, *Thoughts of Sorts*, trans. by David Bellos (Boston, MA: David R. Godine Publisher, 2009), pp. 11–16 (p. 14).

27   From Kafka's letter to Max Brod from June 1921, in *Letters to Friends, Family, and Editors*, trans. by Richard Winston and Clara Winston (New York: Schocken, 1977), as quoted in Rebecca Comay, 'Testament of the Revolution (Walter Benjamin)', *Mosaic: An Interdisciplinary Critical Journal*, 50.2 (2017), pp. 1–12 (p. 6).

impossibility, as a kind of exorcism or sublimation. This is echoed in Anne Boyer's 'Not Writing' from 1995:

> When I am not writing I am not writing a novel called 1994 about a young woman in an office park in a provincial town who has a job cutting and pasting time. I am not writing a novel called *Nero* about the world's richest art star in space. I am not writing a book called *Kansas City Spleen*. I am not writing a sequel to *Kansas City Spleen* called *Bitch's Maldoror*. I am not writing a book of political philosophy called Questions for Poets. I am not writing a scandalous memoir. I am not writing a pathetic memoir. I am not writing a memoir about poetry or love. I am not writing a memoir about poverty, debt collection, or bankruptcy. I am not writing about family court. I am not writing a memoir because memoirs are for property owners and not writing a memoir about prohibitions of memoirs.[28]

The danger is that lists that act as reminders might become repetitive in their attempt to summon something. You might forget or fail to do the task, to respect the power of the list, and you might have to repeat the demand the next day, the next month, still in the hope of its fulfilment. But lists, in some ways, are the hope of living differently, or perhaps even the proof that we already have. Their potential to reduce and expand holds a promise, often broken, yet repeated nevertheless.

---

28   Anne Boyer, 'Not Writing', in Boyer, *Garments Against Women* (Boise, ID: Ahsahta Press, 2015), pp. 41–43 (p. 41).

White Supremacist Capitalist Patriarchy
BEN NICHOLS

Sometimes lists have a peculiar rhetorical force. When bell hooks writes, as she famously does, of 'white supremacist capitalist patriarchy', or 'imperialist white supremacist capitalist patriarchy', she employs the list as a powerful way of evoking an integrated system in which a range of forms of oppression work together in tandem: each one intensifies the effects of the others in one unified direction.[1] The lists to which hooks often returned continue to have currency and have more recently been expanded. In a conversation between hooks and actress Laverne Cox from 2014, for example, Cox gives us a longer list to consider: 'cisnormative, heteronormative, imperialist, white supremacist, capitalist patriarchy'.[2] We could expand the list even further: ableist, anthropocentric, ageist, and so on. The list form here has a crucial role in evoking how disparate phenomena work together as part of what is basically the same systemic force.

What do such lists enable and what do they foreclose? On the one hand, the rhetorical force of lists like these can perhaps get in

---

1   bell hooks, *Feminist Theory: From Margin to Center* (Boston, MA: South End Press, 1984), p. 51; bell hooks, *Feminism is for Everybody: Passionate Politics* (Cambridge, MA: South End Press, 2000), p. 46.
2   The New School, *bell hooks and Laverne Cox in a Public Dialogue at the New School*, online video recording, YouTube, 13 October 2014 <https://www.youtube.com/watch?v=9oMmZIJijgY> [accessed: 8 July 2022].

the way of certain kinds of understanding. For example, in 'Capitalism and Gay Identity' (1983), a famous and formative essay written in an early moment of US-based lesbian and gay studies, the historian John D'Emilio offers an account of how some of the forces in the lists above can also pull against each other or in different directions.[3] D'Emilio argues that it was actually historical developments brought about through capitalism that allowed for the formation of modern homosexual identities and communities in the early twentieth-century US. Rather than upholding heteronormativity, then, capitalism could be seen to have undermined it. The reason for this is that the spread of wage labour played a role in eroding the centrality of family units to human subsistence. Previously, D'Emilio argues, people's lives had been largely defined by subsistence farming, which took place primarily in the context of family units and homes. But the increasing availability of wage labour enabled people to seek employment outside the family unit. This in turn enabled them to act on, and build their lives around, desires in new ways. So, while we can't deny that capitalism and heteronormativity often work in tandem in insidious ways, D'Emilio's analysis shows that sometimes they can work against each other too. However, this does not necessarily happen in isomorphic ways: for example, if capitalism undermines heteronormativity, this does not mean that heteronormativity undermines capitalism. Nevertheless, the picture can be more complex than the list form would suggest.[4]

But perhaps the point of the lists that I've been discussing is precisely to shield us from this kind of complexity. Both hooks's and Cox's

---

3   John D'Emilio, 'Capitalism and Gay Identity', in *Powers of Desire: The Politics of Sexuality*, ed. by Ann Snitow, Christine Stansell and Sharon Thompson (New York: Monthly Review Press, 1983), pp. 100–13.

4   Critics of 'homonormativity', 'homonationalism', and 'queer liberalism' would of course not be surprised by the idea that homosexuality and advanced capitalism ('neoliberalism') could go hand-in-hand. The extent to which they would then seek to dispute the explanatory force of a list like the one given by Cox, which links heteronormativity with capitalism, is however unclear. See Lisa Duggan, *The Twilight of Equality? Neoliberalism, Cultural Politics, and the Attack on Democracy* (Boston, MA: Beacon, 2003); Jasbir Puar, *Terrorist Assemblages: Homonationalism in Queer Times* (Durham, NC: Duke University Press, 2007); David L. Eng, *The Feeling of Kinship: Queer Liberalism and the Racialization of Intimacy* (Durham, NC: Duke University Press, 2010).

lists conjure an integrated system to show the need for systemic up-heaval or transformation. Their lists are basically shorthand for the fact that everything needs to change. Such a process could only ever be overwhelmingly complex: it would involve unpicking every assumption, rebuilding every institution, and recalibrating all social norms. It would be such an enormous undertaking that the desire for it is almost self-defeating: how could it ever succeed? This is where the neatness and coherence of the list offers some solace or encouragement. How could we bear the complexity of actually thinking about everything in the way that hooks's lists seem to encourage us to do without the reduction that they themselves perform? The list gives us a false sense of simplicity, but without it we would arguably not be able to bear the enormity of the task that it points to.

Proust List Impulse

SAM DOLBEAR

For s. m. r.

Lists proliferate in Marcel Proust's work but also his wake.[1] Anne Carson lists 59 instances of Albertine's appearances in *À la recherche du temps perdu* (*In Search of Lost Time*), including the number of pages on which she is mentioned (807) and the percentage of time in which she's asleep (19%).[2] Rebecca Comay lists the remarks made by those who visited Proust on his deathbed, including François Mauriac's comment on the youthfulness of his corpse and Paul Helleu's note that he remained handsome, strange given his diet had consisted of little but *café au lait* for five months.[3] Samuel Beckett lists a number of fetishes in the novel:

---

1   This year I have been reading one volume of *À la recherche du temps perdu* every month, as they were cut into twelve in a particular 1943 publication. At the start of the year I wrapped up the volumes in brown paper, and, at the start of each month, I unwrap a volume to start reading it. I am in a Proust support group with two friends, Lizzie Homersham and Aurelia Guo, who are doing something similar. We send each other voice notes, thoughts, images, and quotes. I have kept a document of notes as I go.

2   Anne Carson, 'The Albertine Workout', *London Review of Books*, 5 June 2014.

3   Rebecca Comay, 'Proust's Remains', *October*, 144 (2013), pp. 3–24 <https://doi.org/10.1162/OCTO_a_00138>.

1. The Madeleine steeped in an infusion of tea.
2. The steeples of Martinville, seen from Dr. Percepied's trap.
3. A musty smell in a public lavatory in the Champs-Elysées.
4. The three trees, seen near Balbec from the carriage of Mme. de Villeparisis.
5. The hedge of hawthorn near Balbec.
6. He stoops to unbutton his boots on the occasion of his second visit to the Grand Hotel Balbec.
7. Uneven cobbles in the courtyard of the Guermantes Hotel.
8. The noise of a spoon against a plate.
9. He wipes his mouth with a napkin.
10. The noise of water in the pipes.
11. Georg Sand's François le Champi.[4]

Beckett ends this list with the comment: 'The list is not complete.'[5]

Anne Borrell collects together the recipes mentioned in the volumes.[6] Eric Karpeles compiles the paintings.[7] Julia Kristeva, in her third lecture on Proust, lists the many stages of the experience of the consumption of the madeleine.[8] Edward Said lists the social institutions that Proust moved through: families, intellectual associations, musical and concert events, philosophical traditions, and academic institutions.[9] Eve Kosofsky Sedgwick lists the various ways in which weather signifies the transmigration of the narrator, when he becomes

---

4   Samuel Beckett, *Proust and Three Dialogues with Georges Duthuit* (London: John Calder, 1949), pp. 36–37.

5   Ibid., p. 37.

6   Anne Borrell, *Dining with Proust* (London: Ebury Press, 1992).

7   Eric Karpeles, *Paintings in Proust: A Visual Companion to 'In Search of Lost Time'* (London: Thames and Hudson, 2008).

8   These are listed in eight stages: 'Stage 1: just a "luminous patch"'; 'Stage 2: the metamorphosis of the dead'; 'Stage 3: I have the luck to taste a madeleine'; 'Stage 4: incest and silence — the disappearance of two women's names'; 'Stage 5: an exquisite pleasure without origin'; 'Stage 6: desire and the visible'; 'Stage 7: a substitution quietens the effervescence — Aunt Leonie in place of Mamma'; 'Stage 8: memory is a cascade of spatial metaphors'. See Julia Kristeva, *Proust and the Sense of Time*, trans. by Stephen Bann (New York: Columbia University Press, 1993), pp. 30–49.

9   Edward Said, *On Late Style: Music and Literature Against the Grain* (London: Blooms-bury, 2017), p. 14.

an 'animated barometer' or is born again after waking up to changed weather. Sedgwick then collates the instances of alchemical changes of state, when air and light are described as:

> 'melted' (5:100), 'glazed' (5:553), 'unctuous' (5:553), 'elastic' (5:555), 'fermenting' (5:555), 'contracted' (5:803), 'distended' (5:803), 'solidified' (6:19), 'distilled' (2:387), 'scattered' (2:387), 'liquid' (2:565), 'woven' (3:474), 'brittle' (3:474), 'powdery' (2:567), 'crumbling' (2:567), 'embalmed' (2:730), 'congealed' (4:721), 'gummy' (1:88), 'flaked' (1:88), 'squeezed' (1:120), 'frayed' (1:214), 'pressed' (1:235), 'percolated' (1:387), 'volatilised' (2:656), or even 'burning' (4:534).[10]

The technique of listing finds its origin in syntax as much as form. Jacqueline Rose remarked in a radio interview that the experience of reading one of Proust's sentences is equivalent to diving into a pool and holding one's breath. You plunge into someone's mind, you have to let yourself go, else you drown.[11] With each comma comes an additional element, an accumulation, ripples that turn into waves. It could go on but it stops. Walter Benjamin also mobilized watery analogues *vis-à-vis* the 'endless sentences'. He says they are like a river, specifically the Nile — a metaphor of Orientalist fancy (of which many lists could be made) — of a language that 'overflows and fructifies the regions of truth'.[12] At another point in his essay on Proust, the sentences are weighted like fisher's catch: 'his sentences are the entire muscular activity of the intelligible body; they contain the whole enormous effort to raise this catch'.[13] For Benjamin, Proust's asthma (part of a list of other illnesses) becomes part of the sentences — or, he says, maybe his asthma is produced by the sentences, as they 'rhythmically and step by step reproduc[e] his fear of suffocating', as if drowning in air.[14]

---

10   Eve Kosofsky Sedgwick, *The Weather in Proust* (Durham, NC: Duke University Press, 2011), p. 9.

11   'Proust', *In Our Time*, BBC Radio 4, first transmitted 17 April 2003 <https://www.bbc.co.uk/programmes/p00548wx> [accessed 6 July 2022].

12   Walter Benjamin, 'On the Image of Proust' [1929], trans. by Harry Zohn, in *Walter Benjamin: Selected Writings*, ed. by Michael Jennings and others, 4 vols (Cambridge, MA.: Harvard University Press, 2004–06), II.1 (2005), pp. 237–47 (p. 237).

13   Ibid., p. 247.

14   Ibid., p. 246.

The above list of lists is incomplete. As each page turns, new ones fall out and in. Other people have no doubt compiled other lists, and other ones have yet to be collated. Each list might also end with an *et cetera*, to mark an inability to reach a final entry. How else to take account of experience if not by piling object on subject on object, social interaction on sensation on memory on habit? How else to make sense of the pages, to remember their contents, against excess and forgetting, when all we have been offered is *durée rélle* (real duration), a pool in which to swim, to come out the other side.

A List of Fears
Eva Kot'átková's *Asylum*
CLAUDIA PEPPEL

> No whole is unified but all is held together
> simply by temporary and contradictory forces.[1]

A two-dimensional black stocking-mask head with an oversized eye hangs from the ceiling by an invisible thread. On a large rectangular table covered in black cloth, a huge number of disparate objects resembling tiny Dadaist stage props, facing in all directions, are arranged in enigmatic order. Cut-outs, collages, and vintage images of human faces and body parts are mounted on slender, mostly bipedal metal stands. They look like miniature billboards. Some objects bear white lines, which often look like seams, a technique of marking and erasing in order 'to counter situations of exclusion and isolation'.[2] Filigree wire sculptures in different shapes and sizes with lattice- and cage-like structures punctuate the scenery. Old photographs, drawings, hand-written notes, and printed pages are laid out in orderly fashion. One piece of paper lists 30 fears, one after the other. FEARS is written above it as the title.

---

1   Eva Kot'átková, *Pictorial Atlas of a Girl Who Cut a Library into Pieces*, 2 vols (Zurich: JRP Ringier, 2015), I, without page numbers.

2   Catherine de Zegher, 'Theater of Speaking Objects: Conversation with Eva Kot'átková', in *Women's Work is Never Done: An Anthology*, ed. by de Zegher (Gent: AsaMer, 2014), pp. 520–33 (p. 520).

FEARS
fear of the dark
fear of physicalf contact
fear of own body
fear of small, narrow spaces
fear of being watched
fear of fragile objects
fear of children
fear of colors
fear of clowns
fear of silence
fear of sudden movement
fear of making decisions
fear of falling a sleep
fear of sharp teeth
fear of objects with some closed content
fear of animal skin
fear of closed doors
fear of being followed
fear of bird wings
fear of opened windows
fear of old furniture
fear of own family members
fear of too friendly people
fear of the outside
fear of having to speak with someone
fear of own ideas
fear of being taken care of
fear of being forgotten in a room
fear of curtains
fear of too many memories[3]

The list contains two typos, 'physicalf' instead of 'physical' and 'a sleep' instead of 'asleep'. The font, the uneven thickness of contour of individual letters, and the errors suggest that the list was written before the age of computers, at a time when typewriters did not have a correction key, or that the list does not claim to be correct but embraces mistakes and uncertainty. Are these fears belonging to one person or are they a compilation of fears of different people? It looks like an ad hoc compilation that does not aim for completeness. At the same time,

---

3   Part of Eva Kot'átková's installation *Asylum*, mixed media, dimensions variable, presented at 55th Venice Biennale, June–November 2013. Courtesy of the artist and Meyer Riegger, Berlin and Karlsruhe.

the list feels exhausting, almost mantra-like; it features many different and very specific fears, some appear more disturbing than others, some seem to contradict each other like the 'fear of being forgotten' and the 'fear of being taken care of'. The recurring phrase *Fear of* ... feels obsessive, but there is also something poetic about it: It's definitely not a to-do list, but rather an artistic-psychological enumeration of anxious states of mind and personal experiences. One feels inclined to look for significance in the order in which the fears are listed, but the list itself seems to frustrate this.[4] Usually, fears and phobias are described in terms of anxiety disorders, and are listed in psychiatric manuals.[5] Their variety seems infinite, and their severity varies from a slight uneasiness or tension to a condition in which a state of great panic is induced by the specific stimulus, which can be an object, an animal, a number, people, spaces, ideas, or a particular situation. For every inexplicable fear the Greeks have something beautiful in store: there is kairophobia, the fear of making decisions, phasmophobia, the fear of ghosts, eisoptrophobia, the fear of mirrors or seeing oneself in a mirror, and paralipophobia, the fear of neglecting duty or responsibility.

The list of fears is part of the installation *Asylum* by Czech artist Eva Kot'átková that was presented at the 55th Venice Biennale in 2013 (Figure 1). The installation is a compilation, collection, and archive, made from found and fabricated objects, blending private and collective history. Kot'átková's works often reflect on the processes that restrict and manipulate people within institutions such as psychiatric hospitals or schools. As Bárbara Rodríguez Muñoz notes, *Asylum* — the title referring to yet 'another example of total institutions that control and administer subjectivities' — is based on Kot'átková's research visits to the Bohnice psychiatric hospital in Prague.[6] It presents 'a collection of fears, anxieties, phobias and phantasmagoric visions of patients and children suffering from communication difficulties or

---

4   Many thanks to Ben Nichols for this thought and his careful and generous reading of the text.

5   *The Encyclopedia of Phobias, Fears, and Anxieties*, ed. by Ronald M. Doctor, Ada P. Kahn, and Christine Adamec, 3rd edn (New York: Facts On File, 2008).

6   Bárbara Rodríguez Muñoz, 'Eva Kot'átková: Mental Armours', *Afterall*, 25 February 2014 <https://www.afterall.org/article/eva-kot_tkov_mental-armours> [accessed 3 June 2022].

Figure 1. Eva Kot'átková, *Asylum*, 2013, mixed media, dimensions variable. Installation view, 'The Encyclopedic Palace', 55th Venice Biennale, June–November 2013. Courtesy of the artist, Meyer Riegger, Berlin/Karlsruhe, and hunt kastner, Prague.

struggling to fit within social structures, a chaotic archive of inner visions'.[7] Is the list of fears a cathartic writing exercise or a mere enumeration? Does it sharpen perception or merely irritate? Can a list of fears evoke or instil fears? Where does one go from here? To list all existing fears seems impossible. Fears are often enduring; they cannot simply be crossed off a list. Instead they pose questions to the body and the mind, to the past and the future. Nevertheless, the form of the list and the enumeration of fears coincide, embedded in a compilation of

---

7   Ibid.

objects. A list combines invocation, presence, intensity. Something abstract emanates from lists, open and yet framed, ephemeral, assembled, wanting to end and endless at the same time. There is also something controlling, restrictive, fearsome, and violent about them. The anxiety that lists can generate is found in the juxtaposition of banality and manipulation. Many things come to mind that can create pressure or trigger anxiety: the task-orientedness, the relentless demand to check items off a to-do list, having to make a list or to continue a list that has been started; having to work things through or to complete actions on the list; forgetting something, excluding something, listing something dangerous or risky, ... Lists can be reassuring too: they grant postponement; what has been noted down does not have to be processed or completed immediately.

Lists have a special appearance and shape. In artworks that operate with or come as lists, the arrangements of entries, the typographical layout, and the formal setting and presentation are of particular importance. This is where aesthetic and conceptual considerations coincide as the following few examples will show: In George Brecht's famous *Water Yam* (1959–63, republished several times since), a tiny box contains a large number of small printed index cards known as event-scores, on which individual instructions for action are listed with bullet points. In Ceal Floyer's *Monochrome Till Receipt* (1998), the receipt from a supermarket, placed in the middle of a white wall, lists the exclusively white products that the artist bought shortly before presenting the work.[8] Kapwani Kiwanga's work *Greenbook* (2019) lists street names of various American states on thirteen archival pigment prints. The prints are extracts of the 1961 edition of the *Green Book*, an annual guidebook for African American road travellers, which was published between 1936–66 by Victor Hugo Green. The book reviewed hotels and restaurants and was a response to the great difficulties that African American people faced — due to the racism of white society — when seeking lodging and food while travelling, from being refused service in shops or restaurants to being denied accommodation in hotels or gas in gas stations, not to mention the constant threat

---

8   *Ceal Floyer: A Handbook*, ed. by Susanne Küper (Ostfildern: Hatje Cantz, 2015), pp. 34–35.

of physical violence. Kiwanga's prints are framed in groups according to state and, depending on the number of places listed, consist of one, two, or three loose sheets, beautifully presented within a plain frame on a moss green background resembling the colour of the original book cover. As noted above, Eva Kot'átková's installation *Asylum* presents a written list on a single sheet amidst a large arrangement of various objects, and it is precisely in this juxtaposition that the big question emerges: Why should a compilation of written items be called a list, while an arrangement or a series of presented, drawn, or photographed objects should not? Would the definitions and forms of series and sequences as well as the cross-connections to series and lists need to be reconsidered in this context? Moreover, her installation shows in a remarkable way the overlaps and correspondences of list-making with basic elements of collage, a technique of arranging and combining given material as well as of detaching items or objects from an original context and rearranging them in another, new context. It does so especially by including a list — the list of fears — that makes the linear order seem unimportant. 'Cutting the images into pieces and rearranging them is for me a way to step actively into history, into a given situation, into already stabilized imagery. It is a form of critical thinking with scissors', says Kot'átková.[9]

9   'Eva Kot'átková', in *The Age of Collage: Contemporary Collage in Modern Art*, ed. by Robert Klanten, Lincoln Dexter, Dennis Busch, and Francesca Gavin, 3 vols (Berlin: gestalten, 2013–20), III (2020), pp. 104–09 (p. 105).

How to Bake X Cake
Notes on the Recipe
IRACEMA DULLEY

INGREDIENTS:

- 4 eggs
- 2 cups of wheat flour
- ½ cup of sunflower oil (You could use other oil. The original recipe said 1 cup but ½ cup will usually do. Add a little more in case the dough needs it.)
- 1 cup of sugar (There were 2 cups in the original recipe. According to your preferences regarding sweetness, something between ½ cup and 2 cups should do.)
- 1 full tablespoon of baking powder
- X
- Optional spice

X stands for a liquid or liquefiable ingredient, such as: the juice of 1 large carrot or 2 small ones; 2 smashed medium bananas; the juice of 1 large orange or 2 small ones; the juice of 2 lemons; the juice of 2 apples.

Optional spice: With carrot, add seeds of cardamom to the dough. With banana and apple, add slices of banana or apple plus cinnamon on top of the cake before baking it. With orange and lemon, add an orange or lemon plus sugar hot sauce on top of the baked cake while still warm.

METHOD OF PREPARATION:

Mix the wet ingredients. Add the dry ingredients. Mix vigorously. Baking powder should be the last ingredient to be gently added to the mixture.

Bake the cake for about 30 minutes (I like it slightly burned). Your oven should be set to 180°C. (Mind the fact that the real temperature of ovens is frequently not what it says.)

THE RECIPE: A LIST WITH A METHOD AND A HISTORY

Recipes are the product of history, but their form can elide this information. This recipe draws from another recipe that was given to me by my daughter's kindergarten teacher so that I could learn how to bake a cake for the celebration of her sixth birthday. I wanted to buy her a cake since I could not bake one, but she resolutely told me that 'all moms can bake cakes'. This is how the experimentation started.

A recipe usually gives you the rules of success but does not address how to avoid failure. This will be the work of experience. For instance, a cake recipe does not say that it can be disastrous to open the oven while baking — it took me a number of ruined cakes to realize this. I have often asked myself why recipes are not more pedagogical and have come to no precise conclusion on this matter. It might be the case that previous cooking experience is just assumed. Or maybe the recipe form implicitly allows the cook to keep their secrets so that the original remains not fully reproducible.

As a purpose-oriented list, a recipe is an attempt to reduce experience to a method and technique aimed at achieving the same, or at least very similar, results. Order can be important and is related to temporality: the results of the recipe depend on the order in which ingredients are added and actions are performed. A recipe is a powerful tool if one starts off to accomplish something without any previous experience. Yet, to the extent that its form cannot contain all the setbacks of chance, its various instantiations will inevitably be somewhat different.

One can approach a recipe from a controlling perspective, in which one tries to reduce the setbacks of chance in order to approximate as closely as possible an imagined outcome. Or else one can approach it from a more experimental stance, in which one takes instructions and ingredients as guidelines and incorporates the variations provided by chance as possible contributions to the end result. I am prone to the latter as long as there are enough ingredients and time to start again before the meal is to be served in case the experiment miserably fails.

The extent to which these notes apply to other recipes or lists shall remain indeterminate.

Walking Away, Walking in Circles, Writing Lists

RACHEL AUMILLER

I make lists at the beginning of the day/week/month/year. I peck away at each item so that I may have that particular joy of crossing each out. The measure of time as the pleasure of erasure, of shedding weight, of leaving you behind.

As I clean out my desk, I find old lists composed of delicately drawn letters. Some lists are like driving by a house I used to live in when I was young or stumbling across an email from a lover who I no longer talk to. Sometimes I'm proud of how far I've come when I encounter the self I left behind in those notes. Tasks that were daunting to her now come to me with ease.

---

* This reflection resulted from a 30-minute timed meditation on lists led by Sam Dolbear. I made very few changes to the original stream-of-consciousness text from the exercise on 3 February 2021: the day after Groundhog Day, a Pennsylvania Dutch tradition founded in Punxsutawney where my extended family still lives. If Phil, the fortune-telling groundhog, does not see his shadow on this day, spring will arrive six-weeks early. If Phil does see his shadow, we are fated to be stuck in winter. The shadow represents a split in one's desire, the impossibility of self-reconciliation or unity. The shadow naturally leads me to Zarathustra, who seeks transformation through his fraught relationship with his shadow and the moment of its disappearance. Nietzscheans who are also Bill Murray fans will get the connection to the eternal return of the same damn day. My chapter in this volume explores the theme of stuckness and transformation on a philosophical register. Friedrich Nietzsche, *Also sprach Zarathustra*, ed. by Volker Gerhardt (Berlin: Akademie Verlag, 2012).

Other lists from years ago are identical to my list from today. '1. Practice German, 2. Write Book, 3. Answer Emails, 4. Run.' Day, I swore I was done with you yesterday. I wake up and write the list, to crumble it up at the end of the day, to wake up to write the same list. I'm *still* writing this beast of a book. The eternal return of the same damn day.

Yesterday was Groundhog Day. A few extra days of winter tacked onto a year that feels like an eternity could be my breaking point. Phil, the groundhog, lives in Punxsutawney, Pennsylvania. My great-grandfather moved to Punxsutawney from Italy when he was a boy. He played the button box and saved up enough money to buy a fruit chart. He sold enough fruit to open Raffetto's Restaurant. My grandpa grew the family restaurant until his brother ran it into the ground. He had drinking and gambling problems. They both fought in the war. After the war my family stopped speaking Italian.

I was always the last one left at the breakfast table with my grandpa after all my cousins had run off to play and my aunts and uncles competed for the shower. He took his time, working his way down the familiar list of his favourite memories, from childhood, from the war. The list was carefully curated for his young audience. When I was home, I would write down the memories, adding the parts he might have left out.

My grandfather told a lot of stories, but there are things that my family still does not talk about, like my uncle Al who died of AIDS when I was a kid. He studied philosophy at Duquesne. My aunt recently sent me his philosophy books. There is a lot about their life that I don't know about.

When I recite my family stories so they won't be forgotten, I try most of all to remember the ones that no one has told me. It's like trying to remember an item on a list that is already crossed off. Like trying to speak in a mother tongue that was never taught.

My favourite list is from Nietzsche's *Thus Spoke Zarathustra*. I memorized it in German (before I 'learned' German. I'll never learn German). I often recite it in my head, counting to twelve:

Eins!
O Mensch! Gib acht!

Zwei!
Was spricht die tiefe Mitternacht?

Drei!
'Ich schlief, ich schlief —,

Vier!
Aus tiefem Traum bin ich erwacht:

Fünf!
Die Welt ist tief,

Sechs!
Und tiefer als der Tag gedacht.

Sieben!
Tief ist ihr Weh —,

Acht!
Lust — tiefer noch als Herzeleid:

Neun!
Weh spricht: Vergeh!

Zehn!
Doch alle Lust will Ewigkeit —,

Elf!
— will tiefe, tiefe Ewigkeit!'

Zwölf!

It is a dancing song that operates as a round. Whenever I recite it in my head, I imagine getting very drunk with friends while toasting to each line. Midnight wakes up abruptly from a deep dream. This day, as every day, she declares, 'So deep is the world that she says to her woe, "Go! but come again!" So deep is joy that it also wants woe. It wants all things again, all things eternally.'

I write lists to externalize what overwhelms me. To be in control. To master and move on. Yet, my lists circle back to me. In Ljubljana we walk the Path of Remembrance and Resistance, a trail that surrounds the city where barbwire was erected during the Nazi occupation. Walking in circles allows us to remember, but it also allows us to forget, or at least to return with a different spirit to what can't be forgotten. The process of writing the same list every day or the same act of writing the list is a looping. I return to myself, to the parts I can remember and to the parts I can't remember, but also can't leave behind.

References

Abraham, Ruth, and K. H. Blacker, 'The Rat Man Revisited: Comments on Maternal Influences', *International Journal of Psychoanalytic Psychotherapy*, 9 (1982–1983), pp. 705–27

Adorno, Theodor W., *Minima Moralia: Reflections on a Damaged Life*, trans. by Edmund F. N. Jephcott (London: Verso, 2005)

—— *Minima Moralia: Reflexionen aus dem beschädigten Leben* [1951] (Frankfurt a.M.: Suhrkamp, 1970)

Ahmed, Sara, 'Home and Away: Narratives of Migration and Estrangement', in Ahmed, *Strange Encounters: Embodied Others in Postcoloniality* (London: Routledge, 2000), chapter 4: pp. 77–94

'Al Qadiri and Al-Maria on Gulf Futurism', *Dazed Digital*, 14 November 2012, <https://www.dazeddigital.com/music/article/15037/1/alqadiri-al-maria-on-gulf-futurism> [accessed 15 October 2020]

Allahyari, Moreshin, and Daniel Rouke, *The 3D Additivist Manifesto*, 2015 <https://additivism.org/manifesto> [accessed 24 February 2021]

Althusser, Louis, 'Ideology and Ideological State Apparatuses', in Althusser, *Lenin and Philosophy*, trans. by Ben Brewster (New York: Monthly Review Press, 1972), pp. 127–86

Andersen, Hanna, 'The History of Reductionism versus Holistic Approaches to Scientific Research', *Endeavour*, 25.4 (2001), pp. 153–56 <https://doi.org/10.1016/S0160-9327(00)01387-9>

Apuleius, *Apologia; Florida; De deo Socratis*, trans. by Christopher P. Jones (Cambridge, MA: Harvard University Press, 2017) <https://doi.org/10.4159/DLCL.apuleius-de_deo_socratis.2017>

Aranke, Sampada, 'Material Matters: Black Radical Aesthetics and the Limits of Visibility', *e-flux Journal*, 79 (February 2017) <https://www.e-flux.com/journal/79/94433/material-matters-black-radical-aesthetics-and-the-limits-of-visibility/>

Archer, Megan, 'Logistics as Rationality: Excavating the Coloniality of Contemporary Logistical Formations' (Doctoral Dissertation, University of Brighton, 2020) <https://cris.brighton.ac.uk/ws/portalfiles/portal/22372242/Archer_Thesis_2020.pdf> [accessed 16 March 2022]

Augustine, *Confessions*, trans. by Garry Wills (New York: Penguin, 2006)

—— *Soliloquies: Augustine's Inner Dialogue*, trans. by Kim Paffenroth (Hyde Park, NY: New City Press, 2000)

Aumiller, Rachel, 'Sensation and Hesitation: Haptic Scepticism as the Ethics of Touching', *A Touch of Doubt: On Haptic Scepticism*, ed. by Rachel Aumiller (Berlin: Walter De Gruyter, 2020), pp. 3–29 <https://doi.org/10.1515/9783110627176-002>

Austin, John, *How to Do Things with Words* (Oxford: Oxford University Press, 1962)

Avanessian, Armen, and Mahan Moalemi, eds, *Ethnofuturismen* (Berlin: Merve Verlag, 2018)

Bachelard, Gaston, *The Psychoanalysis of Fire*, trans. by Alan C. M. Ross (London: Routledge and Kegan Paul, 1964)

Bak, Per, *How Nature Works: The Science of Self-Organized Criticality* (New York: Springer, 1996) <https://doi.org/10.1007/978-1-4757-5426-1>

Barad, Karen, 'Troubling Time/s and Ecologies of Nothingness: Re-turning, Re-membering, and Facing the Incalculable', *New Formations: A Journal of Culture/Theory/Politics*, 92 (2018), pp. 56–86 (p. 60) <https://doi.org/10.3898/NEWF:92.05.2017>

Bazzoni, Alberica, 'Nievo's Pisana and Sapienza's Modesta: Female Heroism as a Challenge to Gendered Configurations of the Nation', *The Italianist*, 39.3 (2019), pp. 332–46 <https://doi.org/10.1080/02614340.2019.1679451>

—— 'Trauma, Sadomasochism, and the Female Body in Elena Ferrante's *I giorni dell'abbandono*', in *Italian Studies Across Disciplines: Interdisciplinarity, New Approaches and Future Directions*, ed. by Marco Ceravolo and Anna Finozzi (Rome: Aracne, 2022), pp. 165–201

Beauvoir, Simone de, *The Ethics of Ambiguity*, trans. by Bernard Frechtman (Los Angeles: Open Road, 2015)

Beckett, Samuel, *Proust and Three Dialogues with Georges Duthuit* (London: John Calder, 1949)

Beigler, Jerome, 'A Commentary on Freud's Treatment of the Rat Man', *Annual of Psychoanalysis*, 3 (1975), pp. 271–85

Belknap, Robert, *The List: The Uses and Pleasures of Cataloguing* (New Haven, CT: Yale University Press, 2004) <https://doi.org/10.12987/yale/9780300103830.001.0001>

Beller, Jonathan, *The Message is Murder: Substrates of Computational Capital* (London: Pluto Press, 2018) <https://doi.org/10.2307/j.ctt1x07z9t>

Benjamin, Walter, 'Berlin Chronicle' [1932], trans. by Edmund Jephcott, in Benjamin, *Selected Writings*, II.2 (2005), pp. 595–637

—— *Berliner Chronik / Berliner Kindheit um neunzehnhundert*, in *Kritische Gesamtausgabe*, ed. by Christoph Gödde and Henri Lonitz, 21 vols (2008–), XI.1, ed. by Burkhardt Lindner and Nadine Werner (2019)

—— 'Berliner Chronik', in Benjamin, *Berliner Chronik / Berliner Kindheit um neunzehnhundert*, pp. 7–102

—— 'Fate and Character' [1919/1921], trans. by Edmund Jephcott, in Benjamin, *Selected Writings*, I (2004), pp. 201–06

—— 'Goethe's Elective Affinities', trans. by Stanley Corngold, in Benjamin, *Selected Writings*, I (2004), pp, 297–360

—— 'On the Image of Proust' [1929], trans. by Harry Zohn, in *Walter Benjamin: Selected Writings*, ed. by Michael Jennings and others, 4 vols

(Cambridge, MA.: Harvard University Press, 2004–06), ıı.1 (2005), pp. 237–47

—— *One Way Street* [1928], trans. by Edmund Jephcott, in Benjamin, *Selected Writings*, ı (2004), pp. 444–88

—— *Origin of the German Trauerspiel*, trans. by Howard Eiland (Cambridge, MA: Harvard University Press, 2019) <https://doi.org/10.4159/9780674916357>

—— 'Schicksal und Charakter', in Benjamin, *Gesammelte Schriften*, ed. by Rolf Tiedemann and Hermann Schweppenhäuser, 7 vols (Frankfurt a.M.: Suhrkamp, 1972–91), ıı (1977), pp. 171–79

—— *Selected Writings*, ed. by Michael Jennings and others, 4 vols (Cambridge, MA: Harvard University Press, 2004–06)

Bergman, Torbern Olof, *A Dissertation on Elective Attractions* [Disquisitio de Attractionibus Electivis, 1775], trans. by Thomas Beddoes (London: Routledge, 2014)

Bergson, Henri, *Matter and Memory*, trans. by Nancy M. Paul and W. Scott Palmer (New York: Dover Publications, 2012)

—— *Time and Free Will: An Essay on the Immediate Data of Consciousness* [1889], trans. by F. L. Pogson (Mineola, NY: Dover Publications, 2001)

Berlant, Lauren, 'First Things', in Berlant and Kathleen Stewart, *The Hundreds* (Durham, NC: Duke University Press, 2019), p. 3 <https://doi.org/10.1215/9781478003335>

—— 'On the Case', *Critical Inquiry*, 33.4 (2007), pp. 663–72 <https://doi.org/10.1086/521564>

Bersani, Leo, *Homos* (Cambridge, MA: Harvard University Press, 1995) <https://doi.org/10.4159/9780674020870>

Betts, Will, 'Interview: Minimalist Electronic Artist Caterina Barbieri', *Sound of Sound*, 31 July 2017 <https://www.soundonsound.com/news/interview-minimalist-electronic-artist-caterina-barbieri> [accessed 2 November 2021]

Biceaga, Victor, *The Concept of Passivity in Husserl's Phenomenology* (Dordrecht: Springer, 2010) <https://doi.org/10.1007/978-90-481-3915-6>

Boccagni, Paolo, *Migration and the Search for Home: Mapping Domestic Space in Migrants' Everyday Lives* (New York: Palgrave Macmillan, 2017)

Boodrookas, Alex, and Arang Keshavarzian, 'Giving the Transnational a History: Gulf Cities Across Time and Space', in *The New Arab Urban: Gulf Cities of Wealth, Ambition, and Distress*, ed. by Harvey Molotch and Davide Ponzini (New York: New York University Press, 2019), pp. 35–57 <https://doi.org/10.18574/nyu/9781479880010.003.0002>

Borrell, Anne, *Dining with Proust* (London: Ebury Press, 1992)

Bousquet, Antoine, *The Scientific Way of Warfare: Order and Chaos on the Battlefields of Modernity* (New York: Columbia University Press, 2009)

Boyer, Anne, 'Not Writing', in Boyer, *Garments Against Women* (Boise, ID: Ahsahta Press, 2015), pp. 41–43

Braidotti, Rosi, *Metamorphoses: Towards a Materialist Theory of Becoming* (Cambridge: Polity Press, 2002)

—— 'The Politics of Life as Bios/Zoe', in *Bits of Life: Feminisms at the Intersections of Media, Bioscience, and Technology*, ed. by Anneke Smelik and Nina Lykke (Seattle: University of Washington Press, 2008), pp. 177–95

Brothers Grimm, 'The Fairytale of Rumpelstiltskin', *Guardian*, trans. by Joyce Crick, 13 October 2009 <https://www.theguardian.com/books/2009/oct/13/fairytales-rumpelstiltskin-brothers-grimm> [accessed 12 Jan 2022]

Brown, Wendy, *States of Injury: Power and Freedom in Late Modernity* (Princeton, NJ: Princeton University Press, 1995) <https://doi.org/10.1515/9780691201399>

Butler, Judith, *Gender Trouble: Feminism and the Subversion of Identity* [1990] (London: Routledge, 1999)

—— 'Imitation and Gender Insubordination', in *Inside/Out: Lesbian Theories, Gay Theories*, ed. by Diana Fuss (London: Routledge, 1991), pp. 13–31

Butor, Michel, 'The Book as Object' (1964), quoted in Brian Dillon, 'Why Literature Loves Lists: From Rabelais to Didion, an Incomplete List of Listmakers', *Literary Hub*, 14 September 2018 <https://lithub.com/why-literature-loves-lists/> [accessed 20 April 2022]

Cappellini, Paolo, Natalino Irti, Andrea Nicolussi, and Aldo Travi, 'Dopo Ratzinger al Bundestag', *Vita e pensiero*, 1 (2012), pp. 61–66

Carson, Anne, 'The Albertine Workout', *London Review of Books*, 5 June 2014

Caruth, Cathy, *Unclaimed Experience: Trauma, Narrative and History* (Baltimore, MD: John Hopkins University Press, 1996)

Casey, Edward, *Getting Back into Place: Toward a Renewed Understanding of the Place-World* (Bloomington: Indiana University Press, 1993)

Castro, Eduardo Viveiros de, 'Perspectival Anthropology and the Method of Controlled Equivocation', *Tipití: Journal of the Society for the Anthropology of Lowland South America*, 2.1 (2004), pp. 3–22 <http://digitalcommons.trinity.edu/tipiti/vol2/iss1/1> [accessed 1 June 2022]

Cavarero, Adriana, *A più voci. Filosofia dell'espressione vocale* (Milan: Feltrinelli, 2003)

Certeau, Michel de, *The Practice of Everyday Life*, trans. by Steven Rendall (Berkeley: University of California Press, 1984)

Cervato, Emanuela, Mark Epstein, Giulia Santi, and Simona Wright, eds, *Mapping Leopardi: Poetic and Philosophical Intersections* (Newcastle upon Tyne: Cambridge Scholars Publishing, 2019)

Chave, Anna C., 'Minimalism and Biography', *The Art Bulletin*, 82.1 (2000), pp. 149–63 <https://doi.org/10.2307/3051368>

Cheiro, *Palmistry for All* [1916] (London: Corgi Book, 1975)

Cherki, Alice, *Frantz Fanon: A Portrait*, trans. by Nadia Benabid (Ithaca, NY: Cornell University Press, 2006)

Chiffoleau, Jacques, 'Contra naturam. Per un approccio casuistico e procedurale alla natura medievale', trans. by Davide Pettinicchio, in Thomas and
Chiffoleau, *L'istituzione della natura*, pp. 47–102.

—— 'Contra naturam. Pour une approche casuistique et procédurale de la
nature médiévale', *Micrologus. Nature, Sciences and Medieval Societies*, 4
(1996), pp. 265–312

Chua, Charmaine, 'Logistics', in *The Sage Handbook of Marxism*, ed. by Beverley Skeggs, Sara R. Farris, Alberto Toscano, and Svenja Bromberg, 3
vols (Los Angeles: Sage, 2022), III

Chun, Wendy H. K., *Programmed Visions: Software and Memory* (Cambridge, MA: MIT Press, 2011) <https://doi.org/10.7551/mitpress/
9780262015424.001.0001>

Comay, Rebecca, 'Proust's Remains', *October*, 144 (2013), pp. 3–24
<https://doi.org/10.1162/OCTO_a_00138>

—— 'Testament of the Revolution (Walter Benjamin)', *Mosaic: An Interdisciplinary Critical Journal*, 50.2 (2017), pp. 1–12

Conte, Emanuele, *Diritto comune. Storia e storiografia di un sistema dinamico*
(Bologna: Il Mulino, 2009)

Contzen, Eva von, 'Theorising Lists in Literature: Towards a Listology',
in *Lists and Catalogues in Ancient Literature and Beyond: Towards a
Poetics of Enumeration*, ed. by Rebecca Laemmle, Cédric Scheidegger
Laemmle, and Katharina Wesselmann (Berlin: de Gruyter, 2021), pp.
35–54 <https://doi.org/10.1515/9783110712230-003>

Coole, Diana, and Samantha Frost, eds, *New Materialisms: Ontology, Agency,
and Politics* (Durham, NC: Duke University Press, 2010) <https://doi.
org/10.1215/9780822392996>

Copeland, Huey, 'One-Dimensional Abstraction', *Art Journal*, 78.2 (April,
2019), pp. 116–18 <https://doi.org/10.1080/00043249.2019.
1626161>

Coquet, Jean-Claude, *Le istanze enuncianti. Fenomenologia e semiotica*, ed. by
Paolo Fabbri (Milan: Bruno Mondadori, 2008)

Cortese, Ennio, 'Per una storia dell'arcivescovo Mosé di Ravenna (m. 1154)
sulla proprietà ecclesiastica', in *Proceedings of the Fifth International Congress of Medieval Canon Law: Salamanca 21–25 September 1976*, ed. by
Stephan Kuttner and Kenneth Pennington (Vatican: Biblioteca Apostolica Vaticana, 1980), pp. 117–55

Damasio, Antonio, *Descartes' Error: Emotion, Reason, and the Human Brain*
(New York: Putnam, 1994)

Darwish, Mahmoud, 'Athens Airport', in Darwish, *Unfortunately, It was Paradise: Selected Poems*, trans. and ed. by Munir Akash and Carolyn Forché
with Sinan Antoon and Amira El-Zein (Berkeley: University of California Press, 2003), p. 12

—— 'Edward Said: A Contrapuntal Reading', trans. by Mona Anis, *Cultural
Critique*, 67 (2007), pp. 175–82 <https://doi.org/10.1353/cul.2007.
0026>

Davachi, Sarah, *Irreal Worlds: Constructions of Phenomenal 'Space' in Experimental Music, 1962–1978* (Master's Thesis, Fine Arts in Electronic Music and Recording Media, Mills College, 2012) <https://www.academia.edu/1961555/Irreal_Worlds_Constructions_of_Phenomenal_Space_in_Experimental_Music_1962-78> [accessed 3 November 2021]

Davidson, Guy, *Categorically Famous: Literary Celebrity and Sexual Liberation in 1960s America* (Stanford, CA: Stanford University Press, 2019) <https://doi.org/10.1515/9781503609204>

—— 'Queer Literary Studies and the Question of Identity Categories', *Literature Compass*, 17 (2020), e12561 <https://doi.org/10.1111/lic3.12561>

Davis, Chloe O., *The Queens' English: The LGBTQIA+ Dictionary of Lingo and Colloquial Phrases* (London: Square Peg, 2021)

de la Torre, Shanna, 'Madness and the Sensitive Anthropologist: Lévi-Strauss's New Structuralism', in de la Torre, *Sex for Structuralists: The Non-Oedipal Logics of Femininity and Psychosis* (New York: Palgrave Macmillan, 2018), pp. 39–59. <https://doi.org/10.1007/978-3-319-92895-1_3>

Deahl, Dani, 'Electronic Music Has a Performance Problem, and This Artist is Trying to Solve It', *The Verge*, 5 April 2019 <https://www.theverge.com/2019/4/5/18277345/chagall-van-den-berg-performance-sensors-gloves-motion-tracking-suit> [accessed 9 November 2021]

Debre, Isabel, and Malak Harb, 'Expo 2020's Workers Face Hardships despite Dubai's Promises', *Associated Press News*, 5 December 2021 <https://apnews.com/article/coronavirus-pandemic-business-health-middle-east-africa-386c8ee45123e7bea212e14cc106adc2> [accessed 4 June 2022]

Deleuze, Gilles, *Negotiations 1972–1990*, trans. by Martin Joughin (New York: Columbia University Press, 1995)

—— 'Postscript on the Societies of Control', trans. by Martin Joughin, *October*, 59 (1992), pp. 3–7

Deleuze, Gilles, and Félix Guattari, *A Thousand Plateaus: Capitalism and Schizophrenia*, trans. by Brian Massumi (Minneapolis: University of Minnesota Press, 1987)

Derrida, Jacques, *On Touching — Jean-Luc Nancy*, trans. by Christine Irizarry (Stanford, CA: Stanford University Press, 2005)

—— 'Plato's Pharmacy', in Derrida, *Dissemination*, trans. by Barbara Johnson (Chicago: University of Chicago Press, 1981), pp. 61–171

Descartes, René, *Meditations on First Philosophy*, trans. by John Cottingham (Cambridge, MA: Cambridge University Press, 2017)

Deuber-Mankowsky, Astrid, and Christoph F. E. Holzhey, 'Vitalismus als kritischer Indikator: Der Beitrag der Kulturwissenschaften an der Bildung des Wissens vom Leben', in *Der Einsatz des Lebens*, ed. by Deuber-Mankowsky and Holzhey (Berlin: b_books, 2009), pp. 9–30

Didion, Joan, *The White Album* [1979] (London: HarperCollins, 2017)

Dinshaw, Carolyn, 'Temporalities', in *Oxford Twenty-First Century Approaches to Literature: Middle English*, ed. by Paul Strohm (Oxford: Oxford University Press), pp. 107–23

Diogenes Laertius, *Lives of Eminent Philosophers*, trans. by R. D. Hicks, 2 vols, Loeb Classical Series (London: Heinemann, 1925; repr. Cambridge, MA: Harvard University Press, 1972)

Doctor, Ronald M., Ada P. Kahn, and Christine Adamec, eds, *The Encyclopedia of Phobias, Fears, and Anxieties*, 3rd edn (New York: Facts On File, 2008)

Dolar, Mladen, 'Freud and the Political', *Unbound*, 4 (2008), pp. 15–29

Dolbear, Sam, 'Reading Wrinkles', 19 May 2021 <https://raeblodmas.substack.com/p/reading-wrinkles> [accessed 1 March 2022]

Dolbear, Sam, and Esther Leslie, *Dissonant Waves: Ernst Schoen and Experimental Sound in the Twentieth Century* (London: Goldsmiths Press, forthcoming 2023)

Downing, Eric, 'Divining Benjamin: Reading Fate, Graphology, Gambling', *MLN*, 126.3 (2011), pp. 561–80 <https://doi.org/10.1353/mln.2011.0036>

Dreyfus, Hubert, 'Foreword to the California Edition', in Michel Foucault, *Mental Illness and Psychology*, trans. by Alan Sheridan (Berkeley: University of California Press, 1987), pp. vii–xliii

Duggan, Lisa, *The Twilight of Equality? Neoliberalism, Cultural Politics, and the Attack on Democracy* (Boston, MA: Beacon, 2003)

Duncan, John, *How Intelligence Happens* (New Haven, CT: Yale University Press, 2010)

Dutta, Aniruddha, and Raina Roy, 'Decolonizing Transgender in India: Some Reflections', *TSQ*, 1.3 (2014), pp. 320–37 <https://doi.org/10.1215/23289252-2685615>

Duverger, Timothée, 'Degrowth: The History of an Idea', *Encyclopédie d'histoire Numérique de l'Europe* <https://ehne.fr/en/encyclopedia/themes/material-civilization/transnational-consumption-and-circulations/degrowth-history-idea> [accessed 12 June 2022]

Dyer, Harriet, *From Ace to Ze: The Little Book of LGBT Terms* (London: Summersdale, 2018)

—— *The Queeriodic Table: A Celebration of LGBTQ+ Culture* (London: Summersdale, 2019)

Easterling, Kelly, *Extrastatecraft: The Power of Infrastructure Space* (London: Verso, 2014)

Eco, Umberto, *The Infinity of Lists: From Homer to Joyce*, trans. by Alistair McEwen (London: MacLehose Press, 2009)

Edelman, Lee, *No Future: Queer Theory and the Death Drive* (Durham, NC: Duke University Press, 2004) <https://doi.org/10.1215/9780822385981>

Edwards, Adrienne, 'Blackness in Abstraction', *Art in America*, 103.1 (2015), pp. 62–69

Eiland, Howard, and Michael Jennings, *Walter Benjamin: A Critical Life* (Cambridge, MA: Harvard University Press, 2014)

D'Emilio, John, 'Capitalism and Gay Identity', in *Powers of Desire: The Politics of Sexuality*, ed. by Ann Snitow, Christine Stansell and Sharon Thompson (New York: Monthly Review Press, 1983), pp. 100–13

Eng, David L., *The Feeling of Kinship: Queer Liberalism and the Racialization of Intimacy* (Durham, NC: Duke University Press, 2010) <https://doi.org/10.1215/9780822392828>

Eng, David L., and Jasbir K. Puar, 'Introduction: Left of Queer', *Social Text*, 38.4 (2020), pp. 1–23 <https://doi.org/10.1215/01642472-8680414>

English, Darby, *1971: A Year in the Life of Color* (Chicago: University of Chicago Press, 2016) <https://doi.org/10.7208/chicago/9780226274737.001.0001>

Eshun, Kodwo, 'Further Considerations of Afrofuturism', *CR: The New Centennial Review*, 3.2 (Summer 2003), pp. 287–302 <https://doi.org/10.1353/ncr.2003.0021>

'Eva Kot'átková', in *The Age of Collage: Contemporary Collage in Modern Art*, ed. by Robert Klanten, Lincoln Dexter, Dennis Busch, and Francesca Gavin, 3 vols (Berlin: gestalten, 2013–20), iii (2020), pp. 104–09

Evans, Martha N., 'Introduction to Jacques Lacan's Lecture: The Neurotic's Individual Myth', *The Psychoanalytic Quarterly*, 48.3 (1979), pp. 386–404 <https://doi.org/10.1080/21674086.1979.11926883>

'Expo 2020 Dubai unveils first permanent public artwork by Kuwaiti creative', *Arab News*, 4 July 2021 <https://www.arabnews.com/node/1888116/lifestyle> [accessed 17 May 2022]

Fadda-Conrey, Carol, *Contemporary Arab-American Literature: Transnational Reconfigurations of Citizenship and Belonging* (New York: New York University Press, 2014)

Fanon, Frantz, *Alienation and Freedom*, ed. by Jean Khalfa and Robert J. C. Young, trans. by Steve Corcoran (London: Bloomsbury, 2018)

—— *Black Skin, White Masks*, trans. by Charles Lam Markmann, forewords by Ziauddin Sardar and Homi K. Bhabha (London: Pluto Press, 2008)

—— 'Day Hospitalization in Psychiatry: Value and Limits', in Fanon, *Alienation and Freedom*, pp. 473–94

—— 'Day Hospitalization in Psychiatry: Value and Limits, Part Two — Doctrinal Considerations', in Fanon, *Alienation and Freedom*, pp. 495–510

—— 'Letter to the Resident Minister', in Fanon, *Alienation and Freedom*, pp. 433–36

—— 'The Meeting Between Society and Psychiatry', in Fanon, *Alienation and Freedom*, pp. 511–30

—— 'Mental Alterations, Character Modifications, Psychic Disorders and Intellectual Deficit in Spinocerebellar Heredodegeneration: A Case of Friedreich's Ataxia with Delusions of Possession', in Fanon, *Alienation and Freedom*, pp. 203–76

—— 'Racism and Culture', in Fanon, *Toward the African Revolution: Political Essays*, trans. by Haakon Chevalier (New York: Grove Press, 1967), pp. 29–44

Fanon, Frantz, and Jacques Azoulay, 'Social Therapy in a Ward of Muslim Men: Methodological Difficulties', in Fanon, *Alienation and Freedom*, pp. 353–72

Fanon, Frantz, and Slimane Asselah, 'The Phenomenon of Agitation in the Psychiatric Milieu: General Considerations, Psychopathological Meaning', in Fanon, *Alienation and Freedom*, pp. 437–48

Fell, Mark, 'Collateral Damage', *The Wire*, January 2013 <https://www. thewire.co.uk/in-writing/essays/collateral-damage-mark-fell> [accessed 2 November 2021]

Ferrante, Elena, *The Days of Abandonment*, trans. by Ann Goldstein (New York: Europa Editions, 2005)

—— *Frantumaglia*, trans. by Ann Goldstein (New York: Europa Editions, 2016)

—— *I giorni dell'abbandono* (Rome: Edizioni e/o, 2002)

Forrester, John, 'If p, Then What? Thinking in Cases', *History of the Human Sciences*, 9.3 (1996), pp. 1–25 <https://doi.org/10.1177/095269519600900301>

—— *Thinking in Cases* (Cambridge: Polity, 2017)

Foucault, Michel, *The History of Sexuality*, trans. by Robert Hurley, 4 vols (London: Penguin, 1978–2021), I: *The Will to Knowledge* [1976] (1998)

—— *The History of Sexuality*, trans. by Robert Hurley, 4 vols (London: Penguin, 1978–2021), II: *The Use of Pleasure* [1984] (1992)

—— 'Introduction', in Georges Canguilhem, *The Normal and the Pathological*, trans. by Carolyn R. Fawcett (New York: Zone Books, 1991), pp. 7–24

—— *The Order of Things: An Archaeology of the Human Sciences* [trans. by Alan Sheridan?] (London: Routledge, 2002)

—— ed., *Moi, Pierre Rivière, ayant égorgé ma mère, ma soeur et mon frère… Un cas de parricide au XIXe siècle* (Paris: Éditions Gallimard, 2007)

Frankl, Viktor, *The Will to Meaning: Foundations and Applications of Logotherapy* (New York: Penguin, 1988)

Franklin, Seb, *Digitality as Cultural Logic* (Cambridge, MA: MIT Press, 2015)

Fraser, Nancy, 'Social Justice in the Age of Identity Politics: Redistribution, Recognition, and Participation', in Fraser and Axel Honneth, *Redistribution or Recognition?: A Political-Philosophical Exchange* (London: Verso, 2003), pp. 7–109

Freud, Sigmund, 'Bemerkungen über einen Fall von Zwangsneurose', in Freud, *Gesammelte Werke*, 17 vols (Frankfurt a.M.: Fischer, 1940–52), VII: *Werke aus den Jahren 1906–1909* (1941), pp. 380–463

—— *Civilization and its Discontents*, trans. by James Strachey (London: Hogarth Press, 1930)

—— *The Complete Letters of Sigmund Freud to Wilhelm Fliess, 1887–1904*, ed. and trans. by Jeffrey Moussaieft Masson (London: Belknap Press, 1985)

—— 'Fragment of an Analysis of a Case of Hysteria (1905 [1901])', in Freud, *The Standard Edition*, VII (1953), pp. 1–122

—— *L'homme aux rats: journal d'une analyse* (Paris: Presses Universitaires de France, 1974)

—— 'Notes upon a Case of Obsessional Neurosis (1909)', in Freud, *The Standard Edition*, X (1955), pp. 153–318

—— 'Recommendations to Physicians Practicing Psychoanalysis (1912)', in Freud, *The Standard Edition*, XVIII (1955), pp. 109–20

—— *The Standard Edition of the Complete Psychological Works of Sigmund Freud*, ed. and trans. by James Strachey and others, 24 vols (London: Hogarth Press, 1953–74)

Freud, Sigmund, and Carl Jung, *Briefwechsel* (Frankfurt a.M.: Fischer, 1984)

Fukuyama, Francis, *Identity: Contemporary Identity Politics and the Struggle for Recognition* (London: Profile Books, 2018)

Gal, Susan, 'Politics of Translation', *Annual Review of Anthropology*, 44 (2015), pp. 225–40 <https://doi.org/10.1146/annurev-anthro-102214-013806>

Galison, Peter, 'The Ontology of the Enemy: Norbert Wiener and the Cybernetic Vision', *Critical Inquiry*, 21.1 (1994), pp. 228–66 <https://doi.org/10.1086/448747>

Galloway, Alexander R., '"Black Box, Black Bloc": A Lecture Given at the New School in New York City on April 12, 2010' <http://cultureandcommunication.org/galloway/pdf/Galloway_Black_Box_Black_Bloc.pdf> [accessed 13 March 2022]

—— *The Interface Effect* (Cambridge: Polity Press, 2012)

Getsy, David J., *Reduction as Expansion: The Queer Capacities of Abstract Art*, lecture, ICI Berlin, 1 February 2021, video recording, mp4, 55:44 <https://doi.org/10.25620/e210201>

Gherovici, Patricia, *Transgender Psychoanalysis: A Lacanian Perspective on Sexual Difference* (London: Routledge, 2017) <https://doi.org/10.4324/9781315745107>

Gibson, Nigel C., and Roberto Beneduce, 'Further Steps toward a Critical Ethnopsychiatry Sociotherapy: Its Strengths and Weaknesses', in Gibson and Beneduce, *Frantz Fanon, Psychiatry and Politics* (London: Rowman & Littlefield, 2017), pp. 131–64

Ginzburg, Carlo, 'Il caso, I casi', *doppiozero*, 12 April 2019 <https://www.doppiozero.com/materiali/il-caso-i-casi> [accessed 2 June 2022]

—— *Il formaggio e i vermi. Il cosmo di un mugnaio del '500* [1976] (Turin: Einaudi, 2009)

Giraldi, Tullio, *Psychotherapy, Mindfulness and Buddhist Meditation* (Cham: Palgrave Macmillan, 2019) <https://doi.org/10.1007/978-3-030-29003-0>

Glück, Robert, *Margery Kempe* [1994] (New York: NYRB Classics, 2020)

Goethe, Johann Wolfgang von, *Elective Affinities* [1809], trans. by David Constantine (Oxford: Oxford University Press, 2008)

Gordon, Lewis, *What Fanon Said: A Philosophical Introduction to His Life and Thought* (New York: Fordham University Press, 2015) <https://doi.org/10.2307/j.ctt13x08sb>

Gragnolati, Manuele, and Francesca Southerden, *Possibilities of Lyric: Reading Petrarch in Dialogue* (Berlin: ICI Berlin Press, 2020), chapter 4: 'Declensions of "Now": Lyric Epiphanies in Cavalcanti, Dante, and Petrarch', pp. 85–108 <https://doi.org/10.37050/ci-18>

Gronlund, Melissa, 'What Monira Al Qadiri's Otherworldly Expo 2020 Dubai Sculpture Says about the UAE', *The National*, 4 July 2021 <https://www.thenationalnews.com/arts-culture/art/2021/07/04/what-monira-al-qadiris-otherworldly-expo-2020-dubai-sculpture-says-about-the-uae/>

Grunberger, Béla, 'Some Reflections on the Rat Man', *International Journal of Psycho-Analysis*, 47 (1966), pp. 160–68

Günel, Gökçe, *Spaceship in the Desert: Energy, Climate Change, and Urban Design in Abu Dhabi* (Durham, NC: Duke University Press, 2019) <https://doi.org/10.1215/9781478002406>

Hacking, Ian, 'Styles of Reasoning', in *Postanalytic Philosophy*, ed. by John Rajchman and Cornel West (New York: Columbia University Press, 1985), pp. 145–64

―― *The Taming of Chance* (Cambridge: Cambridge University Press, 1990) <https://doi.org/10.1017/CBO9780511819766>

Hadot, Pierre, *Philosophy as a Way of Life: Spiritual Exercises from Socrates to Foucault*, ed. by Arnold I. Davidson, trans. by Michael Chase (Malden, MA: Blackwell, 1995)

Halberstam, Jack, *Female Masculinity* (Durham, NC: Duke University Press, 1998) <https://doi.org/10.1215/9781478002703>

Halligan, Neil, 'Expo 2020 Dubai Records More than 24 Million Visits after Late Surge', *The National*, 2 April 2022 <https://www.thenationalnews.com/uae/expo-2020/2022/04/02/expo-2020-dubai-records-more-than-24-million-visits-after-late-surge-in-numbers/> [accessed 17 May 2022]

Halpern, Orit, *Beautiful Data: A History of Vision and Reason since 1945* (Durham, NC: Duke University Press, 2015) <https://doi.org/10.1215/9780822376323>

Halpern, Orit, Robert Mitchell, and Bernard Dionysius Geoghegan, 'The Smartness Mandate: Notes Toward a Critique', *Grey Room*, 68 (2017), pp. 106–29 <https://doi.org/10.1162/GREY_a_00221>

Hammad, Suheir, *Breaking Poems* (New York: Cypher Books, 2008)

Hanieh, Adam, *Capitalism and Class in the Gulf Arab States* (New York: Palgrave MacMillan, 2011) <https://doi.org/10.1057/9780230119604>

―― *Money, Markets, and Monarchies: The Gulf Cooperation Council and the Political Economy of the Contemporary Middle East* (Cambridge:

Cambridge University Press, 2018) <https://doi.org/10.1017/9781108614443>

Hansen, Mark B. N., *Bodies in Code: Interfaces with Digital Media* (London: Routledge, 2006)

Haraway, Donna J., 'A Cyborg Manifesto: Science, Technology, and Socialist-Feminism in the Late Twentieth Century', in Haraway, *Simians, Cyborgs and Natures: The Re-Invention of Nature* (New York: Routledge, 1991), pp. 149–83

Harney, Stefano, and Fred Moten, *The Undercommons: Fugitive Planning and Black Study* (New York: Autonomedia, 2013)

Haslett, Tobi, 'A Philosophy of the Cauterized Wound: Tobi Haslett on the Art of Bouchra Khalili', *Art Forum*, March 2019 <https://www.artforum.com/print/201903/tobi-haslett-on-the-art-of-bouchra-khalili-78669> [accessed 1 March 2022]

Hayles, Katherine, *Unthought: The Power of the Cognitive Non-Conscious* (Chicago: University of Chicago Press, 2017) <https://doi.org/10.7208/chicago/9780226447919.001.0001>

Heidegger, Martin, *Being and Time*, trans. by Joan Stambaugh (Albany: State University of New York Press, 2010)

—— 'Building Dwelling Thinking', in Heidegger, *Poetry, Language and Thought*, trans. by Albert Hofstadter (New York: Perennial Classics, 2001), pp. 141–59

Henke, Robert, 'Live Performance in the Age of Supercomputing', 2007 <https://roberthenke.com/interviews/supercomputing.html> [accessed 8 November 2021])

Hennessy, Rosemary, *Profit and Pleasure: Sexual Identities in Late Capitalism* (London: Routledge, 2000)

Hermitte, Marie-Angèle, 'Le droit est un autre monde', *Enquête*, 7 (1999), pp. 17–37 <https://doi.org/10.4000/enquete.1553>

Hilgers, Philipp von, 'The History of the Black Box: The Clash of a Thing and Its Concept', *Cultural Politics*, 7.1 (2011), pp. 41–58 <https://doi.org/10.2752/175174311X12861940861707>

Holzhey, Christoph F. E., and Arnd Wedemeyer, eds, *Weathering: Ecologies of Exposure*, Cultural Inquiry, 17 (Berlin: ICI Berlin Press, 2020) <https://doi.org/10.37050/ci-17>

hooks, bell, *Feminism is for Everybody: Passionate Politics* (Cambridge, MA: South End Press, 2000)

—— *Feminist Theory: From Margin to Center* (Boston, MA: South End Press, 1984)

bell hooks and Laverne Cox in a Public Dialogue at the New School, online video recording, YouTube, 13 October 2014 <https://www.youtube.com/watch?v=9oMmZIJijgY> [accessed: 8 July 2022]

Hu, Tung-Hui, 'Black Boxes and Green Lights: Media, Infrastructure, and the Future At Any Cost', *English Language Notes*, 55.1–2 (Spring/Fall 2017), pp. 81–88 <https://doi.org/10.1215/00138282-55.1-2.81>

Hughes, John, *The Idea of Home: Autobiographical Essays* (Artarmon: Giramondo Publishing Company, 2004)

Husserl, Edmund, *Ideas Pertaining to a Pure Phenomenology and to a Phenomenological Philosophy, Second Book: Studies in the Phenomenology of Constitution*, trans. by Richard Rojcewicz and André Schuwer (Dordrecht: Kluwer, 1989)

—— *The Phenomenology of Internal Time Consciousness*, trans. by Nancy M. Paul and W. Scott Palmer (Bloomington: Indiana University Press, 1964)

İşcen, Özgün Eylül, 'The Racial Politics of Smartness Urbanism: Dubai and Beirut as Two Sides of the Same Coin', *Ethnic and Racial Studies*, 44.12 (2021), pp. 2282–2303 <https://doi.org/10.1080/01419870.2021.1921233>

ICI Berlin, 'ERRANS environ/s: ICI Focus 2018-20' <https://www.ici-berlin.org/projects/errans-environs-2018-20/> [accessed 22 July 2022]

Jackson, David C., 'Repetition, Feedback and Temporality in Two Compositions by William Basinski', *érudit*, 33 (2019) <https://doi.org/10.7202/1065021ar>

Jackson, Zakiyyah Iman, *Becoming Human: Matter and Meaning in an Antiblack World* (New York: New York University Press, 2020) <https://doi.org/10.18574/nyu/9781479890040.001.0001>

Jameson, Fredric, 'Class and Allegory in Contemporary Mass Culture: Dog Day Afternoon as a Political Film', in Jameson, *Signatures of the Visible* (New York: Routledge, 1992), pp. 35–54

—— 'Cognitive Mapping', in *Marxism and the Interpretation of Culture*, ed. by Cary Nelson and Lawrence Grossberg (Champaign: University of Illinois Press, 1988), pp. 347–60

—— *Marxism and Form: Twentieth-Century Dialectical Theories of Literature* (Princeton, NJ: Princeton University Press, 2017)

—— 'Political: National Allegory', in Jameson, *Allegory and Ideology* (London: Verso, 2019), pp. 159–216

—— *Postmodernism, or, The Cultural Logic of Late Capitalism* (Durham, NC: Duke University Press, 1991) <https://doi.org/10.1215/9780822378419>

—— 'Reification and Utopia in Mass Culture', in Jameson, *Signatures of the Visible* (New York: Routledge, 1992), pp. 9–34

—— *Valences of the Dialectic* (London: Verso, 2009)

Johnson, Mark, *The Body in the Mind: The Bodily Basis of Meaning, Imagination, and Reason* (Chicago: University of Chicago Press, 1987) <https://doi.org/10.7208/chicago/9780226177847.001.0001>

Justo, Gemma, and Ghiwa Sayegh, 'Whose Home Is It? The Workplace of Migrant Domestic Workers Under Kafala', *Funambulist*, 19 February 2021 <https://thefunambulist.net/magazine/spaces-of-labor/

whose-home-is-it-the-workplace-of-migrant-domestic-workers-under-kafala> [accessed 1 March 2022]

Kafka, Franz, *Letters to Friends, Family, and Editors*, trans. by Richard Winston and Clara Winston (New York: Schocken, 1977)

Kahan, Benjamin, *The Book of Minor Perverts: Sexology, Etiology, and the Emergences of Sexuality* (Chicago: University of Chicago Press, 2019) <https://doi.org/10.7208/chicago/9780226608006.001.0001>

Karpeles, Eric, *Paintings in Proust: A Visual Companion to 'In Search of Lost Time'* (London: Thames and Hudson, 2008)

Kauffman, Stuart A., *The Origins of Order: Self-Organization and Selection in Evolution* (Oxford: Oxford University Press, 1993)

Kempe, Margery, *The Book of Margery Kempe* [1501], ed. and trans. by Anthony Bale (Oxford: Oxford University Press, 2015)

—— *The Book of Margery Kempe* [1501], ed. by Barry Windeatt (Cambridge: D. S. Brewer, 2004)

Khalfa, Jean, 'A Theory of Subversion that Could Not Also Serve the Cause of Oppression?', *Interventions*, 23 (2021), pp. 417–31 <https://doi.org/10.1080/1369801X.2020.1784030>

Khalili, Laleh, *Sinews of War and Trade: Shipping and Capitalism in the Arabian Peninsula* (London: Verso, 2021)

Kleinberg, Ethan, 'Presence *in Absentia*', in *Presence: Philosophy, History and Cultural Theory for the 21st Century*, ed. by Ranjan Gosh and Ethan Kleinberg (Ithaca, NY: Cornell University Press, 2013), pp. 8–25 <https://doi.org/10.7591/cornell/9780801452208.003.0002>

Klibansky, Raymond, Erwin Panofsky, and Fritz Saxl, *Saturn and Melancholy: Studies in the History of Natural Philosophy, Religion, and Art* (Montreal: McGill-Queen's University Press, 2019) <https://doi.org/10.2307/j.ctvscxt1r>

Kolenc, Bara, 'Skepticism's Cure for the Plague of Mind', *Women in Philosophy, Blog of the American Philosophical Association* (9 September 2020) <https://blog.apaonline.org/2020/09/09/skepticisms-cure-for-the-plague-of-mind/> [accessed 11 June 2022]

Kot'átková, Eva, *Asylum*, installation, mixed media, dimensions variable, presented at 55th Venice Biennale, June–November 2013

—— *Pictorial Atlas of a Girl Who Cut a Library into Pieces*, 2 vols (Zurich: JRP Ringier, 2015)

Kramer, Jonathan D., 'Postmodern Concepts of Musical Time', *Indiana Theory Review*, 17.2 (1996), pp. 21–62

Krauß, Andrea, 'Constellations: A Brief Introduction', *MLN*, 126.3 (2011), pp. 439–45 <https://doi.org/10.1353/mln.2011.0038>

Kristeva, Julia, *Proust and the Sense of Time*, trans. by Stephen Bann (New York: Columbia University Press, 1993)

Kruks, Sonia, *Retrieving Experience: Subjectivity and Recognition in Feminist Politics* (Ithaca, NY: Cornell University Press, 2001) <https://doi.org/10.7591/9781501731839>

Küper, Susanne, ed., *Ceal Floyer: A Handbook* (Ostfildern: Hatje Cantz, 2015)

Lacan, Jacques, *The Four Fundamental Concepts of Psychoanalysis*, ed. by Jacques-Alain Miller, trans. by Alan Sheridan (London: Routledge, 1998)

—— 'Le mythe individuel du névrosé', *Ornicar?*, 17–18 (1979), pp. 289–307

—— 'The Neurotic's Individual Myth', trans. by Jacques-Alain Miller, *Psychoanalytic Quarterly*, 48 (1974), pp. 405–25 <https://doi.org/10.1080/21674086.1979.11926884>

—— 'Ouverture à la section clinique', *Ornicar?*, 9 (1977), pp. 7–14

—— 'Psychoanalysis and Cybernetics, or on the Nature of Language', in *The Seminar of Jacques Lacan*, ed. by Jacques-Alain Miller (New York: Norton, 1988–), II: *The Ego in Freud's Theory and in the Technique of Psychoanalysis, 1954–1955*, trans. by Sylvana Tomaselli (1988), pp. 294–308

—— *Le séminaire de Jacques Lacan*, ed. by Jacques-Alain Miller (Paris: Seuil, 1973–), XXIII: *Le Sinthome (1975–1976)* (2005)

Lakoff, George, and Mark Johnson, *Metaphors We Live By* (Chicago: University of Chicago Press, 2003) <https://doi.org/10.7208/chicago/9780226470993.001.0001>

—— *Philosophy in the Flesh: The Embodied Mind and its Challenge to Western Thought* (New York: Basic Books, 1999)

Latour, Bruno, 'Note brève sur l'écologie du droit saisie comme énonciation', *Cosmopolitique*, 8 (2004), pp. 34–40

—— *Pandora's Hope: Essays on the Reality of Science Studies* (Cambridge, MA: Harvard University Press, 1999)

—— *We Have Never Been Modern*, trans. by Catherine Porter (Cambridge, MA: Harvard University Press, 1993)

Léger, Nathalie, *The White Dress* [2018], trans. by Natasha Lehrer (New York: Dorothy, 2020)

Leopardi, Giacomo, *Canti* (Milan: Mondadori, 2016)

—— *Canti*, trans. by Jonathan Galassi (London: Penguin, 2010)

—— *Zibaldone*, ed. by Michael Caesar and Franco D'Intino, trans. by Kathleen Baldwin and others (New York: Farrar, Straus and Giroux, 2013)

Lévi-Strauss, Claude, 'A Confrontation', *New Left Review*, 62 (1970), pp. 57–74

—— 'The Effectiveness of Symbols', in Lévi-Strauss, *Structural Anthropology*, pp. 186–205

—— *Introduction to the Work of Marcel Mauss*, trans. by Felicity Baker (London: Routledge, 1950)

—— 'Social Structure', in Lévi-Strauss, *Structural Anthropology*, pp. 277–323

—— *Structural Anthropology*, trans. by Claire Jacobson and Brooke Grundfest Schoepf (New York: Basic Books, 1963)

—— 'The Structural Study of Myth', in Lévi-Strauss, *Structural Anthropology*, pp. 206–31

Lilla, Mark, *The Once and Future Liberal: After Identity Politics* (New York: HarperCollins, 2017)

Lipton, Samuel, 'The Advantages of Freud's Technique as Shown in his Analysis of the Rat Man', *International Journal of Psychoanalysis*, 58 (1977), pp. 255–73

Lochhead, Judy, 'The Temporal in Beethoven's Opus 135: When Are Ends Beginning?', *Theory Only*, 4.7 (1979), pp. 3–30

Love, Heather, *Feeling Backward: Loss and the Politics of Queer History* (Cambridge, MA: Harvard University Press, 2007)

Lukács, György, *Theory of the Novel* [1914–15], trans. by Anna Bostock (Cambridge, MA: MIT Press, 1971)

Luxon, Nancy, 'Fanon's Psychiatric Hospital as a Waystation to Freedom', *Theory, Culture & Society*, 38 (2021), pp. 93–113 <https://doi.org/10.1177/0263276420981612>

Lynch, Kevin, *The Image of the City* (Cambridge, MA: MIT Press, 1960)

Mahony, Patrick, *Freud and the Rat Man* (New Haven, CT: Yale University Press, 1986)

Mailman, Joshua B., 'Cybernetic Phenomenology of Music, Embodied Speculative Realism, and Aesthetics-Driven Techné for Spontaneous Audio-Visual Expression', *Perspectives of New Music*, 54.1 (2016), pp. 5–95 <https://doi.org/10.1353/pnm.2016.0008>

Majaj, Lisa Suhair, 'Departure', in Majaj, *Geographies of Light* (Washington, DC: Del Sol Press, 2009), pp. 43–44

Mannoni, Octave, 'L'homme aux rats', *Les temps modernes*, 20.228 (1965), pp. 2028–47

Mardell, Ashley, *The ABC's of LGBT+* (Coral Gables, FL: Mango Media Inc, 2016)

Marriott, David S., 'Inventions of Existence: Sylvia Wynter, Frantz Fanon, Sociogeny, and "the Damned"', *CR: The New Centennial Review*, 11 (2012), pp. 45–89 <https://doi.org/10.1353/ncr.2012.0020>

—— *Lacan Noir: Lacan and Afro-pessimism* (New York: Palgrave Macmillan, 2021) <https://doi.org/10.1007/978-3-030-74978-1>

Marx, Karl, *Capital: A Critique of Political Economy*, trans. by Ben Fowkes, 3 vols (London: Penguin, 1976), I

Marx, Ursula, and Erdmut Wizisla, 'Zarteste Quartiere: Walter Benjamins Notizbücher. Mit einem Blick in das Jerusalemer "Pergamentheft"', *Yearbook for European Jewish Literature Studies*, 6.1 (2019), pp. 147–69 <https://doi.org/10.1515/yejls-2019-0008>

Maturana, Humberto R., and Francisco J. Varela, *Autopoiesis and Cognition: The Realization of the Living* (Dordrecht: Reidel, 1972)

Mauss, Marcel, *A General Theory of Magic*, trans. by Robert Brain (New York: Routledge, 2001)

—— *The Gift: The Form and Reason for Exchange in Archaic Societies*, trans. by W. D. Halls (London: Routledge, 1990)

—— *Techniques, Technology and Civilisation*, ed. by Nathan Schlanger, trans. by Nathan Schlanger and others (New York: Berghahn Books, 2006)

McAuliffe, Marie, and Binod Khadria, eds, *World Migration Report 2020*, ed. by (Geneva: International Organization for Migration, 2019) <https://publications.iom.int/books/world-migration-report-2020> [accessed 23 July 2022]

McKinney, Cait, *Information Activism: A Queer History of Lesbian Media Technologies* (Durham, NC: Duke University Press, 2020) <https://doi.org/10.1215/9781478009337>

Melman, Charles, 'The Rat Man', in *Obsessional Neurosis: Lacanian Perspectives*, ed. by Astrid Gessert (London: Routledge, 2018), pp. 83–92 <https://doi.org/10.4324/9781003076254-6>

Merleau-Ponty, Maurice, *Institution and Passivity: Course Notes from the Collège de France (1954–1955)*, trans. by Leonard Lawlor and Heath Massey (Evanston, IL: Northwestern University Press, 2010)

—— *The Visible and the Invisible*, trans. by Alphonso Lingis (Evanston, IL: Northwestern University Press, 1968)

Mezzadra, Sandro, and Brett Neilson, *The Politics of Operations: Excavating Contemporary Capitalism* (Durham, NC: Duke University Press, 2019) <https://doi.org/10.1215/9781478003267>

Mirzoeff, Nicholas, *The Right to Look: A Counterhistory of Visuality* (Durham, NC: Duke University Press, 2011) <https://doi.org/10.1215/9780822393726>

—— 'Visualizing the Anthropocene', *Public Culture*, 26.2 (2014), pp. 213–32 <https://doi.org/10.1215/08992363-2392039>

Mitchell, Timothy, *Carbon Democracy: Political Power in the Age of Oil* (London: Verso, 2013)

Morton, Donald, 'Changing the Terms: (Virtual) Desire and (Actual) Reality', in *The Material Queer: A LesBiGay Cultural Studies Reader*, ed. by Donald Morton (Boulder, CO: Westview, 1996), pp. 1–33

Nancy, Jean-Luc, *Listening*, trans. by Charlotte Mandell (New York: Fordham University Press, 2007)

—— *Noli me tangere: On the Raising of the Body*, trans. by Sarah Clift, Pascale-Anne Brault, and Michael Naas (New York: Fordham University Press, 2008)

Napoli, Paolo, 'Indisponibilità, servizio pubblico, uso. Concetti orientativi su comune e beni comuni', *Politica & Società*, 3 (2013), pp. 403–26 <https://doi.org/10.4476/74759>

Neill, Calum, *Lacanian Ethics and the Assumption of Subjectivity* (New York: Palgrave Macmillan, 2011) <https://doi.org/10.1057/9780230305038>

Neimanis, Astrida, *Bodies of Water: Posthuman Feminist Phenomenology* (London: Bloomsbury Academic, 2017) <https://doi.org/10.5040/9781474275415>

Nichols, Ben, 'Library Fever: Lesbian Memoir and the Sexual Politics of Order', *Textual Practice*, early online publication (2022) <https://doi.org/10.1080/0950236X.2022.2032303>

Nietzsche, Friedrich, *Also sprach Zarathustra*, ed. by Volker Gerhardt (Berlin: Akademie Verlag, 2012) <https://doi.org/10.1524/9783050057385>

Nievo, Ippolito, *Le confessioni d'un italiano* (Milan: Mondadori, 1981)

—— *Confessions of an Italian*, trans. by Frederika Randall (London: Penguin, 2014)

Noorizadeh, Bahar, 'Weird-Futuring', *Counter-N*, ed. by Özgün Eylül İş-cen and Shintaro Miyazaki, 12 April 2022 <https://doi.org/10.18452/24452>

O'Brien, Wendy, 'Telling Time: Literature, Temporality and Trauma', in *Temporality in Life as Seen through Literature*, ed. by Anna-Teresa Tymieniecka (=*Analecta Husserliana*, 86 (2007)), pp. 209–21 <https://doi.org/10.1007/1-4020-5331-2_15>

OED Online (Oxford: Oxford University Press, 2022) <https://www.oed.com/>

Oliveros, Pauline, Stuart Dempster, Panaiotis, *Deep Listening* (Important, 473, 2020: reissue).

Online Etymology Dictionary (2022) <https://www.etymonline.com/>

Ostertag, Bob, 'Human Bodies, Computer Music', *Leonardo Music Journal*, 12 (2002), pp. 11–14 <https://doi.org/10.1162/096112102762295070>

Owens, Lama Rod, *Love and Rage: The Path of Liberation Through Anger* (Berkeley, CA: North Atlantic Books, 2020)

Parikka, Jussi, 'Counter-Futuring', *Counter-N*, ed. by Özgün Eylül İşcen and Shintaro Miyazaki, 12 April 2022 <https://doi.org/10.18452/24451>

—— 'Middle East and Other Futurisms: Imaginary Temporalities in Contemporary Art and Visual Culture', *Culture, Theory and Critique*, 59.1 (2018), pp. 40–58 <https://doi.org/10.1080/14735784.2017.1410439>

Pascal, Fania, 'Wittgenstein: A Personal Memoir', in *Wittgenstein: Personal Recollections*, ed. by Norman Malcolm and Rush Rhees (Oxford: Oxford University Press, 1984), pp. 12–50

Passeron, Jean-Claude, and Jacques Revel, *Penser par cas* (Paris: Enquête, 2005) <https://doi.org/10.4000/books.editionsehess.19921>

Pecora, Vincent P., 'Be Here Now: Mimesis and the History of Representation', in *Presence: Philosophy, History and Cultural Theory for the 21st Century*, ed. by Ranjan Ghosh and Ethan Kleinberg (Ithaca, NY: Cornell University Press, 2013), pp. 26–44

Perec, Georges, 'Notes on the Objects to Be Found on My Desk, An Attempt at Exhausting a Place in Paris', in Perec, *Thoughts of Sorts*, trans. by David Bellos (Boston, MA: David R. Godine Publisher, 2009), pp. 11–16

Piattelli-Palmarini, Massimo, 'Introduction', in *Language and Learning: The Debate between Jean Piaget and Noam Chomsky*, ed. by Piattelli-Palmarini (Cambridge, MA: Harvard University Press, 1980), pp. 1–20

Pinker, Steven, *The Blank Slate: Modern Denial of Human Nature* (New York: Penguin, 2003)

Plato, *Phaedrus*, trans. by Alexander Nehamas and Paul Woodruff (Indianapolis, IN: Hackett, 1995)

—— *Symposium*, trans. by Alexander Nehamas and Paul Woodruff (Indianapolis, IN: Hackett, 1989)

Potts, Morgan, *The A-Z of Gender and Sexuality: From Ace to Ze* (London: Jessica Kingsley Publishers, 2018)

Pratt, Mary, 'Ideology and Speech Act Theory', *Poetics Today*, 7.1 (1986), pp. 59–72 <https://doi.org/10.2307/1772088>

Prigogine, Ilya, and Isabelle Stengers, *Order Out of Chaos: Man's New Dialogue with Nature* (London: Heinemann, 1984)

'Proust', *In Our Time*, BBC Radio 4, first transmitted 17 April 2003 <https://www.bbc.co.uk/programmes/p00548wx> [accessed 6 July 2022]

Puar, Jasbir K., *The Right to Maim: Debility, Capacity, Disability* (Durham, NC: Duke University Press, 2017) <https://doi.org/10.1215/9780822372530>

—— *Terrorist Assemblages: Homonationalism in Queer Times* (Durham, NC: Duke University Press, 2007) <https://doi.org/10.1215/9780822390442>

Puar, Jasbir, *Terrorist Assemblages: Homonationalism in Queer Times* (Durham, NC: Duke University Press, 2007) <https://doi.org/10.1215/9780822390442>

Purnell, Bronez, *100 Boyfriends* (New York: MCD x FSG Originals, 2021)

Rank, Otto, 'Bericht über die I. private Psychoanalytische Vereinigung in Salzburg am 27. April 1908', *Zentralblatt für Psychoanalyse*, 1.3 (1910), pp. 125–26

Ratzinger, Joseph, 'The Listening Heart: Reflections on the Foundations of Law', 22 September 2011: <https://www.vatican.va/content/benedict-xvi/en/speeches/2011/september/documents/hf_ben-xvi_spe_20110922_reichstag-berlin.html> [accessed 22 June 2022]

Roads, Curtis, *Composing Electronic Music: A New Aesthetic* (Oxford: Oxford University Press, 2015) <https://doi.org/10.1093/acprof:oso/9780195373233.001.0001>

Robcis, Camille, *Disalienation: Politics, Philosophy, and Radical Psychiatry in Postwar France* (New York: Columbia University Press, 2021) <https://doi.org/10.7208/chicago/9780226777887.001.0001>

Rodríguez Muñoz, Bárbara, 'Eva Kot'átková: Mental Armours', *Afterall*, 25 February 2014 <https://www.afterall.org/article/eva-kot_tkov_mental-armours> [accessed 3 June 2022]

Rowell, Lewis, *Music and Musical Thought in Early India* (Chicago and London: University of Chicago Press, 1992) <https://doi.org/10.7208/chicago/9780226730349.001.0001>

Safouan, Moustapha, 'The Signification of Debt in Obsessional Neurosis', pp. 77–82

Said, Edward, *On Late Style: Music and Literature Against the Grain* (London: Bloomsbury, 2017)

—— *Reflections on Exile and Other Essays* (Cambridge, MA: Harvard University Press, 2000)

Salt of this Sea, dir. and written by Annemarie Jacir, performances by Suheir Hammad, Saleh Bakri, Marwan Riyad Ideis, and Sylvia Wetz (Trigon-film, 2008)

Salzani, Carlo, 'Kafka's Creaturely Life', in *Kafka: Organisation, Recht, und Schrift*, ed. by Marianne Schuller and Günther Ortmann (Weilerswist Metternich: Velbrück Wissenschaft, 2019), pp. 396–407 <https://doi.org/10.5771/9783748906506-394>

Sapienza, Goliarda, *The Art of Joy*, trans. by Anne Milano Appel (London: Penguin, 2013)

—— *L'arte della gioia* (Turin: Einaudi, 2008)

—— *Destino coatto* (Rome: Empiria, 2002)

Schiavone, Aldo, *Ius: The Invention of Law in the West* (Cambridge, MA: Harvard University Press, 2012)

Schneiderman, Stuart, *Rat Man: Freud's 1909 Case* (New York: New York University Press, 1986)

Schwartz, Frederic, *Blind Spots* (New Haven, CT: Yale University Press, 2005)

Searle, John, 'The Storm over the University', *The New York Review of Books*, 6 December 1990 <https://www.nybooks.com/articles/1990/12/06/the-storm-over-the-university/> [accessed 21 July 2022]

Sedgwick, Eve Kosofsky, *Touching Feeling: Affect, Pedagogy, Performativity* (Durham, NC: Duke University Press, 2003) <https://doi.org/10.1215/9780822384786>

—— *The Weather in Proust* (Durham, NC: Duke University Press, 2011) <https://doi.org/10.1215/9780822394921>

Sekula, Allan, 'The Body and the Archive', *October*, 39 (1986), pp. 3–64 <https://doi.org/10.2307/778312>

Sextus Empiricus, *Outlines of Scepticism*, trans. by Julia Annas and Jonathan Barnes (Cambridge: Cambridge University Press, 1994)

Simondon, Gilbert, *L'Individu et sa génèse physico-biologique* (Paris: Millon, 1964)

Soja, Edward W., *Thirdspace: Journeys to Los Angeles and Other Real-and-Imagined Spaces* (Cambridge, MA and Oxford: Blackwell Publishers, 1996)

Sontag, Susan, 'Notes of a Childhood', in *Reborn: Susan Sontag, Early Diaries 1947–1963*, published posthumously and ed. by her son David Rieff (New York: Farrar, Straus and Giroux, 2008), pp. 106–29

Spanò, Michele, '"Perché non rendi poi quel che che prometti allor?". Tecniche e ideologie della giuridificazione della natura', in Thomas and Chiffoleau, *L'istituzione della natura*, pp. 103–24.

Spier, Julius, *The Hands Of Children: An Introduction to Psycho-Chirology* [1955] (London: Routledge, 1999)

Stengers, Isabelle, *In Catastrophic Times: Resisting the Coming Barbarism*, trans. by Andrew Goffey (London: Open Humanity Press, 2015) <https://doi.org/10.14619/016>

Stone, Christopher, 'Should Trees Have Standing? Toward Legal Rights for Natural Objects', *Southern California Law Review*, 45 (1972), pp. 450–501

Strogatz, Steven, Interview, 'Eve Marder on the Crucial Resilience of Neurons', *Quanta Magazine*, 17 May 2021 <https://www.quantamagazine.org/eve-marder-on-the-crucial-resilience-of-neurons-20210517/> [accessed 13 April 2022]

Sutter, Laurent de, and Kyle McGee, 'Introduction', in *Deleuze and Law*, ed. by de Sutter and McGee (Edinburgh: Edinburgh University Press, 2012), pp. 1–14 <https://doi.org/10.1515/9780748664542-001>

Szeman, Imre, 'Who's Afraid of National Allegory? Jameson, Literary Criticism, Globalization', *South Atlantic Quarterly*, 100.3 (2001), pp. 803–27 <https://doi.org/10.1215/00382876-100-3-803>

Tankard, Paul, 'Reading Lists', *Prose Studies*, 28.3 (December 2006), pp. 337–60 <https://doi.org/10.1080/01440350600975531>

Thomas, Yan, 'L'extrême et l'ordinaire. Remarques sur le cas médiéval de la communauté disparue', in *Penser par cas*, ed. by Jean-Claude Passeron and Jacques Revel (Paris: Éditions de l'École des hautes études en sciences sociales, 2005), pp. 45–73 <https://doi.org/10.4000/books.editionsehess.19926> (repr. in Thomas, *Les opérations du droit*, pp. 207–37)

—— 'Fictio legis. L'empire de la fiction romaine et ses limites médiévales', in *Les opérations du droit*, pp. 133–86

—— 'Idées romaines sur l'origine et la transmission du droit', in Thomas, *Les opérations du droit*, pp. 69–84

—— '*Imago naturae*. Note sur l'institutionnalité de la nature à Rome', in *Théologie et droit dans la science politique de l'État moderne. Actes de la table ronde de Rome (12–14 novembre 1987)*, Publications de l'École française de Rome, 147 (Rome: École Française de Rome, 1991), pp. 201–27 <https://www.persee.fr/doc/efr_0000-0000_1991_act_147_1_4171> [accessed 17 July 2022] (repr. in Thomas, *Les opérations du droit*, pp. 21–40)

—— '*Imago naturae*. Nota sull'istituzionalità della natura a Roma', trans. by Giuseppe Lucchesini, in Thomas and Chiffoleau, *L'istituzione della natura*, pp. 13–45

—— *Les opérations du droit* (Paris: EHESS-Seuil-Gallimard, 2011)

—— 'Prefacio', in Thomas, *Los artificios de las instituciones. Estudios de derecho romano* (Buenos Aires: Eudeba, 1999), pp. 9–12

—— 'Prefazione a *L'artificio delle istituzioni*', trans. and presented by Michele Spanò, in *Almanacco di Filosofia e Politica 2. Istituzione. Filosofia, politi-*

ca, storia, ed. by Mattia Di Pierro, Francesco Marchesi, and Elia Zaru (Macerata: Quodlibet, 2020), pp. 249–53 <https://doi.org/10.2307/j.ctvxkn83w.19>

—— 'Présentation', *Enquête*, 7 (1999), pp. 13–15 <https://doi.org/10.4000/enquete.1543>

—— 'The Subject of Right, the Person, Nature', in *Legal Artifices: Ten Essays on Roman Law in the Present Tense*, ed. by Thanos Zartaloudis and Cooper Francis, trans. by Anton Schütz and Chantal Schütz, intro. by Thanos Zartaloudis and Anton Schütz, afterword by Alain Pottage (Edinburgh: Edinburgh University Press, 2021), pp. 107–43

—— 'La valeur des choses. Le droit romain hors la religion', *Annales. Histoire, Sciences Sociales*, 6 (2002), pp. 1431–62 <https://doi.org/10.3406/ahess.2002.280119>

Thomas, Yan, and Jacques Chiffoleau, *L'istituzione della natura*, ed. by Michele Spanò (Macerata: Quodlibet, 2020)

Tiedemann, Rolf, and Hermann Schweppenhäuser, 'Anmerkungen der Herausgeber', in Walter Benjamin, *Gesammelte Schriften*, ed. by Rolf Tiedemann and Hermann Schweppenhäuser, 7 vols (Frankfurt a.M.: Suhrkamp, 1972–91), VI (1991), pp. 623–828

Toscano, Alberto, 'Elsewhere and Otherwise: Introduction to a Symposium on Fredric Jameson's "Allegory and Ideology"', *Historical Materialism*, 29.1 (2021), pp. 113–22 <https://doi.org/10.1163/1569206X-29010101>

—— 'Lineaments of the Logistical State', *Viewpoint Magazine*, 4, 28 September 2014 <https://viewpointmag.com/2014/09/28/lineaments-of-the-logistical-state/> [accessed 28 May 2022]

Tsing, Anna, *Friction: An Ethnography of Global Connection* (Princeton, NJ: Princeton University Press, 2004) <https://doi.org/10.1515/9781400830596>

—— *The Mushroom at the End of the World: On the Possibility of Life in Capitalist Ruins* (Princeton, NJ: Princeton University Press, 2015) <https://doi.org/10.1515/9781400873548>

—— 'Supply Chains and the Human Condition', *Rethinking Marxism*, 21.2 (2009), pp. 148–76 <https://doi.org/10.1080/08935690902743088>

Ty, M., 'Benjamin on the Border', *Critical Times*, 2.2 (2019), pp. 306–19 <https://doi.org/10.1215/26410478-7708371>

—— 'To Break with Fate', talk presented at the conference *Walter Benjamins 'Zur Kritik der Gewalt'*, Humboldt-Universität zu Berlin, 12 February 2021, online video recording <https://symposiumtheoriederpolitik.wordpress.com/programm/> [accessed 26 June 2022]

Vaggione, Horacio, 'Analysis and the Singularity of Music: The Locus of an Intersection', in *Analyse en Musique Électroacoustique, Acts de l'Académie Internationalde Musique Électroacoustique* (Bourges: Éditions Mnémosyne, 1996), pp. 268–74

Valentine, David, *Imagining Transgender: An Ethnography of Category* (Durham, NC: Duke University Press, 2007) <https://doi.org/10.1215/9780822390213>

Varela, Francisco, 'Present-Time Consciousness', *Journal of Consciousness Studies*, 6.2–3 (1999), pp. 111–40

Vismann, Cornelia, 'The Archive and the Beginning of Law', in *Derrida and Legal Philosophy*, ed. by Peter Goodrich, Florian Hoffmann, Michel Rosenfeld, and Cornelia Vismann (London: Palgrave Macmillan, 2008), pp. 41–54

Vogel, Steven, 'Environmental Philosophy after the End of Nature', *Environmental Ethics*, 24.1 (2002), pp. 23–39 <https://doi.org/10.5840/enviroethics200224139>

Walters, Suzanna Danuta, 'In Defense of Identity Politics', *Signs*, 43.2 (2018), pp. 473–88 <https://doi.org/10.1086/693557>

Warner, Michael, 'Introduction', in *Fear of a Queer Planet: Queer Politics and Social Theory*, ed. by Michael Warner (Minneapolis: University of Minnesota Press, 1993), pp. vii–xxxi

Watney, Simon, 'Emergent Sexual Identities and HIV/AIDS', in Simon Watney, *Imagine Hope: AIDS and Gay Identity* (London: Routledge, 2000), pp. 63–80

Weber, Max, *On Law in Economy and Society*, trans. by Edward Shild and Max Rheinstein (New York: Simon & Schuster, 1954)

Wells, Susan, 'Freud's Rat Man and the Case Study: Genre in Three Keys', *New Literary History*, 34.2 (2003), pp. 353–66 <https://doi.org/10.1353/nlh.2003.0024>

Wertz, Frederick, 'Freud's Case of the Rat Man Revisited: An Existential-Phenomenological and Socio-Historical Analysis', *Journal of Phenomenological Psychology*, 34.1 (2003), pp. 47–78 <https://doi.org/10.1163/156916203322484824>

Wildcat, Daniel R., 'Indigenizing the Future: Why We Must Think Spatially in the Twenty-first Century', *American Studies*, 46.3 (2005), pp. 417–40 (p. 434) <https://journals.ku.edu/amsj/article/view/2969> [accessed 1 June 2022]

William Smith, 'inge'nui, inge'nuitas', in Smith, *A Dictionary of Greek and Roman Antiquities* (London: John Murray, 1875), p. 637 <https://penelope.uchicago.edu/Thayer/E/Roman/Texts/secondary/SMIGRA*/Ingenui.html> [accessed 19 July 2022]

Williger, Jonathan, review of Oliveros, Dempster, Panaiotis, *Deep Listening*, *Pitchfork*, 10 February 2020 <https://pitchfork.com/reviews/albums/pauline-oliveros-stuart-dempster-pan-deep-listening/> [accessed 9 November 2021])

Wilson, Scott, 'Caterina Barbieri on Synthesis, Minimalism and Creating Living Organisms out of Sound', *Fact*, July 2018 <https://www.factmag.com/2018/07/08/caterina-barbieri-signal-path/> [accessed 2 November 2021]

Winnicott, Donald W., *The Maturational Processes and the Facilitating Environment* (London: Hogarth Press and the Institute of Psychoanalysis, 1965)

Wittgenstein, Ludwig, *The Blue and Brown Books* (Oxford: Blackwell, 1998)

Wolff, Charlotte, *Bisexuality: A Study* (London: Quartet Books, 1977)

—— *The Hand in Psychological Diagnosis* (London: Methuen, 1951)

—— *Hindsight: An Autobiography* (London: Quartet Books, 1980)

—— *The Human Hand* (London: Methuen, 1942)

—— *Love Between Women* (London: Duckworth, 1971)

—— *Magnus Hirschfeld: A Portrait of a Pioneer in Sexology* (London: Quartet Books, 1986)

—— *On the Way to Myself: Communications to a Friend* (London: Methuen, 1969)

—— *A Psychology of Gesture* (London: Methuen, 1945)

—— *Studies in Hand-reading* (London: Chatto & Windus, 1936)

Wynter, Sylvia, 'Towards the Sociogenic Principle: Fanon, Identity, the Puzzle of Conscious Experience, and What it is Like to Be "Black"', in *National Identities and Sociopolitical Changes in Latin America*, ed. by Mercedes F. Durán-Cogan and Antonio Gómez- Moriana (London, Routledge, 2001), pp. 30–66

Yalom, Irvin D., *The Gift of Therapy: An Open Letter to a New Generation of Therapists and Their Patients* (London: HarperCollins, 2002). Ebook

Zarour Zarzar, Victor H., 'The Grammar of Abandonment in *I giorni dell'abbandono*', *MLN*, 135.1 (2020), pp. 327–44 <https://doi.org/10.1353/mln.2020.0004>

Zegher, Catherine de, 'Theater of Speaking Objects: Conversation with Eva Kot'átková', in *Women's Work is Never Done: An Anthology*, ed. by de Zegher (Gent: AsaMer, 2014), pp. 520–33

Ziadah, Rafeef, 'Circulating Power: Humanitarian Logistics, Militarism, and the United Arab Emirates', *Antipode*, 51.5 (2019), pp. 1684–1702 <https://doi.org/10.1111/anti.12547>

—— 'Transport Infrastructure & Logistics in the Making of Dubai Inc.', *International Journal of Urban and Regional Research*, 42.2 (2018), pp. 182–97 (p. 183) <https://doi.org/10.1111/1468-2427.12570>

Ziporyn, Brook, *Ironies of Oneness and Difference: Coherence in Early Chinese Thought; Prolegomena to the Study of Li* (Albany: State University of New York Press, 2012)

Žižek, Slavoj, *The Sublime Object of Ideology* (London: Verso, 1989)

Notes on the Contributors

Rachel Aumiller is a lecturer in English and Comparative Literature at Columbia University. She received her PhD in philosophy from Villanova University and trained in the Ljubljana School of Psychoanalysis as a Fulbright Scholar in Slovenia. She is the editor of *A Touch of Doubt: On Haptic Scepticism* (2021) and the author of *The Laughing Matter of Spirit* (forthcoming). Her philosophy explores the epistemological, ethical, and political dimensions of affect, sensation, and desire.

Alberica Bazzoni completed her PhD at the University of Oxford, and then was British Academy Postdoctoral Fellow at the University of Warwick. She is the author of *Writing for Freedom: Body, Identity and Power in Goliarda Sapienza's Narrative* (2018), recently published in Italian translation in a revised edition as *Scrivere la libertà. Corpo, identità e potere in Goliarda Sapienza* (2022), and co-editor of *Gender and Authority across Disciplines, Space and Time* (2020) and *Goliarda Sapienza in Context* (2016). Her research interests lie in the fields of modern Italian literature, literary theory, sociology of culture, and feminist, queer, and decolonial studies.

Federica Buongiorno is assistant professor in Theoretical Philosophy and Phenomenology of Technology at the University of Florence. She has been a postdoctoral researcher at Freie Universität Berlin, TU Dresden, and ICI Berlin. Her research combines interest in classical phenomenology with artificial and algorithmic intelligence and digital theory. She is a translator from German into Italian and the Editor-in-chief of the philosophical book series 'Umweg' and the international journal *Azimuth*.

Christopher Chamberlin holds a PhD in Culture and Theory from the University of California, Irvine and is currently in formation as a Research Analyst at the Lacanian School of Psychoanalysis in San Francisco. His work articulates the fields of psychoanalysis and black studies through several projects that examine the history and theory of the 'antiracist clinic'. He serves on the editorial boards of *Psychoanalysis, Culture & Society* and the *European Journal of Psychoanalysis*.

Xenia Chiaramonte is a jurist and a socio-legal scholar. Her research centres on a critique of contemporary ecological discourse especially in relation to environmental struggles and the advancement of a new age of rights, those of 'places'. She published her monograph *Governare il conflitto: La criminalizzazione del movimento No TAV* [Governing conflict: The Criminalization of the No TAV Movement] (2019), which analyses the criminalization of one of the most longstanding and high-profile environmental movements in Western Europe.

Sam Dolbear holds a PhD in critical theory from Birkbeck College, University of London. He largely works on the figures marginalized in Walter Benjamin's work, and has just completed two expansive projects: one on the radio producer and composer Ernst Schoen (1894–1960) and another on the hand reader and sexologist Charlotte Wolff (1897–1986). He teaches at Bard College Berlin and continues as a Visiting Fellow at the ICI Berlin with support from the Leverhulme Trust.

Iracema Dulley holds a BA in philosophy and a PhD in social anthropology from the University of São Paulo. She is also a practicing psychoanalyst. Her research considers processes of subject constitution from an interdisciplinary perspective. She has conducted fieldwork in and archival research on colonial and post-colonial Angola and her publications focus on ethnographic theorization, research methodology, translation, witchcraft, naming practices, and processes of differentiation related to race, ethnicity, gender, and sexuality.

Amina ElHalawani is a Lecturer of English Literature at the Faculty of Arts, Alexandria University. After finishing an MA degree in English Literature, ElHalawani pursued her PhD in Comparative Literature at l'Université de Perpignan and Eberhard Karls Universität Tübingen with the Erasmus Mundus Joint Doctoral Fellowship. Her research interests include: performance studies, twentieth-century literature, contemporary migrant literature, home writing, post-coloniality, and the Global South.

Christoph F. E. Holzhey is the founding director of the ICI Berlin Institute for Cultural Inquiry, which he has led since 2007. He received a PhD in theoretical physics (1993) and another one in German literature (2001). He has run several projects at the ICI Berlin and (co-)edited several volumes, including *Tension/Spannung* (2010), *Multistable Figures* (2014), *De/Constituting Wholes* (2017), *Re-* (2019), *Weathering* (2020), and ERRANS (2022).

Özgün Eylül İşcen received her PhD in Computational Media, Arts, and Cultures from Duke University. She works on computational media as an imperial apparatus within the matrix of racial capitalism and unpacks its geopolitical aesthetic in the context of the Middle East. Her recent research dwells on the idea of counter-futuring at the intersections of materialist media theory, digital arts, and decolonial politics.

Sarath Jakka received his PhD from the TEEME (Text and Event in Early Modern Europe) doctoral program at the University of Kent, Canterbury in conjunction with the University of Porto, Portugal. His doctoral research centered on early modern utopian traditions and seventeenth-century colonial imaginaries. His current research engages a wide range of fields that includes psychoanalysis, discourses on climate change, non-dualist intellectual traditions, and ecological approaches to thinking.

Ben Nichols is Lecturer in Gender and Sexuality Studies at the University of Manchester in the UK and has research interests that span feminist, queer, and trans theory and culture. His monograph *Same Old: Queer Theory, Literature and the Politics of Sameness*, which addresses and interrogates how the field of queer studies has been formed around an aversion to sameness, was published in 2020. He has also published work in journals such as *GLQ*, *Textual Practice*, and the *Henry James Review*.

Claudia Peppel is in charge of Academic Coordination and Communication at the ICI Berlin. She studied Italian and French literature at the Freie Universität Berlin and at La Sapienza in Rome and holds a PhD in Philosophy from TU Darmstadt. Her publications focus on literary and cultural studies, as well as aesthetics, art history, and food studies. She has taught at the Berlin University of the Arts and has curated exhibitions of contemporary art. In 2019, she co-edited the volume *Die Kunst des Wartens* (with Brigitte Kölle) on the topic of waiting in the arts.

Jakob Schillinger is Research Coordinator of the ICI Core Project *Reduction*. A historian of modern and contemporary art, his research focuses on the media-technological and social conditions of art and visual culture and on their connection to gender. He is currently working on a book manuscript titled *Painting Machines*, which takes a media- and systems-theoretical perspective on post-conceptual painting in 1980s and early 1990s Cologne, inquiring how artistic processes affected and connected the artists' bodies that functioned as their media, and how these processes constructed social milieus.

Index

Abraham, Ruth 20 n. 25, 31
Ahmed, Sara 215
Al Qadiri, Fatima 93
Al Qadiri, Monira 10, 91,
    93–96, 107, 108, 111, 112,
    114
Al-Maria, Sophia 93
Alain de Lille 244
Anders, Günther 88
Apuleius Madaurensis 47–49
Archer, Megan 99 n. 21, 100
Augustine of Hippo 48, 49 n. 9
Azoulay, Jacques 62, 75 n. 32
Bachelard, Gaston 160, 161
Bale, Anthony 119, 120
Barad, Karen 227 n. 1, 250
Barbieri, Caterina 11, 178, 179,
    181, 184–188, 190
Basinski, William 186, 187
Beau, Joseph Honoré Simon
    129
Beauvoir, Simone de 55, 56
Beck, Aaron T. 169
Beckett, Samuel 267, 268
Belknap, Robert 255 n. 11, 259
Benjamin, Walter 10, 119 n. 5,
    n. 9, 122–129, 133 n. 65,
    196 n. 16, 269
Bergson, Henri 3 n. 2, 183, 184,
    186, 193, 195, 203
Berlant, Lauren 15, 253
Biceaga, Victor 180, 181 n. 18
Blacker, K. H. 20 n. 25, 31
Boccagni, Paolo 214, 216 n. 11
Borrell, Anne 268
Boyer, Anne 261
Braidotti, Rosi 193, 196, 211
Brecht, George 275

Brothers Grimm 159 n. 7
Butler, Judith 138–140, 150,
    151
Carson, Anne 267
Caruth, Cathy 198, 208
Casey, Edward 216, 223
Cavarero, Adriana 203
Certeau, Michel de 219
Cheiro 127
Cherki, Alice 80
Chiffoleau, Jacques 242 n. 31,
    244, 245
Chua, Charmaine 104
Chun, Wendy H. K. 97 n. 14,
    101, 102
Comay, Rebecca 260 n. 27, 267
Contzen, Eva von 254 n. 6, 255,
    257 n. 17
Coquet, Jean-Claude 199, 200
Cox, Laverne 263, 264
Damasio, Antonio 193
Darwish, Mahmoud 216, 217,
    220
Davachi, Sarah 183, 184
Davidson, Guy 143 n. 26, 150
Davis, Chloe O. 135, 137, 144
Deleuze, Gilles 85 n. 55, 88,
    139, 193, 215, 239, 240
Derrida, Jacques 23 n. 30, 60 n.
    23, 196
Descartes, René 4, 41, 45–47,
    188 n. 38
Didion, Joan 257, 258
Dinshaw, Carolyn 119, 120
Dolby, Thomas 178, 179
Dreyfus, Hubert 168
Duncan, John 162
Durkheim, Émile 77

D'Emilio, John 264
Easterling, Kelly 94
Eco, Umberto 254
Edelman, Lee 139, 140
Éluard, Paul 129
Eng, David L. 140–142, 146–148, 264 n. 4
Ey, Henri 88
Fadda-Conrey, Carol 219
Fanon, Frantz 9, 61–65, 70, 74–89, 143 n. 24
Fell, Mark 177, 178, 181
Ferrante, Elena 206–209
Fliess, Wilhelm 156–158
Floyer, Ceal 275
Forrester, John 6, 7, 34, 35
Foucault, Michel 8 n. 11, 139, 146, 168, 210, 234, 239, 240
Frankl, Viktor 169
Franklin, Seb 107
Fraser, Nancy 147
Freud, Sigmund 8, 13–37, 64, 67, 69, 70, 73, 130 n. 53, 156–159, 166–169
Galison, Peter 98, 99
Galloway, Alexander R. 98 n. 17, 102, 107
Geoghegan, Bernard Dionysius 94
Ginzburg, Carlo 240
Glück, Robert 118, 119, 121, 132
Goethe, Johann Wolfgang von 125, 130
Gordon, Avery 131
Gragnolati, Manuele 133, 197 n. 17, 222 n. 18
Green, Victor Hugo 275
Grund, Helen 123, 128
Guattari, Félix 193, 215
Hadot, Pierre 4
Halberstam, Jack 148, 149

Halpern, Orit 94, 99, 100
Hammad, Suheir 214 n. 3, 217, 218
Hanieh, Adam 110, 111
Hansen, Mark B. N. 175, 176, 190
Haraway, Donna J. 111, 112, 193
Hardell, Ash 145, 146
Harney, Stefano 105
Haslett, Tobi 132
Hayles, Katherine 100
Hegel, Georg Wilhelm Friedrich 40, 42 n. 2, 53 n. 15
Heidegger, Martin 215
Henke, Robert 188 n. 38, 189 n. 40
Hilgers, Philipp von 98 n. 19, 100, 101
hooks, bell 263–265
Hu, Tung-Hui 98
Hughes, John 12, 214, 222–226
Husserl, Edmund 4, 40, 50, 53 n. 15, 60 n. 23, 178–180, 183, 192, 193
Jacir, Annemarie 12, 214, 217, 218
Jackson, David C. 186, 187
Jackson, Zakiyyah Iman 143
Jameson, Fredric 10, 65, 95, 101–103, 106, 112 n. 64, 113, 114
Johnson, Mark 2 n. 1, 193
Joyce, James 196
Jung, C. G. 21 n. 26, 36, 130 n. 53
Kafka, Franz 119 n. 9, 260
Kahan, Benjamin 149
Kant, Immanuel 168, 180
Karpeles, Eric 268
Khalfa, Jean 62 n. 2, 78, 88
Khalili, Bouchra 131, 132
Kiwanga, Kapwani 275, 276
Kot'átková, Eva 271–276

Kramer, Jonathan D. 181, 182, 184

Kristeva, Julia 268

Lacan, Jacques 13, 14, 17, 18, 21–24, 27, 32, 35–37, 64, 67, 70, 71, 80, 84, 102, 140, 164, 165

Lakoff, George 2 n. 1, 193

Lanzer, Ernst 13, 16 n. 12

Latour, Bruno 97, 233 n. 10, 247

Léger, Nathalie 121

Leopardi, Giacomo 197, 200–203

Lévi-Strauss, Claude 9, 62–67, 69–74, 76–79, 84

Lilla, Mark 136 n. 2, 148

Lochhead, Judy 182

Lorde, Audre 212

Love, Heather 150, 153

Lukács, György 102, 133

Luxon, Nancy 87

Magdelain, André 229

Mahony, Patrick 16 n. 12, 18 n. 20, 25 n. 36, 28, 29, 31–33, 36 n. 84

Mannoni, Octave 36

Marder, Eve 171, 172

Margery Kempe 118, 119 n. 6, n. 7, 120 n. 10

Marx, Karl 97, 98

Maturana, Humberto R. 178, 179, 181

Mauss, Marcel 61, 62, 64–67, 77, 78, 85

McGee, Kyle 240

McKinney, Cait 144, 145

Menon, Dilip 121

Merleau-Ponty, Maurice 60 n. 23, 180, 181, 193

Messiaen, Olivier 186

Mezzadra, Sandro 103

Mill, John Stuart 34, 35

Mirzoeff, Nicholas 104, 105, 109

Mitchell, Robert 94

Morante, Elsa 197

Moten, Fred 105, 143 n. 24

Nancy, Jean-Luc 60 n. 23, 165, 166, 169, 193

Neilson, Brett 103

Nietzsche, Friedrich 127, 129, 282

Nievo, Ippolito 204–206

Oliveros, Pauline 176 n. 5, 184 n. 28, 189

Ortese, Anna Maria 197

Ostertag, Bob 175, 177, 190

Owens, Rod 212

O'Brien, Wendy 198, 199, 210

Parikka, Jussi 93

Pascal, Fania 160

Passeron, Jean-Claude 15, 239 n. 25

Perec, Georges 260

Phuture 177, 181

Piattelli-Palmarini, Massimo 161

Pinker, Steven 171, 172

Pirandello, Luigi 196, 197

Plotinus 4

Polignac, Armande de 130

Proust, Marcel 196, 267–269

Puar, Jasbir K. 139–142, 146–148, 264 n. 4

Purnell, Bronez 117, 118

Pyrrho of Elis 47–50, 53 n. 15

Ramondino, Fabrizia 197

Revel, Jacques 15, 239 n. 25

Rieff, David 258

Rivière, Pierre 240

Roads, Curtis 185, 186

Rodríguez Muñoz, Bárbara 273

Rose, Jacqueline 269

Rowell, Lewis 167, 168

Said, Edward 215, 220, 268
Sapienza, Goliarda 197,
    204–206, 208, 209
Sartre, Jean-Paul 103
Schneiderman, Stuart 16 n. 12,
    20 n. 25, 25, 29
Schoen, Ernst 123, 126
Searle, John 256
Sedgwick, Eve Kosofsky 141,
    142, 268, 269
Sekyi-Otu, Ato 65
Sextus Empiricus 51–53, 56 n.
    19
Simon, Claire 121
Socrates 47, 48, 49 n. 9, 51 n. 12
Sontag, Susan 258
Spier, Julius 130
Spinoza, Baruch 193
Stengers, Isabelle 3 n. 2, 246
Sutter, Laurent de 240
Tankard, Paul 253–256
Thomas, Yan 12, 228–249
Toscano, Alberto 104 n. 42, 112
Tosquelles, François 61, 85, 86
Tsing, Anna 96, 104 n. 41, 106,
    246 n. 38
Ungaretti, Giuseppe 197
Vaggione, Horacio 185
Valentine, David 149
Varela, Francisco J. 178, 179,
    181, 192–194, 198
Vionnet, Madeleine 130
Vismann, Cornelia 230
Walters, Suzanna Danuta 136 n.
    2, 152
Weber, Max 231
Wiener, Norbert 99
Winnicott, Donald W. 193, 194
Wittgenstein, Ludwig 160, 162
Wolff, Charlotte 122–131
Woolf, Virginia 196
Yalom, Irvin D. 170

Young, La Monte 183, 184
Young, Robert J. C. 62 n. 2, 78
Ziadah, Rafeef 110, 111 n. 62
Ziporyn, Brook 163, 164

Cultural Inquiry

EDITED BY CHRISTOPH F. E. HOLZHEY
AND MANUELE GRAGNOLATI

VOL. 1   TENSION/SPANNUNG
         Edited by Christoph F. E. Holzhey

VOL. 2   METAMORPHOSING DANTE
         Appropriations, Manipulations, and Rewritings
         in the Twentieth and Twenty-First Centuries
         Edited by Manuele Gragnolati, Fabio Camilletti,
         and Fabian Lampart

VOL. 3   PHANTASMATA
         Techniken des Unheimlichen
         Edited by Fabio Camilletti, Martin Doll, and Rupert Gaderer

VOL. 4   Boris Groys / Vittorio Hösle
         DIE VERNUNFT AN DIE MACHT
         Edited by Luca Di Blasi and Marc Jongen

VOL. 5   Sara Fortuna
         WITTGENSTEINS PHILOSOPHIE DES KIPPBILDS
         Aspektwechsel, Ethik, Sprache

VOL. 6   THE SCANDAL OF SELF-CONTRADICTION
         Pasolini's Multistable Subjectivities, Geographies, Traditions
         Edited by Luca Di Blasi, Manuele Gragnolati,
         and Christoph F. E. Holzhey

VOL. 7   SITUIERTES WISSEN
         UND REGIONALE EPISTEMOLOGIE
         Zur Aktualität Georges Canguilhems und Donna J. Haraways
         Edited by Astrid Deuber-Mankowsky
         and Christoph F. E. Holzhey

VOL. 8   MULTISTABLE FIGURES
         On the Critical Potentials of Ir/Reversible Aspect-Seeing
         Edited by Christoph F. E. Holzhey

VOL. 9   Wendy Brown / Rainer Forst
         THE POWER OF TOLERANCE
         Edited by Luca Di Blasi and Christoph F. E. Holzhey

VOL. 10   DENKWEISEN DES SPIELS
           Medienphilosophische Annäherungen
           Edited by Astrid Deuber-Mankowsky and Reinhold Görling

VOL. 11   DE/CONSTITUTING WHOLES
           Towards Partiality Without Parts
           Edited by Manuele Gragnolati and Christoph F. E. Holzhey

VOL. 12   CONATUS UND LEBENSNOT
           Schlüsselbegriffe der Medienanthropologie
           Edited by Astrid Deuber-Mankowsky and Anna Tuschling

VOL. 13   AURA UND EXPERIMENT
           Naturwissenschaft und Technik bei Walter Benjamin
           Edited by Kyung-Ho Cha

VOL. 14   Luca Di Blasi
           DEZENTRIERUNGEN
           Beiträge zur Religion der Philosophie im 20. Jahrhundert

VOL. 15   RE-
           An Errant Glossary
           Edited by Christoph F. E. Holzhey and Arnd Wedemeyer

VOL. 16   Claude Lefort
           DANTE'S MODERNITY
           An Introduction to the Monarchia
           With an Essay by Judith Revel
           Translated from the French by Jennifer Rushworth
           Edited by Christiane Frey, Manuele Gragnolati,
           Christoph F. E. Holzhey, and Arnd Wedemeyer

VOL. 17   WEATHERING
           Ecologies of Exposure
           Edited by Christoph F. E. Holzhey and Arnd Wedemeyer

VOL. 18   Manuele Gragnolati and Francesca Southerden
           POSSIBILITIES OF LYRIC
           Reading Petrarch in Dialogue

VOL. 19   THE WORK OF WORLD LITERATURE
           Edited by Francesco Giusti and Benjamin Lewis Robinson

VOL. 20   MATERIALISM AND POLITICS
           Edited by Bernardo Bianchi, Emilie Filion-Donato,
           Marlon Miguel, and Ayşe Yuva

VOL. 21 OVER AND OVER AND OVER AGAIN
Reenactment Strategies in Contemporary Arts and Theory
Edited by Cristina Baldacci, Clio Nicastro,
and Arianna Sforzini

VOL. 22 QUEERES KINO / QUEERE ÄSTHETIKEN
ALS DOKUMENTATIONEN DES PREKÄREN
Edited by Astrid Deuber-Mankowsky
and Philipp Hanke

VOL. 23 OPENNESS IN MEDIEVAL EUROPE
Edited by Manuele Gragnolati
and Almut Suerbaum

VOL. 24 ERRANS
Going Astray, Being Adrift, Coming to Nothing
Edited by Christoph F. E. Holzhey
and Arnd Wedemeyer

VOL. 25 THE CASE FOR REDUCTION
Edited by Christoph F. E. Holzhey
and Jakob Schillinger

www.ingramcontent.com/pod-product-compliance
Lightning Source LLC
Chambersburg PA
CBHW030359130626
46549CB00004B/1556